Carmen Dörge

The Notion of Turning in Metap

CW00515122

Religion und Literatur
Religion and Literature

herausgegeben von / edited by

Prof. Dr. Matthias Bauer
(Universität Tübingen)

und / and

Prof. Dr. Birgit Weyel
(Universität Tübingen)

Band / Volume 7

LIT

Carmen Dörge

The Notion of Turning
in Metaphysical Poetry

LIT

Cover Image:
Camille Flammarion, *L'Atmosphère: Météorologie Populaire*
(Paris, 1888)

This book is printed on acid-free paper.

Bibliographic information published by the Deutsche Nationalbibliothek
The Deutsche Nationalbibliothek lists this publication in the Deutsche
Nationalbibliografie; detailed bibliographic data are available on the Internet at
http://dnb.d-nb.de.

ISBN 978-3-643-90991-6 (pb)
ISBN 978-3-643-95991-1 (PDF)
Zugl.: Tübingen, Univ., Diss., 2017

A catalogue record for this book is available from the British Library

© LIT VERLAG GmbH & Co. KG Wien,
Zweigniederlassung Zürich 2018
Klosbachstr. 107
CH-8032 Zürich
Tel. +41 (0) 44-251 75 05
E-Mail: zuerich@lit-verlag.ch   http://www.lit-verlag.ch
Distribution:
In the UK: Global Book Marketing, e-mail: mo@centralbooks.com
In North America: International Specialized Book Services, e-mail: orders@isbs.com
In Germany: LIT Verlag Fresnostr. 2, D-48159 Münster
Tel. +49 (0) 2 51-620 32 22, Fax +49 (0) 2 51-922 60 99, e-mail: vertrieb@lit-verlag.de

e-books are available at www.litwebshop.de

Vorwort zur Reihe
Religion und Literatur / Religion and Literature

Religion und Literatur / Religion and Literature ist mit den vielfältigen Beziehungen zwischen den Religionen und Literaturen befasst. In den hier veröffentlichten Studien geht es insbesondere darum, wie der Bezug zur Religion das ästhetische Potential eines literarischen Textes prägt, und inwiefern religiöse Texte literarisch sein müssen, um ihre Funktion zu erfüllen. Literarische Texte dienen durch ihre Gegenstände und ihren Sprachgebrauch immer wieder dem Ziel der Überschreitung innerweltlicher Wirklichkeiten. Das symbolische Potential religiöser Tradition wird in künstlerisch-kreativer Weise literarisch wirksam. Die Frage nach Gott, die Schilderung religiöser Erfahrungen, Anspielungen auf biblische Erzählungen, zentrale dogmatische Begriffe wie ‚Sünde und Gnade' und ‚Schuld und Sühne,' die Sehnsucht nach Liebe und Erlösung, die Suche nach Identität und die Frage nach Sinn in einem Leben unter den Bedingungen der Endlichkeit setzen Erzählungen in Gang. Engel bevölkern moderne Romanwelten, und Menschen begeben sich auf Pilgerreisen, auf denen sie zugleich bedroht und beschützt sind. Mit dem symbolischen Potenzial christlicher und anderer religiöser Traditionen wird im Verhältnis zu den Ursprungsdokumenten in sehr freier und spielerischer Weise umgegangen, so dass die Religion in der Literatur in ihrem Kontext auf der Basis des jeweiligen poetischen Konzepts analysiert sein will. Dazu gehört auch, dass sich literarische Ordnungsprinzipien auf eine nach Maß, Zahl und Gewicht als göttliche Kunst geschaffene Welt beziehen können. Umgekehrt bezieht sich Religion auf Heilige Schriften, die als literarische Texte menschlicher Autoren wahrgenommen und mit literaturwissenschaftlichen Methoden gelesen werden. Diese ‚Heiligen Texte' sind nur durch Auslegungen zugänglich, die zwar einen mehr oder weniger kontrollierten Textbezug aufweisen, aber zugleich mit dem Anspruch verbunden sind, Anwendungsbezüge in einem sich wandelnden kulturellen Kontext herzustellen.

Die Arbeiten in dieser Reihe zeigen exemplarisch Bezüge zwischen Literatur und Religion auf und tragen zum systematischen Diskurs über die Sakralisierung der Literatur und die Literarisierung der Religion bei.

Preface to the Series
Religion und Literatur / Religion and Literature

Religion und Literatur / Religion and Literature is concerned with the complex relations between religions and literatures. In particular, studies published in this series will explore the ways in which the aesthetic potential of literary texts is influenced by religion, as well as the ways in which religious texts draw on literary aesthetics in order to fulfil their objectives. Works of literature frequently use language and subject-matter with the aim of transcending mundane reality. The symbolic potential of religious traditions is realized in a creative manner by literary artists. Narratives are spurred by questions about God, representations of religious experiences, allusions to biblical stories, reflections on notions such as 'sin and grace' or 'guilt and atonement,' as well as by characters longing for love and redemption, searching for identity or wondering about the meaning of their lives conditioned by mortality. There are angels in modern novels, and there are pilgrims that experience danger as well as protection. The symbolic potential of religious traditions, to be found in the sacred texts of Christianity and other religions, is frequently used by literary authors in a free and playful manner, so that the presence of religion in literature must be analysed in the context of relevant poetic concepts. This includes principles of literary form and structure, which may be linked to notions of a world created by a divine artist ordering all things in measure and number and weight. Correspondingly, religion is based on sacred scriptures which can be perceived, and critically analysed, as literary texts written by human authors. Such 'sacred texts' are accessible only by means of expositions that, however restricted by the linguistic form of the original, claim to relate them to changing cultural contexts.

The studies in this series are meant to explore the relations of literature and religion in an exemplary fashion, and to contribute to the critical debate on literature participating in the sacred and religion participating in the literary.

Table of Contents

Acknowledgements

This study presents a revised version of my dissertation, which was accepted by the Faculty of Humanities at the University of Tübingen in summer term 2016. It was written over the course of several years within the research project A2 "Interpretability in Context" of the Collaborative Research Centre 833 "The Construction of Meaning" located at Tübingen University. This has not only provided me with a stable income but also given me the opportunity (within my research project) to study Emily Dickinson's poetry – so different and yet in many aspects so similar to Donne's and Herbert's poetry. I would like to thank my supervisor and project leader Prof. Dr. Matthias Bauer for his continuous support and valuable feedback on the various drafts of my dissertation. My thanks also go to project leader Prof. Dr. Sigrid Beck and the staff of project A2 for their support and feedback, especially on linguistic issues. I also thank Prof. Dr. Ingrid Hotz-Davies for agreeing to examine my dissertation after it was finished, as well as the staff of LIT Verlag for publishing my thesis and for all help with questions regarding the publication process. Last but not least, I would like to thank my family and friends for the support they offered me over the years.

I. Introduction: Metaphysical Poetry
and the notion of turning

The Poets light but Lamps –
Themselves – go out –
The Wicks they stimulate –
If vital Light

Inhere as do the Suns –
Each Age a Lens
Disseminating their
Circumference –
(Emily Dickinson, J883)

1. Donne's notion(s) of turning

In a sermon "Preached upon the Penitential Psalms, on Psalm 6.4 and 5"
(Donne, Sermons V, no. 18, 364-79), John Donne analyses the notion of
turning in detail. He finds it spelled out in the text for his sermon: "Re-
turn, O Lord, deliver my soul: oh save me for thy mercies' sake. For in
death there is no remembrance of thee: in the grave who shall give thee
thanks?"[1] In his sermon, Donne focuses on the two pleas to "return" and
"deliver" and expands the meaning of "return" to imply three different
aspects: "Returne thy selfe, that is, bring backe thy Mercy; Returne thy
Wrath, that is, Call backe thy Judgements, or Returne us to thee" (370).
That is, Donne takes "returne, O Lord; deliver my soule" as a threefold
plea to God: the speaker of the psalm asks God to return to man (that is,
to turn Himself towards Man); he asks God to take away His anger (i.e.
to turn it away), and he asks God to make man turn towards God (which
implies man's turning away from sin). In the first explication, "returne
thy selfe," "returne" is actually intransitive (God is simply asked to re-
turn), yet by adding "thy selfe" Donne makes it seem transitive (as if God
could return Himself). While "thy selfe" is not necessary to achieve the

---

1   Simpson and Potter list this verse, preceding Donne's sermon, as follows:
    "Returne, O Lord; deliver my soule; O Lord save me, for thy mercies sake. / For in
    death there is no remembrance of thee; and in the grave, who shall give thee
    thanks" (Donne, Sermons V, 364), which makes the reference for the first phrase
    "Returne, O Lord" ambiguous (which would be more in line with Donne's analysis
    of the psalm text). However, there seems to be no official Bible translation
    followed here; all major Bible translations from the Matthew Bible to the
    Auhorized Version have, firstly, no semicolons after "Lord" and "soule," and
    secondly, omit the second "Lord."

meaning intended (simply "return" or "return to us" would have served the same purpose), it adds to the wordplay taking place in these three pleas. This transitive notion becomes even stronger when it is juxtaposed to the second explication. "Returne thy wrath" has the same syntactical structure as "returne thy selfe" (and this phrase is in fact transitive) but it means departure and removal instead of arrival and addition. The last one, "returne us to thee" is also transitive, but carries the intransitive meaning 'make us turn to thee.' Donne plays with the different interpretative possibilities of "returne" and by doing so, draws attention to the words themselves and invites his audience to think about them.

Donne's threefold interpretation is based on two contrary movements, which are also two fundamental characteristics of the notion of turning. Turning in the Early Modern period is distinguished from "modern" ideas of turning by its strongly relational nature. Whereas the use of the word "turn" abounds in modern use (as, for example, in the phrases "turn of the century," "a turn for the worse," or, in a more specialised context, "linguistic turn," or "spatial turn"), these uses are as a rule impersonal. The nature of turning in the 16th and 17th century, however, was always thought of in terms of a relation: not just "a turn", but a turn "towards from or away from." Donne conceptualises turning as a reversal or change (that is, a turning away from someone or something), and on the other hand as a relation and connection (that is, a turning towards someone or something). These go hand in hand: the question of where to turn, and how to orientate oneself, also comprises the choice of turning one way and not another. Both movements show a human concern with how to go through life and how to orientate oneself, and they are also perceived and described in terms of a human relation to God,[2] stressing God's power as the agent behind all "turning" movements and the influence of God's "turning" on man.

In addition to these linear and progressive ways of turning, there is another dimension of turning that is central to an understanding of Early Modern thought: the notion of circular turning found, for example, in the

---

2 This also explains the closeness between secular love poetry and religious poetry, which often use the same vocabulary and conceits, and thus also provides the basis for sacred parody (explored further in the chapter on "The Search") and for including "The Canonization" in a corpus of mostly religious poems as an important example of turning.

classical, medieval and Early Modern astronomical conceptions of re-
volving spheres. As we shall see, this idea is also essential for an under-
standing of metaphysical poetry. In his sermon, Donne also brings in the
cyclical nature of turning, by stressing the recurring nature of life, as well
as God's repeated "returning" to man throughout the life of an individual
and throughout time:

> [A]s God came long agoe, six thousand years agoe, in nature, when
> we were created in Adam, and then in nature returned to us, in the
> generation of our Parents: so our Saviour Christ Jesus came to us
> long agoe, sixteene hundred yeares agoe, in grace, and yet in grace
> returnes to us, as often as he assembles us, in these holy Convoca-
> tions. (372)
> He comes to thee in thy peregrination, all the way, and he returns in
> thy transmigration, at thy last gaspe. So God comes, and so God re-
> turnes. (372)

Donne here places the motions of turning and returning within a spatial
and temporal framework. He also discusses the spatiality implied in the
literal meaning of "returne": "*Shubah, To Returne,* is *Redire at locum
suum,* To returne to that place, to which a thing is naturally affected
[…].[3] But can God returne in such a sense as this? Can we find an *Ubi*
for God?" (368). And Donne likewise discusses the temporal dimensions
implied in the speaker's wish for a return: "[T]he first step in this Prayer,
"*Revertere, O Lord returne,* implies first a former presence, and then a
present absence, and also a confidence for the future" (367).

Donne interprets "returne" as God's turning towards man and simulta-
neously as man's turning towards God, and he emphasises the process of
mutual turning leading to the union with God: "[H]ere is the progresse of
the Holy Ghost, intended to thy soule, that first he comes thus to thee,
and then if thou turne to him, he returnes to thee, and settles himselfe,
and dwels in thee" (371) – thus also linking the different meanings of
"returne." Donne begins his sermon by stressing that this plea is uttered
in the form of a prayer – and a fervent and emotional prayer – addressed
to God and having an effect on God:

---

3   This returning back to the origin, to a place "to which a thing is naturally affected,"
     is also the basis for circular turning such as that of the spheres.

> The whole Psalme is Prayer; and Prayer is our whole service to
> God. Earnest Prayer hath the nature of Importunity; Wee presse,
> wee importune God in Prayer [...]; God flings not away from that.
> [...] Prayer hath the nature of Impudency [...]; And God suffers
> this Impudency and more. Prayer hath the nature of Violence; In the
> publique Prayers of the Congregation, we besiege God [...]; and
> God is glad to be straitned by us in that siege. [...] Prayer [...]
> works upon God, moves God, prevailes with God, entirely for all.
> (364)

By pointing out the function of the psalm as prayer right from the begin-
ning, Donne presents it as a form of communicating with and of estab-
lishing a relation to God, which adds to the reciprocity expressed in his
interpretation of "returne."

Donne arrives at all the different meanings of "returne" through a de-
tailed textual analysis: he looks at the language of the psalm, in particular
the different meanings of Hebrew "shubah," in order to find an adequate
interpretation.[4] Thus, Donne's sermon covers in essence the most im-
portant aspects of turning with which this study will be concerned, and he
does this in a manner similar to the one employed here, through a fine-
grained analysis of different texts. If we, in turn, look at Donne's poetry,
we can see that all these aspects of turning come up again and again, and
if we look further, we can see that turning is a pervasive concern in the
sixteenth and seventeenth centuries.

2.   Turning in the context of the Early Modern period

2.1 Religious turning

Donne found the different meanings of "returne" (including less obvious
meanings, for which he consulted the Hebrew original) important enough
to dedicate the larger part of a sermon to them. If we look at the time in

---

4   Cf. also Goodblatt 2010, 49- 58. Cf. also Eliot's description of Andrewes' method
     of biblical exposition:

> Andrewes takes a word and derives the world from it; squeezing and squeezing the word
> until it yields a full juice of meaning which we should never have supposed any word to
> possess. In this process the qualities which we have mentioned, of ordonnance and preci-
> sion, are exercised. (1972a, 347-408)

     Although Eliot denies to Donne's sermons the quality of Andrewes' texts, the
     process he describes is the same in both authors.

which Donne and Herbert lived, and which shaped their thoughts and works, we see that it was a time in which turning was a pervasive and existential concern. It was a time marked by change and the need for re-orientation, characterised by the lasting repercussions of religious up-heaval and the reformation, and by new scientific and geographic discoveries changing and challenging people's perception of the world and the universe. All this led to a fundamental anxiety about how to lead one's life – especially with regard to the consequences for the afterlife –, about what constitutes a good, "reformed" life, about how to address God and quite generally about what to believe.

The expansion of the reformation and counter-reformation in Europe led to a profound transformation of the foundations of European religious thought and doctrine. While previously there simply was no alternative available, the coming into existence of a reformed church and the abundant discussions of all aspects of religion that accompanied it, created an imperative of choice: a necessity for choosing one's religious affiliation – even when this choice was officially made by local rulers for their subjects, everyone was still able to choose personally either acceptance or rejection (and in the latter case, often persecution and exile). At the same time, this possibility to choose also led to a profound sense of religious insecurity and highlighted the necessity to search for religious truth – a necessity which did exist as an existential religious concern long before the Reformation, but which became even more pressing with the sudden options presented by it.[5] This was accompanied in England by changing monarchs, as well as changing state religions and corresponding regulations. Although by the time most of the poems discussed here were written (i.e., roughly in the first thirty years of the 17th century), these changes had already taken place, and there was an established religion as well as an established monarch, its influence was still palpable. In addition, the reign of James I was also marked by domestic and foreign tension (such as his repeated endeavours to extract more money from parliament, the looming prospect of war with Spain and later the Thirty Years War

---

5   Scarisbrick (81f., 109-21) points out the insecurity created through the frequent changes in religious doctrine as well as ruling authorities, cf. also Duffy (565-93). On the English reformation in general, see Lindberg (309-30), Cummings (2007) and Dickens (1999, 13-24, 378-91). Cf. also Williamson (1935) on the general fear of mutability in the Early Modern period.

on the continent) as well as continuing religious uncertainty (Roman Catholics were still persecuted and conflicts with Puritans arose), and thus a time of persisting and increasing unrest. This becomes visible, for example, in the emergence of different religious movements and sects: thus, there was not only a conflict between Roman Catholicism and Protestantism in general; there were also various Protestant movements in England that conflicted with each other (most notably Calvinist, Puritan and Arminian currents). It is also visible in the flourishing of Bible translations throughout the sixteenth century (which also offered more freedom of choice), and in the endeavours at the beginning of the seventeenth century to create one authoritative Bible translation.[6]

The shaking of religious stability, as well as the freedom it offered, is also reflected in the increased importance of conversion, both in the sense of converting from one denomination to another (which in the 16th and 17th centuries was not restricted to choosing between Roman Catholicism and Protestantism – changes from one Protestant movement to another occurred frequently, as well as to a lesser extent from and to Judaism and Islam)[7] and in the more general religious sense of turning towards God. Both the term and the concept of conversion are closely related to turning: spiritual conversion presents, in a nutshell, the most central characteristic of religious turning: man turns to God, and God turns to man. And, in fact, spiritual "conversion" is defined as the "turning of sinners to God; a spiritual change from sinfulness, ungodliness, or worldliness to love of God and pursuit of holiness" (*OED*, "conversion, n.9"). The term "conversion" is the verbal epitome of the notion of turning: it derives from Latin "con-vertere," "to turn round (*OED*, "conversion, n.")." The term "conversion" refers to the action of "turning round or revolving" (*OED*, "conversion, n.1"), to the action of turning to a particular direction (*OED*, "conversion, n.2.a") and directing one's mind in a particular direction (2.b), and even to "the action of turning back or return-

---

6   On the complexity of thoughts and agendas involved in English bible translations, cf. Tadmor (2015). The same endeavour is found in the history of the *Book of Common Prayer*, which went through several revisions before the final edition of 1662.

7   Cf. also, e.g., Questier 1-11. Stelling (2012) points out the frequent occurrence of conversion (usually from one denomination to another) in 16th-century plays, which also often feature conversions from and to Islam and Judaism.

ing" (*OED*, "conversion, *n.3.a*"), as well as to the "action of turning, or process of being turned, *into* or *to* something else; change of form or properties, alteration" (*OED*, "conversion, *n.*11.a"). Thus, "conversion" always implies turning: turning or returning to God, turning away from sin, being transformed from a sinful to a redeemed human being – and it also offers a sense of orientation, since conversion indicates the "right" direction and the abandoning of the "wrong" way.

In the poetry discussed (in contrast to, for example, the depiction of conversion in plays),[8] there is a clear focus on (individual and personal) spiritual conversion.[9] The basis for the kind of spiritual conversion found in religious metaphysical poetry is found in the Bible, which provides both a vocabulary of conversion and the first conversion narratives. Gaiser summarises the biblical vocabulary used to describe conversion (of which Donne also makes use in the sermon quoted above).[10]

> Biblical studies of conversion [...] regularly examine several Hebrew and Greek terms. The primary Old Testament root is *šûḇ* (to turn back, return). The Greek New Testament uses principally the terms *epistrephō* (to turn, turn around, turn back), *metamelomai* (to change one's mind, regret, repent), and *metanoeō* (to change one's mind, repent, be converted). (93f.)

---

8   Cf. Stelling (2012) in the previous footnote.

9   Even in his "Satire Three," where Donne broaches the issue of how to choose between various denominations in order to find "true religion" (l.43), the important part of conversion is ultimately shown as a personal and individual struggle to reach "Truth":
     [...] On a huge hill,
     Craggèd and steep, Truth stands, and he that will
     Reach her, about must and about [must] go,
     And what the hill's suddenness resists, win so.
     Yet strive so that before age, death's twilight,
     Thy soul rest, for none can work in that night.
     To will implies delay, therefore now do [...] (ll. 79-85)
     The addressee is advised to "Keep the truth which thou hast found" (l. 88) and warned that "So perish souls, which more choose men's unjust / Pow'r, from God claimed, than God himself to trust." (ll. 109-10). At the same time, the individual search for truth presented here also involves turning: "he that will / Reach her, about must and about [must] go."

10   Cf. also Johnson and Malony (1982, 75-85) for a more detailed account of biblical conversion vocabulary.

As can be seen, the main biblical meanings of "conversion" are immediately linked to movements of turning and change, as they are in English. Gaiser also notes that

> Although an examination of the biblical theology of conversion must pay careful attention to the very large number of passages which employ these terms, it cannot be limited to a study of one or several words. The phenomenon of radical change, of transformation, of turning in repentance and faith away from one focus of life to another (or back to a former one) cuts across biblical theology from beginning to end. (94)

This applies equally to the poems discussed here: although "turning" and other words indicating turning are used quite frequently, processes of turning are not restricted to the use of a certain lexicon, but are expressed in various ways. Gaventa (1992) also emphasises the diversity with which conversion experiences are expressed in the Bible and points out that there is no uniform biblical language of conversion.[11]

The biblical vocabulary used to talk about conversion implies not only turning and change, but also, in the words *šûḇ* (to turn back, return) and *epistrephō* (to turn, turn around, turn back) the notion of a return to God. This notion later becomes paramount in St. Augustine's theology: he emphasises conversion as a process of turning back to a sinless state and stresses the importance of relying on memory in order to find this state within oneself. Sherwood summarises St. Augustine's conception of returning to God (and St. Bernard's, which closely follows Augustine's):

> Augustine and Bernard share a psychology of the soul or will 'bent' by Original Sin, needing to 'turn' from the world back to God. Augustine commands the believer, 'converte cor tuum.' The 'heart' or the soul, and alternately the will, are bent (distorta; curva), unlike God's will. 'Distortus tu es, ille rectus es.' Conversion conforms man's bent will to God's straight will. According to Bernard, the soul before returning to God is 'blind, bent' (curvam) earthwards. Its return is a *conversio* that establishes a conformity between the divine and human wills. For both Augustine and Bernard this turn-

---

11   Cf. also Gaventa (1986, 1-3), where she focuses on the metaphors "from darkness to light" and being "born again" as central to descriptions of conversion in the New Testament.

ing to God is the process of erecting the bent soul or, more particularly, the bent will.[12] (1984, 161)

Moog-Grünewald (2008a) elucidates Augustine's concept of conversion as a progressing and simultaneously returning movement:

> 'Conversio" means in a nutshell 'turning back" in the sense of "return"; it is the late Latin equivalent of the Greek words ἐπιστροφή and μετάνοια, which, though they are not synonymous, relate to each other: ἐπιστροφή means a change of direction and implies the idea of a return, be it a return to the origin or a return to itself; μετάνοια means a change of thought, a new way of thinking, and implies the idea of mutation and rebirth. Thus, the Latin 'conversio' is semantically shaped by the polarity of "relating back" and "breaking with" (142; my translation)[13]

This polarity is also characteristic of the conception of turning found in Donne's and Herbert's poetry, where the process of conversion is often depicted simultaneously as progress (involving change and improvement in the speaker) and as a return to God. It becomes especially visible when it is linked to circular movement as in "Riding Westward, Goodfriday 1613," and in poems making use of a circular form, as in Donne's "La Corona."[14]

The experience of conversion is not only a matter of attitude and redemption but also a verbal process: the convert can only attest to his conversion verbally, and he can only verbally reflect about his conversion (though he can also show that he has been converted through his actions,

---

12   The notion of "bending" as an expression of a speaker's turning to God, or God's turning to a speaker will also become important in some of the poems discussed.

13   In the original:
> 'Conversio' – so ist knapp zusammenzufassen – meint 'Umkehr' im Sinne von 'Rückkehr'; es ist das – späte – lateinische Äquivalent der beiden griechischen Wörter ἐπιστροφή und μετάνοια, die ihrerseits nicht synonym sind, doch aufeinander verweisen: ἐπιστροφή meint Änderung der Richtung und impliziert die Vorstellung der Rückkehr, sei es zum Ursprung, sei es zu sich selbst; μετάνοια meint eine Änderung des Denkens, ein Neudenken und impliziert die Vorstellung der Mutation und der Wiedergeburt. Somit ist das lateinische Wort 'conversio' semantisch von der Polarität 'Rückbezug' und 'Bruch' geprägt. (142)

14   The importance of conversion as a return to God also becomes visible, for example, in Donne's emphasis on the role of memory to reach salvation, which he stresses several times in his sermons (see the discussion of memory in the next chapter).

for example by leading a holy life and by trying to convert others). This also becomes visible in the fact that "conversation" was a synonym of conversion (cf. *OED* "conversation, n." 11, for example, from the 1535 Coverdale Bible, Acts XV.A, "They..declared the conuersacion of the Heythen."), a meaning which is also present in e.g., Gal 1.13 and Phil 3.20

> For ye have heard of my conversation in time past in the Jews' religion, how that beyond measure I persecuted the church of God, and wasted it (Gal. 1.13)
> For our conversation is in heaven; from whence also we look for the Saviour, the Lord Jesus Christ: Who shall change our vile body, that it may be fashioned like unto his glorious body, according to the working whereby he is able even to subdue all things unto himself. (Phil. 3.20-21)

"Conversation" is ambiguous here; though its primary meaning may be 'the action of living or having one's being in a place or among persons.' (*OED* "conversation, n." 1), the meaning of "conversion" is also present (in addition to the word's reference to "discourse and interaction with others"). In fact, St. Paul here explicitly describes a conversion when he talks about "chang[ing] our vile body" and provides a model for the speaker's plea to "restore thine image" when he asks to "be fashioned unto his glorious body."

In biblical accounts, spiritual conversion often goes together with a process of transformation, a fundamental change effected through repentance and turning towards God (cf. Gaventa 1992, Gaiser 1992), like the one described by St. Paul in Phil 3. Gaiser (94f.) argues that, in the Old Testament, this experience of transformation is most strongly present in the Psalter. Brueggemann (1974), who focuses on the psalms of lament, combines the finding that the process of transformation is central to the psalms of lament with another important feature of the psalms: their dialogical nature.

> Most importantly, the laments show clearly that *biblical faith, as it faces life fully, is uncompromisingly and unembarrassedly dialogical*. Israel and Israelites in their hurt have to do with God and he has to do with them. The laments are addressed to someone. And precisely in the presence of God himself is where the hurtful issues

must be dealt with. Nowhere but with him does Israel vent her greatest doubt, her bitterest resentments, her deepest anger. Israel knows that one need not fake it or be polite and pretend in his presence, nor need one face the hurts alone. In the dialogue, Israel expects to understand what is happening and even to have it changed. (1974, 4)[15]

Even where the speaker addresses God on behalf of the people of Israel, the Psalms present an individual, personal voice. This personal, dialogical nature is also a central element of most religious metaphysical poetry, which relies heavily on the Psalter's mode of expressing religious anxiety and a speaker's personal relation to God.[16] Both in the Psalter and in many metaphysical poems, transformation comes about while and through addressing God: talking to God functions as a prayer which is at least partly answered as the speaker becomes transformed.

It is important to note that turning is conceived here (in Donne's sermon as well as in the poems discussed) as both momentary and continual. It is defined by single moments in time, at which a speaker goes through an experience of spiritual conversion, of turning towards God or perceiving God's turn towards him. At the same time, it is also characterised as an ongoing process of constant and repeated effort. Even though the poems analysed all present various turns, the end of a poem never marks the end of the speaker's efforts: the speaker has to strive towards God during his lifetime. Thus, the "final" turn in a poem is often projected into the future or just imagined, or, in circular poems like "La Corona," the speaker even turns back to the beginning.

In addition to a vocabulary of conversion that builds on the notion of turning, and a mode of address that presents a turn towards God, the Bi-

---

15 Cf. also Brueggemann (1984), where he classifies the Psalter into Psalms of Orientation, Disorientation and New Orientation.

16 See, e.g., Hamlin (2004, 1-16) on the influence of the Psalter on Early Modern poetry in general, Patrides (Herbert 1974, 10) and Kinnamon (10-11) on their influence on Herbert, and Hunter (2007, 251-53) on their influence on Donne and Herbert. Hunter even argues that Donne's "Lamentations of Jeremy" might be seen as "Donne's contribution to the genre of psalm translation" (253). In addition to the biblical Psalter, the Sidneys' translation – and its personal and intimate style (cf. Niefer 2017) – was also a major influence on Donne's and Herbert's poetry (cf., e.g., Norton 2000, 129-31; Alexander 2006, 107-08, 198, and on their influence specifically on Herbert's poetry, Freer 1972, 1-49).

ble offers a number of conversion narratives that provide models for the speakers in Donne's and Herbert's poetry. The most prominent and, especially with regard to Donne, also the most influential of these is the conversion of St. Paul.[17] The parable of the prodigal son, though it is not explicitly a story about conversion, can be seen as another important and influential conversion narrative (cf. Gaiser 104; this is notably one which does not involve interdenominational change or an amendment and addition of beliefs but presents a purely spiritual conversion). In the sixteenth and seventeenth centuries, the prodigal son becomes a popular and frequent motif in drama.[18] For two reasons, the parable of the prodigal son is also relevant in the context of turning. Firstly, it focuses on the relation between son and father (that is, on a personal and intimate relationship that stands figuratively for the relation between sinner and God). Secondly, the parable presents the process of spiritual conversion within a spatial framework: the son goes away, wanders about and returns to his father; and when he comes back home, his father approaches the son as much as the son approaches the father, resulting in a mutual turn towards each other. The mutuality established by the father's movement towards his returning son is an essential characteristic not just of conversion in general,[19] it is also essential to the way in which conversion is depicted in

---

17 See the next chapter for a more detailed discussion of the account of St. Paul's conversion in relation to Donne's poem.

   With regard to the Old Testament, Gaventa (1992, 43-45) lists the story of Ruth as one of interdenominational conversion, and the calls to Israel to "return" to God in, for example, Jer 3 and 4, and Isa 55 as a reference to spiritual conversion. In the New Testament, and especially in *Acts of the Apostles*, explicit accounts of conversion appear more often: the New Testament is "naturally concerned with conversion, since virtually all members of the earliest Christian communities entered those communities of faith through conversion." (Gaventa 1992, 41). St. Paul's conversion is mentioned several times (in Acts 9, 22, 26; Gal 1; and Rom 7); other explicit conversion narratives are the conversion of the Ethiopian eunuch (Acts 8), the conversion of Cornelius (Acts 10), the conversion of Lydia (Acts 16) and the conversion of the jailer at Philippi (Acts 16) (cf. Johnson and Malony 87ff.).

18 Young (1979) points out the large number of plays having a type of prodigal son as protagonist or character or otherwise picking up the story of the prodigal son.

19 Cf. also Johnson and Malony (73-85), who stress biblical conversion as a process which always involves God and man:

   In a study of conversion in the Bible, one always finds a twin emphasis – on the divine role and on the human role. On the human side, the focus is on the person who turns. On the divine side, God is seen as the One who is active in turning the person to Himself. (73)

the poems discussed here: as the speaker's turning to God and also as God's simultaneous turning to the speaker.

The conversion of Augustine narrated in his *Confessions* provide another important model. It is in turn influenced by St. Paul's conversion narrative (cf. Fredriksen 1986); in addition Augustine casts himself in the role of the prodigal son (cf. Ferrari 1977, Robbins 1991, 21-48). The *Confessions* are especially important for Donne's theological framework as well as for his poetry, not only because of the conversion narrative they offer, but also because of St. Augustine's conception of conversion as a process of turning back.

Augustine describes his own conversion as a change from one religion to another and simultaneously as a spiritual conversion. Similarly, in Donne's biography, both kinds of conversion play a prominent role – the one because of his family's active Catholicism, his covert recusant stance and his later "conversion" to Anglicanism, and the other because of his "transformation" from hedonistic rogue Jack Donne to spiritual and devout Dr. Donne. This importance of both denominational and spiritual conversion in Donne's life led to ample discussions of his work in the context of his religious influences and affiliation.[20]

A number of studies attempt to highlight the influence of one specific denominational tradition. For example, Martz (1955) argues for the strong influence of the Pre-Reformation practice of spiritual meditation (i.e., originally a Roman Catholic practice) on both Protestant and Catholic metaphysical poets. Low (1978) looks at different "devotional modes" in Donne's work as being influenced by existing religious traditions. Young (2000, 2009) argues for a strong though covert Roman Catholic influence visible in Donne's works. Sabine (1992) treats the changing relation to Mary in Donne's works as conditioned by the Protestant prohibition to worship Mary directly. Knox (2011) analyses the influence of Ignatius de Loyola's writings on Donne, with emphasis on what is typically Roman Catholic in Loyola's writings. Lewalski (1979), on the other hand, sees Donne's works as the result of a specifically Protestant attitude taking the Bible as prime model.

---

20 Biographies of Donne consequently also place a heavy focus on his religious affiliation, cf. Bald (1970), Edwards (2001), Stubbs (2006), and especially Carey (1981).

While it is useful for a better understanding of Donne's work to identify influences and literary models, an approach that tries to pin down his works (or beliefs) to just one influence or conviction is problematic because it narrows the perspective down to a limited point of view and thus fails to do justice to the central position the notion of turning occupies in Donne's works. With Herbert, the same problem emerges, although to a lesser extent. Both poets were well-read in authors pertaining to different Protestant developments and used the theological frameworks and concepts that they found necessary or useful to express their understanding of turning and transformation. And although theological discussions and beliefs are vital for analysing their poetry, it does not matter whether they firmly held one opinion or another, or to exactly which denomination they owe a certain conceit, since their poems are not theological treatises. The purpose of this study is not to show to what extent Donne was still a Roman Catholic, a fully reformed Protestant, or a mixture of both at the same time, and whether or not the protestations of his speakers are sincere, but to look at spiritual conversion independently from denominations, as something that concerned all people living in the seventeenth century and is present in the poetry of the time, thus also in Donne's and Herbert's works. Moreover, works focussing on Donne's denominational attitudes tend to present an analysis of Donne's stance towards conversion rather than a close textual analysis of conversion in relation to the notion of turning – when looking at his texts, it emerges that most of them (and especially his poetry) actually reveal a strong engagement with spiritual turning.

Especially in recent years, the distinction between the two roles assigned to Donne, Jack Donne and Dr. Donne, has been challenged and considered in a more critical light. Oliver (1997), for example, looks at Donne's religious writing in the light of his influences and developments, and argues that Donne carefully and artfully construed his spiritual identities. His study is useful, because he points out the consciously constructed nature of these identities in Donne's works, and because he regards religious attitudes in the context of literary analysis (instead of using Donne's works to substantiate Donne's alleged denominational opinions, as is the case in most (older) biographical studies). While he highlights that Donne himself to some extent shaped the story of his spiritual conversion, Oliver focuses on an analysis of how religious stances are presented in Donne's works, and less on the actual turning points where this change happens in the poems, which is in the focus here. Murray (2009, 1-35, 69-104) helpfully considers both kinds of conversion in Donne's work. She suggests that Donne merges the topic of interdenominational conversion with that of spiritual conversion, and argues that Donne to a large extent deliberately avoids taking sides in favour of one religion or other. Her study is also useful as a starting point because it brings in conversion as an independent topic. Conti's (2014, 50-73) analysis of Donne's prose works is valuable because she points out the difficulty in attributing one specific religious stance to Donne and instead foregrounds the diversity of religious influences which invariably had an effect on everyone living in the sixteenth and seventeenth centuries.[21] Conti, like Oliver, considers Donne's religious avowals as a kind of construction or performance:[22]

> Pseudo-Martyr and the Devotions may be Donne's only explicitly autobiographical works, but nearly all Donne's works are strikingly performative, full of the first-person pronoun and monologues that can sound downright confessional. Donne's poems in particular have long tempted readers to interpret them autobiographically [...]. (Conti 2014, 52)

The dialogical nature and the importance of language in the process of conversion, as well as the personal and introspective attitude found in most metaphysical poems dealing with turning and conversion, contrib-

---

21 Cf. also Shoulson, who sees religious dissimulation as the natural consequence of a changing and unstable national religious identity:
> The boundaries between Catholicism and Protestantism, not to mention within and among newly emerging Protestant denominations, remained permeable and shifting; at one time or another throughout much of the sixteenth century most Englishmen and women – whose parents and grandparents very well may have attended a different church than they were attending – would have found it necessary to be somewhat circumspect, if not downright deceptive, about their own religious beliefs and practices. (2)

While Shoulson argues that the figure of the Jew was used to transfer the notion of religious instability to something "alien" (that could, in turn, be converted; cf. also Stelling's study of interdenominational conversions in Early Modern plays) and thus away from English identity, the same insecurity about religious affiliations and beliefs can actually still be seen in the seventeenth century.

22 That is, "performative" in the sense of acting a part, not in the sense of performative speech acts, as used in the chapter on Donne's "The Canonization."

ute to create an affinity to dramatic forms, mostly to the soliloquy (cf. Zirker 2018). Narveson (2004, 111ff.) analyses the genre of the "holy soliloquy," as a specific Early Modern form of devotional literature, which she defines as

> a soliloquizing confession of distress, love, and need, addressed to God by a first person-speaker. [...] In soliloquies, addressing the soul, Christ, or God, the speaker exclaims, exhorts, laments, pleads, and praises, moving among a range of stances, from self-reproach to intimate expressions of love. (111-13)

She classifies Donne's *Devotions* as a prime example of a "holy soliloquy," and this is certainly a text which clearly conforms to her definition, yet many religious metaphysical poems can equally be read as "holy soliloquies." The dramatic character of Donne's works, be it poetry or prose, has been studied on several occasions. Zirker (2018) explores the progress of the speaker's soul in Donne's and Shakespeare's works by analysing the notion of the peripety (as a structural turning point in drama as well as a turning point in a speaker's spiritual development). Fetzer (2010a, cf. also 2010b) takes Austin's theory of performatives as a starting point and combines it with the notion of theatrical performance, highlighting the dramatical nature and role-playing exhibited by many of Donne's speakers, which is also a characteristic feature of those poems concerned with turning. Pebworth (1989 and 1996) also sees Donne's poetry as performance, as does Müller (2010), who looks at Donne's *Songs and Sonnets*, and likewise argues for an understanding of Donne's poetry as both performative and theatrically performing. The closeness to theatrical performance is also a characteristic feature of the poems concerned with turning and analysed here (which explains the affinity to the dramatic soliloquy mentioned above and found in many of these poems), where the emphasis is on psychologically complex individual speakers and their spiritual condition, and although the poems are considerably shorter than plays, they always show a development in the speaker's spiritual condition which is similar to dramatic structure. Moreover, the speakers of the poems act and turn *by* speaking the lines of the poem, which makes their utterances to some extent performative.

Other studies focus on Donne's use of the topic of conversion for the purpose of influencing and improving his readers and audience, rather

than for merely representing his own spiritual development and im-
provement. Shami (1984) argues that Donne, rather than presenting "per-
sonal" experiences, uses models of conversion for rhetorical and didactic
purposes. She focuses on the "Anniversaries" (i.e., a more public kind of
poetry than the poems discussed here) and the sermons, and even argues
that Donne turned from poetry to prose (i.e., to his *Devotions* and Ser-
mons), because prose is easier to understand and therefore more useful
for teaching and influencing others.[23] Shami is useful for analysing the
notion of turning because she focuses on the progress of conversion (ar-
guing that, in order to make this experience more relatable to the audi-
ence, Donne uses commonplace characters to undergo the process of
conversion, as well as similar patterns of development in these charac-
ters). Kneidel (2008, 74-125, cf. also 2001) looks at Donne's treatment of
St. Paul in four of his sermons. Kneidel argues that Donne not only uses
St. Paul as a model for presenting his own conversion, but also that
Donne presents St. Paul's varying self-representation[24] and St. Paul's
rhetorical versatility favourably, in order to justify his own (public) role
as a preacher and as a (rhetorical) manipulator of his audience. Thus,
while Kneidel focuses on sermons, he stresses several aspects of Donne's
writing (the creation of a divided or struggling speaker, the skilful use of
language and to some extent a speaker's self-conscious awareness of this
use) that can also be found in Donne's poems dealing with turning. Yeo
(2012) provides an even larger perspective and sees some elements in
Donne's poetry as symbolic representations of the changing state of Eng-
land, as it becomes transformed from a Roman Catholic to a Protestant
country. Thus, for example, she considers the speaker's occupation with
maps in "Hymne to God my God, in my sicknesse" as a negotiation be-
tween old and new cartographic methods (i.e. medieval T-O-maps cen-
tring on Jerusalem versus more modern and geographically accurate

---

23 Considering the complexity of Donne's sermons and the knowledge and mental
    agility which he exacts from his audience, such a claim seems doubtful. Cf., in
    contrast, Rudrum, who argues that conversion narratives in verse are no more artful
    or less autobiographical than prose narratives (205).

24 Kneidel argues that the presentation of Paul as a divided soul is a rhetorical strate-
    gy (i.e., a performance to some extent) – both by Paul himself and by Donne in im-
    itation of Paul – in order to reach to a larger part of their respective audiences (ap-
    pealing to those that are more and to those that are less convinced).

maps taking new discoveries into account), and she sees the metaphorical
merging of both in the speaker's description of himself (who is on his
way to salvation) as a sign of spiritual advancement – which she inter-
prets also as symbolic of the state of England. While the focus in the po-
ems she discusses is mostly on personal conversion, Yeo argues that

> Donne's poetry constructs an idea of conversion in which internal
> change brings the soul into alignment with a collective experience
> of 'one divine truth'. Conversion is therefore registered less as a
> transfer of religious allegiance than as a reorienting of the self to-
> ward God [which] leads the convert to union with God and, in do-
> ing so, to union with a nation that is itself undergoing the same
> transformative process. Donne's England turns from the Catholic
> Church not in order to embrace the dogmatic truthfulness of Protes-
> tantism so much as to realize its own spiritual regeneration [...].
> (195)

While it is doubtful to what extent this ideal conception of the develop-
ment of English national religion was actually believed in by Donne and
his contemporaries,[25] Yeo's study is useful because she points out the
union of "real" and metaphorical space, that is, the use of geographical
descriptions to talk about a spiritual state and spiritual progress. Like
Shami and Kneidel, Yeo helpfully shows how Donne's treatment of con-
version was embedded in the religious discourses of his time. Their dis-
cussion of the public effect of Donne's work (both poetry and prose) and
of the potential influence on a larger audience provides a context for my
own analysis of the representation of an individual speaker's spiritual
state.

There are several studies focussing on Donne's representation of spir-
itual conversion that take his specific use of language into account.[26] Col-

---

25   Yeo does stress the "construction of an idea of conversion." Also, her citation of
     "one divine truth" refers to Sharpe (2000, 48), where this view is given to com-
     mentators on the function of state and individual, who tried to ensure obedience
     and peace (and thereby to promote the commonweal) by justifying a political and
     religious concept where everybody must conform to parliament and monarch in
     order to keep up the harmony of the state (48-52).
26   Since "Riding Westward, Goodfriday 1613" is so obviously concerned with both
     turning and spiritual conversion, the number of studies relating this poem to as-
     pects of turning is comparatively large; they will be considered in the correspond-
     ing chapter.

lins (1974) looks at "penitential conversion" in the *Devotions*, and while she offers a good overview and covers a broad range of topics, she does not provide detailed linguistic analyses. Guibbory (2011) gives a short survey of Donne's own statements on conversion in both senses (his emphasis is on interdenominational conversion, though he also takes spiritual conversion into account), as voiced in his writings (both prose and poetry); he also sums up what critics have said about Donne's own conversion. Though his listings are inevitably cursory and incomplete (also, not all poems dealing with turning are explicitly about conversion, and not all texts mentioning conversion are important in the context of turning), they provide a valuable overview of the topic of conversion in Donne's own writings. The main concern of Sanchez (2010; 2014, 27-68, 205-12) is interdisciplinary: he compares the treatment of spiritual conversion in Donne's and Herbert's to that in the visual arts, and looks at parallels between representations of Jeremiah (or Jeremiah-like speakers) in Early Modern literature and contemporary depictions of Jeremiah in visual art. While this approach seems at first glance to go in a completely different direction from the one taken here, Sanchez's (2014) study is helpful in that it looks specifically at the notion of turning and at conversion. There is a strong focus on the individual speaker (Sanchez analyses "Lamentations of Jeremy," "Riding Westward, Goodfriday 1613," a sermon and a letter), and he also considers the vocabulary Donne uses in these texts to talk about conversion in general, and turning in particular (including the word "turn" itself). Yearwood (1982) analyses the topic of spiritual conversion in the Holy Sonnets and goes in a similar direction as the one pursued here, arguing that "the poems are not only *about* salvation; they demonstrate it in a way that demands sympathetic participation from the beholders" (208). Yearwood steers clear of attributing a specific denominational stance to Donne. From his sermons, she identifies three doctrines underlying the process of conversion (which she classifies as "the usual Anglican Calvinist blend," 210):

> (1) that God does all, either by his preventing or his sustaining grace; (2) that human action – specifically confession – is a sine qua non of salvation; and (3) that there is predestination only to salvation, not to damnation, consequently that salvation is available to everyone who will confess, and to none who will not. (210-11)

She argues that coming to an understanding of these doctrines is essential for the individual progress. Accepting God's superiority, accepting one's own responsibility, and acting accordingly mark the general process of a speaker's being turned away from God, then towards God and finally being able to imagine their union: "The process [...] thus typically begins in pride, proceeds to confession and despair, and culminates in a humble joy and confidence." (211). It is useful to clarify the structure of this process, since these different states are also found in the poems under consideration (although many poems do not describe the whole process from condemnation to redemption, it provides the basis for a speaker's spiritual development). While Yearwood does not explicitly analyse the notion of turning, she considers conversion as turning, which provides a good starting point for the present study: "The *Holy Sonnets* follow this progress. The persona of the sonnets is a soul undergoing the stages of this theological and emotional turning." (211).

Since Herbert was firmly Anglican, studies of "conversion" with regard to his biography and works usually centre on spiritual conversion (even though Herbert, like Donne, was certainly influenced by various religious currents and tenets). In addition, although Herbert turned from a secular to a religious life in preferring to become a country parson instead of university lecturer, this turn is not as public and spectacular as Donne's turn towards ordination, so that studies of Herbert's poetry less often try to apply the findings from this poetry to definite points in his life.

Soubrenie (1997) looks at Herbert in the context of conversion, regarding *The Temple* as a kind of "spiritual autobiography." In this context, she also stresses the importance of spatiality for depicting and imagining spiritual conversion. Moreover, Soubrenie highlights the connection between spiritual conversion and poetic creativity, and sees conversion as a requirement for poetic accomplishment ("La conversion est donc bien l'événement nécessaire à l'accomplissement poétique," 54). For example, in "The Temper (I)," she sees the speaker's own reinterpretation of his state from torture to "[...] but tuning of my breast, / To make the music better" (ll.23-24) simultaneously as a statement about the speaker's conversion and about his poetical capacity: he will be able to produce better "music" when he is turned to God. Similarly, in "Hymne to God my God, in my sicknesse," she interprets "I tune the Instrument here at the doore" (l.4) as a reference to the speaker's imminent attempt at spiritual improvement and to his ability as a poet (54).

Kneidel (2008, 95-125) looks at Herbert's rhetorical skills in using mercantile and legal metaphors to describe a speaker's process of conversion. He sees Herbert's use of these metaphors as an expression of an ongoing and continually negotiated relationship between believer and God:

> Critics have tended to argue that Herbert appeals to commercial and legal writing to formalize and so finalize the salvific relationship between Christ and the individual Christian. I argue on the contrary, that when Herbert talks about transferring accounts and conveying lordship, he is appealing to forms of commercial and legal writings that establish a continuity of duties and responsibilities between actors. Understood in their historical context, the commercial and legal writings that Herbert appeals to do not document a single, decisive moment in the salvation history of an individual. Instead they frame a span of time [...] – when the Messiah is both behind and ahead, in the past and in the future – that demands continuity between Christ, his worldly church, and especially the rhetorically-skilled pastor or poet who, like Paul, must in the interim negotiate between the two. (95)

Kneidel here stresses the ongoing, continual and repetitive character of the notion of turning. Although the focus here is not on legal metaphors, Kneidel's emphasis on a speaker's turn to God as a fluctuating, flexible and evolving relationship also forms the basis for the analysis of turning in this study: even though the general progress of a speaker's conversion follows the same order (that is, the steps outlined by Yearwood above), this process of turning is always dynamic and evolving.

Sanchez (2014, 71-134, 205-12) also considers Herbert's poems in the context of spiritual conversion, and as with Donne's works, he compares the persona of the speaker to representations of Jeremiah in visual arts. In analysing Herbert, he does not explicitly focus on the vocabulary of turning, as he does with Donne's texts; instead he places metaphors of reading and writing in the foreground and links them explicitly to turning: writing and understanding what is written becomes part of a speaker's process of conversion.

2.2 Turning within the world and cosmos

Geographically, the knowledge of the world was expanding in the six-teenth and seventeenth centuries, and therefore changing the view of the world at large. The lasting impact of the discovery of America, the explo-ration of the new continent and the ongoing efforts to explore routes to the East likewise changed the outlook and attitudes of Early Modern people, which was also reflected in the ongoing development of cartog-raphy and cosmography. In metaphysical poetry, the metaphorical use of geographical features (such as cardinal directions, poles or the auxiliary lines of longitude and latitude), maps and globes often provides an im-portant means for expressing a speaker's progress through life (that is, to exploit the concept of the path of life and of life as a journey), as well as his inner, spiritual development (which is also regularly depicted as a voyage), and for illustrating a speaker's (changing and evolving) rela-tionship to God. Donne's interest in maps and geography can be seen, e.g., in the speaker calling himself a "map" in "Hymne to God" and spir-itually "travelling" the earth on his way towards death, or in "The Good-Morrow," where the lovers turn away from an exploration of the world and towards each other: "Let sea-discoverers to new worlds have gone, / Let Maps to other, worlds on worlds have showne" (ll.12-13).

At the same time new scientific discoveries challenged people's per-ception of the world. The Copernican, heliocentric model of the universe was still a novel idea, having emerged in the middle of the 16th century and being perpetuated and refined by scientists throughout the 16th and 17th century. This fundamental change in how to view the earth's role in the cosmos carried implications for how to view man's role in the cos-mos. Turning an established hierarchy upside down and assigning to the earth a dependent and off-centre place in the universe also means that man is no longer the centre of the cosmos, but a dependent and displaced being.[27] The new way of seeing the world was not only intimidating, it also offered new ways of expression – it provides the opportunity to re-late an individual's journey (physical and spiritual) and an individual's feeling out of place and out of touch with God, to the larger movements of world and cosmos. Thus, for example, in the *First Anniversary*, Donne

---

27   Cf., e.g., Crane 1-18.

expresses the speaker's spiritual sense of confusion and loss of orientation in view of the revised world picture:

> And new Philosophy cals all in doubt,
> The Element of fire is quite put out;
> The Sunne is lost, and th'earth, and no mans wit
> Can well direct him where to looke for it.
> And freely men confesse that this world's spent,
> When in the Planets, and the Firmament
> They seeke so many new; they see that this
> Is crumbled out againe to his Atomis.
> 'Tis all in pieces, all coherence gone;
> All iust supply, and all Relation (ll. 205-14)

New inventions and improvements such as the microscope and telescope, the exploration of magnetism or the laws of gravity and free fall, allowed for a better study of the natural world but also induced thoughts about the relation between nature and creation.[28] The impact of all these diverse changes is also visible in the poetry of the time, where it is often placed in relation to turning. For example, in his Holy Sonnet "Thou hast made me" Donne uses the concepts of magnetism and gravity to describe the speaker's relation to God (and his salvation): in spite of the heavy weight of his sins, the speaker is drawn up to God, as the power of gravity is reversed and superseded by God's superior, magnet-like power.

Quite generally, space plays an essential role in metaphysical poetry, and especially with regard to the notion of turning. Since turning is a categorically spatial concept, the use of spatial constructions and images – be it geographical details, maps or the moving spheres – serves to substantiate the notion of turning and makes it more palpable. Geographical and cosmological constructions also form the basis for microcosm-macrocosm analogies that occur frequently in Early Modern poetry.

There are several studies considering the treatment of space in the works of Donne, Herbert and other metaphysical poets. Schleiner (1970), for example, looks at a number of metaphors, among them the concept of life as a journey, and provides a structured overview of Donne's imagery.

---

28 On the development of the various scientific developments and discoveries detailed here and in the previous paragraph, see Windelspecht (2002) and Krebs (2004). Cf. also Briggs 127-35.

Although he restricts himself to Donne's sermons, the images he identifies can also be found in Donne's poetry. Though his compilation of imagery is not complete, it is comprehensive, and as he not only lists different metaphors but orders them, he shows that many of the metaphors Donne uses can be grouped into a small number of thematic fields, several of which are relevant with regard to turning (most notably the notion of life as a journey, cf. 85-94).

Gorton (1998 and 1999) gives a short overview of "Donne's Use of Space," which shows how deeply Donne was influenced by spatial conceptions (and especially by the notion of circularity) and could build on a tradition of spatial imagination ranging from Plato's spherical notion of the cosmos shown in the *Timaeus*, to the Copernican model, allowing Donne "to imagine metaphysical relationships in spatial terms; in terms of the sphere, circle, centre, circumference and set of concentric circles that gave shape to space in the closed cosmos, where space took shape and meaning from the forms that filled it" (1998, §8). Falck (2011) and Pando Canteli (2000) look at the conceptualisation of space in Donne's love poetry. Falck focuses on how the individual relationships celebrated in Donne's epithalamia are presented as part of a cosmic, universal framework. Pando Canteli focuses on the representation of small, confined space in some of Donne's love poems, on the gradual diminution of space and the concentration and depiction of the speakers' love in small poetic forms, such as the sonnet. Though they both analyse secular poetry, their central concerns, opposite but related, are both important here as well: a speaker's integration into a higher order or macrocosmos, and the microcosmic representation of a speaker as a world in itself are both attitudes that emerge regularly in poems concerned with turning. The microcosm-macrocosm analogy offers a way to deal with the question of orientation and integration, that is, where to turn and how to position oneself in the world and afterlife, since it provides a universal spatial concept that a speaker can adapt to his individual situation. Friederich (1978) analyses spatial relations in Donne's *Devotions* and shows how the speaker's changing and wavering perceptions of space – from minute to vast and from openness to closeness – merge in the notion of a divine space that combines big and small and "differs from the negative closeness which dominates many devotions, but it never is the opposite extreme of unlimited space" (30).

The form and structure of *The Temple*, with its explicit references to architectural and ecclesiastical space lend themselves to investigations of space and spatial relations. Higbie (1974) analyses space in *The Temple*, and he regards images of enclosure and enclosed space in The Temple as self-referential allusions to the small poetic forms *The Temple* consists of, arguing for a changing emphasis from the space of man to the space of God expressed in these images (a development which is also visible, for example, in "The Search" and "The Temper (I)," which will be analysed in detail here). Ford (1984) sees the poems of *The Temple* and their arrangement as an imitation of the various elements of a liturgy, progressing in time as well as in space, just as the liturgy takes place over a certain period of time and involves movement in the space of the church. The emphasis on spatial relations in metaphysical poetry is further developed by Lang-Graumann (1997), who focuses on notions of smallness (such as the point as the smallest geometrical unit or a grain of dust as the smallest unit of matter) as constitutive elements of *The Temple*, and shows the extent to which Herbert's poetry relies on spatial perception, which is a basis for the equally spatial notion of turning.

Geometrical constructions provide the basis for more tangible concepts of space, which is also why they are essential for understanding the notion of turning in metaphysical poetry. The use of geometry has been considered in analyses of metaphysical poetry as a way of expressing and understanding the ordered construction of the universe and its reflection in the order of the world (in this sense geometry is also related to musical concepts and the idea of world harmony). With regard to the study of individual poems, naturally more attention has been paid to those poems where geometrical form becomes manifest, like Herbert's "Coloss. 3.3," Donne's "La Corona" and Herbert's "A Wreath" (which will be discussed in detail in the corresponding chapters).

The most pervasive geometrical construction found in metaphysical poetry is the circle. Circularity is linked to turning (and used in metaphysical poetry to illustrate turning) in two ways. Firstly, because the circle is a symbol of divine perfection and therefore provides a notion that is used frequently within the spatial framework of religious turning.

It is also constitutive of the spherical conception of the world that under-
lies many metaphysical poems concerned with turning. Secondly, be-
cause the action of turning also comprises circular revolution and repeti-
tion: Repetition and recommencement stress a speaker's continual effort
to turn towards God and thus emphasise the continual and ongoing aspect
of turning (whereas, for example, the depiction of a single, momentary
experience stresses the other side of turning, a concrete turning point).

Donne was especially fascinated by the idea of circularity – circular
imagery and references to circles as an expression of divinity abound in
his works, and have been analysed to a vast extent (mostly in connection
to specific texts). Thus, for example, Nicolson (1950), Fleissner (1961),
Sullivan (1995/96), Freccero (1963), Spenko (1975), Morillo (1966),
Thomas (1976), Hall (1983), Fischler (1994), Divine (1973), Lobsien
(2009), Salenius (2001) and Schleiner (1970) all treat Donne's use of
circles. Herbert uses circular imagery to a lesser extent than Donne,
though still frequently and the presence of circles and the notion of circu-
larity in his works has been studied, for example, by Carpenter (1970),
Sullivan (1995/96) and Bell (1982), who regards Herbert's use of circular
structure in the light of Ben Jonson's influence (thus showing, how Jon-
son, too, made extensive use of this notion).

2.3 Turning towards harmony

Up to the seventeenth century, geometrical and mathematical construc-
tions play a major role in conceptualising and construing the order of the
universe and the world. Most notably, the notion of the harmony of the
spheres, and of its correspondence in nature and man, still has a decisive
influence (in spite of the change from Ptolemaic to Copernican world
model).[29] Consequently, it is a concept that comes up regularly in meta-
physical poetry, and is used to situate a speaker and his movements in the
world. Moreover, while the notion of the music of the spheres (as devel-
oped in Boethius' De Institutione Musica, which was a major influence
on later philosophers and writers)[30] is one of abstract proportional and

---

29   Kepler's Harmonices Mundi is a good example of this: Kepler tries to conciliate
     his new insights on planetary motion with the idea of celestial and worldly harmo-
     ny. Cf. also Leimberg 1996, 23-31.
30   Cf. Hollander 24-26, Finney x-xi.

mathematical harmony rather than of actual music, it is often depicted in musical terms. Thus, in metaphysical poetry, musical imagery is used to show turning as a kind of tuning: a speaker feels out of tune and wants to be in harmony and concord with God. In analyses of Donne's poetry, the use of musical images is often treated in relation to larger spatial concepts, i.e., in relation to cosmology and the notion of the music of the spheres. Baumgaertner (1980), for example, considers Donne's poetry in the light of contemporary ideas of (world) harmony, while, for example, Pollock (1978) and Baumgaertner (1984) look at Donne's use of the concept of harmony in individual poems, Pollock focussing on "Hymne to Christ" and Baumgaertner (1984) on "La Corona" and "Upon the Translation of the Psalms."

Due to Herbert's biographical affinity to music, the relation between musical notions and metaphysical poetry has been studied more in connection with Herbert's poetry. Diaconoff (1973) looks at how the notion of the music of the spheres is reflected in *The Temple*. Several others show how much Herbert was influenced by contemporary musical developments, and how pervasive musical ideas and notions are in his poetry, for example Boenig (1984) argues for the influence of the structure of lute songs on Herbert's poetry, Tuve (1961) shows how the concept of "sacred parody" employed by Herbert is taken over from "parody" in a musical sense and Wilcox (1987) argues that many of the visual and aural elements in Herbert's poetry are due to his intense occupation with music. Summers (1954, 156-70) highlights the extent of musical imagery in *The Temple*, Elsky (1981) argues that the often dialogical nature of Herbert's poems is taken over from polyphonic music and McColley (1989) shows Herbert's consciousness of various musical forms in several of the poetic forms used in *The Temple*. All these studies show how strongly Herbert was aware of and influenced by musical ideas (including not only the use of metaphors relating to music and harmony but also the use of structural elements and musical forms and genres), and in many of his poems he also makes use of these notions to present a speaker's turning to God.

3.   Why Metaphysical Poetry?

The notion of turning in metaphysical poetry is distinguished from that found in other kinds of poetry, firstly, by its pervasiveness, and secondly by its importance for the individual speaker of a poem. Aspects of turning are of course also found in other kinds of poetry, as well as in other literary genres. For example, if we compare religious metaphysical poetry to contemporary secular love poetry, we can see many similarities with regard to turning, especially in an individual speaker's focus on the object of his love (to whom the speaker turns, and whose turn the speaker desires).

In the English poetry up to Donne and Herbert, we see the strong and widespread influence of Petrarchan love poetry (and thus of a poetic tradition treating an individual's feelings as well as the absence of a beloved) in the whole development of English love poetry from, e.g., Wyatt to Shakespeare, foregrounding an individual speaker and his or her concerns. This personal stance also holds for a large body of religious literature that emerged in the sixteenth and seventeenth centuries. The notion of turning emanates from an individual's perspective and always has a personal component, and a poem's potential for individual expression makes it an ideal medium for staging a speaker's soul-searching and self-analysis and thus for exploring spiritual states of mind.

In addition, the notion of turning comprises two sides – an individual speaker's experience of his own journey through life, his concern with where to turn and how to turn, as well as making sense of this journey by integrating and understanding it within a larger formal and structural framework. And since poetry combines content and form in the smallest, most condensed and most intimate space, its formal devices are well-suited for doing justice to both of these aspects.

The different facets of turning examined here are also at issue in other kinds of poetry, of course. Thus, for example, in his sonnets Shakespeare places human relationships in the context of universal musical harmony (e.g., sonnet #8 and #128), uses the motif of a journey or pilgrimage (e.g., #27 and #50), examines the inward state of a speaker in spatial terms (e.g., #27 and #113), discusses the matter of orientation and where to turn (e.g., #116 and #143) and uses geographical metaphors to expresses relations and states of mind (e.g., #132 and #146). Yet, in metaphysical poetry, the engagement with turning and its various characteristics is intensified, it is conspicuously prominent – almost pervasive –, as turning comes up again and again in various shapes. This is because in the poetry of Donne, Herbert and their followers, the question of how to turn and where to turn is an essential and existential concern, since receiving a response from God is a vital and life-changing matter for the speakers of the poems, with consequences for life, death and afterlife. Moreover, the beloved in Petrarchan love poetry is by definition inaccessible,[31] while the religious metaphysical speaker must strive to make God accessible – for Donne's and Herbert's speakers turning away from God, accepting that God is out of reach or not interested in the speaker, is no option at all.

In this connection, it is worthwhile to consider what makes the poetry of Donne, Herbert and their successors "metaphysical." Although the expression "Metaphysical Poetry" is a fixed term in literary studies nowadays, from the first use of the term it has been difficult to provide a precise definition, and no "final" or definitive definition exists, both with regard to the authors constituting this movement and with regard to their "typical" style.[32] The focus in criticism is mostly on their sophisticated

---

31 A prominent exception is found in Spenser's *Amoretti*; it is significant that here God is made part of the lover's union through their (holy) marriage (cf. also Klein 1992 and Kaske 2004).

32 The term was first used by Dryden to refer to Donne's love poetry as "nice speculations of philosophy" (19). Samuel Johnson shares this notion:

> The metaphysical poets were men of learning, and to shew their learning was their whole endeavour [...] But wit, abstracted from its effects upon the hearer [is] a kind of *discordia concors*; a combination of dissimilar images, or discovery of occult resemblances in things apparently unlike. (24ff)

In 1921, Grierson likewise places focus on an intellectual approach and philosophical interest:

> [Donne was] inspired by a philosophical conception of the universe and the roles assigned to the human spirit in the great drama of existence. [...] his deep reflective interest in the experiences of which his poetry is the expression, the new psychological curiosity with which he writes of love and religion. (1-2)

In addition, Grierson sees in metaphysical poetry a "blend of passion and thought, feeling and ratiocination" (3). T. S. Eliot tried to provide some sort of classification:

> the elaboration of a figure of speech to the farthest stage to which ingenuity can carry it [...]. (1972b, 281f.)

> The *structure* of the sentences, on the other hand, is sometimes far from simple, but this is not a vice; it is a fidelity to thought and feeling.

and complex style, reasoning and imagery, but rarely on the question *why* this is so. Here, it is worthwhile to note that the notion of turning is also present, quite literally, in the idea of a literary trope, that is, turning the meaning of an expression into a different meaning,[33] thus comprising metaphors, ambiguities, *apo koinou* constructions, and generally any word, phrase or sentence that can be read in more than one way. All these are used frequently in metaphysical poetry and form the core of what is typically called metaphysical conceit. Thomas Wilson in *The Art of Rhetoric*, explains the purpose of tropes as follows:

> When learned and wise men gan first to enlarge their tongue and sought with great utterance of speech to commend causes, they found full oft much want of words to set out their meaning. And therefore, remembering things of like nature unto those whereof they spake, they used such words to express their mind as were most like unto others. (196)

That is, he sees tropes as a means to convey something that cannot be expressed otherwise – which, too, seems quite fitting in the context of metaphysical poetry, for it helps explain the religious motivation for its characteristic style.

When looking at what is considered "metaphysical poetry," it becomes apparent that much of it is religious poetry (which is unsurprising considering that the poets typically called metaphysical were situated in a context characterised, among other things, by the prominence of religion and religious discourses). And as a matter of fact, the writers who are taken to

---

[...] Tennyson and Browning are poets, and they think; but they do not feel their thought as immediately as the odour of a rose. (1972b, 285ff.)

Bennett continues to place emphasis on metaphysical poets' intellectual approach and calls them "self-conscious and analytic" (5), without denying them emotion (135). Gardner, too, focuses on the poets' intellectual and elaborate style:

desire [...] for concise expression, achieved by an elliptical syntax, and accompanied by a staccato rhythm in prose and a certain deliberate roughness in versification in poetry. (xxi) [...] Argument and persuasion, and the use of the conceit as their instrument, are the elements or body of a metaphysical poem. Its quintessence or soul is the vivid imagining of a moment of experience or of a situation out of which the need to argue, or persuade, or define arises. (xxvi)

33   Etymologically, "trope" comes from Greek τρέπειν, literally meaning "to turn" (OED, "trope, *n.*"). Cf. also Murray 5-7 on the conceptual closeness between tropes and the notion of conversion.

be the most important or typical metaphysical poets are all (partly or completely) writers of religious poetry.[34] Leimberg (1996) goes one step further and sees the quest for salvation as the main incentive of (a significant part) of metaphysical poetry. She argues that the poetic speakers' personal anxiety for the salvation of their soul, as a driving force for the turn towards God, is a general and recurring feature of religious metaphysical poetry:

> If one tries to find a common denominator for the impulses giving rise to the religious poetry of the time [...] one will think of the concern for assurance of salvation and, in doing so, probably first consider Milton. At a time when there was, so to speak, a competition between certainty of knowledge and fundamental doubt as regards the beginning of all inquiry, the concern for assurance of salvation became as urgent in religious poetry as it had last been (seen from an English perspective) in the Psalms of David. It is one of the common themes of Donne, Herbert, Crashaw, Milton, and Bunyan. Against this strong common feature all possible differences pale. (11; translation Matthias Bauer)

This approach provides a unifying element that is useful for understanding metaphysical poetry as a whole – this anxiety for the future of a human being's soul is found in all religious metaphysical poetry and explains why so much of metaphysical poetry is religious poetry. Even though (and especially since) in the sixteenth and seventeenth centuries fundamental doubt became a serious option, the concern for one's own salvation became all the more pressing. Both spiritual anxiety and the quest for salvation driven by this anxiety are, moreover, expressed within the notion of turning – the question of where to turn and how to turn is essential for establishing a relation to God and for achieving hope or an assurance of salvation. This anxiety also forms the core for the notion of

---

34   That religion seems to play an important role in metaphysical poetry also becomes visible in the more limited choice of poets to be included in collections of metaphysical poetry after Grierson's rather inclusive anthology.Cf., for example, Helen C. White's *The Metaphysical Poets*, which focuses on Donne, Herbert, Crashaw, Vaughan and Traherne; Inge Leimberg's *Heilig Öffentlich Geheimnis*, analysing Donne, Herbert, Crashaw, Vaughan, and Matthias Bauer's *Mystical Linguistics* with a focus on Herbert, Crashaw and Vaughan.

spiritual conversion discussed above: conversion as a turning towards God.[35]

It should be noted that in the instances of turning analysed in this work there is always an expectation of reciprocity that goes beyond mere hope: the speaker (even when describing forsakenness and disorientation) can expect a reciprocal turning (in sacred poetry, because the speaker assumes the presence of God – and therefore salvation; in the love poetry analysed, that is, mainly in "The Canonization," because the lovers' feelings are reciprocated). This is different in texts where the expectation of reciprocity remains unfulfilled: in love poetry, for example, where the speaker's love is not requited. A prominent example is Wroth's "Pamphilia to Amphilanthus": the speaker seeks to turn towards the beloved but feels stuck in a labyrinth of love and does not know *where* to turn:

> In this strange Labyrinth how shall I turne,
> Wayes are on all sides, while the way I misse:
> If to the right hand, there, in loue I burne,
> Let mee goe forward, therein danger is.
> If to the left, suspition hinders blisse;
> Let mee turne back, shame cryes I ought returne:
> Nor faint, though crosses which my fortunes kiss,
> Stand still is harder, although sure to mourne. (Sonnet lxxvii, ll.1-8)

Yet here, too, the speaker, while making an effort to turn towards the beloved, lives in the hope of reciprocated feelings, and can use her love as a guide: thus, she is able to pick up and follow the "threed of Loue" (sonnet lxxvii, l.14). Only when she ends up where she began ("In this strange Labyrinth how shall I turne"), which is due to the poem's Crown form, do her expectations get frustrated (and on a larger scale, the same happens as she progresses through the whole sonnet sequence and gradually has to abandon her hope of mutual love).

With regard to a speaker's personal relation to God, a complete and final state of despair is very rarely found. It is notable, for example in Marlowe's *Doctor Faustus*. When Faustus still has a chance to repent, he declares:

---

35   While Leimberg (1996) is not explicitly concerned with turning, conversion in the sense of searching for and turning towards God plays a central role in her study.

Now, Faustus, must thou needs be damned,
And canst thou not be saved.
What boots it then to think on God or heaven?
Away with such vain fancies and despair!
Despair in God and trust in Beelzebub.
Now go not backward. No, Faustus, be resolute.
Why waverest thou? O, something soundeth in mine ears:
'Abjure this magic, turn to God again!'
Ay, and Faustus will turn to God again.
To God? He loves thee not.
The god thou servest is thine own appetite,
Wherein is fixed the love of Beelzebub.
To him I'll build an altar and a church,
And offer lukewarm blood of new-born babes.
(II.i., ll.1-14, A-Text)

Doctor Faustus is exceptional not only because of the protagonist's damnation but also because he rejects God and salvation: whereas the speakers in the poems analysed here feel that they may have turned away from God because of their general human sinfulness, Faustus actively turns away from God and towards the devil instead. Therefore later on, when he does wish to repent in the face of imminent damnation, his wish becomes futile.

The anxiety about the soul is not only a common feature found in metaphysical poetry, it is also reflected in the poets' use of language. If we look at the style of their poems, at the use of vocabulary and syntax, at the imaginative use of imagery and conceit, it becomes apparent that the perceived complexity and union of "thought and feeling" found in metaphysical poetry is actually due to a faithful expression of the poems' content within the poems' language.[36]

The special and peculiar use of language in metaphysical poetry has been considered not only in (both censuring and praising) attempts at

---

36 Leimberg (1996, 13) also points out Thomas Browne's positive use of the term "metaphysical," firstly, to describe deliberate and careful thinking ("a Metaphysicall and strict examination," Browne 1981, 543), and secondly, to refer to a justified belief in the resurrection and everlasting life:

To subsist in lasting monuments, to live in their productions, to exist in their names and predicament of chimeras, was large satisfaction unto old expectations, and made one part of their Elysiums. But all this is nothing in the metaphysicks of true belief. To live indeed, is to be again ourselves, which [is] not only an hope, but an evidence in noble believers [...]. (Browne 1958, 50)

defining what metaphysical poets are, but also, of course, comes to play in most analyses of their poetry. There are several works that explicitly focus on Donne's and Herbert's conception and use of religious language. A number of studies treat the language of Donne's sermons, for example, Asals (1979), points out Donne's continuing emphasis on the importance of dissecting biblical language and grammar as a way to approach God, and takes this emphasis as a basis for understanding his use of language in the Holy Sonnets. Goodblatt (2010 and 2003) focuses explicitly on Donne's interpretations of the Hebrew roots of certain words, including "turning," and Crawforth (2013, 102-46) likewise analyses Donne's use of etymology to show, among others things, Donne's discussion of the "place" of God in relation to man. Clutterbuck (2005, 1-30, 111-148) argues that Donne's religious poems present a "seeker" verbally attempting to get closer to God, while Magnusson (2006) argues that, within different genres, including his sacred poetry, Donne's speakers act rhetorically, using whatever rhetorical strategy is necessary to achieve their goals.

Herbert's use of language is considered, for example, by Merrill (1981), who sees Herbert's poetry as sacred parody, arguing that religious poetry is generally distinct from secular poetry but uses the same strategies to approach God, and can therefore generally be seen as a kind of sacred parody. Martz (1989) argues that in *The Temple* Herbert in many instances deliberately offers ambiguous readings, in order to avoid strictly Calvinist doctrine and offer a more inclusive view on God's love and the promise of salvation. Asals (1981) explores Herbert's use of synonyms and ambiguity (what she calls "holy equivocation") as a way to express the divine.

As we have seen, the analysis of metaphysical poetry in literary scholarship does take all the aspects found in this study into account. Sometimes there is a focus either on non-poetical works such as Donne's sermons, or on a single poem or very restricted number of poems (such as only the Holy Sonnets, or only a couple of poems from *The Temple*). Often, poems are used to illustrate a specific argument or claim, but without a close textual analysis. However, there is no study which focuses on turning as a general notion and on its diverse aspects, nor is turning analysed consistently in connection to a systematic and detailed textual analysis. This is surprising, since the notion of turning does appear so frequently in Early Modern poetry, and since turning provides a unifying perspective and a means of understanding the spiritual anxiety that seems to pervade both Early Modern thought and metaphysical poetry.

4. Approach and structure

The different facets of turning analysed in this study will be approached through close analyses of single poems. All the poems discussed are highly complex, and can only be understood in their entirety; this requires a full analysis. Although each chapter centres on a different aspect of turning, the poems analysed usually contain most or all of these aspects, and they are often combined with each other. Though other poets are drawn on where it seems expedient, the main focus is on the poetry of John Donne and George Herbert, the most prominent metaphysical poets, for two reasons. Firstly, they constitute the first two "generations" of metaphysical poets, and later metaphysical poetry is largely based on or inspired by them.[37] Secondly, Donne's and Herbert's religious poems are simultaneously similar and different – similar in their topics and concerns and their use of imagery and language, yet different in tone and style – thus providing two contrasting approaches within the same tradition, which is useful for illuminating the notion of turning from different angles. The poems chosen here thus present aspects of turning (and poetical realisations of turning) that are sufficiently similar to allow for a literary analysis in one monograph, and at the same time varied enough to provide *one* good and thorough insight into how turning was treated in Early Modern poetry – without claiming to be exhaustive or complete – inevitably, within the scope of this work, the number of texts selected for discussion must be limited and is therefore to some extent restrictive.[38]

---

37 Cf., for example, the imitation of Herbert's title *The Temple: Sacred Poems and Private Ejaculations* by Harvey, Crashaw and Vaughan (On the implications of this title for the status of religious metaphysical poetry as both sacred and intimately personal, see also Bauer 2015a, 110).

38 While the core canon of Metaphysical Poetry comprises only male (and mostly Protestant) authors, a similar occupation with a speaker's relation to God (often including the notion of turning) can be found in a number of sequences by female authors, e.g. Catherine Parr's "The Lamentacion of a Sinner" (1547), Anne Locke's "A Meditation of a Peninent Sinner" (1560), Mary Sidney's psalm

The structure of this study reflects the two extremes of immediate experience and formal abstraction, beginning with a poem that depicts turning in a very concrete way and ending with a poem in which progress and turning are inextricably linked to the poem's formal and circular structure. Donne's poem "Riding Westward, Goodfriday 1613" provides a vivid example of how different notions of turning are treated (and combined) in a poem. It unites all aspects of turning under consideration and serves to give an overview over the different kinds and concepts of turning this study is concerned with, and will therefore be taken as the starting point for a detailed analysis of turning in metaphysical poetry. "Goodfriday, 1613" centres on turning in the sense of a spiritual conversion and on the process of the speaker establishing a relation to God. The poem does so through a reinterpretation of the speaker's movements, merging the worlds of speaker and Christ, creating a spatial and temporal state in which both are simultaneously present and converging, and allowing the speaker to establish a connection to Christ (which enables his conversion). The poem integrates the speaker's literal journey (westwards, for "pleasure or businesse") into a larger structural concept of the world, both on a small, human level ("Let mans Soule be a Sphaere," l.1) and a large, universal level ("those hands which span the Poles, /And tune all spheares at once," ll.21f.). This world view implies a circularity that allows for a reinterpretation of the speaker's movements: looking away from Christ is turned into looking towards Christ, moving towards death is turned into moving towards life, and moving away from Christ is thus turned into moving closer to (and communicating with) Christ.

Thus, the poem shows the combination and interplay of two perceptions of the world, which are central to the notion of turning in Early Modern poetry and found in many contemporary poems. On the one hand, the speaker's direct experience of his progress through life and towards death (seen as a literal journey) is based on the ancient and universal metaphor of the "path of life." In a Christian context, this journey is often interpreted as a "pilgrimage" through life and towards God. The

---

translations (1599), Elizabeth Melville's "Ane Godlie Dreame (1603) or Aemilia Lanyer's "Salve Deus Rex Iudorum" (1611). Similarly, while Donne and Herbert are both Protestants, the stances found in their poems can also be found in the works of Catholic authors such as Robert Southwell and Richard Crashaw.

concept of a life-journey is combined with a highly sophisticated formal and geometrical construction of the world (that allows for the journey to death to become a journey to life), a view based on spherical order and harmonic patterns. The poem also illuminates aspects of orientation and movement that are inherent to the notion of turning, of the speaker's movement in space and time, and his search for guidance and orientation. And all this is made accessible through the poem's language. An analysis of the poem shows how turning comes about in a lyrical text, how turns are both depicted and addressed in the text and also how turns are constructed and performed through the use of a variety of linguistic mechanisms.

Its inherent spatiality is a fundamental characteristic of the concept of turning, and will therefore provide the main focus of the next chapter. The notion of life as a journey or pilgrimage is a spatial concept, as is the notion of a structured world following harmonic principles. Herbert's "The Search" will serve as the main text for a detailed analysis of turning in the context of space (and to some extent, time). Herbert's poem combines the speaker's literal searching for God (that is, his wandering around) with metaphorical and spiritual motion (the speaker's journey through life, his perceived distance and closeness to God), and it uses spatial conceptions to imagine the prospect of a union between speaker and God (again, spatial and spiritual). At the same time, the speaker's description of his search, combining the notion of a journey through space with his progress through time and towards death, lends itself to a discussion of the notion of life as a pilgrimage (which is intimately linked to and based on the notion of turning). "The Search" also makes use of sacred parody – the desire to be close to God parallels the desire to be close to the beloved in secular love poetry –, and Herbert in fact borrows much from this tradition, which shows the transformation of genres to be included in the multiple processes of turning involved.

Turning is expressed in language and through language. In all poems analysed, besides literal and metaphorical conceptions of turning, various linguistic means are used to describe turning and to make turning happen within a poem. Thus, word meaning and lexical ambiguity (e.g., the various meanings of "turn," "tune," "bend" or "temper") are exploited to approach different ways of turning. Syntactical ambiguity is used to allow a simultaneous turning in two directions (e.g., "Turn, and restore me" in "The Search" can be read as "God, turn Yourself towards me", or as "God, turn me towards You," similar to the possibilities explored in Donne's sermon). The form of a poem underlines processes of turning and may in itself contain a kind of turn (e.g., in Donne's "Thou hast made me," the speaker's change of perspective is linked to the sonnet's form and rhyme scheme, which contains a volta or turn after the eighth line).

The role of language in turning is foregrounded in the analysis of Donne's "The Canonization," which highlights the transforming potential of language in bringing turns about. The two lovers the poem is about are transformed into saints with help of the poem's language. At the same time language is made a subject of the poem itself, which is also a poem about speaking or "hold[ing] your tongue," about "verses," "sonnets" and "hymns," the preservation of love in poetry, the invocation of saints, and the power of "calling" someone a certain way and thereby changing them. As mentioned above, "The Canonization" is distinguished from the other poems under consideration by treating a secular love relationship; however, this relationship is explicitly characterised as a sacred one, and religious vocabulary is used throughout the poem, thus making it a religious poem as much as a love poem.

The next chapter links the immediate experience of turning to formal structural and harmonic principles, and the speaker's experience and movements to a larger order and harmony of the world. These structuring principles are harmonic, in the sense of mathematical proportion and in the sense of musical harmony, and a speaker's position within the larger context of world and universe is often seen and described in musical terms. Likewise, the turn towards God and a desired union with God are often perceived musically as a tuning of the speaker in order to achieve a harmony with God. Herbert's "The Temper (I)" will serve as the main example to show how turning is connected to tuning and to structural and musical principles.

The last chapter then focuses on circular form as the defining element of Donne's "La Corona." Like "Goodfriday, 1613," this poem unites all other aspects discussed, it contains a journey through life, as well as spatial movement and orientation, it is based on musical notions and it relies on language to maintain both progress and circularity. Yet the focus here is different: while the same structural conception informs all the poems discussed previously, structure and form are in the foreground here, and they define and are essential to the speaker's turning. "La Corona" hence provides a counterpoint to "Goodfriday," it gives insight into turning from a different perspective and thus rounds off the examination of notions of turning in metaphysical poetry.

The aim of this study is thus threefold. In the first place, it adds to a deeper understanding of Early Modern poetry, by showing how one central concern of Early Modern life, the anxiety about man's spiritual fate and the salvation of his soul, is linked to and expressed in the notion of turning. Secondly, on a smaller level, it adds to the understanding of a particular number of poems, which are analysed in detail. Thirdly, on a broader level, it gives a deeper insight into certain mechanisms of language, into how the notion of turning is conceived and depicted within a poem's text, and how turns are shown and come about in these poems.

II. Turning in "Goodfriday, 1613. Riding Westward"

The face I carry with me – last –
When I go out of Time –
To take my Rank – by – in the West –
That face – will just be thine – [...]
(Emily Dickinson, J336)

1.   A paradigm of turning

"Goodfriday, 1613. Riding Westward" provides an excellent example of turning, as it deals with turning both explicitly and implicitly and contains in a nutshell all aspects of turning this study will consider. It describes different kinds of movement and a dynamic relation between the individual speaker, the speaker's world and God. The poem shows how turns take place on a linguistic level, and it provides numerous examples of how turning is conceptualised in metaphysical poetry. At the same time, it shows the religious aspect of turning by exemplifying an individual's spiritual struggle for salvation, which, in turn, reflects a general religious concern of the 17th century. Lastly, the poem integrates the topic into contemporary engagements with other disciplines and illustrates the diverse ways in which the notion of turning is present in 17th century thought and imagination.

In this poem, the speaker tells how he rides westwards on Good Friday 1613, while at the same time describing Christ crucified in the East. Within the poem's language, turns take place or are made possible on multiple levels (for example, by exploiting ambiguities, using different tenses or changing pronouns), resulting in the speaker's explicit verbalisations "I turne my back to thee" and "I'll turne my face" at the end of the poem. The speaker's final turn is made possible through the intersection of the speaker's time and space and Christ's time and space (enabling the speaker to establish a personal connection to Christ and to actively pursue his own salvation), which is achieved by linguistic means:

01 Let mans Soule be a Spheare, and then, in this,
02 Th'intelligence that moves, devotion is,
03 And as the other Spheares, by being growne
04 Subject to forraigne motions, lose their owne,
05 And being by others hurried every day,
06 Scarce in a yeare their naturall forme obey:

07 Pleasure or businesse, so, our Soules admit
08 For their first mover, and are whirld by it.
09 Hence is't, that I am carryed towards the West
10 This day, when my Soules forme bends toward the East.
11 There I should see a Sunne, by rising set,
12 And by that setting endlesse day beget;
13 But that Christ on this Crosse, did rise and fall,
14 Sinne had eternally benighted all.
15 Yet dare I'almost be glad, I do not see
16 That spectacle of too much weight for mee
17 Who sees Gods face, that is selfe life, must dye;
18 What a death were it then to see God dye?
19 It made his owne Lieutenant Nature shrinke,
20 It made his footstoole crack, and the Sunne winke.
21 Could I behold those hands which span the Poles,
22 And tune all spheares at once, peirc'd with those holes?
23 Could I behold that endlesse height which is
24 Zenith to us, and to'our Antipodes,
25 Humbled below us? or that blood which is
26 The seat of all our Soules, if not of his,
27 Make durt of dust, or that flesh which was worne
28 By God, for his apparell, rag'd, and torne?
29 If on these things I durst not looke, durst I
30 Upon his miserable mother cast mine eye,
31 Who was Gods partner here, and furnish'd thus
32 Halfe of that Sacrifice, which ransom'd us?
33 Though these things, as I ride, be from mine eye,
34 They'are present yet unto my memory,
35 For that looks towards them; and thou look'st towards mee,
36 O Saviour, as thou hang'st upon the tree;
37 I turne my backe to thee, but to receive
38 Corrections, till thy mercies bid thee leave.
39 O thinke mee worth thine anger, punish mee,
40 Burne off my rusts, and my deformity,
41 Restore thine Image, so much, by thy grace,
42 That thou may'st know mee, and I'll turne my face.

1.1 Turning – the central concern of the poem

The central concern in "Goodfriday" is that of turning, and this choice has consequences for the whole poem: it leads to an overall importance of spatial relations and movement. Underlying the notion of turning is the conception of life as a voyage from cradle to grave, and beyond, to heaven. By choosing the image of the soul as a (moving) sphere, the speaker introduces turning right at the beginning and establishes the spatiality necessary for describing his experience, making movement and turning central aspects of his descriptions. They are further exploited in situating the moving speaker between East and West, in the "bending" of his soul, in his conflict of looking or not looking eastward, in describing how God "tunes [or turns] all spheares" and in the speaker's explicit statements "I turne my back" and "I'll turne my face." The speaker creates a two-dimensional space by setting himself between East and West (using East and West as points of reference between which he moves on the surface of the earth). This space is then expanded to a three-dimensional one, as God is shown to be above (his hands spanning from pole to pole, and his "endlesse height" being "zenith to us, and to 'our Antipodes") and below ("humbled below us [and our Antipodes]") as well as around everything (his hands spanning from pole to pole). The notion of the moving spheres in ll.1-8, although presenting an imaginary setting, already anticipates this three-dimensional space.[1] In "Goodfriday," turning also becomes a temporal process, as the speaker's perception moves between different times (he changes between his own time frame on "this day" – ostensibly Good Friday 1613 – and the first Good Friday) and he goes through a process of transformation and conversion.[2] Turning is thus described (and performed) on several levels.[3]

1　Cf. also Herbert's depiction of God's all-encompassing arms in "Prayer (II)": "Of what supreme almightie power / Is thy great arm which spans the east and west, / And tacks the centre to the sphere" (ll.7-9); and in "The Temper (I)": "Whether I fly with angels, fall with dust, / Thy hands made both, and I am there" (ll.25-26).

2　"Space" is used as much for "denoting time or duration" (*OED*, "space, *n*.1" I.) as for "denoting area or extension" ("space, *n*.1" II.). The expression "space of time," which accentuates the perception of time in terms of spatial relations, has been in use since the beginning of the 16th century (cf. *OED* "space, *n*.1", P2 b.).

3　Cf. also Marvell's "To his Coy Mistress" (Marvell 2005):

　　But at my back I always hear
　　Time's wingèd chariot hurrying near:
　　And yonder all before us lie
　　Deserts of vast eternity. (ll. 21-24)

　　While the setting described is similar to that of "Goodfriday" and Marvell, too, uses a spatial metaphor to show the fugacity of life, there is a reversal in the speaker's attitude. In "Goodfriday," the speaker is driven by "pleasure or

The setting of the poem incorporates another metaphor relevant in the context of turning, which is that of the crossroads. A crossroad is, literally, a point where two roads cross. At the same time, it is a prominent metaphor for a point at which someone has to come to a decision (cf. Hercules at the crossroads), that is, it marks a place where turning (in one direction or other) must take place. In "Goodfriday" the idea of a crossroad is implied in the (unmentioned but certainly present) road on which the speaker moves and Christ's Cross: the presence of the Cross in the speaker's memory creates an "alternative" path, and the speaker must decide which one to follow (ultimately he chooses to return to Christ, toward whom the speaker's soul already bends).

In "Goodfriday," turning is characterised not only as a physical and spiritual process; it is in equal measure a verbal process. The speaker not only *thinks* about his struggles for being able to turn, he verbalises his struggles and describes turning explictly, while at the same time turning also takes place through the poem's language (that is, turns are made possible and performed through a special use of language).

1.2 The worlds of the poem

The speaker's statement in ll. 9-10, "I am carried towards the West / This day" marks the poem as an occasional poem (and the various titles for the poem likewise suggest a specific occasion for writing the poem) and thus raises the question of the poem's relation to Donne's biography, that is, the poem's status as a nonfictional (in this case then autobiographical), or a fictional text.

A reading of the poem as a fictional text is suggested, firstly, by the fact that the text is presented in the form of a poem (and not, for example, as a letter, sermon or devotion), and, linked to this, the degree of elabo-

---

businesse" to move westward and towards his death while he strives to look behind at Christ (and thus, towards resurrection and an eternal life). In Marvell's poem, the speaker is driven on by "Time's winged chariot" (situated behind the speaker) and a disregard for "deserts of vast eternity." Both time and eternity seem to press down on him and create the expectation of a change in the speaker – however, neither makes him turn back or move forward. While the speaker in "Goodfriday" decides to turn to Christ, the speaker in "To his Coy Mistress" instead interprets the pressure of time and eternity as a reason to focus on the present and on momentary "pleasures," as well as a reason for him and his beloved to turn towards each other.

rateness and careful composition of the text (which does not exclude a nonfictional reading, but it presupposes that the text has been thought-through and carefully constructed, which does not accord with a purely biographical account). To this is added the fact that the speaker several times stresses the imaginary nature of what he describes (which, too, does not exclude a biographical reading, but it foregrounds imagination and not reality). Further, there are parallels to other works (such as St. Paul's description of his own conversion), which, too, point at the constructed nature of this experience (and are less likely to depict the author's spontaneous epiphany). Therefore, without deciding conclusively, the poem will here be interpreted as a fictional text.

The implications of choosing a fictional or nonfictional reading lie less in different interpretations and more in how the poem will be related to the world of the reader. A nonfictional reading (equating the speaker of the poem with the author) places more emphasis on the author's personal relation to what he describes (in this case, influencing the reader's evaluation of Donne as author). A fictional reading, on the other hand, offers more possibility for an individual reader to relate the poem to his own world and establish a relevance to him- or herself, since it is not presented as a biographical incident (whose general significance and validity may be challenged), but as a potentially universal experience, left to some extent uncontested because it is of a fictional nature. As the speaker in "Goodfriday" describes an experience which is both personal and can at the same time be regarded as a universal Christian experience, this is a further point in favour of a fictional reading.[4]

---

4   We may consider a sentence as providing a number of possible worlds which are like the actual world but differ from the actual world with regard to what the sentence states. The sentence offers logical possibilities, which are carried out in that particular sentence, even if not in the actual world. Accordingly, a whole text, made up of several sentences, may offer a logical possibility of what the world could look like (Lewis 1-7). In fictional texts, the case is slightly different, though the general mechanism is the same. The assertions made in a fictional text only refer to the world of this fictional text, and are therefore not "possible" in the sense of being viable in the actual world. Still, what is asserted in a fictional text is usually consistent and presents a "world" that is congruent and logically possible in itself. Moreover, in spite of not being part of the actual world, the world created in a fictional text stands in a certain relation to the actual world (i.e., the reader's world). Even though the text does not assert a truth in the real world, it does assert a "fictional truth" (called "FictionAssert" by Bauer and Beck 251f.) which allows

In addition to the question of the poem's fictionality, there is the question of what is "material" or immaterial (spiritual or imagined) within the poem. The speaker creates and combines several imagined worlds in the poem. In ll.1-8, he opens up the world of the spheres, beginning with "let mans Soule be a Spheare," which establishes the realm of thought and imagination. In addition, the speaker here uses an old-fashioned world model (the planets arranged in a series of concentric circles, moved by a "first mover"), a choice which already shows that what he describes is a theoretical and imagined construct, chosen because it is well-suited to draw an analogy to his spiritual conflict, and not because it is a faithful description of astronomical facts. At the same time, the idea of the moving spheres relies on the existence of "material" planets. Thus, although there is a dichotomy between material and immaterial fields, both are connected from the beginning.

Ll. 1-8 also introduce the realm of the soul, whose form, as it is not graspable, can only be imagined by the speaker. Only after establishing this hypothetical image does the speaker refer to himself, stressing the time and place of his voyage: "Hence is't, that I am carryed towards the West / This day, when my Soules forme bends toward the East." In 11-32, he describes the crucifixion at once as an historical event and as a sight he imagines at the point of speaking, that is, he combines a past world with the realm of his imagination. In ll. 33-42 the speaker goes back to his own material world and present, and gives an outlook on his future. Now, however, Christ seems to become part of the speaker's

---

for the reader to establish a connection and to perceive the text as relevant. That is, the reader can relate a fictional text to himself (i.e., there is a relation R between text and reader, cf. Bauer and Beck 256f.).

Cf. Lewalski (1973) on the use of first person singular in Donne's sermons:

[...] in his sermons at least Donne accommodated himself to a general Protestant norm regarding the use of the self as paradigm. He constantly spoke to his auditory in the first person, creating a typical or symbolic "I" to whom all the biblical texts could be applied in the first instance, and in whom the pattern of salvation was manifested. (105f.)

Kneidel (2008), on the other hand, sees Donne's use in several of his sermons both of St. Paul's writings and of St. Paul as a persona as a strategic move, not in order to focus on St. Paul as an Augustinian "paradigmatic divided self" (93) but in order to further an inclusive and communal "ethic of corporate Christianity" (3), stressing on "we" and "us" as presenting a "collective body of believers" (78).

world and time.[5] Thus, in the end, a merging of both material and imma-
terial fields is announced (which goes along with the spatial and temporal
approximation of the speaker and Christ): the speaker still describes what
he sees with his memory (that is, what he imagines), but states that he
will "turn his face" (that is, a specific part of his body).[6]

This interplay between different times and places corresponds to an in-
terchange of inner and outer worlds and of public and private spheres.
The poem goes from a general perspective on men's souls to a personal
localisation of the speaker to a general description of the crucifixion to a
personal encounter between the speaker and Christ. The reader gains in-
sight into the speaker's innermost thoughts and emotions and witnesses
his personal conversion. The speaker's recourse to his memory, that is, to
finding Christ's image within himself also presents an inward turn, which
emphasises the interiority of the speaker's experience: everything in the
poem (apart from his riding) takes place within the speaker's imagina-
tion.

At the same time, "Goodfriday" depicts not only a personal experience,
but an exemplary conversion narrative, which ties in with a (Christian
and 17th-century) reader's experience on several levels. For instance, the
speaker's struggle for contrition and salvation is an essentially Christian
struggle (and therefore relevant to most readers of the poem in Donne's
time). The depiction of the crucifixion in ll. 11-32 relies on communal

---

5   Goldberg sees the speaker's westward movement as an imitation of Christ: "to
     follow the sun from east to west means to follow the Son from his east to his west,
     that is, to imitate Christ [...] by taking up the cross of the world" (472).

6   Bellette sees the figure of Christ turning the spheres as the central ordering and
     harmonising element in the poem and as its climax:
         Time, in its disordered state represented by the "whirld" and "hurried" spheres of the
         opening, is here redeemed as all spheres turn at once. Space, in its disorder represented by
         conflicting East and West, and later polarized into Zenith and Antipodes, is reconciled by
         "those hands which span the Poles." At this moment when man and God are one, the or-
         der in which we customarily live (described in the dry and almost pedantic tones of the
         opening) is fully transcended. (345)
     The lines before ll.21-22 he sees as an approximation towards Christ, the lines
     following the central couplet, however, as a receding movement away from Christ,
     though leaving hope for a future union:
         They are full of anguish [...]. But the reality of Christ, experienced once through contem-
         plation, though it recedes, is not effaced. The retreating back, the growing distance in time
         and space from Calvary, do not ultimately affect the felt proximity, the reality of Grace
         extended. (346)

Christian knowledge (which also becomes evident in its depiction as a "spectacle"), and the speaker uses first person plural in several instances (ll. 24-25, "Zenith to us, and to'our Antipodes, / Humbled below us," l.26, "The seat of all our Soules," l.32, "that Sacrifice, which ransom'd us") – indicating that all Christians are included in the observation of this "spectacle" and showing the global impact of the crucifixion (which affects also the Christian reader: "But that Christ on this Crosse, did rise and fall, / Sinne had eternally benighted all" (l.13-14)). In addition, he can base his experiences on existing models of conversion (see below), with which a Christian in the 17th century would have been familiar. Thus, the general, "public" side of the speaker's experience is just as important as the speaker's private experience in "Goodfriday."

   With the opposition of the spheres and his own body and soul in ll.1-8 and ll.9-10, the speaker also introduces the conventional distinction between the macrocosm of the world, and its reflection in the microcosm of man and man's soul, thus showing himself to be part of the world and obeying natural laws (regardless of whether he wants to or not).[7] In the last part of the poem, this link to the world at large does not count any longer, as the movement towards the east or west is replaced by a movement "towards them" and "towards mee" and the focus shifts exclusively to the relationship between the speaker and Christ.

1.3 Imagination, memory and vision

The speaker is aware that what he describes emanates from his imagination. He hints at the fact that he is talking about imagined, constructed worlds by beginning with a thought experiment and presenting a "spectacle" as well as a process of change that (at the moment of speaking) happen only in his imagination. While his "statement of facts" in ll.9-10 provides a counterpoint to the thought experiment of ll.1-8, the reference to his "Soules forme" immediately goes back to a realm that is not tangible or physically visible – which is then continued with the description of the crucifixion that the speaker does *not* see, and with a vision of Christ, whom the speaker likewise cannot see physically. Thus, apart from the

---

7   By linking large, planetary movements to the movements of his mind, the speaker also opposes turning on a very large scale to turning in a space which is simultaneously very small (nonspatial, because nonphysical) and immense.

speaker's riding, the main action of the poem is situated either in the speaker's imagination, or the speaker's memory, and concerns most importantly his soul. At the same time, the fact that the spectacle of the crucifixion takes place in the speaker's memory allows for a merging of the speaker's world and Christ's world (which cannot be linked except in the speaker's imagination), both spatially and temporally.

The speaker displays a threefold way of looking at the invisible, as he unfolds his story by recurring to imagination, memory and vision: with his physical eyes, he looks westwards, though he does not mention in any way what he sees there.[8] Instead, with his memory, he looks East and describes his vision. This is only possible through his imagination, which allows him to picture what he remembers. This triad of vision, imagination and memory corresponds to the speaker's use of present, past and future tense, which are interwoven. To talk about his actual vision (that is, about the fact that he sees something with his memory),[9] the speaker uses the present tense (i.e., "They'are present yet unto my memory"), as he also does when he situates his body and his soul in the present ("I am carried," "my Soules forme bends," "as I ride," "that [memory] looks towards them," "I turne my back"). The spectacle he sees with his

---

8   It is, however, clear that West is the direction of the setting sun and of death and darkness. Cf. Donne's "Hymne to God my God, in my sicknesse," where the speaker simply states "I see my West" to indicate that he looks forward to his death, as a desirable event leading to his resurrection, and Henry King's "Exequy," which likewise depicts the way towards death as a journey towards the west and as desirable (leading towards life after death as well as to a reunion with his deceased wife):

     Each minute is a short degree,
     And ev'ry houre a step towards thee.
     At night when I betake to rest,
     Next morn I rise neerer my West
     Of life, almost by eight houres saile,
     Then when sleep breath'd his drowsie gale. (1657, 56)

9   Schleiner points out the importance of the image of the "Eyes of the soul," and Donne's idea that God can only be seen with these, explicit at various points in Donne's sermons (Schleiner 138-45). Cf. also the Holy Sonnet "What if this present," where the speaker exhorts himself to "Mark in my heart, O soul, [...]/ The picture of Christ crucified, and tell / Whether that countenance can thee affright, and in "This is my play's last scene" the speaker states "my'ever-waking part shall see that face," just as in "Goodfriday," the speaker's "ever-waking part," that is, his soul is looking towards Christ.

memory is described simultaneously as a past event ("Christ on this Crosse, did rise and fall") and an hypothetical vision ("There I should see") – an event that happened in the past but can be seen by the speaker because he remembers it (or rather, could be seen if he turned round) and which he can describe with the help of his imagination.[10]

The speaker's reliance on his memory has several functions within the poem. In the first place, it contributes to the spatial setting of the poem and the speaker's conflicting movements. The speaker explicitly states that his memory "looks towards thee," that is backwards and eastwards, and his recurrence to memory thus increases the tension between the contrary movements found in the poem.[11] Temporally, "memory" indicates

---

10 Especially in Vaughan's and Traherne's poems, the recourse to memory is often a recourse to the innocence of childhood, too. Cf. Leimberg on Vaughan's "The Retreate":

> Anders als viele seiner Weggefährten möchte der Sprecher nicht vorwärts, sondern zum Ursprung zurückgehen, doch dieses Ziel ist paradoxer Weise nur durch Weiterschreiten zu erreichen, denn der Durchgang zur wiedergewonnenen Kindheit – jeden Tag hier im Leben oder am letzten Tag – ist das Sterben [...]. Weil die Lebensbahn als Kreisbahn gedacht ist, dann ist der Weg zurück auch immer schon der Weg nach vorn, ähnlich wie bei Donne der Ritt nach Westen letztlich zum Sonnenaufgang hinführt. (1996, 441)

Cf. also Vaughan's "Child-hood":

> Dear, harmless age! the short, swift span
> Where weeping Virtue parts with man;
> Where love without lust dwells, and bends
> What way we please without self-ends.
> An age of mysteries! which he
> Must live that would God's face see (ll.31-36)

Ll.35-36 are ambiguous; they may refer simply to the fact that everyone necessarily passes through childhood (and may see God's face in this state of innocence) or it may be a moral demand to "live childhood" (that is, to go back to a state accompanied by virtue and love without lust) in order to see God's face.

11 There are two further spatial aspects associated with memory. Traditionally, memory was seen as located at the back of the head: behind this lies the idea that information enters the mind through sensual perception; the information passes first to fancy or imagination (located in the front of the brain), then to reason (located in the middle) and is then stored in memory (located at the back); cf., for example, Draaisma 26, Lees-Jeffries 13f. In addition, the resort to memory was often associated with spatial constructs serving as mnemonic devices, such as that of wax tablets stored and ordered in a certain way or a storehouse in which information was arranged in different places (Carruthers 37-55). Masselink points out that Donne himself uses loci as mnemonic device in several sermons, not simply to make it easier for the congregation to follow him, but also to

> encourage listeners to participate mentally in the sermon. By asking members of the congregation to join him in a tour of, in this case, a palace, Donne actively involves their fac-

the past, and thus provides a counterpoint to the speaker's present in which he rides westward. Paradoxically, then, the speaker's memory (turning his thoughts backwards in space and time) is also the point of origin for his progress and turn towards Christ, providing the image that makes it possible for the speaker to "see" Christ's looking at him.[12] Secondly, by placing the image of the crucifixion in his own memory, the speaker also marks it as a personal experience (and not just as a collective Christian memory passed on to him through his religious education), an integral part of the speaker and ingrained in his past, an event that is now "from" his eyes but a long time ago was actually seen by his eyes.

Most importantly, the fact that the speaker resorts to his memory can in itself be seen as a way of turning towards God. Donne expounds his notion of divine memory in a sermon. He distinguishes between "three faculties of the soul, the *Vnderstanding*, the *Will*, and the *Memory*."[13] While the first two are often hard to control (people do not understand, or presume to understand too much about God, and their will is often unmanageable), memory offers the most straightforward access to God:[14]

---

ulties. Instead of allowing their memories to receive his message passively, he tells them, in effect, that unless they actually accompany him to the various rooms, they will not be able to "see the sights" (i.e., learn the lessons) he has prepared for them. (105)

12   Carruthers points out the pre-eminence of vision with regard to classical and medieval views on memory and the process of memorisation: Although in a few, select cases memory is triggered acoustically, in most instances what is to be memorised is visualised in one way or other (31-33).

13   This distinction is taken over from St. Augustine and St. Bernard. Guite points out that in differentiating these three faculties in the mind, St. Augustine does not intend them to be considered as entirely separate entities. Rather, they work together, so that "the whole soul is memory, the whole soul is will, the whole soul is intelligence" (Guite 1):

What Augustine and his followers understand by memory then includes within it not only specific memories of the past, but also the whole of what we would call consciousness, together with what we would call the unconscious, and beyond that [...], a special and unsearchably deep memory which corresponds to the Presence of God himself in the soul, or as Augustine often prefers to put it, the soul's presence in God. [...] The exercise of memory for Augustine leads not just to a renewed awareness, in the present, of the past, but to a deeper consciousness of the present moment, of our own true nature and ultimately, of God Himself. For stored in the memory is the image of our own soul as it was created by God in his own image, which calls to us. (2)

14   "Donne's conception of memory as a faculty of great spiritual significance derives directly from the Augustinian tradition [Quinn refers to *Confessions* X], which makes memory the instrument of self-knowledge, which is in turn the key to the self-knowledge of God" (Quinn 283). Cf. also Sherwood (1984, 161) quoted in the

But the *memory* is so familiar, and so present, and so ready a facul-
ty, as will always answer [...] The art of *salvation*, is but the art of
memory. [...] And when we expresse Gods mercy to us, we attrib-
ute but that faculty to God, that he *remembers* us; *Lord, what is
man, that thou art mindfull of him?* And when God works so upon
us, as that *He makes his wonderfull works to be had in remem-
brance*, it is as great a mercy, as the very doing of those wonderfull
works was before. [...] Plato plac'd *all learning* in the memory;
wee may place *all Religion* in the memory too: All knowledge, that
seems new to day, says *Plato*, is but a remembering of *that*, which
your soul knew before. All instruction, which we can give you to
day, is but the remembering you of the mercies of God, which have
been *new every morning.* Nay, he that hears no Sermons, he that
reads no Scriptures, hath the Bible without book; He hath a *Genesis*
in his *memory*; he cannot forget his *Creation* [...]. (Sermon
Preached at Lincolns Inne, on Psalm 38.3, Donne, *Sermons* II, no.
2, 73-74)[15]

---

introduction. Sherwood (161f.) also points out another instance where Donne
explicitly takes up St. Augustine's notion of memory: "*Mine iniquities are as a
burden, Inclinant*, they bend down my soule, created straight, to an incurvation, to
a crookednesse" ("Sermon Preached at Lincolns Inne, The Third Sermon on
Ps.38.4," Donne, *Sermons* II, no. 5, 133).

Chambers (1987) notes that the homiletic text for Good Friday 1613 was Zech.
12.10., "They shall look upon me whom they have pierced" (a verse which is
meaningful also with regard to the speaker's struggle to look at Christ) and stresses
the importance of Zechariah for the prominence of memory in "Goodfriday":

> The etymology of "Zechariah" is, in fact, "God" (Jah or Yah) is "renowned," but at one
> time the import of "renown" was thought to be of a kind which may not be obvious today.
> Isidore of Seville translates "Zecharias" with "memoria Dei," which appears to mean
> "memory of God." John Stockton (citing Isidore) re-translates with "*Zacharias,* The re-
> membrance of the Lord." What is signified, as both writers immediately add, is that the
> Lord remembered his people when, thanks in part to Zechariah's preaching, they were
> mindful of him. The "populus," moreover, consequently was "reversus," as Isidore puts it
> – "turned back," that is – for the rebuilding of Jerusalem and the temple. (190-94)

15   Hickey argues that Donne's abundant use of imagery (especially in his later
    sermons, when he had gained more experience as a preacher) is due to exactly this
    "belief that the understanding and the will are best reached by appealing to the
    memory" (36). This is also how the three faculties are presented in "Goodfriday."
    In the beginning, the speaker seems understanding and knowledgeable in detailing
    a complex argument (which syntactically is also presented in a complex way).
    Then he argues that he cannot look back, in a manner which makes it apparent that
    he is unwilling to look behind. His memory serves as a tool through which he can
    reach a higher (and true) understanding of his relationship to God, as well as the
    will to turn (that is, to announce, "I'll turne my face").

While "these things" in l.33 refers primarily to the "spectacle" of the crucifixion, it can also be seen as a reference to the catechetical truths contained in ll.11-32, that is, to God saving humankind, and the speaker's plea to be restored in God's image in l.41 also hints at this broader conception of memory.[16] Thus, memory serves to retrieve a knowledge that the speaker already possesses – not just a memory of the crucifixion but of everything the crucifixion entails, and a memory of his untarnished relation to God.[17] In "Goodfriday" the speaker goes even further: In general, if there is a need to resort to memory, this happens because what is to be remembered is *not* present, either because it is spatially distant or because it lies in the past (that is, temporally distant), and memory serves to bring it to mind. What the speaker remembers in "Goodfriday," becomes present to him, and, moreover, he recognises that it has been present all along.[18]

Thus, although physically, the speaker situates himself in the present and the crucifixion in the past, in l.35 the fact that Christ looks at the

---

16　Cf. also the role of memory in a "Sermon Preached upon Whitsunday, on John 14.20." Significantly, the verse chosen for this sermon ("At that day shall ye know, that I am in my Father, and ye in me, and I in you") stresses the mutuality of the believer's relationship to Christ which is also found in "Goodfriday":

But come to know that Christ is in thee, and expresse that knowledge in a sanctified life: For though he be in us all, in the work of his Redemption [...], yet onely he can enjoy the chearfulnesse of this unction, and the inseparablenesse of this union, who [...] always remembers that he stands in the presence of Christ, and behaves himselfe worthy of that glorious presence [...], who having done well from the beginning, persevers in well doing to the end, he, and he onely shall finde Christ in him. (Donne, Sermons IX, no. 10, 249)

17　Leimberg points out a similar recourse to memory in Herbert's "The Sinner:" "Lord, how I am all ague, when I seek / What I have treasur'd in my memorie! [...] Yet Lord restore thine image [...] (ll.1-2, 12):

[...] wo sich der Mensch, in der Rückbesinnung am siebten Wochentage, als Perversion des Kosmos, als Ruine eines Tempels und als zerstörtes Ebenbild sieht, um dessen Wiederherstellung er (gleichsam den westwarts reitenden Donne zitierend) seinen göttlichen Werk-Meister bittet (1996, 195)

18　Guibbory highlights the uniting power of memory:

Not only does memory transcend time, making the past present, but it also establishes that special intersection of God's vision and man's. [...] While man goes forward in time, memory can move backward to repair in part the bond with God that was severed, thus enabling him with God's grace to complete the circle and regain paradise. [...] But there is still one further sense in which memory brings us closer to our first perfection. As Donne often observes, remembering is "recollection," a bringing together of things that were previously united but since have become separated, and in this sense it is an attempt to restore original wholeness or, as Donne says, "integrity." (2015, 42f.)

speaker is presented in the present tense ("thou look'st towards mee"). This vision is a product of combining memory (the speaker sees the crucifixion through his memory) and imagination (the speaker imagines Christ looking at him from the cross) with the speaker's actual vision: by using present tense he creates the impression that he is already looking at Christ – and Christ at him – at the moment of speaking.[19] By explicitly locating Christ on the cross at the moment of looking at the speaker ("thou look'st towards mee, / O Saviour, as thou hang'st upon the tree" the speaker merges his own present and Christ's present (which is a distant past to the speaker) and turns a general religious event into an event of personal importance to himself.

Lastly, with his imagination the speaker construes a future event: his own future turn, both physical and spiritual. It is already implied in the ambiguity of "I should see" (since its basic form "shall" also indicates futurity) and made explicit in the last line, when the speaker uses the future tense: "I'll turne my face." In contrast to the description in ll.11-34, what the speaker "should see" in the last lines of the poem is not just the crucifixion he remembers as a religious "spectacle" but Christ's looking

---

19 The present tense used for Christ's looking at the speaker can indicate either that Christ has looked at the speaker all the time, or that he only just now turned his attention to the speaker. The mention of the speaker's memory suggests the former, while the fact that Christ's glance was not mentioned before and is suddenly in the focus in l.35 creates the impression that the speaker has only now become aware of Christ's glance. In order to illustrate God's all-seeing gaze, Cusa compares it to that of an omnivoyant painting (that is, one where the person depicted seems to look directly at everyone who looks at the painting, even when the spectator moves and no matter in which direction he moves past the painting):

And while [the spectator] considers that this gaze does not desert anyone, he sees how diligently it is concerned for each one, as if it were concerned for no one else, but only for him who experiences that he is seen by it. [... He] will also notice that (the image) is most diligently concerned for the least of creatures, just as for the greatest of creatures and for the whole universe. (*De Visione Dei* 1988, 681f.)

Cf. also Donne's "Epistle to Sir Edward Herbert," "Since then our business is to rectify / Nature, to what she was" (ll. 33-34), and a passage from one of Donne's sermons:

[...] go to thine own memory [...] we may be bold to call it the Gallery of the soul, hang'd with so many, and so lively pictures of the goodness and mercies of thy God to thee [...] And as a well made, and well place'd picture, looks alwayes upon him that looks upon it; so shall thy God look upon thee, whose memory is thus contemplating him, and shine upon thine understanding, and rectifie thy will too. ("Sermon of Valediction at my going into Germany, at Lincolns-Inne, April 18, 1619, on Eccl. 12.1," Donne, *Sermons* II, no. 11, 237)

at him. At the same time, Christ's gaze towards the speaker fuses past and present: the temporal gap between the time of the speaker's westward journey and the time of the crucifixion disappears, and they both seem to exist in the same time frame (which is requisite for their looking at each other). Thus, turning is also characterised as a reciprocal process: the speaker turns to Christ and Christ turns to the speaker.

Throughout the poem, there is a strong emphasis on vision, as well as on the direction of the speaker's (and later also Christ's) glance.[20] The speaker's physical eyes are turned westward. However, there is not a single word to describe what lies before him and what he can see with his eyes;[21] instead, he elaborately describes what he cannot see – so much that he creates a detailed image of it. The speaker in "Goodfriday" does not want to look when Christ is above him, since he claims that it is too terrible to see God's greatness (it would kill him), but neither does he want to look when Christ is beneath him, for then he claims that he cannot bear to watch Christ's humiliation. In the middle part of the poem, the speaker thus oscillates between descriptions of both kinds. On the one hand, he considers God's greatness: "God's face, that is self-life" (l.17); "those hands, which span the Poles / And turn all spheres" (l.21f.); "endlesse height, which is / Zenith to us" (l.23f.); "blood, which is / The seat of all our souls" (l.25f.). To this is opposed the image of Christ's suffering: "to see God die" (l.18); "pierced with those holes" (l.22); "Humbled below us" (l.25); "Made dirt of dust" (l.27); "ragg'd and torn" (l.28).

---

20   Sanchez points out the strong emphasis on "beholding," which "Goodfriday" shares with the "Lamentations of Jeremy" (2014, 47-48). Cf. also "The Crosse" (ll.1-2, 35-36), where the speaker exhorts himself, first, not to look away from the Cross, and as a result, become Christ:

Since Christ embrac'd the Crosse it selfe, dare I
His image, th'image of his Crosse deny? [...]

Let Crosses, soe, take what hid Christ in thee,
And be his image, or not his, but he.

21   Carey points out the stark contrast between the rich landscape Donne was purportedly traversing while writing the poem, and the non-existence of this landscape in the poem:

Warwickshire and Shropshire, with their rivers, birds, trees and sizeable populations, have been obliterated – as, for that matter, Donne's horse. It is no earthly terrain he passes across. The poem's geography is surreal. He moves like a planet away from a giant crucifix, the landscape's only feature, which he dare not look at, and on which Christ hangs, watching him. In all of the two counties, Donne and Christ are the sole figures (1981, 121).

By the time the speaker's thoughts reach line 33, the "there" from line 11, indicating distance between the speaker and Christ, has been turned into "these" (instead of "those," which would be expected if the speaker still assumed a distance between him and Christ), but the oscillation between varying descriptions of God is necessary in order for the speaker to reach one level with Christ (and to mentally bring Christ to his own level). Though the speaker has not in fact turned and seen "these things," he has recreated them in his mind and made himself a witness with a correspondent memory. Thus, although the speaker does not achieve a oneness with God at the end of the poem, he has attained the necessary requirements for salvation and is therefore able to look into the future confidently and to promise, "I'll turne my face."[22]

2.   Turns performed on the level of language

As mentioned above, apart from explicit references to turning, the speaker uses a number of linguistic strategies that in themselves constitute processes of turning, as well as a number of tropes that make it possible to talk about and imagine the process of his turning and conversion. Gradu-

---

22   Ettenhuber (205-24) stresses that Donne's notion of the vision of God (i.e., as an immediate, face to face encounter) as a way to eternal happiness and salvation derives largely from St. Augustine. Sherwood points out Donne's threefold and gradual characterisation of vision in a sermon "Preached at Hanworth, to my Lord of Carlile, Aug. 25. 1622, on Job 36:25": Beginning with a "rational 'knowledge' of God from his creatures", leading to a "rational knowledge of Christ gained from actual Christian experience: 'it is a *seeing of God*, not as before, in his *works* abroad, but in his *working* upon himself, at home' [Donne, *Sermons* IV, no. 6, 173]" and culminating in a beatified 'sight' of God in glory with the 'eyes' of the soul" (1984, 166). Cusa (on which the spatial depictions of both Donne and Herbert are based to a considerable extent) also describes the personal relation to God in terms of vision, and in a way very similar to the one found in "Goodfriday":

   I stand before the image of Your Face, my God – an image which I behold with sensible eyes. And I attempt to view with my inner eyes the truth which is pointed to by the painting. And it occurs to me, O Lord, that Your gaze speaks; for Your speaking is none other than Your seeing. (*De Visione Dei*, 1988, ch.10)

   And Donne himself describes the prospect of God turning away from man in terms of seeing and being seen:

   To fall out of the hands of the living God, is a horror beyond our expression, beyond our imagination. [...] that God, who [...] did yet see me, and see me in mercy, by making me see that he saw me, [...] should so turne himself from me ("Sermon Preached to the Earle of Carlile, and his Company, at Sion," Donne, *Sermons* V, no. 13, 266).

ally, the boundaries between present and past (the speaker's time and the time of Christ's life and death), as well as between the speaker's space and Christ's space become blurred, since many expressions can be interpreted with reference to either's space and time. The speaker exploits modality, adverbials, determiners, pronouns, verb forms and syntax to transcend the boundaries between the speaker and Christ and to bring the speaker closer to God. Most of these contain a deictic component, and show to some extent the speaker's relation to what he describes. The use of indexicals (which appear prominently in the poem) assumes an antecedent: it is given by situating the poem on Good Friday, which entails that Christ on the cross is present in some way according to the speaker's perception. In addition, while not being part of its strictly linguistic features, the way in which the poem is structured contributes to its meaning and to the identification of turns within the poem.

2.1 The title

The first hint at the poem's temporal and spatial placement is the title of the poem. It varies between different manuscripts (none of them originally by Donne), but the poem is in most cases either titled "Goodfryday. 1613. Ridinge towards Wales" or "Goodfryday / Made as I was Rideing westward, that daye". Exceptions are, for example, "Riding to Sr Edward Herbert in wales" and "Mr J. Dun*ne* goeinge from S^r H[enry] G[oodyer]: on good fryday sent him back this Meditacion on the waye" (Gardner 98). Gardner adopts the title from the 1633 edition, "Goodfriday, 1613. Riding Westward."

The titles are interesting in themselves, since they, too, indicate spatiality and spatial orientation. All titles have in common that they provide a temporal and spatial placement of the speaker: the action of the poem ostensibly takes place on a Good Friday during the speaker's voyage, likely to have been in 1613. The speaker is "riding" and his direction is indicated, "westward." From some of these titles is seems likely that "Goodfriday" is an occasional poem, but even if not, it becomes clear from the text that the speaker takes the crucifixion as an occasion for meditating about God and about his own relation to God.[23]

---

23   The scene is set not only by the title but also by the specification of the speaker's situation in lines 9-10 and by his description of the crucifixion. Thus, even if the

Especially the addition "[...] sent him back this Meditacion" marks the text itself as something that is turned back (coming into existence during the speaker's voyage, and then being sent back as a finished text). Considering that the speaker's turn takes place in the poem and through the poem, that is, that the text itself becomes part of the process of turning, this is an apt movement. At the same time, it also attributes a larger impact to the poem, since sending the poem to others also affects the real world.

The title also contains the expectation of another, even more significant turn, since Christ's crucifixion will lead to his ascension, his subjugation will be turned to elevation, and his pain will be turned to glory. "Goodfriday" thus stands for a turning point in eschatological history. On a more personal level, the title also joins a central turning point in the life of Christ (taking place on Good Friday) to a central turning point in the speaker's life (taking place while he rides westwards), so that, by setting the speaker's conversion on Good Friday, the title also foreshadows the speaker's emulation of Christ – his suffering and subsequent deliverance.

At the same time, the title contains the temporal (and consequently spatial) possibilities unfolded in the poem. "Goodfriday" in the title alludes not only to one specific day in 1613, but also to a single event in the more distant past as well as to a yearly, recurrent holiday. The combination of these three references provides two events marking specific points in time (and two places where these events take place), as well as a recurrent event perpetuating the actual crucifixion up to the speaker's time (a kind of annual return to the crucifixion) and prompting the speaker's reflections in 1613. Which of these is referred to in the poem is often left unclear, and this openness carries a potential for transcending the boundaries of space and time, which is precisely what happens in the course of the poem.

2.2 Structure

Notably, though the poem is fairly long and contains a number of distinct changes, it is not divided into stanzas. The development shown in the

---

title were unwarranted (which seems unlikely, considering that the poem was consistently handed down *with* a title), the poem gives enough indication to support the setting presented by the title.

poem is an inner one – the speaker's outward movement does not change, though his interpretation of his own situation changes. Therefore it is quite fitting that the outer form does not change – just as the speaker steadily moves westwards, the reader steadily moves on through the poem.

However, within the poem there are some fairly clear demarcations on a contentual level, dividing the poem into three parts, which are indicative of turning points.[24] The poem consists of 42 lines, and although the rhyme scheme (consisting only of rhyming couplets) does not create structural division,[25] the content allows for several possible divisions. The following have been suggested: 8-2-4-6-2-6-4-2-8, or 10-22-10, or 10-4-18-4-6 (see Donne 2010, 102f.), or even 14-14-14 as a set of three sonnets (DiPasquale 119). A division into 10-22-10 lines seems to be the most plausible: ll.1-10 presenting a general explanation of the scene described in the poem (man's soul as sphere) and a localisation of the speaker; ll.11-32 showing what the speaker would see in looking behind; ll.33-42 going back to the speaker's place and time (as described in ll. 9-10 but containing a change of perspective (visual and temporal), which makes it possible for him to leave the hypothetical description of ll.11-32 and to look behind (not with physical eyes, but with the eyes of the soul). This change of perspective creates a personal connection to Christ, a kind of pre-turn, which makes it possible to ask Christ for a "real" turn. At the same time, while the speaker is torn between two opposite directions (spiritually) and changes his course, the image of Christ as all-encompassing is exactly at the centre of the poem (ll. 21-22), providing a structural and thematic turning point.

Almost every movement in the poem has its counterpart: the speaker's westward journey is contrasted to the eastward movement he perceives he should make, the spheres move either to their own motions, or to "for-

---

24 Sullivan argues that "the poem falls into two parts, and in each, the meaning of death is different" (1987, 4). For most of the poem (i.e., ll.1-32), the speaker fears and avoids death, while in ll.33-42 the speaker looks forward to death as a redeeming punishment (1987, 5-6).

25 Although rhyme it not used to structure the poem, there are two instances which show a meaningful deviation from perfect rhyme: O'Connell (1985, 17, 24) points out the imperfect rhymes in ll. 9-10 ("East" and "West") and ll. 33-34 ("eye" and "memory"), which contribute to the incongruity between the speaker's body and soul and their divergent movements.

raigne motions," the speaker talks about looking up at God's "endlesse height" and immediately describes it as "humbled below us," Christ is a sun "by rising set" who "should rise and fall," the speaker looks and is simultaneously looked at, restoring the speaker's image creates an implicit contrast between a sinful and a sinless state, and the speaker turns his back while announcing that he will also turn his face (although this movement is not yet complete, since the fulfilment of this promise lies in the future). Only one movement in the poem is unique, which is the central one of Christ moving the spheres. This revolving movement is, firstly, self-contained (there is no power moving God, and God moves *all* the spheres), and, secondly, a circular movement (intrinsically so, in contrast to the speaker's movements: he has to bend and turn back in order to achieve circularity). At the same time, l.21 hints already at the poem's ending: if God literally turns *all* spheres, this necessarily includes the speaker's soul-sphere, showing God as the cause of the speaker's westward movement and the speaker's turning his back.[26]

The first and third parts lend themselves to further division: ll.1-8 explain the speaker's turning through a thought construct, followed in ll.9-10 by a resuming explanation that applies the general argument from ll.1-8 to the speaker: "Hence is't, that I am carryed towards the West / This day, when my Soules forme bends toward the East." Similarly, ll.33-34 go back from the general description found in the middle part to the speaker's personal situation ("Though these things, as I ride, be from mine eye, / They'are present yet unto my memory"), and then seamlessly go on to detail what can be found in the speaker's memory (maintaining the emphasis on the speaker's personal state).[27]

---

26 O'Connell points out that Christ only *seems* to move (from the speaker's perspective) when he is described as rising and falling in ll.11-14, but is in fact motionless, firstly, because He is nailed to the cross, secondly, because He is equated with the sun, i.e., apparently moving but actually surrounded by moving planets (1985, 19).

27 Severance considers the poem as consisting of three parts and nine parts at the same time. The division into nine smaller parts, with Christ at the centre, creates a symmetrical and circular structure (1987, 25-26), while a division into three larger parts (that is, ll.1-10, ll.11-32, ll.33-42) reflects the speaker's linear journey and interior development. In the latter division, the first and third part show the speaker's perception and the middle part a divine truth; the speaker's perception changes because of the middle part, leading from incomprehension to an

The speaker's development within the poem essentially follows a symmetrical structure: his turning (and riding) away from God is followed by an ekphrastic description, which, in turn, is followed by the speaker's prospective turning towards God. Thus, through the course of the poem, the speaker switches between different spatial and temporal frames. Throughout the poem, there is an interplay between abstract and concrete, and between (spatial and temporal) distance and closeness. The first eight lines generally explain a separation between speaker and Christ, without referring to him and without specifying the time and place of the poem's action (the speaker is torn between "pleasure or business" and "devotion" and chooses the wrong turn, which is amended in the last part of the poem, where the speaker and Christ are reunited).

The middle part of the poem describes the crucifixion mostly from a communal viewpoint as a religious spectacle,[28] employing ekphrasis to describe the imagined picture that is "present" to the speaker's memory. The use of ekphrasis is significant, because it enables the speaker to describe what he perceives as impossible to look at, giving him the means to describe it in just as much detail as if he were actually looking. The description of the crucifixion is an important step towards the speaker's conversion, since it allows the speaker to approach Christ in his imagination and make Christ "present," which is a prerequisite for establishing a connection to him. This ekphrastic description serves a double purpose: It presents an image of the crucifixion that promotes the speaker's conversion by letting him "look back" in spite of his unwillingness and to imagine Christ's gaze at him. In addition, it presents an event, which reminds the speaker of the remission of his sins *through* the crucifixion, and therefore also of being an image of God. What seems at first glance like an evasive strategy, employed in order to avoid turning backwards, thus turns out to be a successful way of approaching God.

---

understanding which allows him to "see" truly (1987, 30-32). The combination of both structures results in "a numbered, linear journey through life and a circling to and with God" (38).

Herman also argues for such a threefold structure and calls it, quite aptly, "triptych-like" – the middle part of the poem corresponds to the central panel of the triptych, while the first and last part, showing different attitudes of the speaker, are opposed to each other, like the side panels of a triptych (n.p.).

28   Oliver compares ll.11-32 to a "versified sermon" (107).

But ekphrasis is not only important in allowing the speaker to "see" without "looking back." Its use is also important as a statement about the speaker as a poet, since it presents a creative act on part of the speaker: his verbal description is so detailed, that, instead of circumscribing the dreaded image he allegedly does not want to picture, the speaker creates (or rather re-creates) through his words an image in its own right.[29] In addition, the ekphrastic description also unites the faculties he employs in approaching Christ, that is, memory, imagination and vision: the speaker resorts to his memory, in order to find the original model, which he then "paints" with his imagination and thus visualises.

The last ten lines then show the speaker's private involvement in the crucifixion, which has become personal through focussing on Christ's glance at the speaker (consequently, the speaker also turns from ekphrasis to direct description and even direct address). In order to make this turn possible, the speaker has to bridge the gap between Christ and himself by bridging the temporal and spatial distance between Jerusalem 30-33 AD and Britain in 1613 with the help of his memory.

2.3 Adverbials

Adverbial adjuncts are of course the most self-evident way of setting time and space. They are used not only to indicate time and place, but also to distinguish and establish a connection between different points in time and different points in space and thus also show intervals and

---

29 Hartwig compares the depiction of the crucifixion in "Goodfriday" to similar depictions in Renaissance paintings (270-78), while Malpezzi stresses the visual nature of the speaker's description:

> The visual image of the horse and rider juxtaposed with the figure of the crucified Christ at the poem's center accomplishes exactly what those prominent figures of horses in so many crucifixion paintings do. It emblematises for us the consequences of all such errant wanderings. [...] Through the image of his errant rider Donne exemplifies the unbridled corporate pride and lust of humanity which led to Christ's sacrificial assumption of mortal flesh. (26f.)

Moog-Grünewald, in discussing the prototypical model of ekphrasis, Homer's description of the Shield of Achilles, highlights the creative significance of ekphrastic description:

> Die 'Beschreibung' des Schildes des Achilleus ist zum einen Modell, weil sie auf ein Werk der bildenden Kunst sprachlich Bezug nimmt, um mit ihm textuell an Bildlichkeit zu konkurrieren; zum anderen aber – und dies ist wesentlich – ist sie Modell, weil sie intendiert, Sprache metaphysisch zu fundieren – nicht, indem sie auf einen 'Schild' Bezug nimmt, vielmehr indem sie den 'Schild' hervorbringt. (2008b, 196)

movements. In the first eight lines, "every day" and "scarce in a year" show the general course of time and its repetition and monotony; in a similar vein, "eternally," "endless day" and "endless height" describe events on such a large scale that they are not graspable by the mind of a human being ("endless height," too, contains a temporal component, since the speaker would never finish looking up at this height).

In l.34, in contrast, the speaker describes the crucifixion as "present," which specifies not only the temporal actuality it has for the speaker but also its spatial placement, i.e., its "presence" in the speaker's memory. Time thus alternates between the immediate present (in ll. 9-10 and from l. 33 on) and eternal, repeated cycles (both secular and sacred). The speaker's experience is immediate and unique, limited to a single moment in the present, which is decisive for the speaker's conversion.

Spatial references are similarly used to differentiate the world at large from the spot where the speaker experiences his conversion (whether this refers to a region in Britain through which the speaker is riding or to a position in front of the cross is left open). "In this" in l.1 is a special case, since it refers back to the mental construct began with "let mans soule" and underlines the circular motions described in ll.1-8. "Towards the west" and "to the east" provide the horizontal range for the world the speaker constructs in his poem, the points of reference between which the speaker is moving. On a vertical level, this world is defined by "too much weight," "endless height" and "humbled below us," i.e., by dimensions that do not accord with the speaker.

The speaker adjusts what he needs (i.e., Christ's height and presence) to his own level (or closer to his own level – Christ is still *up*-on the tree, so, though closer, not exactly on the same level). Thus, the speaker moves from a relationship to God that carries "too much weight for me" to one that is easier to bear for him. Moreover, the speaker, after creating a "hurried" and "whirling" movement right at the beginning of the poem by describing planetary motions and keeping it up in the middle part with Christ's turning of the spheres, reduces movement in the last ten lines. Christ's movement is described as "rise and fall" in l.13; in l.36, Christ just "hangs upon the tree." The speaker now focuses on turning his back and face (i.e. physically very small movements), while in l.9 and l.33 he still talked about riding away, that is, about moving on a larger scale.

Correspondingly, this adjustment and reduction of movement goes to-
gether with the change from past to present: in ll.9-10 the speaker situates
himself in the present, which he takes up in l.33. In l.13 the past tense is
used to describe the crucifixion, while in l.36 the speaker does the same
in the present tense, thus bringing Christ and the crucifixion to his own
temporal level, the present – which the speaker states explicitly with
"they are present yet unto my memory." "Yet" is ambiguous here: either
the crucifixion is *still* present in the speaker's memory (that is, as a past
event which is still fresh in his memory – but may fade over time), or it is
already present (that is, the speaker was successful in envisioning the
crucifixion as an event taking place at the present moment of speaking).
The ambiguity thus provides a temporal bridge in bringing past and fu-
ture closer together.[30]

Similarly, "hence" is ambiguous in several ways, and its ambiguity
works like a hinge that allows movement (both spatial and temporal) in
both directions. In addition to its meaning as a logical term (cf. *OED*,
"hence, *adv*. III.7": "(As an inference) from this fact or circumstance;
from these premises or data; for this reason; therefore"), "hence" can also
refer to spatial and temporal movement. Spatially, it means "away from
here, away from this place" (*OED*, "hence, *adv*. I.1.a") and in a more
specific and religious sense, "from this world, from this life" (that is into
the next world or life, cf. "hence, *adv*. I.3.a"). But it can also be used to
indicate the goal of this departing movement (*OED*, "hence, *adv*. I.3.b":
"in the next world"). Temporally, its primary meaning is "From this time
onward, henceforward, henceforth" ("hence, *adv*. II.4.a"), and in a more
specific sense, "from now" ("hence, *adv*. II.4.c").[31] Thus, "hence" serves
to logically deduce a reason for the diverging movements of body and
soul, but it also connects these movements in in its different meanings.

The prepositions used in these adverbial clauses are telling, too. The
speaker rides "towards" the West and bends "to" the East – "towards"
and "to" straightforwardly indicate opposite and divergent directions. In
l.33, "these things" are still "[away] *from* mine eye" but present "*unto* my

---

30   Taking the merging of separate spaces literally, at the end of the first part, the
     speaker needs two lines to describe the central movements (i.e., ll.9-10), while later
     on they are joined in a single line (l.35).
31   Brooks points out that that the connotation "from now" creates a "growing
     immediacy of the meditative experience" (1995, 292).

memory" – although the speaker uses idiomatic expressions, "from" and "unto" are also directional.[32] Considered on its own, "from" marks a point of origin from which "these things" have a certain distance ("these things" are *away from*, i.e., literally *at some distance* from his eyes). Thus it contributes to demarcate the distance between the speaker and the crucifixion: "these things" on the one side, the speaker's "eye" on the other.[33]

"From mine eye" is paralleled to "unto my memory" in the next line. This expression is likewise both idiomatic and has a spatial connotation. "Unto" can be used to indicate "the recipient of an impression, the holder of an opinion or the like; used esp. after verbs, as appear, seem, †think, etc." (VIII.26.b. b.) and this is the primary sense in "Goodfriday." But "unto" also contains "to" and expresses "motion directed towards and reaching (a place, point, or goal)" (*OED* "unto, *prep.* and *conj.*" A.I.1.a) or simply "in the direction of; directed towards" (A.I.2.a).[34] It can also be used for "indicating the limit or dimension of a movement, extension, or continuance in space" (*OED* "unto, *prep.* and *conj.*" A.I.3.a) and often denotes closeness.[35] Thus, while "from" implies an increase of distance and expands the space described in the poem (and literally, the speaker rides westwards, away from the crucifixion in the East), "unto" implies

---

32   Cf. some examples given in the *OED* ("eye, *n.*1" I.5.b): "too hyde this blemish from the eye." (from Golding's translation of the *Metamorphoses* (new ed. 1567, ix. f. 112), "Masking the Businesse from the common Eye." (*Macbeth* (1623), iii. i. 126) and "we cannot withhold it from the eye of the learned" (*Monthly Rev.* Oct. 316, 1783). These examples have in common that they contain a verb showing that something is *kept away* from the eye; the speaker in "Goodfriday," in contrast, just says "be from mine eye," which is a more neutral statement with regard to the cause of "these things" being invisible to the speaker and at the same time puts more emphasis on the preposition itself.

33   The phrase "from mine eye" may hint at the ancient idea that vision originates in the eye, which sends out rays of light.

34   The title "Mr J. Dun*ne* goeinge from Sr H[enry] G[oodyer]: on good fryday sent him back this Meditacion on the waye" suggests the same kind of movement and gives an explicit recipient.

35   Cf. *OED* A.I.4.a, "Upon (and in contact with); on, against" and A.I.4.b, "in contiguity or proximity to; in front of; by, close beside," as well as A.I.5, "expressing relative location (esp. with nigh or near)" and V.15.a, "Denoting attachment, union, adherence, or kinship to a person." The opposite sentiment can also be expressed with "unto" (cf. VII.23, "Against, in respect of opposition or hostility") but is much rarer.

an increase in proximity and orientation towards a goal and delimits the poem's space.

The use of "present" may also be seen as a spatial reference indicating direction in this context (especially in combination with "*unto* my memory" and in opposition to "from mine eye"): when read as "pre-sent" it shows God's approximation towards the speaker: the image of the crucifixion has been sent to the speaker's memory. In this regard, the choice of "present" alludes to another meaning as well: "these things" can be seen as a present (that is, as a gift) from God to the speaker, both with regard to the crucifixion itself (Christ has given himself to redeem humankind) and the image of the crucifixion in the speaker's memory (which helps him to establish a connection to God). And just as "present" can be understood in a temporal or spatial sense, when it is read as "pre-sent" both notions are preserved: the (image of the) crucifixion is spatially sent unto the speaker' memory (that is, displayed in front of his memory), and temporally, Christ was sent to earth before the speaker's time.

"Unto" is also close to "onto", evoking the image of "these things" being placed upon the speaker's memory from above. Furthermore, "present" is acoustically similar to "pressed" or "pressing" (i.e., "these things are pressing, from above, onto my memory), which may be seen as a continuation of the speaker's previous evasive strategy, as it takes up the description of the crucifixion as a "spectacle of too much weight" bearing the speaker down in l.16, but also in a positive light, since a pressing down of this "spectacle" on the speaker's memory simply overturns his reluctance to look behind.[36]

As mentioned before, although there is an approximation between the speaker and Christ from l.35 on, this distance is never cancelled completely, and the speaker seems to be aware of this. He cannot behold "that endlesse height [...] humbled below us," nor can he look at Christ's blood in the dust (i.e., down on the ground). In l.29, the speaker states that he cannot look "*on* these things" and in l.30 he asks himself whether he can look "*upon* his miserable mother" – in both cases he is unable to

---

36   Moreover, the idea that picturing the crucifixion is (permanently) pressed upon and imprinted in the speaker's memory evokes the idea of stamping a coin and thus ties in with the "metal" qualities associated with the plea "burn off my rusts" in l.40.

look. Two things should be noticed here. Firstly, in the middle part of the poem, the speaker is concerned with his actual vision – he imagines the crucifixion (effectively *seeing* it) but does not dare to look. In l.35, it is his memory that looks, with which he had been able to see the crucifixion all along. So, externally nothing changes: the speaker had accessed his memory in describing "that spectacle" and "these things" and is still accessing his memory when he "looks towards them" with his memory. Internally and psychologically, however the speaker goes from a state of not seeing to a state of seeing (and, what is even more, from not seeing Christ to seeing Christ) and thus experiences a kind of epiphany. Secondly, the speaker changes his perception from focussing on the crucifixion as a whole, a "spectacle" (which you can only look at but are no part of), to focussing on Christ alone, as a fellow human being communicating with the speaker. This contributes to reassuring the speaker that Christ will be there for him and that he can hope for his own salvation.

In l.35, the speaker's memory looks "towards" "these things" and Christ looks "towards me." Here too, "towards" shows two movements, but this time they are convergent. Moreover, the doubling of the identical construction "towards …" makes these two movements seem identical and increases the reciprocity of the speaker and Christ looking at each other. In contrast to the unequal and disproportionate movement of body and soul in ll. 9-10, the ocular movements of memory and Christ in l.35 are symmetrical. Thus, the most explicit prepositions regarding directional movement are used at two central points in the poem, and the directions indicated by them are completely reversed. There is, however, one restriction: in ll.9-10, the speaker talks about actual movements (physical and spiritual), while in l.35, although the movements go in the right direction, there is only eye movement, which consequently can only lead to eye contact and not to an actual convergence (though it facilitates the speaker's prospective turn in l.42).

While "toward" and "towards" in ll.9-10 open up the space described (leading to an increasing distance, which then becomes even larger with God's "endlesse height"), the double use of "towards" in l.33 (describing an approach, decreasing distance) delimits it. Similarly, "till" in l.38 provides an explicit temporal limitation – there is an end in sight for the speaker's misery.

2.4 Determiners

The use of determiners, and especially demonstratives, is another way to indicate the speaker's stance towards Christ, and, conspicuously, the speaker uses a great many of them. "In this" in the first line is already ambiguous; it either refers to man's soul as a sphere within which devotion is situated, or to the theoretical construct within which man's soul is imagined as a sphere. "This day" in l.9 is at once specified and unspecified: it refers to a certain day, but it does not state which day that is (whether the original Good Friday, or the holiday in 1613). It indicates proximity to the speaker and refers to the time of speaking (which is also emphasised by the present progressive "I am carried"). Still, it remains unclear when exactly "this day" takes place and whether the crucifixion is included in this proximity (i.e., part of "this day").

With regard to the use of determiners, "this day" is central, because it may explicitly point at the speaking time but also at "this Good Friday/this holiday." "This day" refers generally to the point in time when the speaker is speaking, moreover it may refer more specifically to one day in 1613 (namely Good Friday), but it may also refer to the first Good Friday (that is, to a day in the distant past, which the speaker perceives as present) or to Good Friday as a yearly, recurrent holiday. It seems clear at first glance (I ride this day, i.e., at the moment of speaking), but, as we have seen, its reference is in fact ambiguous. It is meant to be ambiguous, in order to create an intimate connection between the speaker and Christ and to create the possibility for the speaker to communicate with Christ. And it becomes ambiguous through the speaker's alternation between past and present, which obscures whether the speaker refers to his own time, Christ's time or a yearly holiday – or, in fact, to all three of them at the same time). As a result, Christ seems to be present and part of "this day."

Up to line 35, the speaker's relation to Christ alternates between distance and proximity. "There" in line 11 shows the distance between the speaker and whatever is located East. The same holds for "that setting" in l. 12. In line 13, however, the speaker switches to a demonstrative expressing nearness again: "this cross." Then he switches back to a distant stance: "that spectacle" (1.16), "those hands" (1.21), "those holes" (1.22), "that height" (1.23), "that blood" (1.25), "that flesh" (1.27) and "that sacrifice" (l.32). In between these is found "these things" (ll. 29 and 33), which, though less distant, is deliberately vague and vacant.

The speaker's stance then changes. In l.35, the speaker begins with "that [memory] looks towards them" but goes on with "and thou look'st towards me." Although "thou" and "me" belong to different grammatical categories, they are juxtaposed to "that" and "them." Proximity seems to come from Christ, who seems to turn toward the speaker. At this point the speaker finally switches from a general to a personal description and from public worship to a private relation to Christ, which initiates the speaker's conversion. It is accompanied by the use of the present tense in ll. 33-34, which refers again to the speaker's time of speaking. The last determiner to be found is "the tree" in l.36. It refers back to "this crosse," one of the few demonstratives indicating proximity in the middle part, but at the same time it also presents "the tree" (i.e., "this crosse") as a landmark known to the speaker which requires no further specification.

2.5 Pronouns and forms of address

As already indicated, pronouns are similarly used to indicate the speaker's changing relationship to Christ. Significantly, the poem presents a first-person narrator, thus making the conversion experience depicted in the poem more accessible and relatable. It is also noticeable that the speaker talks about himself a lot. After the general musings in ll.1-8, the speaker emphasises his own actions and his own perception of the world: "I am carried," "my soules forme," "I should see," "dare I [...] be glad I do not see," "too much weight for me," "could I behold," "could I behold" again, "I durst not looke," "durst I," "as I ride." This stands in contrast to the general "way of the world" described in the first eight lines and to the general doctrines of Christianity described in ll.11-32. For these he uses either a generic singular or plural forms: "man," "our souls," "sinne had [...] benighted all," "to us and our antipodes," "humbled below us," "all our Soules," "which ransom'd us." In ll. 11-32, the crucifixion is described as a "spectacle," a general tableau complete with running blood, torn flesh and weeping Mary. Still, it is a spectacle the speaker does not dare to look at, and which consequently does not encourage him to repent and turn the right way.

In 1.35 the speaker switches from a third-person description of his memory and "these things" to directly addressing God and naming himself ("thou look'st towards mee"), a mode which he keeps till the end of the poem. Among the use of pronouns, forms of address play a special role in the last part of the poem –directly addressing Christ enables the speaker to establish the connection to Christ necessary for his personal conversion. The speaker's thoughts and perception circle again and again around himself and Christ: "thou," "me," "thou," "my back," "thee," "thy mercies," "thee," "me," "thine anger," "me," "my rust," "my deformity," "thine image," "thy grace," "thou," "I," "my face."[37] The personal address is intensified by the use of imperatives in ll. 39-41 and the vocative "o" in ll. 36 and 39, giving the last lines the character of a prayer-like invocation, which stands in stark contrast to the impersonal, hypothetical reasoning of the poem's openings lines 1-8, and which is also indicative of the change that has taken place in the speaker and his relation to Christ.

Thus the speaker opposes general knowledge and doctrine to his personal experience – his immediate experience as a sinner being led astray, but also his experience of seeing and perceiving the presence of Christ.[38] There is a gradual movement from an impersonal and detached description in the beginning (which includes the speaker's description of himself in ll.9-10 – while he turns to himself and his own soul, he does not go beyond a mere statement of facts) to a personal and emotional experience in the end.

---

37 Frontain sees here a "widening of the viewer's perspective":
    With the introduction of "thou" in line 35, "Goodfriday" abruptly changes mode of address, in effect requiring the speaker to step back and view the scene of the poem's action from a perspective broad enough to include the hitherto unnoticed Saviour. (2006, 86)
    At the same time, the use of imperatives in the last lines of the poem leads to
    a shift from the written to the oral performance mode [...], an attempt to conjure God, to elicit a word or action from the only being who has the power to save the speaker's soul. Donne's desire to "make something happen" through the medium of a poem is no doubt modelled as much upon the biblical premise of the creating Word as upon the magical powers of oral formulae (2006, 87f.)

38 Although there is a personal relation between the speaker and Christ, the speaker's still allocates himself to the community of men – he is included in "we" and "our," while his connection to Christ, even though it is intimate, is described in terms of "me " and "thou", and not "us."

2.6 Verbs

The tense, mood and aspect of verbs indicate whether something is "real" in the poem, and also what the speaker's relation to his depictions is. Lines 1-8 are in the present tense, yet not in the speaker's present; they describe a thought experiment presenting an analogy, which, though it is applicable to the speaker's individual situation, is of a very general nature. Lines 9-10 are also in present tense, but they present the speaker's actual position in space and time. After this placement of the speaker, he switches to the subjunctive and gives a hypothetical description of the space and time of Christ which the speaker does not see. This is interspersed with a reference back to the speaker's space and time (lines 15-16) and some general truths about God ("Who sees God's face, [...] must die," "those hands which span the Poles [...]," "that endlesse height, which is [...]," "that blood which is [...]), before going back to a hypothetical thought in line 18, followed by another statement about God's past situated in Christ's space and time in lines 19-20. (i.e., this is not a hypothetical description but one of times past). The hypothetical questions in lines 21-30 then continue the description of what the speaker does not see, while lines 31-32 again state a "historical" truth and are in simple past tense.

In line 33, the speaker switches back to his own space and time and a present tense description of his actual situation. In lines 33-38, the speaker's and Christ's space and time are united through the use of present tense – in l.35 the simple present is used for the first time to describe Christ's action, "Thou look'st towards mee." Although l.35 is set in the present tense, it joins past and present: while memory, in the present, performs the action of looking backwards, it sees only what is past. The continuation "thou look'st towards me," however, is not a statement about the past but about the present time. The approximation between the speaker and Christ increases in lines 39-24, in which the speaker is able to use imperatives in addressing God. In line 42, the speaker even makes a promise for the future, showing his prospective salvation ("I'll turne my face"). Thus, through the course of the poem, the speaker switches between different spatial and temporal frames.

In the first eight lines, the soul-sphere's impotence is suggested by the passives "growne subject," "being hurried," "are whirld," and "I am carried." The soul "admit[s a] first mover,"[39] albeit the wrong one, so that the soul, like the spheres, deviates from the right course and is "whirld." However, the "Soules forme" still "bends toward the East." Though devotion entails submission, it is not a passive action. It is related to "to vow," (that is, "the action of devoting or consecrating [...] by vow," cf. *OED*, "devotion, *n*") which is both a verbal statement and a performative, and in the last line of the poem, the speaker will indeed vow, "I'll turne my face." Because of its lack of an object, "move" is also ambiguous, its primary meaning here is of course that of an action creating movement, but "move" also has the sense of "affect emotionally." Considering the speaker's emotional response to the image of Christ crucified, this meaning of "move" is also present. Not only does devotion get the soul into motion, but the "intelligence" (i.e., in the sense of information) of Christ crucified can also be seen as something that touches the speaker's emotions (i.e. moves him) so much that it incites devotion.

In line 9, the speaker states that he is "carried" towards the west. On the one hand, the passive "carried" refers to the different forces moving the speaker as if he had no will of his own. Additionally, "carried" refers to the speaker's means of transport. If he is "carried," he will either be using a horse that carries him, or be sitting in a wagon or coach drawn most likely by horses. In line 33, the speaker states "as I ride," which, again, can refer to either a horse or a coach (and if one of the poem's titles is indeed originally by Donne, the action of "riding" there would also highlight the presence of a horse in the poem). In both cases, the image of the horse, even though not mentioned explicitly, contributes to the idea of the speaker being dragged by other forces. The horse as a symbol of the force of passion brings to mind Plato's chariot allegory in *Phaedrus* (69-71; ch. IX, 246A-247C), in which the intellectual part of the soul is compared to a charioteer being driven by two horses representing reason and passion, respectively. The horses in Plato's allegory pull in different directions and need to be reined by the charioteer.

---

39 Friedman points out that even "admit" is ambiguous and can be read as a "purely physical action, involving neither will nor agency" (423n10).

St. Augustine, too, uses a similar notion in comparing the human body to an unruly horse, an image which Donne adopts in a sermon:[40]

> *Caro mea jumentum meum*, says S. *Augustine*, my body is the horse I ride; *iter ago in Jerusalem*, my business lies at *Jerusalem*, thither I should ride; *De via conatur excutere*, my horse over pampered casts me upon the ay, or carries me out of the way (Sermon Preached at St. Paul's on Midsommer Day 1622, on John 1.8, Donne, *Sermons* IV, no. 5, 152)

In another sermon, Donne takes up the psalm he is preaching on, "Be not as the horse, or the mule, who have no understanding; whose mouth must be held in with bit and bridle, lest they come neere unto thee" (which is preceded by the verse "I will instruct thee and teach thee in the way which thou shalt go: I will guide thee with mine eye"), and links the command of the horse or mule to turning towards God:

> If a man, having opportunities […] to be better instructed, […] doe but lay himselfe downe as a leafe upon the water, to be carried along with the tide, […] if […] he keepe not his understanding awake […], I would it were true of them, *Facti sicut*, you are like the Horse, and the Mule. […] Affection and calamity are the bit and bridle, that God puts into our mouth sometimes to turne us to him. […] God bits and bridles us, he whips and scourges us, sometimes lest our desires should mislead us a wrong way, sometimes, if they have, to turne us into the right way againe. (Preached upon the Penitentiall Psalmes, on Ps. 32.9, Donne, *Sermons* IX, no. 17, 385-87)

This passage neatly sums up the development found in "Goodfriday": rather than being "carried along," the speaker needs to be (and wants to

---

40 Malpezzi (24f.) notes that the analogy of horse and rider to body and soul is also pervasive in the emblem tradition as well as in English Renaissance love poetry, mostly as a symbol of lust, sensual appetite or unreined passions which must be controlled, seen for example in Wyatt's "The long love that in my thought doth harbour" (ll.6-7, "my trust and lust's negligence / Be reined by reason, shame, and reverence"); in Sidney's *Astrophel and Stella*, as a central conceit in sonnet #49 ("I on my horse, and *Love* on me doth trie / Our horsemanships") and the Fifth Song (l.15, "For rage now rules the reynes, which guided were by Pleasure.").

be) "bit and bridled" in order to be turned to God (that is, in order to effect the final turn announced in the last line, "I'll turne my face").[41]

The "spectacle" described in ll. 11-32 is introduced by "There I should see," which substantially emphasises its material and graspable character for the speaker. The ambiguity of "should" is most significant here, since it is indicative of the speaker's attitude towards Christ and towards his own religious obligations. The modal verb "should" can be read either as indicating weak obligation (i.e., "I ought to see") or as (part of) a conditional II indicating a weak possibility (i.e., "If I turned round, I should see"). The first reading is quite straightforward – the speaker, as a good Christian, is morally obliged to find the strength necessary to look at the crucifixion – to open himself up to the vision of Christ and to participate in the celebration of Good Friday as a religious holiday. This obligation exists regardless of whether the speaker actually turns or not.

The second reading is more complex, since it touches the question whether the speaker actually sees something and whether there *is* anything to see – which in turn is complicated on several levels (because it can be read in several ways). It should be noted that, in the first place, "should" indicates a possible reality, so that whatever he may describe is not actually happening physically. However, it is still "real" to the speaker, on the one hand as a vision he perceives in his memory (as an image of an event he witnessed in the past or feels to have witnessed, so that it has become part of *his* memory), and on the other hand as a permanently

---

41 Westerweel (1989) points out the traditional allegorical depiction of Temperance as a woman wearing bit and bridle and lists several literary examples taking up this image, among them Herbert's "Christmas (I)," which also depicts the speaker's life as a journey (214-16):

   All after pleasures as I rid one day,
   My horse and I, both tir'd, bodie and minde,
   With full crie of affections, quite astray,
   I took up in the next inne I could finde. ((ll.1-4)

Westerweel also points out that the use of "Corrections" finds a parallel in Herbert's "The Church-porch" (ll. 261-64) where it is associated with horsemanship (218):

   "Be not thine own worm; yet such jealousie,
   As hurts not others, but may make thee better,
   Is a good spurre. Correct thy passions spite;
   Then may the beasts draw thee to happy light"

present reality (so vivid to him that he did not have to witness it personally in order to "see" it).

That the image of the crucifixion is engrained in the Christian speaker can be taken for granted, moreover it remains vivid through yearly repeated religious holidays (involving textual descriptions of the crucifixion, too), as well as through visual depictions. The fact the speaker characterises the crucifixion as a "spectacle" also brings in a dramatic element evoking mystery plays and pageants: the crucifixion is something designed to be "seen." Apart from textual and visual reminders, the crucifixion is present as a historical event of which the speaker is at all times aware and which is thus permanently present in the his memory. In contrast to this universally present event, Christ's glance at the speaker is depicted as a sudden occurrence (or at least a sudden perception, which the speaker does not notice till the moment of speaking). While God's eye on men (including the speaker) is of course permanent, it is not perceived as such by the speaker. Only when he considers himself to be looking at Christ (which he does explicitly in l.35, even though only with his memory), that is, only when he is attentive and focussed on the right course, does he become aware of the reciprocity of this glance. Thus, the crucifixion is set in the past tense (apart from the general truths noticed above), remote and removed from the speaker, while the speaker's personal involvement is present to him and consequently set in the present tense. To some extent, the change from ll. 11-32 to ll.33-34 mirrors that from ll.1-8 to ll.9-10, leading from distance to intimacy; now, however, the poem stays personal and l.35 then leads over to the most intimate part, concerning only the speaker and Christ.

By switching from past to present, and from passive to active, the speaker thus changes his own stance towards the crucifixion and reinterprets both Christ's and his own action. The crucifixion is turned from a general, impersonal "spectacle" into an event witnessed by the speaker – at least in the speaker's mind and imagination. The use of active tense also has another consequence. Not only does it create more immediacy, it also puts an emphasis on choice: although he needs the assurance of Christ's glance as a trigger for his conversion (and help in the form of "corrections"), the speaker chooses to turn his back and his face. The "real" meeting between the speaker and Christ is still to come, however, which is why the speaker uses future tense in the last line. "I'll turne my face." The contraction "I'll" further reduces the distance between the speaker and God, as it takes away the possibility to distinguish between "I will" and "I shall" and thus merges the two options: an expression of the speaker's wishes thus becomes a factual statement about a future event, and vice versa, the speaker not only talks about what will happen in the future, but also about what he really wants.

2.7 Syntax

The poem's syntax partly reflects the poem's structure, most notably at the beginning of the poem. The complexity of ll.1-8 stands in contrast to the syntax of the remaining lines and serves two main functions. Firstly, it reflects the disorder of the twisted world it describes, so that it becomes iconic of the hurrying, whirling and losing of "natural forme" it shows. Secondly, their syntactical complexity also contributes to make the first eight lines appear abstract, impersonal and scholarly, which is in accordance with their abstract, logical argumentation and creates the impression of an erudite and learned speaker.[42]

The first sentence is made up of eight full lines, divided into three main clauses. The first main clause, "Let mans Soule be a Spheare," is ambiguous (either introducing a thought experiment or stating a wish for man's soul to be a sphere) but not yet problematic. The second main clause is somewhat more complex and continues the construct established in the first clause: "and then." It contains an ellipsis, "in this," which may refer either to man's soul, the sphere or the construct of man's soul as a sphere, but the ellipsis does not obscure the phrase, since the meaning remains the same. It also contains an inversion in moving the subject to the end, which, again, does not obscure the phrase, but it contributes to make "th'intelligence that moves" appear as a faculty for which there is an alternative ('the intelligence that moves not,' for example). Still, the second main clause is not problematic.

---

42   Sicherman notes that a process of discovery similar to that found in "Goodfriday" – where the speaker's apparent confidence in his knowledge serves to initiate a process of self-examination that leads to deeper understanding – can also be found in several other poems by Donne, both secular and sacred (74-88).

The third main clause, covering lines 3 to 8, however, is very difficult to process. It begins with a subordinate clause, followed by an insertion: "*And* as the other Spheares, [by being growne subject to forraigne motions, (*subordinate clause*, insertion)] lose their owne." The ellipsis in "their owne," is likely to refer to the motions the spheres had prior to being influenced by foreign motions, but it could also refer to the spheres' own intelligence, or to the spheres' form (anticipating "natural forme" in line 6). This subordinate clause and insertion are directly followed by yet another subordinate clause and insertion: "*And* [being by others hurried every day (subordinate clause, insertion)] scarce in a year their naturall forme obey."

Since the subordinate clauses are paratactic, no hierarchy can be established between their statements. The second subordinate clause in line 5 continues the comparison from line 3 but omits the "as," making it more difficult to follow the speaker's reasoning. "Others" might refer to other spheres, the forces produced by other spheres, or even completely different entities influencing the spheres' motion. In line 6 there is yet another inversion, with the verb "obey" in the last position. Furthermore, through its position in the sentence, "scarce" is ambiguous, and it is not clear whether it refers to "in a year" or "obey," i.e., whether it refers to the fact that the planetary movements of the spheres do not take exactly one year, or to the fact that their movement is not perfectly circular.

This is followed by another main clause, again with its own subordinate: "Pleasure or businesse *so* our souls admit for their first mover, [*and* are whirld by it" (*subordinate clause*)]." Again, there is an inversion in putting "pleasure or business" in the front. "Whirled" is homophonous with "world" – the celestial bodies not only spin around, they "are world" or "worldly" by this movement. If we apply this description to the speaker, whose movement is analogous to that of the spheres, then the speaker will also be whirled and "be world"[43] by pleasure or business.[44]

The first ten lines of the poem present a logical argumentation in the form of deductive reasoning. They establish the metaphor of turning right

---

43   Cf. Donne's Holy Sonnet "I am a little world made cunningly."
44   Cf. also the negative influence of "business" in Vaughan's "Child-hood": [...]
     Those observations are but foul, / Which make me wise to lose my soul. / And yet
     the practice worldlings call / Business, and weighty action all" (ll.25-28).

from the beginning of the poem and thus provide the basis for describing the speaker's relation to God in terms of movement and spatial relations. The use of "let," "then," "and as," "and," "so," "and," "hence," and "when" in ll. 1-10 emphasises the reasoning character of the poem's beginning.

The first line "Let mans Soule be a Spheare" establishes a first premise, namely that man's soul *is* a sphere. The continuation "in this, / Th'intelligence that moves" contains another (implicit) premise, namely that all spheres *are* moved by something (an intelligence of some sort). From this it is concluded that the intelligence of the soul (i.e., the mover of the soul) is devotion (there is no further explanation: *if* man's soul is a sphere, *then* it is moved by devotion). This statement thus also contains an implicit equation of intelligence and devotion.

After establishing devotion as the mover of the soul, the speaker in ll.3-8 then adds a restriction and explains it by comparison with "the other Spheares," i.e. celestial bodies (thus also making his own soul's deviance more pardonable – if not even whole planets can stick to their natural movement, how should the speaker's soul). Ll. 3-4 present the image of celestial spheres (with which the soul-spheres are being compared), while l.5 is simply a paraphrase of l.4, repeating and thus stressing again the *external* influence on the spheres. L.6 then shows the consequence of this deviation: "scarce in a yeare their naturall forme obey." In l.7 and 8, the speaker applies the explanation from ll.3-6 to men's souls: just as celestial spheres admit "forraigne motions" as their first mover, the soul admits "pleasure or businesse" as its first mover.[45] The reference to the first mover is significant and further links the two parts of the analogy: in both cases it is God who should be (and remain) the first mover, and who is replaced by inferior forces (God as first mover is later described explicitly in ll.22).

---

45   Cf. also Donne's Holy Sonnet "Oh, to vex me," which, too, depicts the speaker's inability to look at God ("I durst not view heaven," l.9) as the result of different, conflicting forces influencing the speaker and leading to a change in "devotione":

Oh, to vex me, contraryes meet in one:
Inconstancy unnaturally hath begot
A constant habit; that when I would not
I change in vows, and in devotione. (ll.1-4)

The speaker characterises this influence distinctly as a "forraigne motion," "hurried by others," while devotion in contrast is the spheres' "owne" and "naturall forme," which they "lose" (which, too, implies that they possessed it first). "Pleasure and business" are not part of the soul's movement in the first place, but need to be actively "admitted" (which presupposes some kind of resistance before their acceptance and – understanding "admit" in a spatial sense – the admission *into* the spheres of something that was not in there before).

In l.9, the speaker then draws a final inference from the general to the specific, deducing his own misbehaviour from the state of spheres and souls. By presenting his explanation of the soul's deviance as a logical argumentation (in principle indefeasible), the speaker thus provides a backdrop and a justification for his own movements: just as the other spheres in general "scarce in a yeare their naturall forme obey," his own soul in particular does not move freely but is "whirld." The distinction between the "owne" and "naturall" movement inherent to the soul-spheres and an unnatural intrusion is important to the speaker's personal experience later in the poem. The speaker talks not simply about his soul in contrast to his body, but about his "Soules forme." He thereby takes up the expression "naturall forme" from l.6, and links the description of the celestial bodies in l.6 to the description of himself in l.10. By repeating it, he also stresses the importance of the "forme," and he implies that the soul's form is also its natural form. Though his body moves the wrong way, his "Soules forme" already bends the right way and he only needs to be "restored" to a previous state.[46]

---

46   Cf. also Donne's "Second Anniversary," where the soul (on earth) is unable to
"see" truly:

> In this low forme, poore soule, what wilt thou doe?
> When wilt thou shake off this Pedantery,
> Of being thought by sense, and Fantasy
> Thou look'st through spectacles; small things seem great
> Below; But up unto the watch-towre get,
> And see all things despoyld of fallacies (ll. 290-95)

Powrie, however, points out that the image of the watchtower as a symbol for spiritual enlightenment is rejected by St. Augustine, who takes care to distinguish it from the image of the mirror: whereas the idea of looking into a mirror helps in pursuing introspective contemplation and in finding the image of God within the soul, the watchtower distances the watcher from what is to be looked at. The use of the watchtower in the Second Anniversary thus hints at the speaker's implicit

In Plato's Theory of Forms,[47] the form is the idea after which objects in the world are modelled, however, the term "form" can also be used for the visible product, i.e. the form resulting from an idea.[48] In "Goodfriday," both uses seem to coexist: the spheres' "naturall forme" is the original, unchanging pattern, which becomes visible in the spheres but also subject to change. The "soules forme" seems to refer to the soul's original, pure and uncorrupted state, since the speaker states that his "Soules forme bends toward the East" (i.e. towards Christ), even though he is unwilling to actually look or turn East. At the same time, in line 40 the speaker mentions his "deformity," which he asks Christ to "burne off," which then must be taken as referring to a deviation from the ideal form, while at the same time the speaker uses an image – cleansing through fire – that is quite physical and material.[49]

The first eight lines also establish the temporal range that is inherent to "Goodfriday" as a specific day (at the moment of speaking and in the past) and a yearly holiday: the spheres are hurried "every day" and thus "scarce in a yeare their naturall forme obey." But the state described in lines 1-8 provides not only an analogy to the speaker's personal situation; due to its general nature, it can also be seen as an analogy to the Fall. As

---

unwillingness to dedicate himself wholly to spiritual matters and shows him torn between "secular and spiritual aspirations, between the horizon of business and that of Christian devotion, between the art of salvation and poetic artistry" (10-13).

47 Cf. e.g., *Phaedo* (253-281; chapters 73A-80E), which also discusses the role of memory as a recollection of the knowledge which the soul already possesses prior to birth (to which Donne probably alludes in the "Sermon Preached at Lincolns Inne, on Psalm 38.3," cited above under 1.3).

48 The use of "forme" is ambiguous, since the terminology is irregular. While Plato uses different terms (mostly ἰδέα or εἶδος) for the ideal prototype, Aristotle uses ἰδέα for the prototype and εἶδος for the externally visible realisation of this prototype. In English, both "idea" and "form" are used to denote the ideal prototype, while "form" of course also strongly suggests the physical materialisation.

49 Cf. also Verse Letter "To Mr Rowland Woodward."

If men be worlds, there is in everyone
Some thing to answer in some proportion
All the world's riches, and in good men this
Virtue our form's form, and our soul's soul, is. (Donne 2010, ll. 29-32).

Here, "soul" and "form" are simultaneously separated ("form's form," "soul's soul") and joined ("this Virtue" is made up of both "form's form" and "soul's soul").

a consequence, man is "whirld" (or "world") – thrown out of Eden into the world. Since the 16th century, "world" could also be used as a verb, meaning "to provide a world with people" or "to bring a child into the world by birth" (*OED* "world, *v*") – childbirth being another consequence of the Fall.

The speaker's uses of parataxis, insertions, inversions and ellipsis make the first eight lines extremely complex. Lines 9 to 10, which end the mental construct of the previous lines and provide the conclusion to the premises previously given, are distinguished by their simplicity and thus stand in contrast to ll. 1-8. Through the first eight lines (which, further-more, are applicable to all celestial spheres and all human beings), the speaker creates a foil against which the speaker stands out as an individ-ual.

The speaker uses a large number of conjunctions to join phrases and sentences: "and," "but," "yet" and "or" come up several times throughout the poem. "Hence" in l. 9 and "for" in l.35 stick out, since they do not only link phrases but prove logical conclusions (although "hence" is an adverb, its function is the same as that of "for" in the poem), giving the impression of an objective, impersonal argumentation. The complexity and style of the first eight lines stand in contrast to the rest of the poem, whose syntax is much more simple in comparison and which focuses more on the speaker's feelings. In ll. 11-34, where we would expect justi-fications for the speaker's inability to look back, these are only given on the level of content. The speaker uses rhetorical questions, to which the answer is "no, I could not" and "no, I durst not," but with regard to syn-tactical conjunctions he does not underline why he cannot turn back.[50]

It is noticeable, however, that the speaker's placement of himself in ll.9-10 but also in ll.33-34 are given in simple, short, clear and confined

---

50   Cf. Stirling:

> The question 'could I' is not a question simply of volition but of ability: is it possible for me to contemplate these things now? And the answer seems to be, 'not in this lifetime', as Donne, paraphrasing Exodus 33.20, makes quite clear: 'Who sees Gods face, that is selfe life, must dye' (l.17). And so, in the deferral of the final confrontation between man and God that is typical of Donne's religious poetry, Donne's speaker postpones his 'turn' to-wards God's face.

The result is a poem that "incorporates past, present, and future in its meditation: the past event that is to be commemorated; the present act of memory; and the future justification" (238).

sentences, each spanning two lines (l.34 is continued in l.35, but complete in itself). These two sentences provide, firstly, localisations not argumentation (though they are of course integrated into the poem's reasoning), and, secondly, points of orientation within the poems structure – for both purposes their simple structure is helpful and appropriate. It is also noticeable that the speaker's explicit mentions of turning, ""I turne my backe" and "I'll turne my face," are also syntactically very simple statements (again, embedded in a more complex sentence with more complex argumentation), each consisting in a short clause. Thus the two most central statements the speaker makes with regard to his conversion stand out.

3. The genre of "Goodfriday" – turning as conversion

Apart from the poem's presentation as an occasional poem, other genres seem to play a role in "Goodfriday." The poem's motifs and its structure suggest a reading as either (or both) a formal religious meditation and a conversion narrative. Further, especially the last part of the poem, with its direct invocation of God, also has the character of a prayer. In all three cases, while focussing on a personal experience, the poem also contains a public side, showing not only the speaker's personal development but also a text that is meant to be read by others (a characteristic which the poem shares with the conversion narratives discussed below, as well as with written accounts of meditations and with most prayers).

3.1 "Goodfriday" as a conversion narrative

"Goodfriday" essentially constitutes a conversion narrative: the speaker, who at first (at least physically) renounces God, receives an impetus to turn towards God – by perceiving God's turn towards the speaker in Christ's look *at* the speaker – and experiences a spiritual conversion, turning (i.e. "bending") first his mind, then his back (though his back is turned in the opposite direction, this becomes a requisite for looking at Christ with his memory), and announcing to turn his face as well (that is, going round full turn); and he describes these different stages as the poem progresses.

In addition to "conversion" as the "turning of sinners to God" (*OED*, "conversion, *n.* 9") and physically or mentally turning in a particular direction (towards or away) from something or someone, or returning to a previous place or state (cf. the various meanings of conversion discussed in the introduction), the term is also used specifically for "the turning back of the sun in its apparent course on reaching the tropic; the solstice" (*OED*, "conversion 3.a"), so that the motion of Christ's turning and tuning of the spheres and the motion of the speaker's tuning and turning of himself coincide in the notion of "conversion."

The double movement entailed in the concept of conversion, turning back (i.e. return or reversal) and turning into something new (i.e., transformation) (cf. Moog-Grünewald 2008a, 142) is also essential in "Goodfriday." The notion of "bending" or "turning" implies a continuum; the speaker is not looking for a new beginning but for a change of direction which entails at least a partial return to a previous place (literal or metaphorical). The speaker's pleas to "burn off his rusts" and to "restore" his image imply a return to a previous, unfallen state of his soul, which also entails a radical separation from his sinful state. Such a view ties in with the speaker's emphasis on memory, and the role of memory (as shown in Donne's sermon quoted above) in reminding the speaker that he is made in the image of God (that is, straight, unbent). Thus, in spatial terms, the motion of the speaker's soul, bending backwards (while the speaker's body seems to be bent forward, presenting his back to God for future corrections), can also be seen as a rectification, a bending that ultimately straightens the soul and returns it to its original, sinless state.[51]

The speaker's experience is also evocative of the conversion of St. Paul, as there are several parallels to St. Paul's experience.[52] The speaker,

---

51 Sherwood (1984, 161) points out that the same motion is present in "Batter my Heart": "That I may rise, and stand, o'erthrow mee,'and bend" (l.3). Cf. also the speaker's description of the crucifixion as a "spectacle of too much weight" (that is, it would drag him down if he were to look) while he is yet unwilling to look back with his memory.

52 Hartwig points out that in depictions of St. Paul's conversion, he was traditionally shown travelling on horseback, and either falling or lying on the ground during his conversion (277). Sherwood distinguishes the speaker's state in "Goodfriday" from that of St. Paul:

> Donne's primary interest is not in the sudden conversion of Paul, but in the more protracted kind of conversion, with its centre in repentance, that fulfils time. Every believer, misdirected by fallen selfishness, repeatedly turns away from God, then repeatedly is turned back by repentance. (1984, 159)

like St. Paul, is going *away* from Jerusalem, and he, too, experiences a vision of Christ. In both narratives there is a strong emphasis on sight (and lack of sight). In 1 Cor 15.5-8, St. Paul lists those who have seen Christ, including himself:

> And that he was seen of Cephas, then of the twelve: After that, he was seen of above five hundred brethren at once; of whom the greater part remain unto this present, but some are fallen asleep. After that, he was seen of James; then of all the apostles. And last of all he was seen of me also, as of one born out of due time.

In Acts 9.3-18, St. Paul is first blinded by a bright light and later has his vision restored:

> And as he journeyed, he came near Damascus: and suddenly there shined round about him a light from heaven: And he fell to the earth, and heard a voice saying unto him, Saul, Saul, why persecutest thou me? [...] And the Lord *said* unto him, Arise, and go into the city, and it shall be told thee what thou must do. And the men which journeyed with him stood speechless, hearing a voice, but seeing no man. And Saul arose from the earth; and when his eyes were opened, he saw no man [...]
> And immediately there fell from his eyes as it had been scales: and he received sight forthwith, and arose, and was baptized.

Instead, Sherwood sees St. Augustine and St. Bernard as main models for the speaker's contemplative stance in "Goodfriday," both because of their reflexive attitude towards conversion and their explicit considerations of turning and bending discussed above. However, there is no contradiction here: Donne may simultaneously depict the setting of St. Paul's conversion (and, similarly, allude to St. Augustine's conversion in the garden) as well as the (ongoing) psychological process of repentance.

Brooks points at the "present-mindedness" which such an ongoing process of repentance entails:

> [B]oth Augustine and Donne's speaker [...] share in protracted conversions in which the will is slowly but surely brought into alignment with the will of God. And thus both also create narratives that capture the timelessness of their individual spiritual journeys. Augustine's is embodied in the tripartite structure of his spiritual autobiography: Books I-IX focus on his past sins; Book X addresses the present, converted state of his soul; and Books XI-XIII look to the future. But the whole of the narrative is uttered out of and informed by the present, converted state of this soul, imparting to the *Confessions* its overall sense of timelessness. Donne's poem [...] is likewise organized around the present-mindedness of the soul's "attention." (1995, 299)

In Acts 22 and 26, St Paul marks noon as the time for his conversion:

> And it came to pass, that, as I made my journey, and was come nigh unto Damascus about noon, suddenly there shone from heaven a great light round about me. (Acts 22.6)
> At midday, O king, I saw in the way a light from heaven, above the brightness of the sun, shining round about me and them which journeyed with me. (Acts 26.13)

Noon as the point in time where the sun changes its course from rising to falling and from being in the East to being in the West lends itself as a natural turning point. While the speaker in "Goodfriday" does not mention an exact time, in l.20 he states that Christ's death "made [...] the Sunne winke" (l. 20) – which is a reference to the sudden darkness before Christ's death that occurred "at the sixth hour" (cf. Matt 27:45, Mark 15:33 and Luke 23:44), that is, at noon. Fittingly this implicit reference to noon is found in the middle of the poem.

The verbal and dialogical nature of conversion stressed in the introduction is also crucial in "Goodfriday." As has been pointed out there, "conversation" in the sense of "conversion" is used by St. Paul to describe his own experience (see Gal 1.13 and Phil 3.20), and in "Goodfriday" all three meanings of "conversation" (that is, conversion, discourse and dwelling place) come together. The first one, "conversion" is of course present when the speaker is converted and becomes ready to "turn [his] face" towards God at the end of the poem. Secondly, the speaker describes the process of his conversion in terms of a "conversation": not only does he begin to talk directly to God, he creates the impression that God is at least listening, since afterwards there is eye contact between them. Thirdly, the poem also deals with "conversation" in the sense of "residence": since the speaker dwells *not* in heaven but on earth, he is distracted by "pleasure or businesse" and has to turn back to the right course to be saved (and his salvation also entails the prospect of dwelling in heaven after his death). Also, it is precisely the fact that the speaker is *not* stationary, in his usual dwelling place where he would be able to worship on a holiday, which leads to the poem's initial situation – a situation which is resolved (and thus takes a turn for the better) when the speaker turns to his memory, where God's image dwells, and which makes him turn to God.[53]

The *Confessions* of St. Augustine offer another conversion narrative with which "Goodfriday" shares a number of decisive characteristics. In the first place, it presents an individual's written autobiography, providing details of St. Augustine's life and thoughts which will be irrelevant to an omniscient God, that is, only be of interest to other men. In "Goodfriday," the speaker does not disclose much information about himself, but he does give some clues (riding westward on Good Friday), which place him in a mundane context, and he describes a decisive incident in his life that is part of his process of conversion – and all this happens in writing. The *Confessions* are, as the title says, a "confession" – they are a verbal statement (either oral or written).

The speaker's conversion in "Goodfriday" bears several similarities to the key scene of St. Augustine's conversion in the *Confessions*.[54] The poem's speaker is situated in the open air and seems to be alone (if there are other people present, they are irrelevant to the speaker's experience). St. Augustine is in his garden (as far away from the house as possible) when he experiences his conversion, and although he is initially accompanied by a friend, he does not interact with him and later leaves him to be in complete solitude. Even though the poem's speaker is passively "carried" throughout his conversion, the poem describes a lot of move-

---

53   In a sermon ("Preached at a Christning, on Rev 7.17"), Donne dwells on this notion of "conversation":

> when our *soul*, our *devotion*, by such a conversation in heaven, associates it self with all this blessed company that are met in this Chapter [i.e., Revelation 7], that *our fellowship may be with the Father, and with his Son Jesus Christ*, and with all the *Court* and *Quire* of the Triumphant Church. (Donne, *Sermons* V, no. 4, 96)

In order for the soul to "associate it self" with God, it must already have been converted in the sense of being turned away from sinfulness. At the same time, the poem is indeed a conversation between the speaker and God. The speaker begins the poem without determining an addressee (either human or divine), but towards the end converses directly with God ("thou look'st towards mee").

54   With regard to its communicative form, "Goodfriday" is also similar to another one of St. Augustine's works, the *Soliloquies*. They take the form of a dialogue between St. Augustine and the voice of reason (which begins with the speaker 'turning' ("volventi," Augustine 1965, 6) thoughts in his mind and storing thoughts in his memory for further reflection). In both cases, the action of speaking is important for reflecting on one's own sinfulness and developing the right disposition of mind, necessary for turning away from sinfulness.

ment. Similarly, there is an emphasis on movement in the *Confessions*, even though St. Augustine does not move out of the small garden.

St. Augustine struggles to arrive in the garden as much as he struggles to go "into God's will and covenant":

> For, not to go towards only, but to arrive fully at that place, required no more but the will to go to it, but yet to will it resolutely and thoroughly; not to stagger and tumble down an half wounded will, now on this side, and anon on that side; setting the part advancing itself to struggle with another part that is falling. (Augustine 1912, 445; bk. VIII, ch. viii)

St. Augustine also describes his inner turmoil in terms of conflicting forces and diverging movements:

> Thus soul-sick I was, and in this manner tormented; accusing myself much more eagerly than I was wont, turning and winding myself in my chain, till that which held me might be utterly broken; which though but little, yet held it me fast enough notwithstanding. And thou, O Lord, pressedst upon me in my inward parts, by a most severe mercy redoubling my lashes of fear and shame, lest I should give way again, and lest that small and tender tie, which now only was left, should not break off but recover strength again, and hamper me again the faster. (bk. VIII, ch. XI, 457)
> And what were those things which they [i.e., his seductresses] suggested to me in that phrase this or that, as I said, what were those which they suggested, my God? Such, as let thy mercy utterly turn away from the soul of thy servant. [...] For on that side which I set my face towards, and whither I trembled to go, was that chaste dignity of Continency discovered [...] stretching forth those devout hands of hers [...], both to receive and to embrace me. (bk. VIII, ch. XI, 459)
> Myself when sometime I deliberated upon serving of the Lord my God, (as I long had purposed) it was myself who willed it, and myself who willed it ; it was I myself. I neither willed entirely, nor yet willed entirely. Therefore was I at strife with myself, and distracted by mine own self. Which distracting befell me much against my mind, nor yet shewed it forth the nature of another man's mind, but the punishment of mine own. I therefore myself was not the causer of it, but the sin that dwells in me: from the punishment of that more voluntary sin, because I was a son of Adam. (bk. VIII, ch. X, 451)

Thus, St. Augustine's depiction of his inner conflicts prior to his conversion is very similar to that of the speaker in "Goodfriday" – and Donne was certainly just as familiar with it as with St. Paul's narratives.

The experience described in "Goodfriday" shares with St. Paul's and St. Augustine's accounts an emphasis on space: St. Paul is on a journey to Damascus, St. Augustine moves within the garden, the speaker in "Goodfriday" travels westward. At the same time, the choice of this space allows for a focus on the individual speaker: while none of the three speakers is necessarily alone, they do not move in large crowds, and, moreover, they seem to move individually. St. Paul's servants, St. Augustine's friend, and potential travel companions in "Goodfriday" stay in the background and do not interact with the speaker during his conversion experience. Lastly, all three conversions are characterised by inner turmoil and an inner change.

3.2 "Goodfriday" as a meditation

While "Goodfriday" adheres to St. Paul's and St. Augustine's models of a conversion narrative, it also follows the traditional tripartite structure of a meditation best exemplified by Loyolas's *Spiritual Exercises* (cf. Martz 1955, 25-29). These genres do not exclude each other, rather, they can be seen as complementary, since the meditation aimed at an experience of spiritual conversion. Thus, "Goodfriday" begins with a composition of place setting the scene (ll.1-10),[55] which is followed by a contemplation of divine matters (ll. 11-32) and ends with a colloquy with God (ll.33-42).[56] In "Goodfriday," the composition of place begins already in the title of the poem, which, although it does not give a *precise* location (which is not usually demanded in a meditation), provides an imaginative setting imitating a real-life situation. After the composition of place, lines 11-32 present both a parallel and a counterpoint to the meditative con-

---

55   More precisely, the first ten lines form a "composition by similitude" (Martz 1955, 54), which is designed to make something invisible and ungraspable clearer (the human soul cannot be directly examined or comprehended, while planetary motions can be measured and depicted).

56   Martz also points out that the three parts of a meditation – composition, analysis and colloquy – are often seen to correspond to the acts of memory, understanding and will, respectively (1955, 37f.).

templation of God. The speaker professes to be unable to look at Christ, and in describing what he does not dare to look at, provides a detailed description of Christ on the Cross.[57] This contemplation becomes intermingled with the final colloquy, since Christ's gaze towards the speaker in line 35 (even though it is only imagined by the speaker at this point) is a powerful communicative act, which is crucial for the speaker's relation to God.[58]

Francois de Sales distinguishes the strict practice of meditation (as a mental exercise) from the notion of what he calls contemplation (quoted in Martz 1955, 15-17): "meditation is an attentive thought iterated, or voluntarily intertained in the mynd, to excite the will to holy affections and resolutions," so that "[m]editation considereth by peecemeale the obiectes proper to move us; but contemplation beholdes the obiect it loves, in one simple and recollected looke, and the consideration so united, causeth a more lively and strong motion."

Both a Loyolan and a Salesian approach are found in "Goodfriday." The speaker displays an intellectual and reiterated preoccupation with his own turning, presenting a sophisticated and methodical composition. At the same time, he emphasises the immediacy of a single moment and a single look: the direct, wordless communication in line 37, which, while it cannot happen without the intellectual, verbal reflection preceding it, has the power to create closeness between the speaker and Christ. Of course, the colloquy with God does not entail an actual divine answer,

---

57 Hurley argues that in addition to the meditative tradition outlined by Martz, "Goodfriday" also stands in a tradition of visualising the crucifixion for meditative practices, using graphic verbal descriptions (often accompanied by illustrations), and that the middle part thus presents an entirely conventional image. She sees the poem's ending as an unfinished meditation, because the speaker turns his back "not, as anticipated by one tutored in the meditative tradition, in compassion to receive the blows intended for the Lord, but in guilt to receive the blows deserved by the self" and concludes that "the poem thus documents a failure or, at best, an interruption, in the meditative process. The speaker cannot paint the image he sees before him in his heart; his image-making faculty in fact turns away" (1955, 76). She concedes, however, that "resolution is implied [...] in a not-yet-imagined future where 'I'll turn my face'" (76).

58 Martz actually uses "Goodfriday" as an example of a poetic meditation (1955, 54-56). Cf. also Slattery:

Prayer and poetry share a kindred recognition of how important it is to move the imagination into a meditative space, there to shift one's normal mode of perceiving, moving into a deeper seeing than simple perception. (40)

but Christ's imagined gaze in line 37 gives the very strong impression of an answer, affirming God's turn towards the speaker. This is also emphasised by the speaker's subsequent direct address of Christ.

Lewalski sees the poem somewhat differently, as a "Protestant occasional meditation upon experience" (1979, 277), in this case, the experience of riding westward on an important holiday instead of worshipping.[59] She names two features that "especially characterize Protestant meditation [...]: a focus on the Bible, the Word [...]; and a particular kind of application to the self [...]" (148):

> In [Ignatian or Salesian meditation], the meditator typically seeks to apply himself to the subject, so that he participates in it; he imagines a scene vividly, as if it were taking place in his presence [...]. The typical Protestant procedure is very nearly the reverse: instead of the application of the self to the subject, it calls for the application of the subject to the self – indeed for the subject's location in the self (1979, 149)

This application to the self she sees in the speaker's own efforts: "the speaker must finally "turne my face" rather than recognize that his journey has taken him to the right place after all" (279), a turning, however, which is facilitated by what he imagines and "sees" with his memory as if it were present.[60] No matter which exact model Donne had in mind (if any separate model at all), "Goodfriday" shares with the religious meditation the process of visualisation: the speaker makes something visible which he did not perceive before, and which helps him in getting closer to God.

---

59   Cf., however, Halewood: "I read the poem as a radically Protestant meditation on sin and salvation – thus *about* sin and salvation, not about meditation" (218).

60   Cf. also Friedman:

> Donne is in effect reinterpreting or expanding the [Jesuit] meditative procedures. [...] The "composition of place" and the "composition of similitude" are introduced, exploited, and then transcended as the poet finds other means of conveying truth into the human spirit. [...] In Donne's treatment that feeling [of being present at the scene imagined] is transmuted into physical and emotional empathy that dissolves the barrier between the contemplator and the object of his contemplation. (431f.)

3.3 "Goodfriday" as a prayer

The notion of "Goodfriday" as prayer (already inherent to its reading as a meditation) deserves an extra mention, firstly, since "Goodfriday" is a poem, that is, a verbal statement (like most prayers, and like all written prayers), and secondly, because it ends in a direct address of God. In the third part of the poem, the speaker gains confidence in his own devotion to God and in God's devotion for him. Imagining and describing their mutual gaze creates a bond between them and the speaker truly converses with God, addressing him.[61] In this respect, "Goodfriday" can be seen as a prayer, starting with a focus on the speaker's own concerns and ending with addressing God and praying for salvation (a progress that is found, for example, in numerous Psalms). In a broad sense, the nature of prayer is simply "human communication with divine and spiritual entities" (Gill 7367).[62] The *OED* defines prayer as a "solemn request to God, a god, or other object of worship; a supplication or thanksgiving addressed to God or a god," ("prayer, n." 1.a), which shows another characteristic, also

---

61 Considering that the final aim of a meditation is the colloquy with God, viewing "Goodfriday" as a prayer goes hand in hand with viewing it as a meditation. Prayer is not necessarily voiced aloud, nor are the speaker's invocations in "Goodfriday" necessarily vocal. Considering that he imagines the backward glance of his memory, he may also imagine (that is, think) all his utterances. Cf., for example, "The Exstasie," where the lovers' communication is described as a "dialogue of one" (l.74) and, outwardly, consists entirely in holding hands and looking at each other, which is also made explicit in the poem: "Wee like sepulchrall statues lay; / All day, the same our postures were, / And wee said nothing, all the day" (ll.18-20). Leimberg sees "The Exstasie" as a precursor to "Goodfriday," especially with regard to the use of spherical imagery (cf. ll.51-52: "Wee are / Th'intelligences, they [our bodies] the spheare"), but she also points out the deeply religious undertones of the lovers' union, describing "The Exstasie" as "ein Lobpreis des gottgeschaffenen Menschen" and a poem in which "ein Mensch im anderen sich selbst findet, weil der Körper seiner Beseeltheit gewahr wird" (1996, 135).

62 An alternative view to this would be a ritual model of communication, in which prayer creates "a situation in which nothing new is learned but in which a particular view of the world is portrayed and confirmed" (Carey 1992, 20), i.e., a "sacred ceremony that draws persons together in fellowship and commonality" (18) – however, this view only applies to public prayer.

essential to "Goodfriday": the speaker addresses God in order to attain his own salvation.[63]

Renaissance prayer theorists distinguish between public ("common") and private prayer. That 16th and 17th century poets were also aware of this distinction can be seen, for example, in the subtitle to Herbert's The Temple: "Sacred [i.e., public and liturgical] Poems and Private Ejaculations." While public prayer is integrated into the liturgy and uttered by a community (or a priest on behalf of the community), private prayer belongs to the individual:

> Public prayer was fixed in form to guarantee uniformity, and its proper locale was a sacred place such as a church. Private prayer, on the other hand was solitary; it could occur anywhere and in a form of the speaker's choosing. (McGuire 63)

According to this description, "Goodfriday" would pertain to private prayer. However, the distinction made here between public and private is not as clear as it seems. The Psalms, for example, are on the one hand considered private, on the other hand an integral part of any (Anglican) service and therefore also public. While "Goodfriday" is clearly an instance of private prayer (the single speaker speaks to Christ as an individual penitent sinner), it can, similar to the Psalms, also be seen as an expression of the feelings pertaining to Christian religion: the speaker's state of agitation and penitence (turning his back to God in order to "receive corrections") is not a singular state but an essential requirement for Christian salvation and the speaker also presents himself as an example of humankind by beginning the poem with a general statement about "mans Soule" which he then applies to himself. In addition, the poem is also a fictional text, written down in a "public," accessible poetic form, so that others can read the poem and relate the (fictional) speaker's situation to their own.

Prayer is characterised by a personal and intimate relationship to God. Renaissance prayer handbooks also stressed the fact that prayer is to be

---

63   Sanchez (2014, 51) sees the last ten lines of "Goodfriday" as a prayer, following the structure of a collect comprising invocation (ll. 33-36), petition (ll. 37-41) and pleading (l.42).

considered as reciprocal communication (Garrett 331).[64] Equally, the speaker in "Goodfriday" stresses God's reciprocity from line 37 to the end of the poem and addresses him directly.[65]

Through the poem, there is a change in the speaker's potential address-ees, and a turn towards Christ as (exclusive) conversational partner.[66] In ll.1-34 the speaker mainly talks to himself (constituting a kind of solilo-quy) and maybe to other believers who find themselves in the same pre-dicament, and, further, he talks *about* God. Ll.35-42, however, are di-rected at Christ, and at Christ only. There is thus a change from descrip-tion to invocation:[67] the speaker's initial abstract and rational considera-tions are transformed into a personal and passionate expression of his anguish, and the pleas in ll. 39-41 become the speaker's personal pleas,

---

64   Cf. Heiler:

> Das Gebet ist kein bloßes Erhabenheitsgefühl, keine bloße weihevolle Stimmung, kein bloßes Niedersinken vor einem höchsten Wert; das Gebet ist vielmehr ein wirklicher Um-gang des Menschen mit Gott, ein lebendiger Verkehr des endlichen Geistes mit dem un-endlichen [...] Beten heißt mit Gott reden und verkehren. (494)

Cf. also Sanchez:

> No longer does the poem function as a meditation, but rather as a dramatic supplication imploring direct intercession from God on behalf of the speaker's desired conversion. The *turn*, therefore, involves both parties turning *toward* each other. The speaker must act; so too must God, whom the speaker implores (2014, 48)

65   With regard to linking a personal encounter to the use of direct address, Clutterbuck sees a parallel procedure in Dante's *Paradise* and in *Piers Plowman* (20). A similar turn to God through direct address can be found in Donne's "Corona," which begins with direct address (when the speaker asks for his own glory). Then the speaker, though addressing Mary and Joseph, talks about Christ only in the third person. At the end of sonnet 5, when the speaker asks for his own salvation, he again addresses Christ directly: "Now thou art lifted up, draw me to thee."

66   In a sermon, Donne states,

> And turne all those his Commandments into prayers, till thou come to his *Faciamus hom-inem*, *Let us make man according to our own Image*; Pray that he will restore his Image in thee, and conforme thee to him. ("Sermon Preached upon the Penitential Psalmes, on Ps. 6.2 and 3," Donne, *Sermons* V, no. 17, 362)

67   Halewood states that the last eight lines of "Goodfriday" find

> a suggestive parallel in the prayers that complete each of the *Devotions on Emergent Oc-casions*, also in the prayers with which Donne ends *Essays in Divinity*. The latter, too, are apostrophes (as the apostrophe in the poem is a prayer) and releases from more ordinary and restrictive kinds of discourse. Their double process both petitions for and assumes di-vine presence: "I beseech thee, that since by thy grace, I have thus long meditated upon thee, and spoken *of* thee, I may now speak *to* thee." (228)

his personal prayer to God, directed at the most accessible manifestation of God, Jesus Christ.[68]

4.   Turning as pilgrimage – turning and spatial relations

Spatiality serves an important function with regard to turning: since turning is a spatial notion, many of its occurrences are also related to concepts of space. Donne makes use of different spatial conceptions to present and characterise the speaker's journey and his relation to God. On a more abstract level, basic geometrical concepts are used to create the space in which the poem's speaker is situated and to relate him to God. To this basic spatial structure, references to the "real" world are added, which link the speaker to this world and world view. On a smaller scale, this happens with geographical references showing him to be "on earth" (which creates a largely two-dimensional space). On a larger scale, there are references to the cosmos and the whole of creation (creating a three-dimensional space, including the whole earth and other planets). This makes geometry, astronomy and geography important subjects with regard to turning, which come up in many metaphysical poems that are engaged with the topic. All three fields are prominent in "Goodfriday," where the relation between the speaker and God is thus presented within a carefully constructed spatial construct, which also allows for physical and spiritual movement within this space.

The poem's setting with a travelling speaker, combined with the speaker's concern of turning towards God, characterises this journey as a spir-

---

68   Clutterbuck calls this mode of addressing God a "plea-dialogue": even though God does *not* answer directly, there is an expectation of a divine answer, which gives this kind of communication the character of a dialogue. Clutterbuck distinguishes between "giving" and "demanding" types of dialogue (pleas clearly belonging to the latter), and states that

[...], in demand function, the conversation could not possibly end there. The interrogatives and imperatives that express demands initiate an ongoing movement into the *immediate future:* the speaker expects a response. Even if the response is silence, this continues the conversation by rejecting the demand. The forward impulse of demand function can also increase further when the speaker promises to engage in future action if the demand is met [...]. (24)

This is also what happens in "Goodfriday": the speaker ends the poem (and thus his conversation with God) by promising his own future turn – after having received God's corrections and thus creates an expectation of his future salvation beyond the poem.

itual pilgrimage: The poem combines a literal, temporally limited journey (taking place on Good Friday 1613), with the speaker's journey through life and towards death, and with his spiritual journey in his memory.[69]

4.1 Geometry

The speaker's movement takes place on a plain. The speaker, while speaking, is continually moving westwards, or rather, he is moved by his horse or carriage. Christ, on the other hand, does not move and provides a fixed point of reference. The speaker is unable to turn and look at the "spectacle of too much weight," yet his "soul's form" is drawn towards it (the bending soul in l. 10 already indicates, though not a complete turn, at least a tendency or wish for a turn; the bending is a kind of oblique instead of straightforward turn). Thus, there are two opposing forces tearing at the speaker.[70]

In addition, the spheres in ll. 1-8 and the turning of the spheres in l.22 transform the setting described into a three-dimensional, spherical one: the plain on which the speaker and Christ are situated is part of the earthly sphere, and the poem also contains the circular movement of the celestial spheres in ll.1-8 and in l.22, which contrasts with the linear East-West movement. However, both kinds of movement are connected through the analogy between celestial spheres and the human soul, which

---

69   Cf. Archer:

> From the motif of a non-specific, incongruous journey, the purpose becomes clear and acceptable [...]. Still, the journey is no quest for adventure, nor is it a specific mission; it is a time of suffering as the speaker is prepared for death through the power of grace. The conclusion "I'll turne my face" means a readiness for death, since it harks back to verse 17, "Who sees Gods face, that is selfe life, must dye." (178)

70   In his sermons, Donne saw weight or "spiritual ballast" (Schleiner 92) as a helpful means on the journey towards God (Schleiner 92f.), maybe based on Augustine's *Confessions*:

> All things pressed by their own weight go towards their proper places. [...] Things a little out of their places become unquiet: put them in their order again, and they are quieted. My weight is my love: by that am I carried, whithersoever I be carried. (Augustine 1912, 391; bk. XIII, ch. 9; cf. also Gorton 1998 n8)

In the poems, especially in "Goodfriday," weight as an impeding force seems to be more frequent.

Cf. also one of Donne's sermons: "[repentance] is *Aversio*, and *Conversio*; it is a turning from our sins, and a returning to our God" (Sermon Preached to the Household at White-hall, April 30, 1626, on Matt. 9.13," Donne, *Sermons* VII, no. 5).

also explains the opposition between eastward and westward movement (the soul is pulled away from its right course, be it linear or circular, by "pleasure or businesse") and joins a small-scale perspective to a more global point of view. The combination of different points of reference also creates a three-dimensional picture: the plain on which the speaker rides is defined by East and West, while the description of Christ on the cross as "endlesse height [...] humbled below us" and as a "zenith to us, and to'our Antipodes" adds a vertical reference line, thus adding three-dimensional space.[71]

Similarly, the soul bending backwards draws a semi-circle that contributes to create three-dimensional space. Seen purely in spatial terms, this semi-circular movement could imply that half of the soul's movement is still missing – another bending back to close the circle and reach completion. When considered in the context of St. Augustine's and St. Bernard's conception of the bent, distorted soul, it becomes apparent that the missing semi-circular movement already happened: the soul's bending towards God is already the second bending, which repairs the soul's deviancy (that is, its bending away from God). In the last line, the speaker promises to turn his face, too, which would make him whole again, joining body and soul as they move in the same direction. This wholeness, however, will only be reached after his death: his body necessarily moves westward and towards death; through his conversion, however, he knows that this westward movement corresponds to going east, as he will be joined to Christ after death.

The description of God as "zenith" in l.24 contributes to the geometrical construction presented in "Goodfriday." God thus provides the most important point of reference in the poem, as well as being linked to circular movement. But God is not only situated at the highest point above the speaker, he also symbolises a turning point at which the speaker's attitude changes. The speaker's perspective is in principle rather restricted,

---

71   Fischler notes the importance of a combination of circular and linear space and movement:

But Donne's ultimate concern is with a linear imposition that provides paths to redemption not just for individual souls but for all humankind. As noted earlier, the contrary rotations of his divine and human circles put them in potentially fruitful dialectic opposition to one another [...]. [T]he cross not only provides the connections between the divine and human circles but is itself a meeting place for these two contraries – in other words, the cross, too, becomes an emblem of the final synthesis. (178)

horizontal and two-dimensional – he looks in front of himself (i.e. west-wards), where he might notice earthly things (i.e., "pleasure or busi-nesse") with his eyes, but in fact does not seem to notice anything, since he is concerned with the vision of his memory. A larger perspective is presented when he describes the scene of the crucifixion, which, though it is marked as present only in the speaker's memory, adds the vertical dimension. This description also includes Christ turning the spheres and thus gives an outlook on the earth as a whole, as does the thought exper-iment at the beginning. Thus, although the speaker can only "see" with his eyes on a limited horizontal level, with his imagination he can see and create a three-dimensional space, including the earth, the sun and other spheres. The speaker's physical linear movement shows in a small, indi-vidual context (in the personal perspective of the speaker) the same movement and conflict that (or so ll. 1-8 claim) concerns the whole world and every man's soul.

The single speaker appears like a spot in the landscape (otherwise void of description) and his individuality is emphasised by the repeated refer-ence to himself: "I." Christ is equally only a spot in the landscape but he is immobile and provides orientation to the speaker. Through the speak-er's observation of and communication with Christ, an additional linear relationship is created: speaker and Christ are connected through their gaze, which transcends time and space. The soul's bending, and the speaker's verbal (not yet physical) turning form a sinuous motion; the line connecting but also separating the speaker and Christ is bent so that, ultimately, the two terminal points, speaker and Christ, will be joined.

4.2 Geography

Geographical elements are used in "Goodfriday" to support the place-ment of the speaker and his movement in space. After the hypothetical exposition in ll. 1-8, the dichotomy between East and West in ll. 9-10 provides a reference to the speaker's physical world. However, this posi-tioning remains very vague; there is no further indication of place. West is simultaneously the direction of the speaker's purported voyage and of his physical death, while East is the direction in which Christ's death lies, but also the way towards the speaker's salvation and resurrection.[72]

By referring to the crucifixion, which the speaker "sees" in the East, he implicitly restricts the general geographical information "East" to mean "Jerusalem," and even more specific, "Golgotha." Thus, the imaginary "East" seems much more real than the "West" towards which the speaker physically moves. The "tree" in l.36 is the only landmark present in the poem and also contributes to anchor Christ's cross in the landscape and make it appear more real (while it is impossible for the speaker in 1613 to see the cross with his physical eyes, it would easily be possible for him

---

72   Cf. Chambers (1961):

> When John Donne rode westward on Good Friday, 1613, he travelled in large company; most of the universe – as he knew it, at least – was moving westward too. The heliotrope, a favorite example, arched its stem in order to follow the course of the sun. Gasparo Contarini had noted that the ocean flowed to the west; Peacham said that only the Mediterranean refused to obey this general law; and Donne himself discovered that the currents of the south-west straits never flow eastward. [...] Aeneas went west, Constantine went east; one followed the divine will, and one did not. (31f.)

Glaser sees the different directions in "Goodfriday" as symbolic of Catholicism and Protestantism:

> The course of European history was westward, from the Near East to England and beyond, and this scheme was widely applied to church history as well [...] East is the authoritarian structure of the Catholic Church, and behind that the Old Law. West is the reformed Protestant present and future with its enlightened insistence on each Christian's personal relationship with God. (171)

The speaker's looking back towards the east he sees as a remembrance of Donne's "ardent Catholic childhood" and a look "toward the iconography of baptism, when his soul was awakened like the red clay of Adam or the dust at the foot of the Cross" (172). Yet Glaser concedes that, even when applied to Catholic and Protestant churches, the movement found in "Goodfriday" is ultimately a concurring one and cites a similar notion from Donne's *Essays in Divinity*, where Catholicism and Protestantism, though they develop in opposite directions stem from the same root: "[Y]et though we branch out *East* and *West*, that Church concurs with us in the root, and sucks her vegetation from one and the same ground, *Christ Jesus*" (Donne 1952, 50). On a smaller scale, "by travelling westward [the speaker] is actually imitating Christ's final journey. The *Via Dolorosa* in Jerusalem runs westward toward Calvary" (Glaser 173).

Goldberg, however, notes that (especially in 17th-century Christian poetry) the journey to the East is found frequently, as a "vehicle for the presentation of dogmatic and poetic truths" – Donne's poem seems to be exceptional in so far as it is the only Good Friday poem to make use of this trope (470).

to see a tree on the ground).[73] The "tree" serves a number of functions: Firstly, it makes Christ small (smaller than a tree) and more or less the same size as the speaker. Secondly, it makes Christ accessible by showing him (visually) as a sinner (that the speaker actually is). Thirdly, (as a landmark) it ingrains and fixes Christ in the landscape, providing a better anchor for the inconstant speaker. Lastly, it appeals at Christ's mercy (according to the *Golden Legend*, the cross was made from wood from the "tree of mercy" in Paradise, Caxton, 180f.).

The "Sunne" which the speaker would see "there" is both the spherical sun and the son of God. Taken literally, east is of course the direction of the rising sun, the word "orient" deriving from oriens, "rising" (*OED*, "orient, n. and adj."), and the direction from which light (and therefore vision) comes. Correspondingly, the West or occident is literally the direction of death, coming from "occidens," falling or going down (*OED*, "occident, n. and adj."). At the same time, the orient gives orientation to the speaker (which is especially meaningful, since the speaker in ll-1-8 had presented himself as lacking orientation): in spite of being carried westwards, he perceives in Christ's cross a fixed point of reference in the east.[74]

In addition to East and West, measuring the world on a horizontal line, the speaker introduces a vertical dimension by referring to the "Poles in l.21 and to "zenith" and "antipodes" in l.24 (i.e. to the speaker's zenith and to the one visible in the antipodes). By introducing the poles and the antipodes, as well as the tuning/turning of the spheres in l. 22, the two-dimensional, map-like image of a plain between East and West becomes a three-dimensional, globe-like image of the world.

In one sermon, Donne uses an image which differs from the conception presented in "Goodfriday," but has similar implications for the meaning

---

73 In *De Visione Dei* (1988, 690-91), Cusa describes the experience of seeing and comprehending the vision of God by comparing this experience to seeing a nut tree in all its details.

74 Chambers (1961, 64) points out that in Zech 6.12, Jesus is called "Oriens": "ecce vir Oriens nomen eius." With regard to "Goodfriday," it should be noted that "Oriens" is translated into "Branch" in English: "Behold the man whose name is The Branch" (KJV). The same correlation can be found in Zech 3.8, which reads "servum meum orientem" and "my servant the Branch," respectively; while in Isa 4.2, Isa 11.1, Jer 23.5 and Jer 33.15, the English "branch" has a Latin equivalent (cf. also Spear 36).

of East and West. In imagining a flat map rolled up and thus forming a circle, Donne describes West and East as two faces of the same coin:

> Take a flat Map, A Globe *in plano*, and here is East, and there is West, as far asunder as two points can be put: but reduce this flat Map to roundnesse, which is the true form, and then East and West touch one another, and are all one: So consider mans life aright, to be a Circle ("Sermon Preached to the Lords upon Easter-day, on Ps. 89.48," Donne, *Sermons* II, no. 9, 199).[75]

Thus, beginning with a two-dimensional movement on a plane, the speaker's soul bends back (as in a semicircle) to Christ, and he turns his back (again, bending, a semicircular movement) to Christ.

These two contrary movements (each of which contributes towards three-dimensional circularity but does not form a complete circle on its own) become one in the circularity inherent to a spherical globe – which was introduced in ll.1-8 with the mention of the revolving spheres.[76] In his sermon, Donne achieves with this graphic image a sense of circularity and a union of life and death, as well as of Christ and the speaker, which is also present in "Goodfriday": if East and West become one, the speaker not only rides away from Christ, but ultimately towards him.[77]

---

75 One way of understanding this process is imagining a flat map that is rolled up and thus becomes a tube on which east and west touch, forming a circle. Another possibility is that of a two-dimensional map literally becoming a three-dimensional globe. This idea is not Donne's; at the beginning of the 17th century, Martin Waldseemüller published gores for constructing globes. These consist of a number of vertical stripes, connected in the middle and decreasing towards the upper and lower edges, which can be cut out and joined to make up a three-dimensional globe. In this case, East and West do indeed touch each other, and a three-dimensional space is constructed similarly to the speaker's movement in "Goodfriday."

76 Taken very literally, a complete (threedimensional) little world emerges from a flat, twodimensional piece of paper.

77 The same image is used in Donne's "Hymne to God my God in my sicknesse," and with the same conclusion: Moving through life towards death is nothing to be afraid of, since it brings one closer to eternal life: "What shall my West hurt me? As West and East / In all flatt Maps (and I am one) are one, / So death doth touch the Resurrection" (ll.13-15).

   Also, as in "Goodfriday," in "Hymne to God" Donne adds a temporal concurrence to this spatial union:

   We thinke that Paradise and Calvarie,
   Christs Crosse, and Adams tree, stood in one place;

4.3 Astronomy

The first eight lines rely heavily on astronomical ideas. Donne combines two astronomical models in "Goodfriday." On the one hand, the planetary motions the speaker of "Goodfriday" describes are usually associated with a geocentric world model, and the notion of a "first mover," which originally comes from Aristotle, also belongs to this traditional world picture. On the other hand, the role of the "Sunne" conforms to a heliocentric model, which is also reflected in the structure of the poem: The Sun/son stands at the centre of the poem (lines 21-22) and causes the movement of "all spheares."

The analogous relations established between spheres and human souls can be presented in the following way, assuming a Ptolemaic, geocentric model behind the description of the spherical motions.

positive motion (rational)	*negative motion (irrational, sensual)*
theory	
duration: day	duration: year
agent: prime mover	agent: individual planets
direction: westward	direction: eastward
manner: being moved	manner: move by themselves
spheres	
duration: "in a yeare"	duration: "every day"
agent: "their owne [motion]"	agent: "forraigne motions"
direction: eastward	direction: westward
manner: "scarce [...] their naturall forme obey"	manner: "by others hurried"

Looke Lord, and finde both Adams met in me;
As the first Adams sweat surrounds my face,
May the last Adams blood my soule embrace. (ll.21-25)
Cf. also "Upon the Annunciation and Passion falling upon one day. 1608": "Th'Abridgement of Christs story, which makes one / (As in plain Maps, the furthest West is East)" (ll.20-21). In this poem, too, events taking place in different time frames seem to converge till they are joined in a single day. Cf. also the discussion of map imagery in "The Search" in the next chapter.

> *speaker*
>
> duration: Good Friday (=yearly)   duration: "this day"
> agent: "devotion"   agent: "pleasure or businesse"
> direction: eastward   direction: westward
> manner: "Soules forme bends"   manner: "I am carryed"
>   (spiritually)   (physically)

There are different opinions on whether the westward motion of distract-
ed spheres and men is ultimately contrary to or in accordance with the
natural course of the stars (depending on which astronomical treatise
Donne could have read).[78] No matter which, there can be no doubt that
going westward, in this poem, means going towards death, and is (at least
initially) linked to "pleasure or businesse," that is to worldly and sinful
matters, and that going eastward means approaching God.[79]

---

78 Chambers notes several possible models for the speaker's use of astronomy to
    draw an analogy, among which are Plato, Aristotle, Sacrobosco, Boethius, Kepler
    and their commentators, perpetuating this analogy to Donne's time (1961, 32-42).
    Gardner sees Donne's particular depiction of the spheres in "Goodfriday" based
    largely on Johannes de Sacrobosco's treatise *De Sphaera* (though reversing
    rational and irrational motion as presented by Sacrobosco) (Donne 1978, 99,
    156f.). Beck notes that the same reversal can be found in a poem by Lydgate,
    which, significantly, is based on the same general metaphor as "Goodfriday,"
    Pilgrimage of the Life of Man (166-69). Westerweel (1989, 117) cites the same
    poem as a possible source for the use of horse imagery in "Goodfriday":
     [...] Sensualyte;
     'The wych wyl nat bridled be,
     But ffroward euere in hys entent,
     Mevying toward the occident,
     [...]
     Al-though the spyryt (in hys entent)
     Meueth toward the orient,
     Wych thenys kam. & iff he sholde
     Thyder ageyn, fful ffayn he wolde:
     Toward the Est, in alle thing,
     He travaylleth in hys mevying
     Wych (be my red) shal neuere tarye,
     But labour, & be contrarye
     To the meying off the body,
     And contynue virtuously
     Bexaumple [...] off the boterflye,
     Wych ay ffro the occident
     Tourneth toward the orient. (ll.12291-12314)
79 However, applying the model shown in the previous table, the westward movement
    would in theory actually be seen as positive and rational.

The most important step the speaker makes with regard to his movement is the reinterpretation of his apparent deviance. His outward movement in the poem does not change (therefore, neither does his movement within the analogy of ll.1-8). However, his attitude changes, and he reinterprets the cause for his westward movement. Now that he has established a connection to God, he states that he turns his back to God (that is, continues westward) "but to receive / Corrections."

In all three fields – geometry, geography and astronomy – it becomes apparent that there is a distinction between linear and circular movement, and that circularity is what the speaker considers to be the most important and desirable movement. Circularity is attributed to God and (yet) lacking in the speaker. Accepting this circularity entails not only repetition but also progress: a true understanding of the speaker's westward course, a change from reluctant to contrite and a vision of the way to God.

5. Turning and music – turning as tuning

Although musical imagery is not found abundantly in "Goodfriday," it is literally central to the poem. The image of God turning or tuning the spheres is located exactly in the middle of the poem, in ll.21-22. "Tune all spheares" in l.22 reads "turne all spheres" in three manuscripts (Gardner 31).[80] This variation also indicates the merging and to some extent inseparability of the notions of turning and tuning. Although this is no indication of whether such a pun was intended by Donne, the apparently interchangeable use of "turn" and "tune" (and their conceptual relation) shows that there is a relation between them (and no matter which word was used originally, the image of Christ turning/tuning the spheres is always both spatial and musical, since it is linked to the notion of the music of the spheres, derived from Boethius). Christ's pierced hands in this image are comparable to the tuning pegs of string instruments, which are turned in order to tune the instrument.[81]

---

80 Todd examines the poem's different manuscript and print versions in detail, without coming to a conclusive decision about the variants "turne" and "tune" (208f., 211). A similar confusion can be found in Herbert's "The Search," where ll.21-22 reads either "I tun'd another [sigh] into a grone" or "I turned another [sigh] into a grone," depending on the edition (cf. Herbert 2007, 556).

81 Cf. O'Connell: "Whether the correct reading of line 22 be "turne all spheares" or "tune all spheares," the picture is definitely one of cosmic harmony" (1985, 22).

The movement of the spheres described in ll.1-8 also alludes to the music of the spheres conceptualised in Boethius's *De Institutione Musica*, with its underlying idea of a celestial harmony which extends to humankind: the large-scale planetary music (Boethius's "musica mundana," which in "Goodfriday" is disturbed by "forraigne motions"), corresponding on a smaller scale to the harmony of man's body and soul (Boethius's "musica humana"). The contrary movements of the spheres in general and the speaker in particular (as they are described in ll.1-8) create a tension and discord which stands in contrast to Christ's turning (or harmonious tuning) of the spheres in l.22.[82] Getting on one level with Christ can likewise be seen as a process towards harmony (similar to the process of musical tuning): finding the equilibrium between perceiving Christ as too far above the speaker (an "endlesse height" and a "zenith to us, and to'our Antipodes," ll.23f.) or unbearably below the speaker ("humbled below us," with his blood making "durt of dust" and his flesh "rag'd, and torne," ll.25-28) in a mutual gaze on (almost) equal terms: "For that looks towards them; and thou look'st towards mee" (l.35).

6.   Turning as transformation

The speaker's conversion also entails his transformation from unruly and sinful to contrite and cleansed. While outwardly the speaker does not change and continues riding westward, he is inwardly transformed from a misled sinner into a contrite sinner, and he asks for a further transformation and a restoration from his sinful state to an unfallen state through God's "corrections." Thus, there are two kinds of transformation in the poem. The first is the one that simply happens through the speaker's speaking: in uttering the poem, the speaker is changed, he becomes contrite and brings himself closer to God. The second transformation is one which he cannot perform alone, or through the power of words, and which he accordingly asks from God and situates at a future point in time.

---

82   Severance sees the desire to be a sphere already as a desire to be in tune with God: "A Litanie" promises: "A sinner is more musique, when he prayes, / Then spheares, or Angels praises bee" (ll. 200-1). The opening words of "Goodfriday, 1613," "Let mans Soule be a Spheare," spoken from an awareness of contrary motion, of disjuncture and disharmony, are such a prayer. To be a sphere is to be "in line" and "in tune" – at one with God. (29)

The corrections the speaker wishes for are part of a process of purification and catharsis and will have a double effect on the speaker: they will cleanse him (i.e. burn off his rusts), and they will take away his deformity. Rust and deformity are both properties that affect and alter something that is already there. Rust settles on the surface of materials, and a deformity presupposes the existence of a form which can be "de-formed." Removing the rust and reversing the deformity of the soul to its proper form is a process of restoration, and this is indeed what the speaker wishes for: "Restore thine image." In l.10, the speaker attributes "form" to his soul, which is taken up in the "deformity" that he asks God to remove.[83]

Robbins lists several possible parallels to the expression "burn off my rusts," all related to metalwork (Donne 2010, 566).[84] The *OED* ("deform-

---

83   Lewalski points out the superficiality of these "rusts" and "deformity," which can taint the soul but not ultimately dissolve it:

> Because he took the image to be in the powers of the soul themselves, Donne held with Augustine and the Roman Catholic theologians generally that original sin could not efface it. Bernard's striking comment, "*Imago Dei uri potest in Gehenna, nonexuri*" [quoted in Donne's sermon, 81] comes close to being his favorite quotation: "Till the soule be burnt to ashes, to nothing, (which cannot be done, no not in hell) the Image of God cannot be burnt out of that soule." ["Sermon Preached to the King, at the Court, The Second Sermon on Gen 1.26," Donne, *Sermons* IX, no.2, 81]. (1973, 121)

Such a view also corresponds to Donne's use of "burne off" in "Goodfriday": the use of "off" suggests that "rusts" and "deformity" are only external and can therefore be taken "off" the speaker's soul.

Glaser (173) points out the image of a "rusty copper" in one of Donne's sermons:

> I consider Christ to have been [...] and to be still the Image of the Father, the same stamp upon the same metall; and my self a peece of rusty copper, in which those lines of the Image of God, which were imprinted in me in my Creation, are defaced, and worn, and washed and burnt, and ground away, by my many and many and many sins. ("Sermon Preached at the marriage of Mistress Margaret Washington, May 30, 1621, on Hos 2.19," Donne *Sermons* III, no. 11, 250).

Significantly, this example is used by Donne to affirm the union (i.e., "marriage") of God and man's soul after death.

84   Cf. also the related verb "burnish": "To make (metal) shining by friction" (*OED*, "burnish, *v*.1 1.a"), and "To make bright and glossy (*OED*, "burnish, *v*.1 2.a), which was also used metaphorically.

Brooks (1995, 296f.) points out St. Augustine's description of the state of his soul, which is similar to both the beginning and ending of "Goodfriday":

> I fall into dissolution amid the changing times, whose order I am yet ignorant of; yea, my thoughts are torn asunder with tumultuous vicissitudes, even the inmost bowels of my soul; until I may be run into thee, purified and molten by the fire of thy love. (Augustine 1912, 281; bk. XI, ch. 29).

Cf. also a passage from the *Devotions*, where turning is also linked explicitly to receiving God's corrections:

ity, 4.a") lists an example with a very similar twofold expression: "Purged and clene of all vice and alkyn deformitee" (from Mandeville's Travels, c.1400). Here, too, deformity is linked to the spiritual sphere and connected to "vice." While "rusts" in "Goodfriday" can of course be read metaphorically,[85] the image it evokes is primarily physical. The use of "rusts" therefore continues the interplay between the inner and outer part of the speaker: between his physical and material part and his spiritual and immaterial part, between body and soul, rust and deformity (both in a literal and metaphorical sense).[86]

In the end, the speaker has thus neither changed physically nor changed his direction, and, as a mortal being, he will of course continue his journey westwards (towards his death), but through the reciprocity of his look at Christ and Christ's look at him, he becomes assured of Christ's

---

There is then a middle kinde of *Hearts*, not so perfit, as to bee given, but that the very giving mends them: Not so desperate, as not to bee accepted, but that the very accepting dignifies them. This is a *melting* heart, and a *troubled* heart; and a *wounded* heart, and a *broken* heart, and a *contrite* heart; and by the powerfull working of thy piercing spirit, such a *Heart* I have; *Thy Samuel* spake unto all the house of thy *Israel*, and sayd, *If you returne to the Lord with all your hearts, prepare your hearts unto the Lord*. If my heart bee *prepared*, it is a *returning* heart; And if thou see it upon the *way*, thou wilt carrie it *home*; Nay, the *preparation* is thine too; this *melting*, this *wounding*, this *breaking*, this *contrition*, which I have now, is thy *Way*, to thy *Ende*; and those *discomforts*, are for all that, *The earnest of thy Spirit in my heart*." (XI. Expostulation, 59f.)

The vocabulary used here is also relevant with regard to Herbert's "The Temper (I)" and the notion of tempering (that is, heating something up but *not* melting it completely) as a means of turning. Cf. also the XVII. Prayer:

And being thus, O my *God*, prepared by thy *correction*, mellowed by thy chastisement, and conformed to thy will, by thy *Spirit*, having received thy *pardon* for my *soule*, and asking no *reprieve* for my *body*, I am bold, O *Lord*, to bend my *prayers* to thee for his assistance, the voice of whose *bell* hath called me to this devotion. (90)

85   "Rust" in this sense is often used in combination with the verb "canker," in which case rust refers to a herbal disease, cf. *OED*, "rust, n. 1": "From canckred rust Christ shall make iust," (1577); and "May not we be busie in soliciting for unnecessary favours to others, .. and yet our souls contract a rust, whose cancker may make it at last moulder away to nothing?" (G. Mackenzie *Moral Essays*, 1665).

86   Hamlin, in discussing "A Litanie," reads the speaker's desire for restoration as a two-fold one, voicing a concern of the poem's speaker as well as of Donne as a poet: "Donne's "ruinous" state and his desire for re-creation can thus be read in terms of his poetic as well as his religious self, or rather of a single multifaceted self with both artistic and spiritual anxieties." However, while Hamlin sees the same desire for spiritual restoration in "Goodfriday," he denies the speaker the "intense self-examination" he finds in "A Litanie" (2008, 201).

presence in his life and gains the strength necessary to deal with his sin-
fulness and become contrite, which in turn assures him of his own salva-
tion and anticipates a wholeness of body and soul (in the double sense of
completion and integrity).[87]

7. Circular turning and self-referentiality

From the poem's first line, the speaker stresses circular movement: the
spheres are circular, their movement is (roughly) circular, the sun – an-
other sphere – is circular, God turns or tunes the spheres in circular revo-
lution, the implied union of East and West leads to circularity, the speak-
er's recourse to his memory – turning back to previous events – implies
circularity, as does the restoration of his image, and the speaker's bend-
ing, turning his back, and (at some point in the future) turning his face,
also creates a circular motion.[88]

Within all these circular movements, two stand out. The first is God's
turning or tuning of the revolving spheres, which places God at the centre
of all things and relates circularity to perfection, and secondly, the speak-
er's movement, which is characterised as a double turning and as a circu-
lar (though yet unfinished) movement. The promise of the speaker's final

---

87   Harland sees the speaker's turning as an overcoming of his self-love and a
     willingness to imitate Christ:
     > When one, afflicted and suffering, as all persons are, catches a glimpse of oneself in
     > Christ's suffering and sees one's personal story there reflected, one's heart is melted by a
     > com-passion, and through this recognition, freed to love this other suffering being. Fur-
     > thermore, one is granted the ability to enhance this identification, by taking up the other's
     > burden as one's own. [...] initial fear and rejection of the crucifixion, based on narrow
     > self-love, [is] followed by a compassion that occurs when self is mirrored in the tortured
     > Christ (170-72).

88   Nicolson highlights the pervasiveness of the symbolic use of the circle image both
     in 16th and 17th- century literature and in Donne's works (34 -63). Cf. also
     Fischler (169):
     > In the works of John Donne, the circle assumes the status of controlling metaphor: it is a
     > figure which at once represents the refection of God, the cycles of Nature and of the hu-
     > man beings caught up therein, and the solipsistic repetitions of sin. "God hath made all
     > things in a *Roundnesse*," he maintains in a sermon, "from the round superficies of this
     > earth, which we tread here, to the round convexity of those heavens which (as long as they
     > shall have any beeing) shall be our footstool, when we come to heaven, God hath wrapped
     > up all things in Circles" ("Sermon preached to the King, at White-Hall, the first of April,
     > 1927, on Mark 4.24," Donne, *Sermons* VII, no. 16, 396).
     Cf. also "Upon the Annunciation and Passion falling upon one day. 1608": [My
     soul] sees [Christ] man, so like God made in this, / That of them both a circle
     emblem is, / Whose first and last concurre" (ll.3-5).

turn marks the end of the poem and the result of previous turns. It is no coincidence that it occurs at the end of the poem – a traditional place for determined statements, conclusions or sudden turns in argumentation. Like a sonnet's last line, the last line of "Goodfriday" contains the central message of the poem in condensed form (which, in this particular case has been prepared from l.37 onwards). And, since the poem ends here, there is no further turn (away from God) possible; the speaker cannot retract his statement any longer.

The turn in line 42 is both a turning point in the speaker's relation to God, and the speaker's goal in this poem. It is a turning point, since the speaker has been riding in the opposite direction and has *not* looked back with his face. It is the speaker's goal, since through the poem, the speaker is striving to look at God and is trying to attain the restoration and salvation that goes along with being able to look at God. At the same time, this final turn is already a re-turn to God, made possible by a previous turn in the opposite direction. In l.10, the speaker states that his "Soules forme bends toward the East" while his body rides to the West. The soul has already turned back, or is at least trying to ("bending" east against the straight westward path of the body and, in this bending and therefore humble movement, showing the devotion which is God's due).

Although it looks at first glance like a contrary movement, the speaker's turning his back to God also serves the higher purpose of making him turn (wholly and completely) towards God. In l. 37, when the speaker says, "I turne my back to thee," he immediately follows with a reason for doing so, "but to receive / Corrections." The speaker's turning his back is thus a threefold action. He must present his back to God in order to get punished (to be beaten on his back). Literally, he is riding away from Christ, thereby showing him his back. And idiomatically, his stance seems to be one of rejection: the phrase "to turn one's back" means "to turn away" (*OED*, "turn, v.", VII.48). However, "I turn my back" sounds very similar to "I turn me (i.e., myself) back," and "turn" can also be used reflexively ("I turn me ..." is documented up to the 19th century. This hint at a movement *towards* God is supported by the preposition "to" ("turn one's back *upon* or *on*" would be much more common than "to").

So, no matter which reading is chosen, the speaker's turning his back to Christ only seems disobedient at first glance.[89] It actually shows the speaker's understanding and prepares the proper turn in the last line. Accordingly, the speaker marks his turning away from God as a prerequisite for turning his face by continuing with "but to receive corrections" in l.37. The corrections have a positive association: the speaker has to be "worth" God's anger; the corrections are accompanied by God's "mercies" and they (and the restoration of God's image) will take place through God's "grace."[90] Thus, although his journey takes him further

---

89   Schoenfeldt (2001) sees the speaker's turning his back to Christ as an "act of overt defiance" (569) and cites from the sermon on Ps. 6.4-5 (discussed in the introduction), where Donne explicitly condemns it: "When the Lord comes to us, by any way, though he come in corrections, in chastisements, not to turne to him, is an irreverent and unrespective negligence" ("Sermon Preached upon the Penitentiall Psalmes, on Ps. 6.4 and 5," Donne, *Sermons* V, no. 18, 370). Powrie likewise sees the speaker's turning his back to Christ as the "posture of defiance" of a speaker "vexed by opposing desires for enlightenment and for secular pleasures" (12) However, as just shown, the speaker in "Goodfriday" does not simply "turn his back." He turns towards Christ with his memory, and he even solicits the presence of God by asking for God's punishment. Thus, he turns his apparent "irreverent and unrespective negligence" (which he cannot change anyway, since he is "carryed" westward) into an action necessary for his salvation (and he also qualifies it as such: "but to receive / Corrections"). Strier (2008) considers the speaker's "I turne my back" as a true turning away from God, a "fantasy [...] to avoid acknowledgement of one's own imperfection and infinitude, to avoid seeing another in order to avoid being seen, in the deepest sense, by another" (23f.) – arguing that the speaker will not turn back until he has become perfect (22f.). This reading, however, seems to be difficult to support when regarding the poem as a whole.

90   Cf. Sanchez: "The 'Corrections' the speaker requests come from God's active participation (in the form of anger, punishment, and burning), but also from the individual eventually turning towards God to accept the corrections" (2014, 54). Halewood reads the "but" in l.36 not as "in order to" but as "nonjustifying, nonexplanatory, having nothing to do with intention" and meaning "'only,' 'merely,' 'nothing more than,' 'with no worse result than'" (219ff.), leading to a reading of "Corrections" not as frightening or distressing but just as a sign of God's attention and mercy:

> There is no boldness in the word, then, and it does not belong to the language of condition-making, or insubordination, but to the language of thanksgiving. It is the same "but" understood without difficulty in "Batter my heart ... for you as yet *but* knocke, breathe, shine, etc." [The speaker's] his sinful desertion has produced not the deserved penalty but only (nothing but) corrections designed by mercy.

Halewood also cites Job 5.17, "happy is the man whom God correcteth" and one of Donne's sermons, "O Lord be angry with me, for if thou chidest me not, thou

away from Christ in the east (riding westward and not turning his face),
the speaker can only be saved because he is riding away from God, al-
lowing his soul to "bend" and presenting his physical back for God's
physical cleansing punishment – and thus ultimately towards God.[91]

The notion of looking backward and forward, of seeing (oneself and
others) and being seen (by oneself and others), and of having an "image"
is prominent in "Goodfriday" and evokes the process of looking into a
mirror (this process also implies some kind of circularity, as the specta-
tor's image is "returned" by the mirror to the spectator).[92] Early mirrors
were made of metal (steel or silver, cf. *OED* "mirror, n." II.4 and Kalas
519f.), which goes along with the idea of "restoring the speaker's image"
by burning off his rusts.[93] When he will be cleansed, the speaker will

---

considerest me not, if I taste no bitternesse, I have no Physick; if thou correct me
not, I am not thy son" ("Sermon Preached at White-Hall, March 3, 1619, on Amos
5.18," Donne, *Sermons* II, no. 18, 362) as examples of a positive view on being
corrected by God.

91   Cf. Leimberg (1996, 48):

> Der scheinbare Zufall [that is, his westward journey on Good Friday] gibt sich also als of-
> fenbare Notwendigkeit zu erkennen. Die Geste der Mißachtung wird als Bedingung von
> Reue und Buße verstanden, und das Davonlaufen vor dem Kreuz, das Schauen in die an-
> dere Richtung, ist im sphärisch gestalteten Kosmos eigentlich schon immer ein Hinschau-
> en, während es heilsgeschichtlich auf das Angeschautsein von Gott als Ursprung der
> Erkenntnis verweist.

Chambers (1987, 199) points at a sermon by Andrewes, written for Ash
Wednesday 1619, which uses exactly the same imagery that can be found in
"Goodfriday":

> The text announced is from Joel 2.12-13, "Turne you unto Me ... turne unto the Lord your
> God," and one of the points heavily stressed *(XCVI Sermons,* 204) is that the text is itself
> "a circle ... which circle consists of *two turnings;* (for, twise he repeats this word)." Re-
> pentance, metaphorically, also "is nothing else, but a kind of circling." "First, a *turne*
> wherein we look forward to GOD, Then, a *turne* again, wherein we look backward to our
> *sinnes.*" Each of these, by itself, is "but the *halfe-turne*" (205), and since that is true, the
> common preference for looking forward will not serve. Past sin must also be recalled:
> "the *Hemisphaere* of our *sinnes* (not to be under the *Horizon,* cleare out of sight) must as-
> cend up" (208). When both half turns are made, however, "the two between them, make
> up a complete *repentance,* or (to keepe the word of the text) a *perfect revolution*" (205).
> "And when our *turne* is done; GOD shall begin His" (213).

92   Ure points out that there is a general "tendency [...] to associate the mirror with
truth-telling" (219f.), found across the various symbolic associations of the mirror,
from being a representation of Vanity and Lust to being a symbol of Chastity and
Prudence.

93   Mirrors could be and were used to create fire since antiquity, so that they are also
linked to fire. Most prominent is the story of Archimedes burning ships attacking
Syracuse by reflecting sunlight on the ships with the help of large mirrors.

reflect God once more. Lines 37 to 42 can be seen as an allusion to 1 Cor 13:12, "For now we see through a glass, darkly; but then face to face: now I know in part; but then shall I know even as also I am known."[94] Christ's returning gaze in l.35 promises a vision of God "face to face," the impossibility of which is stated in line 17. Since the speaker is not looking back with his physical eyes but with his memory (creating a certain level of indirectness which reflects the process of looking into a mirror), he is able to stand Christ's returning gaze.

Ironically, the image of Christ in a church would be veiled on Good Friday. It is because the speaker is on the road, where he can only visualise Christ through his memory, that he is able to see Christ face to face: firstly, because seeing God face to face in real life would mean his death, whereas the memory provides a degree of indirectness that makes it possible to look; and secondly, because during a service in church the speaker would not be able to see Christ at all because of the veil, which does not exist in the speaker's memory of the original Good Friday.[95]

---

94 Cf. also a sonnet by Drummond, which, though being a secular love poem, nonetheless shows the same kind of inner self-examination using similar imagery.

In mind's pure glasse when I my selfe behold,
And vively see how my best dayes are spent, [...]
My begunne course I, wearied, doe repent,
And would embrace what reason oft hath told, [...]
Yet when I think vpon that face diuine, [...]
Malgre my heart, I ioye in my disgrace. (30)

The mind is depicted as a "pure glasse," showing the speaker his true self, although when he thinks about "that face diuine" (which is *not* divine but the human face of a woman) the poem takes a different turn and his repentance turns into joy.

Cf. also the idea of a mirror as an instrument for self-examination and consequently self-correction reflected in book titles such as *A Mirror for Magistrates* or Clarke's *A Mirror or Looking-Glass for both Saints and Sinners*. In this connection, the image of the mirror also makes visible a link between "seeing" and "knowing" or "understanding" (made explicit in the poem's last line "That thou may'st know mee," but implicitly also present in the speaker's exploration of his own state (cf. also Severance 30, Schleiner 137).

95 Sherwood (1979, 119f.) also points at Zech 1.3: Turn ye unto me, saith the Lord of hosts, and I will turn unto you, saith the Lord of hosts." In "Goodfriday," this double turning seems to happen simultaneously: in the moment the speaker states "that looks towards them," he also states "and thou look'st towards mee" (though syntactically this could also imply a temporal succession). DiPasquale points out that what happens in Donne's poem is actually a reversal of Zech 1.3, as the speaker "reserves his 'turn' for last" (128). She highlights the similarity to Psalm

Apart from this conceptual closeness to mirror imagery, the poem is to
some extent self-referential. The poem's occasional character, with a title
such as "Made as I was riding ..." not only marks the poem as an occa-
sional poem but also as one "written on the way" so that "as I ride" be-
comes inseparable from "as I write" (and although both verbs are not
homophonous, an acoustical closeness is already evident) and thus points
at the poem itself.[96] "Goodfriday" is a poem exploring language, but also
a poem about language. God speaks to St. Paul and God speaks to St.
Augustine. God does not speak to the speaker in "Goodfriday," but the
speaker recalls (and also re-calls) God through the words of the poem
and finds a response in Christ's glance at him. The speaker makes this
glance come into existence through the text of the poem and especially
through the ekphrastic middle part.[97]

The speaker's projected turn is made possible because he does possess
the right disposition from the beginning of the poem (even though he first
needs to overcome his aversion of looking behind): his soul in line 10
already "bends towards the East." Lines 33 and 34 are, in a way, a repeti-
tion of lines 9 to 10: the speaker states once more where his body is situ-

---

80, with a threefold repetition of "Turn us again, O God, and cause thy face to
shine; and we shall be saved":

> The prayer at the conclusion of "Goodfriday, 1613" revises the psalmist's prayer, invert-
> ing its emphasis: the Psalm speaks of *God's act of turning man*, presenting a sequence in
> which salvation follows from that turning and from the shining of the divine face; the po-
> et/speaker of "Goodfriday, 1613" speaks of his own face and his own act of turning (128)

> Cf. also a statement from one of Donne's sermons on the power of God's glance
and the reciprocity it creates: "[God's] guiding us with his eye, manifests it selfe in
these two great effects; conversion to him and union with him. First, his eye works
upon ours; His eye turns ours to looke upon him" (Preached upon the Penitentiall
Psalmes, on Ps. 32.8," Donne, *Sermons* IX, no. 16, 367).

96   Cf. also Schoenfeldt:

> The poems [...] are not so much vivid dramatizations of the sacrifice as they are perfor-
> mances of the enormous difficulty of apprehending what is, in Donne's words, a "specta-
> cle of too much weight." These writers ask how the immense suffering of the Christian
> sacrifice can be represented in poetry, free of the inevitable anesthesia of memory and the
> distorting fictions of the imagination. (562)

97   At the same time, the written form of the poem creates another kind of spatial
relation: seen from outside the poem, the speaker's voyage is retained on paper,
while within the poem there is a nonphysical description of both a physical and a
nonphysical event – both are linked through the text of the poem, which preserves
the speaker's words (and thus Donne's work of art) and creates the speaker's
experience.

ated. However, there a change has taken place and the speaker's relationship to Christ has become more personal. Though the speaker's body is still in as much need of correction as it was in the beginning, the speaker is now ready and willing to be corrected, and to continue his journey westwards – knowing that he is at the same time journeying to the east and towards being joined to Christ in his life after death.[98]

8. Conclusion

The analysis of "Goodfriday" has served to illustrate a number of points that are important with regard to turning: it is a poem full of turns, and everything in the poem serves to turn and direct the speaker. This happens by creating a connection to Christ through visual communication, and this act of communication is central in effecting the speaker's conversion. Thus, the speaker envisions something that is invisible through a number of means. He turns his literal journey into a metaphor for his spiritual way through life and his conversion and expresses his changing spiritual state through physical images. He describes a double process: from literal journey to metaphors for conversion, which are made visible through turns of phrase. The speaker uses multiple linguistic mechanisms and thematic areas to talk about this experience, and to create multiple turns throughout the poem.

"Goodfriday" is marked by all sorts of movement: there is a linear movement in the speaker's riding westward, in his development from a general to a personal relation to Christ and from focussing on a public spectacle to experiencing a personal gaze, and in the speaker's gradual recognition that he moves in the right direction. There is a circular movement in the revolving spheres (both in the beginning and centre of

---

98   Friedman (442) and Chambers (1961, 52) see the speaker's initial stance on his westward movement as a mistake – the fact that a westward movement is not only right, but the only right one can only be understood towards the end of the poem:

> The journey westward to death is both right and inevitable. Donne has therefore followed natural, uniform and direct motion throughout his poem. [...] Devotion, leaning to the east, thus becomes the irrational motion within Donne's sphere, becomes a "passionate" and "sensual" movement toward Christ. The divine contemplation of Good Friday's Passion creates in Donne the irrational desire to move eastward at once, the desire to avoid that longer and harder westward path. This devotion can scarcely be called bad; indeed, it is that which makes the westward movement good, for only Donne's awareness of Christ at his back makes possible the final touching of east and west. (Chambers 1961, 52)

the poem) and the speaker's realisation that going westward means going eastward (that is, a mental turning).

The speaker achieves his conversion by bringing Christ from a distant past to his own present (and into his own presence). This enables him to communicate directly with Christ. The speaker visualises and approximates Christ through language, which also enables him to reinterpret waywardness into obedience: he turns his back "but to receive / Corrections." Thus, at the end of the poem, the speaker's outward movement has not changed. He is still riding westwards. Instead of seeing his journey as one that takes him away from Christ in the east, however, he can now perceive it as a movement towards Christ: Christ is already present to the speaker and in the speaker (who, through recourse to his memory, has established a connection to Christ), and the speaker can look forward to his final salvation, announced in the prospective "I'll turne my face."

III. Spatial turning in Herbert's "The Search"

Prayer is the little implement
Through which Men reach
Where Presence – is denied them.
They fling their Speech

By means of it – in God's Ear –
If then He hear –
This sums the Apparatus
Comprised in Prayer –
(Emily Dickinson, J437)

1. Turning as a spatial notion

Herbert's "The Search" will serve to illustrate the spatial relations under-lying the notion of turning. Turning is in itself a spatial concept and en-tails movement and progress, and (especially gradual, progressive) turn-ing can also be seen as a kind of journey. In the context of religious poet-ry, this is linked to the idea of pilgrimage (i.e., a journey in order to come closer to God or to salvation). At the same time, the speaker also takes up motifs of love poetry and uses them for his own purpose of addressing God and writing about his relation to God (that is, he turns these motifs into sacred poetry).

The speaker of "The Search" tries to find God, who he feels has turned away from him, and constructs a spatial framework within which his spiritual search for God takes place – until the speaker realises that he has to give up his active search (marked by his insistence on his own will and wilfulness) in favour of simply accepting God's will and admitting God to himself. The speaker describes not only his search for God, but also his prospective goal: a turning towards God on his side, and a turning towards the speaker on God's side. The poem ends with a prospect of the speaker's union with God, which is made possible through this imagined double turn. The meeting with God is conceptualised as a complete union of the speaker and God, to the point at which both distance (i.e., space in general) and all differences between speaker and God are cancelled.

The same special emphasis on spatial relations and movement can be found in Donne's Holy Sonnet "Thou hast made me" and in Herbert's "Coloss. 3.3" – and, as we shall see, in these poems, too, there is a focus on the mutuality of turning and on a final union with God. They share with "The Search" the speaker's need for orientation and for a sign from

God. In "Thou hast made me," the speaker's struggle is completely internalised: although the speaker describes his options for moving in different directions, these are detached from any real or metaphorical scenery or surroundings. In "Coloss. 3.3" the way to God is already paved within the written poem (which might explain the speaker's confident approach) and only remains to be "found." And in both poems there is a development towards the recognition that God is there for the speaker: in "Thou hast made me" the speaker's final focus is on God above, in "Coloss. 3.3" there is the recognition that both ways described in the poem inevitably lead to God.

The speaker's most pressing concern at the beginning of "The Search" is *where* to find God. Thus, the relation between the speaker and God is conceptualised as a spatial relation right from the beginning, and the speaker is presented as an active seeker (even though he does not seem to move his body from one place to another). The speaker's world is one which he simultaneously constructs and mentally perambulates. It is characterised by his relation to God, which is expressed as a spatial distance and taken as the measure of all things (cf. ll. 45-47, "Since then my grief must be as large / As is thy space, / Thy distance from me" and ll. 57-58, "thy absence doth excell / All distance known."). Consequently, when the speaker feels the distance between him and God to lessen, space in general is likewise minimised: "What edge so keen, / What point so piercing can appear / To come between?" (ll.54-56). The changing distance between the speaker and God is representative of the speaker's changing attitude towards God (which lets him imagine their eventual union). Space in the poem is thus a dynamic concept relying on movement and relation. Like "Goodfriday, 1613," "The Search" can be seen as a formal Loyolan meditation, with a composition of place in stanzas 1-4, a more abstract contemplation in stanzas 5-13, and finally a colloquy with God in stanzas 14-15. The use of spatial metaphors provides a thought pattern and a way of approaching God and imagining union.

There are several references to space and turning in the poem, beginning with the title and the activity of searching and seeking (implying movement to and fro); the mention of earth and sky, sphere and centre, and herbs and stars, which encompass the smallest as well as the biggest entities imaginable; the references to archery, which also rely on spatiali-

ty as the arrow moves through space; the activities of bending and turn-
ing, and God's will as a "distance" that must be turned into "nearnesse,"
so that nothing can come between.

Another spatial aspect of importance in "The Search" is that of the ex-
ploration of different proportions. There is an alternation between big and
small entities, between large-scale and small-scale descriptions, which
runs through the poem and which illustrates the speaker's perception of
distance and disparity. In the end, the oppositions between big and small
are evened out, as space is minimised and eventually cancelled while
"two" become "one."[1]

A progression in space is necessarily linked to a progression in time.
The speaker marks his searching as a habitual action, his "daily bread"; at
the same time he indicates that this unsuccessful search has been going
on for a while (l.17, "I sent a sigh," l.21, "I tun'd another"). In the pre-
sent, he stays immobile ("My knees pierce the'earth, mine eies the skie";
"Yet can I mark"), while the feeling of God's non-attendance is shown as
a past event ("art thou fled"). The final union with God is envisioned as a
future event ("When thou dost turn, and wilt be neare"), yet, as space
(and therefore also movement through space) disappears, the ending be-
comes timeless, which is expressed by the (grammatically non-finite)
gerund: "making two one" (which also implies that this "making" goes
on infinitely).

Behind the spatial construction of "The Search" lies the conception of
God as geometer, designing the universe after geometrical principles as a
harmonious, well-proportioned mathematical construction.[2] The speaker

---

1   This is also reflected in the poem's stanza form and stress pattern: every stanza has
    four lines, and in each stanza, the stress pattern continually alternates between four
    and two stresses.

2   This idea goes back to Plato's *Timaeus*, where God is called a demiurge or
    "artificer" (δημιουργός, sec.3), who in the manner of an artisan designed and
    crafted the whole world and everything in it according to geometrical principles,
    and was still present in the 16th century, being taken up, for example, by Kepler in
    his *Harmony of the World*. Cf. also the image of God as architect with a compass
    piercing the centre of the earth in Codex Vindobonensis 2554 (Österreichische
    Nationalbibliothek), available on: <http://en.wikipedia.org/wiki/Bible_moralisée>.
    Cf. also a passage from Donne's sermons:
    First then, Christ establishes a Resurrection, A Resurrection there shall be, for, that makes
    up Gods circle. The Body of Man was the first point that the foot of Gods Compasse was
    upon: First, he created the body of Adam: and then he carries his Compasse round, and

hints at God's creative power when he describes how God can create and
reduce distances, it becomes visible in God's "making two one," (1.60),
and it is also verbalised when the speaker is concerned about God
"moulding" a "new fabric" (1.25).[3]

1.1 Geometry and mystical geometry

The title "The Search" and the opening of the poem (asking "whither"
God is fled and stating "my searches are my daily bread" introduce a
spatial setting right from the beginning. The speaker looks around him,
"below" and "above," he sends his sighs upwards to God, he searches for
God's "hidden place" and describes his spiritual separation from God as
a "distance."

The representation of space found in "The Search" has at its core a ge-
ometrical conception, which depends on basic geometrical forms –point,
line, circle and sphere – and their combination. In "The Search," they are
combined, at first, to illustrate the distance between speaker and God,
and later, to show how this distance is taken away.[4]

---

shuts up where he began, he ends with the Body of man againe in the glorification thereof
in the Resurrection. God is Alpha and Omega, first, and last: And his Alpha and Omega,
his first, and last work is the Body of man too. ("Sermon Preached at the Earl of Bridge-
waters House, November 19, 1627, on Matt. 22.30," Donne, Sermons VIII, no. 3, 97)

3   The ordered construction of the world is frequently compared to the creation of art.
Kepler, for example, states that the Soul has "been designed by God in the
harmonic proportions" (312) but also makes clear that, analogously, harmony is
also found in the (man-made) proportions of dancing, poetry, drama and
architecture (314f.). Puttenham, for example, matches geometrical figures, some of
which he explicitly characterises as architectural figures, to similarly shaped
poems. Cf. also Ohly on God as (artistic) creator and architect of the world (557).

4   Geometrical imagery as a way to express distance or union is found frequently in
metaphysical poetry, for example in the compass image in Donne's "Valediction
forbidding Mourning," the beginning of Donne's Holy Sonnet "At the round
earth's imagined corners," the first stanza of Vaughan's "The World" (describing
eternity "Like a great ring of pure and endless light [...]/ And round beneath it,
Time in hours, days, years, / Driv'n by the spheres / Like a vast shadow mov'd; in
which the world / And all her train were hurl'd." (ll.2-7), or Marvell's "Definition
of Love" (Marvell 2005), where Fate placed the lovers "as the distant poles" (1.18):
   Unless the giddy heaven fall,
   And earth some new convulsion tear;
   And, us to join, the world should all
   Be cramp'd into a planisphere.

As lines, so loves oblique may well

A spatial conception is also the basis for the way the speaker imagines his union to God (or rather, God's approach to him): as a union in one point so small that nothing can "come between" (1.56), and at the same time as an ongoing movement ("Making two one," 1.60). While the speaker's focus is on God's nearness, the unfathomable distance does not necessarily disappear (and the speaker still uses present tense in the last stanza to talk about God's absence (ll. 57-58, "as thy absence doth excell /All distance known,"); however, it retreats behind the nearness with which the poem ends when God is no longer distant from the speaker. Thus, in "The Search," as mentioned above, there is a contrast between entities of different sizes as well as distances, which are set in proportion to each other. These relations allow the speaker to imagine how his prayers will be answered and how he, as an insignificant human being, will be saved.

A necessary step towards this union is the acceptance of God's will as the reason for the speaker's perceived abandonment. In 1.32, the speaker first begins to consider God's will, and in stanzas nine to eleven, he tries to conceptualise God's will through spatial imagery. He describes God's will consecutively as "thy ring," an "intrenching" that "passeth thought," and a "strange distance." The speaker states that he "will passe" a ring made of brass, steel, or mountains, yet not a ring consisting of God's will. While "ring" primarily refers to some kind of fortification (cf. *OED* "ring fence, *n.*", Herbert 2007, 558), it also serves to characterise God (literally, a ring is a circle and thus symbolises perfection; in addition, it is closed on all sides so that, literally, nothing can get in or out). At the same time, "ring" also alludes to marriage and to music, hinting at the poem's harmonious ending.

"Ring" in the sense of a fence or fortification is picked up in the next stanza, where God's will is called an "intrenching." The speaker immediately clarifies that he does not refer to an earthly fortification (like one

---

Themselves in every angle greet;
But ours so truly parallel,
Though infinite, can never meet.

Therefore the love which us doth bind,
But Fate so enviously debars,
Is the conjunction of the mind,
And opposition of the stars. (ll. 21-32)

made of brass, steel or mountains), but to one that "passeth thought" and to which "strength" and "subtilties" are "things of nought." In stanza 11, the speaker goes even further: "Thy will such a strange distance is, / As that to it / East and West touch, the poles do kiss, / And parallels meet," that is, a distance so immense that even the greatest irreversible distances are nothing compared to God's will. The speaker then puts this distance in relation to his own – equally immense – grief, and pleads to God to take the distance between them away (which would also take away his grief). The prospect given in the last two stanzas of a union between God and the speaker presents a closeness which is just as immense as the previous distance, so that the spatial relations between the speaker and God seem to be reversed: immeasurable distance has become immeasurable nearness.

This use of spatial (and especially mathematical and geometrical) conceptions as a way to imagine God finds a prominent precursor in the ideas of Nicolas of Cusa.[5] In particular, Cusa's doctrine of the unity of opposites (coincidentia oppositorum),[6] that is, the idea that everything (even things or ideas that logically exclude each other) coincides in God,[7] and

---

5   Leimberg argues that Herbert was familiar Cusa's works, both because he uses similar spatial constructs and because he picks up specific words and wordplays (1996, 238). Cusa (and the reception of Cusa by other philosophers) is central in imparting and spreading ideas that were present in all of Europe (Mahnke VI, 76f.)

6   Hopkins points out that, while Cusa's *Of Learned Ignorance* to a large extent treats the concept of the unity of opposites, Cusa does not explicitly use the term there (6).

7   Such as, within the poem, the logical impossibility of joining geographic directions, poles and parallels, respectively.
     Related to this idea, there is another concept, which does not come from Cusa but influenced his works (cf. Mahnke 84-86) and is also present in "The Search," namely that of God as an infinite sphere, whose centre is everywhere and circumference nowhere: "Deus est sphaera infinita cuius centrum est ubique, circumferentia vero nusquam" (Second Definition from the *Liber XXIV Philosophorum* (Hudry, 152) – Poulet (xi-xxvii) points out that the concepts presented in the *Liber XXIV Philosophorum* also had a strong influence on poetry in general). In calling God's will a "ring," the speaker may be alluding to this image. Cf. also the line God "fils all place, yet none holds him" (l.3.10) in "La Corona" and a passage from Donne's *Devotions*:
     As he that would describe a circle in paper, if he have brought that circle within one inch of finishing, yet if he remove his compass he cannot make it up a perfect circle except he fall to work again, to find out the same centre, so, though setting that foot of my compass upon thee, I have gone so far as to the consideration of myself, yet if I depart from thee,

his doctrine of God enfolding and unfolding everything seem to lie behind the spatial setting in "The Search." Both doctrines are related and illuminate different aspects of divinity. Jasper Hopkins, in his introduction to Cusa's *De Docta*, states that:

> [Cusa's] doctrine of enfolding overlaps with the doctrine that in God opposites coincide, though it is primarily correlated with the theology of creation, whereas the doctrine of *coincidentia* is primarily correlated with the *via negativa* and with God's inconceivability and simplicity. Of course, Nicholas does not hesitate to state that "God is the enfolding of all things, even of contradictories" (I,22), and here the topic is not creation. But it is a topic directly associated with creation; and what is said to be enfolded is *all things*, not simply *contradictories*. (*De Docta* 1981, 13)
> The word "in" is all-important. For Nicholas nowhere states that all things are the Absolute Maximum, or God, but maintains only that *in* God all things are God; ontologically prior to their creation they are "enfolded" in God as God; and the act of creation is God's act of "unfolding" them from Himself. (*De Docta* 1981, 12)

So, how are these concepts relevant to the speaker's attempt to find God in "The Search"? The speaker sees the unfolding of creation everywhere around him: he contemplates the stars and the herbs and he considers a "new fabrick" (implicitly characterising himself as the "old fabrick"). Yet although the speaker knows that he, too, is God's creation, he does not feel it. He feels only the "distance" and "absence" of God, which motivates his search for God's "nearnesse." Moreover, the speaker does not simply want to be "neare" God, he wants to be so near that nothing can come between. That is, in Cusa's terms he wants to be (inseparably) enfolded in God rather than just being a part of God's unfolded creation.[8]

1.2 Geography

The poem contains several references to nature and geography. Quite generally, the speaker mentions the earth and the sky, as well as herbs

---

my centre, all is imperfect. This proceeding to action, therefore, is a returning to thee [...]. (20th Expostulation, 107f.)

8 Cf. also the last stanza of "The Temper (I)," where the same notion is described: "Whether I fly with angels, fall with dust, / Thy hands made both, and I am there; / Thy power and love, my love and trust, / Make one place ev'rywhere."

and stars, but also more specific landmarks (mountains and entrenchings), and even specific cartographic reference points (the cardinal directions and the poles). The literal meaning of "search" as well as the beginning "whither art thou fled" imply travelling and, while not excluding other spaces (such as heaven, hell and the cosmos), suggest an earthly location that is actually searchable by the speaker. Like geometry, geography is important with regard to turning because it contributes to create spatiality and thus provides a metaphorical foundation within which turning can take place, albeit from a different and more palpable angle than geometry (which is more abstract) and astronomy (which is more remote).

The speaker attempts to survey as well as measure and classify the world he perceives. He makes reference to "sphere and centre," "above and below" as well as "distance," "barres," and "lengths," and thus to spatial expansion and directions. He sends a "sigh [...] deep drawn" to "seek thee out," which indicates his desire to measure and fathom. He fails, however, when confronted with the unfathomable distance to God.

One image related to geography (and also to astronomy) that appears in several metaphysical poems, is the image of the map.[9] The notion of a map is particularly relevant to a poem concerned with journeying and orientation, as maps offer guidance and structure and are essential for travelling. With regard to the depiction of space, a map combines geometrical elements, two- and three-dimensional space as well as abstract and concrete representation. While maps are not mentioned explicitly in "The Search," ll. 43-44, "East and West touch, the poles do kiss, / And parallels meet," strongly suggest the idea of a map, as they combine sev-

---

9   Cf., for example Donne's "Hymne to God my God, in my sicknesse": "Whilst my physicians by their love are grown / Cosmographers, and I their map, who lie / Flat on this bed" (ll.6-8) and "As west and east / In all flat maps (and I am one) are one" (ll.13-14); "To Mr Thomas Woodward": "My verse, the strict map of my misery, / Shall live to see that for whose want I die" (ll.8-9); "To the Countess of Bedford": "I can study thee / [...] and so can make by this soft extasie, / This place a map of heav'n, my selfe of thee" (ll. 10-14); "The Good-Morrow": "Let sea-discoverers to new worlds have gone, / Let Maps to other, worlds on worlds have showne, / Let us possesse one world, each hath one, and is one." (ll.12-14); and "Upon the Annunciation and Passion falling upon one day": "Th'Abridgement of Christs story, which makes one / (As in plain Maps, the furthest West is East)" (ll.20-21). In Herbert's "Holy Scriptures (I)," the speaker says about the Bible "heav'n lies flat in thee" (ll.13).

eral features of cartography: cardinal directions, geographic locations and geometrical lines (which in cartography are used as reference lines to depict latitude and longitude). "Parallels" is ambiguous – it may refer simply to two straight lines that run parallel to each other, but it may also directly refer to the auxiliary lines indicating latitude in maps or globes, therefore providing a direct reference to cartographical representation.[10]

As mentioned in the last chapter, Donne uses the image of the rolled up map to imagine the resurrection.[11] In "The Search," the same idea is present in connecting East and West (rolling up a map, or creating a globe) and the poles (equally possible by rolling up a map sideways). Similarly, on a globe – as a three-dimensional realisation of a map – East and West are always connected as the globe is turned round, and the auxiliary lines indicating longitude do meet at the poles. Significantly, "The Search" mentions the meeting of parallels, i.e., lines indicating latitude, which is not possible nor represented on maps and globes (since they are truly parallel to each other) and which makes the task of joining them appear even more impossible and supernatural.

Within the poem's landscape, the speaker thus presupposes God's omnipresence in addressing God without seeing Him, an assumption which proves true in the end.[12] The imagined bending of natural laws shown in

---

10 Apart from these textual links, there is another important parallel between a poem like "The Search," dealing with a speaker's spiritual journey, and maps (or at least some kinds of map). One medieval use of maps was that of facilitating a "spiritual, imagined or interior pilgrimage" (Connolly 28, cf. also Kupfer 119, and Dyas 205-18) for those who could not go on an actual pilgrimage to a sacred place (that is, usually to Jerusalem). Bitton-Ashkelony points out that "idea of wandering as a metaphor for the pious life" is already present in Greek philosophy (111) and that

> From the fourth century onward, and especially in the Middle Ages, the conception of spiritual pilgrimage as the antithesis of earthly pilgrimage became widespread in monastic circles in both the East and West. An emphatic preference for *peregrinatio in stabilitate* over *stabilitas in peregrinatio* was articulated in monastic rules, since physical pilgrimage came to be seen as contrary to the monastic way of life.

11 Shami argues that, while Donne uses both the microcosm-macrocosm concept and map imagery to represent man's relation to the world and to God, he draws on maps in order to express separation as well as the possibility to bridge gaps (163-64):

> The old geography seems inadequate, connecting men in misery rather than in harmony. This leads [Donne] to search instead for connections […], for metaphors that can make sense of the changing, obviously uncorrespondent world. (163)

12 In cartography, a visualisation of this divine omnipresence can be found in a number of medieval maps which show Christ encompassing and holding the world

lines 43-44 (which can be visualised with the help of maps) is significant with regard to turning, because it provides an additional framework to imagine mutual approximation (especially in spite of a distance that is felt to be impossible to bridge). In the case of "The Search," this image also serves to adjust the speaker's view of his own power(lessness), since it is not him but God who has the power to do so.

1.3 Astronomy

On a grander scale, the speaker in "The Search" also alludes to astronomical conceptions. While the speaker depicts an earthly landscape and situates himself kneeling on the ground with herbs below him, he simultaneously looks up to sky and stars, thus creating a three-dimensional space that includes the cosmos. At the same time, he differentiates between what he is physically touching and what he can only look at from a distance. To this measurable and comprehensible distance (even the movements and relations of stars and planets can be calculated to some extent), the speaker then adds the unfathomable distance to God. Thus the speaker creates a model of the world where God is both near (making herbs "grow green and gay") and far (making stars "simper and shine"), all-encompassing and everywhere – though not perceived by the speaker who stands in the midst of everything.

The speaker's description of his grief in ll.45-46, which is "as large as is thy space," i.e., infinite and never-ending, and becomes transformed into a never-ending union, likewise shows his awareness of infinite (i.e., cosmic) space. The ongoing movement of "making two one" shows a conception of God as the first and supreme mover of all things (it is a movement that appears to be outside human perceptions of time, as it seems to have neither beginning nor ending), as well as a continuation of their union through eternity (implying the existence of a – positive – afterlife for the speaker).

---

depicted in the map (Kupfer points out the characteristic "*syndesmos* figure, [...] the cruciform pose assumed by Christ's members" (106) in these maps). A special case is the Ebstorf Map, which shows Christ's hands, feet and head inside the circle containing the world. Kupfer argues that this particular depiction, where Christ is shown within and not outside the map, creates a "divine immersion in the earthly realm [...] God takes the place of man, and the earthly sphere overtakes the cosmos" (107f.).

The musical connotations of the final union "making two one," leading from discord to concord and finally to the elimination of distance, indicating harmony and unison, point at the concept of cosmic harmony as found in Boethius and Kepler (and analysed in more detail in the context of Herbert's "The Temper (I)"). The description of the stars as "having keyes unto thy love" already hints at the idea of musical harmony in implying that, musically, the stars know the right keys (in the sense of tonality) to be in harmony with God. While the speaker's concern lies with his own exclusive relationship to God, he also turns from the position of an outsider, who watches how "herbs below / Grow green and gay" (ll.9-10) and "starres above / Simper and shine" (ll.13-14), while he "decays" (l.12) and "pines" (l.16) to becoming part of this universal cosmic harmony in the course of the poem. The speaker's vision turns from seeing himself as a lonely individual to seeing himself as one with God, that is, no longer as a separate entity – which also entails his union with everything else, including herbs, which, too, seem to "meet" God" and stars, who seem to have "keyes unto thy love." This means that, at the same time as he reaches his goal of being joined to God, the speaker's existence concurs with everything else in existence (becoming a "thing of nought," so to speak) creating a meaningful "one" in contrast to the insignificant "one" of l.24.

2. "The Search" as a sacred parody

Before we turn to an analysis of the poem, the concept of sacred parody, which informs the poem as a whole and is therefore important for its analysis, should be discussed. The speaker of "The Search" alludes to the Song of Songs, which presents an amorous relationship and stands in a long tradition of exegesis in terms of religious poetry, as well as to the Psalms, which to a large extent chronicle the personal relationship between a speaker and God, that is, to two biblical texts which each contain sacred and secular elements. In addition, the speaker takes up motifs from secular, Petrarchan love poetry and applies them to his relationship to God. He stresses his loneliness and exclusion from the company of others (in the poem, herbs and stars).[13] He feels excluded from God's

---

13 Cf., for example, in secular love poetry, Wyatt's "They flee from me, that sometime did me seek" and "My galley charged with forgetfulness," Surrey's "O

presence and presents himself as jealous of those who seem to have a connection to God (elements of nature and possible other "new" creations).[14] By using a possessive pronoun and addressing God as "*My* Lord, *my* Love" and "*my* God," the speaker claims God for himself and characterises their (potential) relationship as an intimate one, in addition, he explicitly calls God his "Love."[15] He desires the presence of his beloved and a union, and last but not least tries to achieve his goals through his poetry (i.e., through the text of the poem, which in this case is addressed to God).[16] The idea of love as a chase or strife (and also as a battle) is also prominent in secular love poetry.[17]

---

happy dames," Sidney's "Because I oft in dark abstracted guise" (*Astrophel and Stella* #27), Daniel's "Lo here the impost of a faith entire" (*Delia* #57), Greville's "Who grace for Zenith had," ll. 159-168 ("Since then this is my state [...]," *Caelica* #84), Spenser's "Lyke as the Culuer on the bared bough" (*Amoretti* #89) and Shakespeare's "When in disgrace with Fortune and men's eyes" (Sonnet #29).

14 Cf., for example, Greville's "Love, I did send you forth enamelled fair" (*Caelica* #71), Shakespeare's "Whilst I alone did call upon thy aid" (Sonnet #79) and "Was it the proud full sail of his great verse" (Sonnet #86) and Sidney's "O how the pleasant ayres of true loue be" (*Astrophel and Stella* #78).

15 Cf. also Sherwood 1989, 51:

[The speaker in "The Search"] echoes the unrequited secular lover separated from the beloved or suffering from Cupid's disfavour. By identifying the divine person and, reflexively, himself as well, the speaker thereby clarifies the nature of their relationship. [...] Herbert's fondness for explicitly calling on God expresses possession self-consciously [...]. Herbert persists throughout *The Temple* in examining the relationship of 'mine' and 'thine' between God and man. [...]The object of the 'hearts desire' ('Discipline,' 5), the love parody assumes, is union with the beloved, expressed as mutual possession, 'mine' and 'thine.' [...] For Augustine, and Herbert after him, both desire and its fruition in the enjoyment of God are components of love. Love's desire is the will's movement to enjoy the love object.

16 Cf., for example, Daniel's "Go, wailing verse" (*Delia* #2), "These plaintive verse" (*Delia* #4) and "Tears, vows and prayers gain the hardest hearts" (*Delia* #11), Drayton's "Go you, my lines, ambassadors of love" (*Idea* #72), Sidney's "Loving in truth, and fain in verse my love to show" (*Astrophel and Stella* #1) and "Come, let me write. And to what end?" (*Astrophel and Stella* #34), Spenser's "Happy ye leaues when as those lilly hands" (*Amoretti* #1).

17 Cf., for example, Wyatt's "The long love that in my though doth harbour" and "I find no peace and all my war is done," Surrey's "Love that doth reign and live within my thought," Drayton's "Truce, gentle Love, a parley now I crave" (*Idea* #63), Spenser's "So oft as homeward I from her depart" (*Amoretti* #52), "Dayly when I do seeke and sew for peace" (*Amoretti* #11) and "One day I sought with her hart-thrilling eies" (*Amoretti* #12), Sidney's "I on my horse, and Loue on me, doth trie" (*Astrophel and Stella* #49) and "Stella, whence doth this new assault arise"

There are also some specific allusions to a love relationship in "The Search." The speaker's arrows are comparable to Cupid's arrows, "the poles do kiss" suggest intimacy and the "ring" in l. 35 makes one think of a wedding ring. The last line of the poem, "making two one," can likewise be seen as an allusion to the marriage service, which states that "they two shall be one flesh" and "those whom God hath joined together let no man put asunder" – a state of inseparableness which is emphasised in "The Search" with the rhetorical questions in ll.54-56, "What edge so keen, / What point so piercing can appear / To come between."

The speaker takes these secular poetic terms and motifs and turns them into sacred poetry, that is, he parodies existing literary traditions for his own purposes. "Parody" is taken here in the sense of Rosemond Tuve's discussion of Herbert's concept of parody. Tuve sees the difficulty of defining what exactly the purpose of parody is when it is not used for mockery, and considers poetic parody in analogy to musical parody as the overlay of a new element over an existing structure (such as a new text for a specific existing rhyme pattern, or, musically, a new text for an existing melody, 1961, 254f.; Cf. also Tuve 1959, 329f.).[18] This process, whether musical or literary, is in itself a kind of turning: a secular melody is turned into a sacred one, secular poetic themes and motifs are turned into sacred ones. The use of parody and the choice of an existing model does of course have consequences for the interpretation of the new text (or piece of music), ranging from mere satire to new works that are enriched by the original model. Thus, one point that is made apparent through the use of parody in "The Search," is the closeness between certain conceptions of secular and sacred love (a notion which is of course not exclusive to this particular poem).[19]

(*Astrophel and Stella* #36) and Shakespeare's "Mine eye and heart are at a mortal war" (Sonnet #46).

18   Cf. in this context also the tradition of "madrigali spirituali" (sacred madrigals) – especially with regard to the madrigal-like opening of "The Search" discussed in 3.2.

19   Merrill points out the difficulty in regarding sacred parody merely as a replacement of secular motifs by religious motifs and of a human beloved by God, and points out the asymmetry in talking about secular topics and talking about God (and in making statements about worldly things and stating the same things about God (196-99). He also stresses the mutual enrichment of love poetry and devotional poetry that is engendered through parody:

This turning from secular to sacred happens in the act of speaking and addressing God. From the beginning "Whither, O, whither art thou fled, / My Lord, my Love," which could just as well be the beginning of a secular love poem, the speaker goes on towards "making two one" – which *could* in theory be part of a love poem, but is explicitly shown as a union between man and God.

As for the speaker in "The Search," his use of parody emphasises both his turning away from the world and wholly towards God (he abandons stars, herbs and the idea of a "new fabric" and centres his thoughts and feelings on God alone), as well as his close relation to God. It shows the speaker's relationship to God as a loving relationship. The parodic use of love poetry found in "The Search" leads to the depiction of the speaker's strong personal feelings for God, and emphasises his view of a possessive and exclusive relationship.[20] It also stresses the speaker's loneliness and longing as an emotional need and the prospective union between the speaker and the object of his desire. Paradoxically, while this union is often hindered or made impossible in secular love poetry (which to some degree lives on the beloved's absence as a prerequisite for expressing the speaker's longing),[21] in religious poetry an eventual union can be presup-

---

> Instead of a wholesale replacement of the human for divine being [...], I see something more like interaction occurring – two structurally similar yet essentially different loves informing one another I precisely the way Max Black [describes as] bringing "two separate domains into cognitive and emotional relation by using language directly appropriate to the one as a lense for seeing the other. (210)

20   In this, the speaker's stance is also comparable to that of the psalmist, offering an instance of deeply personal religious communication and invocation.

21   This comprises the vast majority of Petrarchan love poetry, beginning with Petrarch's *Canzoniere*, where Laura is unattainable, because she is first married and then dead. For example, in Wyatt's "Whoso list to hunt" the beloved belongs to "Caesar," in Sidney's *Astrophel and Stella* Stella gets married, in Greville's *Caelica*, the beloved casts Philocell out, and in Shakespeare's Sonnets the speaker is abandoned by both his loves. Spenser's *Amoretti* are a notable exception, and they are based on a religious conception of love that leads to marriage. Cf. also the Pilgrim Scene in *Romeo and Juliet* (I.5.92-105), which combines secular and sacred elements in reverse – using religious motifs to convey amorous feelings –, and Siegel's discussion of *Romeo and Juliet* in the context of Christianity as presenting a transgression against contemporary Christian morality but also a manifestation of divine (cosmic) love (383-87). Love poetry is also linked to pilgrimage, as lovers are often depicted as pilgrims (as in *Romeo and Juliet*). Hahn (in analysing Spanish examples) points out that in "all of the examples in which the figure of the *peregrino de amor* occurs, the type of love described is either

posed as the consequence of God's love, even when the speaker of a poem is in doubt about his hopes.

The echoes of love poetry found in "The Search" thus provide a strongly subjective and introspective attitude to the speaker's quest for salvation: the speaker uses love poetry as a medium to communicate a religious pursuit in a personal way, making it both reflecting and emotional, and marking the mutual turning and final union as an act of love and not just as a development and consequence of religious doctrine.[22]

3. Turning in "The Search"

3.1 Title and structure

The engagement with space expressed by the title of the poem may refer either literally to the activity of going around and looking for something, or, figuratively, to the seeking of something immaterial. In either case, a search is a dynamic activity, and the seeker aims to get (physically or spiritually) closer to a desired entity. Both activities are combined in the poem: the speaker is in fact searching for something immaterial (the union with God), yet he describes his search within the setting of a physical environment (he depicts the scenery around him, and he shows his emotional state and his actual as well as desired relationship to God through spatial metaphors).[23]

---

unhappy or at last problematic" (64), which can be extended to English texts, too – the concept of pilgrimage entails that a goal is envisaged but (not yet) reached.

22 Another poem which, even more clearly than "The Search," can be considered as sacred parody is "The Canonization." Brooks goes in a direction similar to Tuve's when he writes about "The Canonization":

The basic metaphor which underlies the poem [...] involves a sort of paradox. For the poet daringly treats profane love as if it were divine love. [...] The poem then is a parody of Christian sainthood; but it is an intensely serious parody of a sort that modern man, habituated as he is to an easy yes or no, can hardly understand. [...] Either: Donne does not take love seriously [...] Or: Donne does not take sainthood seriously [...] Neither account is true; a reading of the poem will show that Donne takes both love and religion seriously; it will show, further, that the paradox is here his inevitable instrument. (1949, 10-11).

23 Within *The Temple*, "The Search is preceded by "Priesthood" – a poem expressing humility and meekness – and followed by "Grief," which goes back to the stance found at the beginning of "The Search." Martz sees the poem as part of a "plateau of assurance" comprising four poems from "The Search" to "The Flower" (1955, 309-20). While this grouping does not take into account the variability of the

The title thus sets the tone of the poem: the emphasis is on searching, not on finding God. Although the union with God is the central aim of this search, it is only possible *through* the process of searching.[24] The necessity of a search presupposes that God is absent from the speaker, or rather, that the speaker perceives God to be absent, and it also assumes a motivation on the part of the speaker to change this state. In contrast to "Goodfriday," where the soul's deviancy is presented from the beginning as a conflict of "devotion" versus "pleasure or businesse," that is, where the problem of turning towards God is presented as a moral problem requiring in the first instance a change in the speaker, the speaker's main motivation in "The Search" is his own sense of loneliness and his feeling of being deserted by God, and his primary wish is for God to turn towards him (thus, he asks "whither art thou fled," (l.1) and "Where is my God?" (l.29), and he entreats God to "see my charge" and "see my case" (ll.47-48), and to "turn" and "be neare" (l.53)). This attitude is reflected in the speaker's loving stance (he addresses God as "My Love" (l.1) and shows himself pining and sighing (ll.16-17), full of grief "as large /as is thy space" (ll.45-46)) and also in the speaker's jealousy of those who seem to have a connection to God (i.e., those whom God seems to favour with His attention, a potential "new fabric [...] which favour winnes, / And keeps thee present," ll.25-27). However, although the speaker's main concern is to make God turn, it is the speaker who must search for God, and their union is not possible without the speaker's simultaneous turn.

In many respects, the poem makes heavy use of numerical (mostly binary) structures. Each stanza has four lines, which are divided into two

---

speaker's feelings, it highlights a strong thematic link between the opening of "The Search" and the last stanza of "The Flower":

> These are thy wonders, Lord of love,
> To make us see we are but flowers that glide:
> Which when we once can finde and prove,
> Thou hast a garden for us, where to bide. (ll.43-46)

The ending of "The Flower" thus provides a counterpoint both to the searches that do not "prove" and to the speaker's "decay" in "The Search."

24 Cf. Strier, 1983, 234:

> The poem [...] will not only be expressing a feeling but exploring a typical way of conceptualizing it. The extreme regularity and compactness of the stanza form – as contrasted, for example, with the stanza of "Longing" – perhaps itself suggests this.

parts by the rhyme scheme (abab) and stress pattern (4+2+4+2 stresses),
which also links the first and third, as well as the second and fourth line,
respectively.[25] Repetitions of two grammatically equal or similar ele-
ments are found frequently, both within one line or stanza ("whither, o
whither," "my Lord, my Love," "my knees [...], mine eies," "sphere and
centre," "green and gay," "simper and shine," "all strength, all subtilties,"
"East and West,"[26] "these barres, these lengths," "see my charge [...] see
my case," "edge so keen, point so piercing") and across stanzas ("Yet can
I mark"; "herbs" and "stars"; "while I decay" and "while poor I pine";
"Thy will is such"; "I sent a sigh" and "I tun'd another").[27] This empha-
sis on duality (and the impression of division, separation and contrast it
implies) is kept up till the end, where duality is transformed into oneness
with the statement "making two one." At the same time, this repetitive
use of expressions creates a kind of echo effect, which contributes to the
spatiality of the poem. Ironically, the speaker does not even hear an echo
as response to his own efforts at communicating with God, and every-
thing stays "dumbe" till the end.[28]

---

25 Schliebs sees Sidney's version of psalm 59 as a model for the stanzaic form of
    "The Search" (Schliebs 274). However, Sidney's stanzas in psalm 59 consist of 6
    lines, with the rhyme scheme ababcc and the stress pattern 4-2-4-2-4-4, making
    only the first four lines of each stanza similar to "The Search." There is a much
    stronger similarity to another poem of *The Temple*, "Praise (II)," which does
    exhibit the same rhyme scheme and number of stresses. Schliebs argues that in
    "The Search" the stress pattern creates a tension between the longer and shorter
    lines of a stanza, which in "Praise (II)" is weakened, because the short lines end in
    feminine rhyme, while they are masculine in "The Search" (Schliebs 286).

26 The same duality is inherent to the concept of (two) poles and parallels (i.e., two
    lines) in st.11.

27 The frequency of analogous expressions is also reminiscent of the Psalter's use of
    parallelism.

28 Herbert's "Heaven" provides a counterweight to the initial situation in "The
    Search." Here too, the speaker is alone, but through the use of prosopopeia, he
    creates a dialogic situation, which thus turns into divine communication. In the first
    line, the speaker does not know yet where to turn and asks, "O who will show me
    those delights on high." This question is taken up and reflected by an echo, which
    not only "answers" the speaker's questions, but additionally points at another, less
    ephemeral instance to which the speaker can turn: the "holy leaves" (l.11) of the
    Bible. Thus, although the speaker notes "just" an echo, instead of meaningless
    reverberations, a dialogue between a human being and a divine voice emerges,
    reassuring the speaker of the existence of "light, joy, and leisure" (l.19), as well as
    pointing him the speaker towards the Bible (and thus indirectly towards heaven).

3.2 The first stanza: establishing space and relation

The poem begins with:

> 01 Whither, O, whither art thou fled,
> 02   My Lord, my Love?
> 03 My searches are my daily bread;
> 04   Yet never prove.

The first stanza points out the necessity of searching by asking *where* God is *fled* and by repeating the description of the speaker's activity as a search, and thus reinforces the spatiality of this search. By beginning with "whither, O, whither," the speaker presents his search as a physical and spatial one – "whither" is an interrogative asking "to what place." This spatial impression is strengthened by the echo effect created through the repetition (as mentioned above). Also, the word "whither" already contains" hither" (i.e. the answer to the question "whither"). In the first printed version of *The Temple* (1633), the initial "whither," printed as "VVHither," illustrates the coexistence of both meanings (cf. facsimile in Herbert 2002, 322).[29]

The first line not only implies a spatial perception of the speaker's relationship to God, it is also the first hint at a love relationship between the speaker and God. The initial situation in "The Search" is also quite similar to the one found in the second chapter of the Song of Songs, which begins with a description of the speaker's search for her beloved. While the searches in Herbert's poem are the speaker's *daily* bread, the speaker in the Song of Songs searches at night:

> By night on my bed I sought him whom my soul loveth: I sought him, but I found him not. I will rise now, and go about the city in the streets, and in the broad ways I will seek him whom my soul loveth: I sought him, but I found him not (Cant. 3.1-2)

Echo effects of this kind (i.e., repetitions of the same musical phrase (and often the same text) through two or more parts) are also used in musical compositions, either to exploit existing architectural conditions (cf. the Venetian polychoral style) or to imitate such a style later on. Thus, the many twofold elements in the poem contribute not only to the creation of space but also hint at a musical approach.

29 Cf. also the description in Donne's "Sermon Preached upon the Penitentiall Psalmes, on Ps. 6.4 and 5," quoted below: The Lord may return "hither," and men will be called "hither" by God.

And at the beginning of chapter 6, the female speaker is asked, "Whither is thy beloved gone, O thou fairest among women?" (Cant. 6.1). Thus, the beginning of "The Search" is based on a tradition merging secular and religious love.[30]

The beginning "Whiter, O, whither" is also reminiscent of the beginning of several madrigals, most of them secular and amorous.[31] For example, Thomas Morley's "Whiter away so fast" (the repetition of the text in each part also leads to a repetition of "whither"), Robert Jones's "Whither runneth my sweet heart" (the first line is repeated), Thomas Bateson's "Whither so fast? See how the kindly flowers" and, similarly, in Robert Jones's "Stay wandering thoughts, o whither do you hast" (the text of this madrigal leaves it open whether it talks about love or just

---

30   Apart from the Song of Songs, Wilcox (Herbert 2007, 555) also names Acts 17.27, "They should seek the Lord" as a biblical predecessor; other examples would be Job 11.7, "Canst thou by searching find out God? canst thou find out the Almighty unto perfection?" and Ps. 27.8, "When thou saidst, Seek ye my face; my heart said unto thee, Thy face, Lord, will I seek." Inversely, in Ps. 139.23, for example, the speaker asks for God's approach: "Search me, O God, and know my heart: try me, and know my thoughts." All these biblical models present the same tension between a literal and figural interpretation of searching and seeking that is already inherent to the title and first stanza of the poem.

Low argues that the opening of "The Search" places the poem in the tradition of mysticism and mystical contemplation. Low points out that Cant. 3.1 "came to be read as an expression of the soul's spiritual desolation or sense of abandonment at certain stages of the mystical way" (104) and cites the beginning of St. John of the Cross's "Spiritual Canticle" (based on Cant. 3.1) as another important influence (103-05). The first stanza of the Spiritual Canticle does indeed bear a lot of resemblance to "The Search":
   Where did you hide,
   My Love, and left me thus to moan?
   Like the stag, you fled,
   Leaving in me this wound;
   I ran calling loud, but you were gone. (St. John of the Cross 117)
The poem shares further characteristics with "The Search" in presenting the interior striving for God as a search out-of-doors. In contrast to Herbert's poem, the "Spiritual Canticle" is dialogical: the soul/bride does receive an answer from God/the bridegroom. Cf. also Clements, who demonstrates the strong influence of the mystical tradition, including St. John of the Cross, on metaphysical poetry (2011, 1-18).

31   "The Glimpse" begins in a similar way, with "Whither away delight," and is called by Miller "a premature aubade" (142).

hope). The repetitive beginning is also taken up in *The Winter's Tale* (4.4, l.297 and l.306), where Autolycus offers to sing an amorous ballad containing the words "Whither? O Whither? Whither?" (spread over three parts) and later "Then whither goest? Say whither."

"Fled" again allows for a literal interpretation ("to run away," "withdraw" or "disappear," see *OED*, "flee, v. I.1; 3.a.; 5") or a metaphorical one (cf. *OED*, "flee, v., I.5.", which provides mostly figurative examples). Equally, the plural use of "searches" in l.3 could be read as the speaker's daily setting out on a physical journey or as a daily mental exercise intended to bring him closer to God. The use of "prove" is ambiguous, too. In the first place, the speaker complains that his searches never prove successful, i.e., that he searches but does not find God. We would usually expect an object with "prove," i.e., that his searches prove well, or prove (to be) successful. The intransitive use (without any adverbial complement such as "prove well") would more commonly be found to mean "to prosper, thrive; to succeed" (*OED*, "prove, v. I.3.b.). While the primary meaning is still that of searching unsuccessfully, one may wonder what it means for a search to (not) "prosper and thrive": literally the speaker's searches thrive, because the fruit of the speaker's unsuccessful search is the poem itself, coming into existence as an expression of his feelings: the speaker's "Search" is from the beginning thriving as a poem (and it is precisely God's absence which provides an occasion for the speaker's speaking and the making of the poem – a similarity which the poem shares with the majority of Petrarchan love poetry).[32] However, "prove" could also refer to "demonstrat[ing] the truth of [something] by evidence or argument" (*OED*, "prove, v., I.1."), i.e., demonstrating something through logic, in which sense it is also used for mathematical proofs, and in order "to show the existence or reality of" something

---

32 In this regard, another sense of searching becomes prominent, namely the search for words and topics, which is also a poet's daily bread. In classical rhetoric this finds an analogy in the process of *inventio*, the searching and finding of appropriate thoughts and arguments. This searching and finding is described in spatial terms, as the consideration of a number of *topoi* or *loci* (i.e., literally "places") where one can search for arguments (cf. Lausberg 119). In a similar way, the speaker in the poem explores different *topoi* which might help him in addressing God (comparing himself to nature, talking about his sighs and groans, envying about potential rivals, discovering God's will, and eventually imagining God's turning, and their final union).

(*OED*, "prove, *v*., I.2.a". In this sense, the speaker's searches never prove anything, in particular, they do not prove the presence of God – the speaker has to believe instead of waiting for a visible or audible proof.

By calling his searches his "daily bread," the speaker alludes not only to the Lord's Prayer (substantiating the status of his poem as a plea to God) but also to Psalm 42, "my tears have been my meat day and night: while they daily say unto me, where is now thy God" (Herbert 2007, 558), which shows the same mixture of hope and desolation (and which, though not speaking explicitly about a search, nevertheless implies the speaker's restlessness, "disquieted soul" and longing).[33] There is however, one important difference between "The Search" and Psalm 42: The speaker here asks, "whither art thou fled, / My Lord, my Love?", showing his own doubts; the speaker in Psalm 42 is merely asked by his enemies "Where is now thy God?" while he is in fact remembering and addressing himself to God. The speaker in "The Search" thus turns round the setting found in Psalm 42: he presents himself simultaneously as a man praying to God and as his own enemy (lacking faith and therefore unable to notice the presence of God).

Ryley points out that the speaker's searches actually fulfil everything they should fulfil. They are "1. Constant: *my daily bread*. 2. Humble: upon the *knees*. 3. Universal: his *knees* on *earth*, and his *eyes* in heaven. Nay they *pierce* the earth and *skies*, as not satisfied with a superficial scrutiny." (226). Further, the speaker's groans "one would have thought could not have failed of success, for nothing is so dear to God as *one good groan* (*Sion*)" (226). What is missing from the speaker's efforts, however, is the right disposition – an absolute faith in God, and it is this lack which makes the speaker his own enemy.

At the same time, by stating that his searches are his "daily bread," the speaker shows his searches to be his main occupation and probably main way of earning his living. In combination with his searching for someone

---

33 The repetitive exclamations "Whither, o, whither" and "My Lord, my love" are also reminiscent of Jesus's exclamation "My God, my God, why hast thou forsaken me" (Mark 15.34 and Matt 27.46). The same exclamation is found at the beginning of Psalm 22, which continues by stressing God's perceived distance from the speaker, "why art thou so far from helping me, and from the words of my roaring? O my God, I cry in the day time, but thou hearest not; and in the night season, and am not silent," before turning to the speaker's assurance of God's help.

who has "fled" and in connection to the poem's setting in the open air, this statement suggests a shepherd's search for his lost sheep[34] (which, in turn, recalls the image of Christ as the Lamb of God). Thus the speaker as shepherd searches for what he has lost, God, Christ, his lamb. In this search he is initially unsuccessful, because he assumes the wrong role: he should not be the one searching but the one who is lost and found (i.e., instead of asking "whither art thou fled, / My Lord," he should be exclaiming "The Lord is my shepherd").[35]

Herbert's spatial approach to a spiritual search for God also finds a precedent in Donne's sermon quoted in the introduction, where Donne deals explicitly with God turning toward man. He describes the Eucharist in a way which shows in many respects a conception of approaching God similar to the one found in "The Search."

> [...] whosoever says, *O Lord return,* says all this, Lord thou wast here, Lord thou art departed hence, but yet, Lord thou mayest return hither againe.[36] [...] Can we find an *ubi* for God? A place that is his place? Yes; and an earth which is his earth [...]. So the church,

---

34   At the same time, a reference to the shepherd and his flock also hints at Herbert's own occupation as a pastor (i.e., literally a "shepherd," cf. *OED* "pastor, *n.*") responsible for his own salvation as well as for that of his parish.

35   Cf. also the beginning of "The 23 Psalme":

> The God of love my shepherd is,
> And he that doth me feed:
> While he is mine, and I am his
> What can I want or need? (ll.1-4)

This poem combines the biblical model presenting God as shepherd with motifs of secular poetry, stressing "love" and mutual possession.

The setting of searching for something lost is also reminiscent of the parable of the prodigal son. The speaker searches for a beloved who has "fled," while it is in fact the speaker who has gone astray and must be found and acknowledged by his Father (when the prodigal son returns, his father actually runs toward him, cf. Luke 15.20).

36   Although in the psalm text for this sermon (i.e., Ps. 6.4-5) the speaker laments Gods absence, the psalm ends on a positive note: "The Lord hath heard my supplication; the Lord will receive my prayer" (Ps. 6.9). In the psalm, as also becomes clear in the passage from Donne's sermon, the speaker is not moving but asks for God's return to him, moreover, he also asks for a transformation of his enemies: "Let all mine enemies be ashamed and sore vexed: let them return and be ashamed suddenly" (Ps. 6.10). Thus, similar to Psalm 42 discussed above, the speaker contrasts himself to his enemies (whereas the speaker in "The Search" is in the enemies' position and has to be (re)turned by and to God).

which is his vineyard, is his *ubi,* his place, his centre, to which he is
naturally affected. And when he calls us hither, and meets us here
[...], he returns to us here, as in his *ubi,* as in his own place. And as
he hath a place of his own here, so he hath an earth of his own in
this place. Our flesh is earth, and God hath invested our flesh, and
in that flesh of ours, which suffered death for us, he returns to us in
this place, as often as he maketh us partakers of his flesh, and his
blood, in the blessed Sacrament. So then, though in my days of sin,
God have absented himself from me, (for God is absent when I do
not discern his presence) yet if to-day I can hear his voice, as God is
returned to-day to this place, as to his *ubi,* as to his own place; so in
his entering into me, in his flesh and blood, he returns to me as to
his earth, that earth which he hath made his by assuming my nature,
I am become his *ubi,* his place [...] ("Sermon Preached upon the
Penitentiall Psalmes, on Ps. 6.4 and 5," Donne, *Sermons* V, no. 18,
367-68)

Donne describes the Eucharist not just as a union, but as a return of God
to an identifiable, material place (the church in general, and man in par-
ticular). While the speaker in "The Search" is in a different position, feel-
ing God's absence and still unable to "hear his voice," the coming to-
gether in one place and the becoming one with God is imagined in very
similar terms, stressing the *ubi,* the place where God may be found.

The idea of the Eucharist also resonates in the speaker's description of
his searches as his "daily bread,"[37] which, however, "never prove": his
"daily bread" appears unsatisfactory to the speaker because it consists in
searching, not in finding Christ as his daily bread and the bread of life.
This allusion to the Eucharist also shows the speaker's aim at a union
with God right from the beginning (a union that with regard to the Eucha-
rist is also reflected in the term "Holy Communion"). In "The Search,"
other members of the Christian community are notably absent from this
union – the communion the speaker aims at is exclusively with God –
other people are not involved, neither as participants in an act of commu-
nal worship nor as other believers with their own relationship to God.[38]
Accordingly, the speaker does not mention other people in the poem; the

---

37   Cf. also Patrides in Herbert 1974, 168.
38   While he does not exclude other Christians when talking about the "blessed
     Sacrament," the focus in Donne's passage also switches to an individual's relation
     to God.

contestants for God's attention are herbs and stars, and very vaguely, "some new fabric." On the other hand, the public nature of *The Temple* as a whole (and thus also its individual poems), is made clear in the cycle's complete title as well as the fact that it was published, and the speaker's individual strife can also be seen as an exemplary model of a Christian's relation to God.

3.3 Stanzas two to six: the speaker as the centre of attention

After establishing his search for God as the main subject of the poem, the speaker focuses on a description of himself. Although he talks about his "searches," he is physically kneeling down and looking towards heaven, that is, he is not physically moving:[39]

> 05 My knees pierce the'earth, mine eies the skie;
> 06   And yet the sphere
> 07 And centre both to me denie
> 08   That thou art there.

He states, however, that "my knees pierce the'earth, mine eies the skie" (l. 5), a description which, even though it means that he is kneeling down, implies a double movement: his knees point downward, while his eyes glance upwards. Moreover, he performs an important movement with his eyes and his vocal exclamations and indicates this movement in several places. Again, the speaker combines inner and outer states: his external posture is one that reflects or serves to create a mental attitude, devotion. After describing his position as a praying man, he goes on with "and yet," showing that his supplicating stance does not lead to the desired result, as God's presence is denied to him.

With his mention of the "sphere and centre," the speaker captures the whole earth, as well as his own complete (and restricted) perspective: above himself, he can see the sky (i.e., the heavenly sphere), beneath his knees, he touches the earth (a sphere, too, as well as a "centre" surrounded by the sky). By placing his knees and eyes in relation to earth and sky

---

39 Asals (talking about "Antiphon II") sees the kneeling posture as a unifying gesture: "this gesture which finally *makes one* of the heaven and earth which the poem echoes between: 'Praised be the God alone, / Who hath made of two folds one.'" (1981, 31).

(and to sphere and centre), and by stressing up and down, the speaker
may also allude to the conception of man as a microcosmos reflecting the
order and processes of the macrocosm of earth and universe.[40] Thus, alt-
hough the speaker verbally distances himself from the world and cosmos
surrounding him, he implicitly creates a connection which entails God's
working in him, just as in earth and sky (and herbs and stars).

The relation between "sphere" and "centre" is made clearer by "both to
me denie" in l.7: this indicates that they refer to two different things (just
as the speaker distinguishes between "herbs below" and "starres above"
in the next two stanzas). By using the terms "sphere" and "centre," the
speaker, firstly, alludes to a world picture based on the notion that the
world consists of several spheres, secondly, continues the opposition of
earth and sky (the "centre" may also refer to the earth itself, cf. *OED*,
"centre, *n.* and *adj.* I.2.b"), and thirdly, presents a view of the world in
terms of geometry. However, at this point, the speaker lacks insight into
this world; he cannot see God in sphere and centre, herbs and stars. The
denial of God's immediate presence is ascribed to sphere and centre, i.e.,
to entities other than the speaker, even though it is of course the speaker
who feels that God is no there (and knows that he should not feel this
way).[41] At the same time, the speaker addresses God from the beginning,
so he does trust in God's attention to some extent. Only later, in stanza
11, does it become clear to the speaker that God can join sphere and cen-

---

40   His emphasis on surveying up and down, while keeping his eyes fixed and
     immobile seems to be another allusion to the correspondence of microcosm and
     macrocosm – it is rather similar to a pair of complementary emblems in Tycho
     Brahe's *Astronomiae instauratae Mechanica*, one framed by the text "Suspiciendo
     despicio" (title page) and one framed by "Despiciendo suspicio" (final page), i.e.,
     "in looking upwards, I look downwards" and "in looking downwards, I look
     upwards."

41   Cf. Strier, 1983, 234f.:

     The sense in which "the sphere / And centre … denie" to Herbert that God is "there," in
     either place, is an extremely important matter in "The Search." This would seem to mean
     that Herbert is unable to find any traces, *vestigia*, or "footprints" of God in these places. It
     turns out, however, that this is not the case, since the next two stanzas expressly deny this
     conclusion […]. Herbert is unable to find God "there" in the creation even in the fact of
     the very evidence for the view that the created things he is contemplating are in touch
     with God – or that God is "in" them. Herbert leaves the question open as to whether or not
     these things are "in touch" with God. The "as if" and "as" here seem to be genuinely neu-
     tral rather than skeptical. The important point, however, is that […] God is not "there" *for
     the speaker* in these things even if He is literally there.

tre, and in the last two stanzas, it becomes evident that sphere and centre *are* God – to which the speaker wants to be joined.

The next two stanzas continue the complaint about God's absence from the speaker's life, both beginning in the same way. The use of "yet" in the "The Search" is conspicuous: it is used four times in the poem, but only in the first four stanzas. In l.4, "Yet never prove" it indicates simply an opposition (i.e., as a conjunction meaning "but"). The same happens in l.6-7: "And yet [they] denie." In both cases, the speaker contrasts his efforts (he searches for God daily, he assiduously kneels and contemplates the sky) to their lack of a result (his searches do not prove, God's presence is denied to him).

> 09 Yet can I mark how herbs below
> 10   Grow green and gay,
> 11 As if to meet thee they did know,
> 12   While I decay.
>
> 13 Yet can I mark how starres above
> 14   Simper and shine,
> 15 As having keyes unto thy love,
> 16   While poore I pine.

In stanzas three and four, "yet" is used somewhat differently. "Yet can I mark" in ll.9 and 13 indicates a turn towards something positive: the herbs are "green and gay," the stars "simper and shine" ostensibly because they *are* connected to God. However, while the speaker can "mark" the herbs' and stars' happy state, he does not perceive God's presence, so that his search continues. As in the first stanza, where the repeated exclamation "Whither, o whither" suggests a physical turning to and fro, the repetition of "yet can I mark" in ll. 9 and 13 suggests a turning from one thing to another – and quite literally a turning of the head is necessary to see first herbs and then stars. This literal turn does not happen, however, as the speaker states in l.5 that his eyes pierce the sky, which characterises his sights as mental images.

"Mark" carries a multiplicity of connotations, which are relevant in the context of "The Search." In the first place, of course, it here means "to notice or observe" either mentally or physically (*OED* "mark, *v.*, III."). But "mark" can also mean "To record, indicate, or represent by a mark, symbol, or marker; to record, note, or represent in writing" ("mark, *v.*, II.19.a") or "To fashion or make; to conceive (an idea)" ("mark, *v.*, I.1.b"). That is, the speaker as poet can imagine or "make" herbs and stars in his poem and "record" them in the text of the poem (though he cannot "mark" God). In the context of the following two stanzas, another meaning of "mark" is relevant, too. Though already obsolete at the time when Herbert was writing *The Temple* (the last recorded use in the *OED* is from 1540), "mark" could also mean "To aim a blow or missile at" (*OED*, "mark, *v.*, IV.30.a"), and "markman" and later "marksman" have been in use since the 16th century.[42]

The connotations of "piercing" in l.5 and "marking" in lines 9 and 13 precede the central metaphor of stanzas 5 and six, where the speaker describes his sighs and groans as arrows he shoots towards God.

> 17 I sent a sigh to seek thee out,
> 18   Deep drawn in pain,
> 19 Wing'd like an arrow: but my scout
> 20   Returns in vain.
>
> 21 I tun'd another (having store)
> 22   Into a grone;
> 23 Because the search was dumbe before:
> 24   But all was one.

This action is not entirely hostile but can also be seen as an attempt at communication – as a way of reaching God.[43] The speaker states that he

---

42   Herbert uses "Mark-man," albeit in a different sense, in "Constancie" (l.34), where it refers to an exemplary and ideal model; according to Wilcox, "mark" is used there in the sense of "an attestation of quality, rank or distinction" (cf. OED "mark, *n.*, III.9,"; see Herbert 2007, 265). Wilcox also points at Herbert's introduction to *A Priest to the Temple*, where he states,

> I have resolved to set down the form and character of a true pastour, that I may have a mark to aim at; which also I will set as high as I can, since hee shoots higher that threatens the moon, then hee that aims at a tree. (Herbert 1902, 214).

Here, too, Herbert combines the notions of "mark" as a term of archery, and a spiritually desirable goal.

43   Cf., for example, Jonathan shooting arrows as a secret message for David: "And I will shoot three arrows on the side *thereof*, as though I shot at a mark," 1 Sam 20.20), and "Prayer (I)," where the speaker describes prayer as "Christ-side-piercing spear" (l.6). In Vaughan's "The Feast," the speaker describes it as "O spear, the key / Opening the way!" (ll.64-65).

sends a sigh in order "to seek thee out," which is ambiguous and can re-
fer to a number of possible aims. "Seek out" may mean "to attack"
(*OED*, "seek, v. I.6.a."), but it may also simply refer to the fact that the
speaker is searching for God (i.e. "seek" in the sense of "to go in search
of" someone or something, *OED* "seek, v. I.1."), or "To search, explore
(a place) in order to find something" (10.a) and "To search, examine,
consult" (10.b). "Seek" was also used frequently with the more specific
meaning of "draw[ing] near to (God), in prayer (I.5.b).[44]

Huttar (69) points out an emblem that may have served as a model for
Herbert's use of shooting imagery (and also for the description of the
speaker as a praying man) in "The Search" but also in "Artillerie,"[45]
"Prayer I," "Prayer II," and "Deniall."[46] The first emblem in Hugo's *Pia
Desideria* (Hugo 1624) shows a kneeling man out of whose breast arrows
aim upwards into a cloud containing God's eye and ears. The subscrip-
tion (from Psalm 38) also shows a situation similar to the one in "The
Search": "Domine ante te omne desiderium meum, et gemitus meus à te
non est absconditus" ("Lord, all my desire is before thee; and my groan-
ing is not hid from thee.").[47] Further, Huttar mentions an observation by

---

44   Used idiomatically, the infinitive "to seek" can also describe the state of being "at
      a loss or at fault; unable to act, understand, etc.; puzzled to know or decide
      (III.20.a) or "astray from the truth, mistaken" (III.20.c). For example, as in "We
      were exceedingly to seek how to settle things." (Oliver Cromwell, speech on 12
      September 1654, quoted in *OED* "seek, v. III.20.a). Although this use does not fit
      grammatically in *The Search*, it aptly describes the speaker's emotional state in the
      poem.

45   Clements discusses the same emblem in connection to "Artillerie" (1973, 269-71).

46   "Longing" and "Praise (I)," while not containing shooting imagery, show the same
      movement upwards to God. Cf. also Leimberg (1996, 453) on the conceptual
      proximity of "shooting" and "praying":

      Die erste Variante, die das Schulkind fand, wenn es "*to Shoote, to Hurle, to Fling*"
      nachschlug, was "*Jaculari*," und "*an Arrow, a Bolt or Dart*" hieß (und heißt) "*Jaculum*".
      Unter den englischen Bildungen aus *iaculari* gab es nun ein im 17. Jahrhundert gebräuch-
      liches "jaculatory" als Beiwort zu "prayer" in der Bedeutung: "a short prayer 'darted up'
      to God"; das *OED* erwähnt in diesem Zusammenhang das französische *oraison jacula-
      toire* und gibt als geistesgeschichtliche Quelle Hieronymus an: "*preces jaculatoriae*". So
      ist also der *arrow way* (an Herberts "Ejaculations" erinnernd) tatsächlich ein *narrow way*.

47   Psalm 38 is also connected to the imagery of "The Search" through its beginning
      (ll.1-2), where arrows are seen in a different light, coming from God and reaching
      (and hurting) the speaker: "O Lord, rebuke me not in thy wrath: neither chasten me
      in thy hot displeasure. For thine arrows stick fast in me, and thy hand presseth me
      sore."

Eleanor James, namely that "the labels on Hugo's arrows (Ah!, vtinam!, Heu!) identify them not just as prayers but prayers of a very specific kind, namely "sighs and groans."[48] The accompanying poem also mentions "sighs and groans" and at the same time stresses the closeness between God and the speaker by concluding with "Nemo meos gemitus, suspiria, votaque novit, Nemo, duo nisi nos, et duo sufficimus" (in the later English translation: "None knows my secret GROANS, and VOWS, and SIGHS, None but *we Two*, and only *we* suffice").

There is, however, one crucial difference between Hugo's emblem and "The Search," owing to the fact that Hugo's emblem is based on Psalm 38, which, though it shows the speaker in a state of misery, also shows his confidence in being heard by God, while Herbert's speaker still lacks this confidence. In Hugo, as in Psalm 38, the speaker's desire is laid open and his groans are *not* hid from God; in Herbert, the speaker's sighs and groans do not seem to reach God, who is apparently hidden from the speaker. Thus, in the emblem, God's eye and ears are visible, and the praying man can be sure that his arrows are reaching God. At the point at which the speaker of "the Search" unsuccessfully shoots his arrows, he can only "mark" herbs and stars but not see God, nor does he get a response from God, so that, when his arrows return, he complains that God is concealed in a "hidden place" and God's face "eclipsed" by a "covert." In Hugo's emblem, the speaker exposes himself to God knowing that he is seen and heard, while the speaker in "The Search" is less confident and consequently has a desire to actively "seek God out", not just to be seen by God.[49] As with Psalm 42 discussed above, here too, the situation encountered in the psalm is reversed in "The Search": the speaker obstructs his own endeavours to reach God, because he assumes that he can find God, instead of waiting (and praying) till God reaches out to him.

---

48 Huttar (69), summarising James, "The Emblem as an Image-Pattern in Some Metaphysical Poets" (Diss. University of Wisconsin, 1942, 272-75).

49 Cf. also "Sion," where groans are depicted as a suitable way of addressing God:

> But grones are quick, and full of wings,
> And all their motions upward be;
> And ever as they mount, like larks they sing;
> The note is sad, yet musick for a king. (ll.21-24)

In "The Search," the problem lies not in sending out sighs and groans, but in the speaker's lack of confidence in God's presence on the one hand and in placing too much emphasis on his own will and ability to find God.

The idea of sighs and groans shot off at the beloved in order to elicit a response hint of course at bow and arrow as attributes of Cupid (and, similarly, the speaker shoots at God to draw God's attention to himself), while the speaker's sighs – sent out to move his addressee – are also a motif found in love poetry. The allusions to secular love poetry from the first stanza are thus continued, and are also taken up again later in the poem: the "poles do kiss," "ring" in line 35 primarily refers to earthwork or fortifications but also hints at a wedding ring (as a physical sign of a physical and spiritual union) and "[m]aking two one," i.e. the prospective union with God, implies physical closeness and intimacy between the speaker and God.[50]

In stanzas 5 and 6, however, the speaker describes his efforts as "vain" and the search as "dumb," and both descriptions also tell something about the speaker himself. That the search is "vain" means that it is futile, but the speaker is also "vain" (i.e, full of vanity) in assuming that he can reach God. The opposite is of course true – God can reach the speaker, but this does not mean that the speaker can do the same (hence his sigh "returns in vain"), and the speaker has to recognise that he must surrender to God and that it is up to God to take "these barres, these lengths away" and to "turn and restore" the speaker.[51]

---

50   Cf. also Herbert's poem "Hope," where the speaker exchanges a variety of presents with personified Hope, and, when he becomes disappointed with what he gets in return ends with "I did expect a ring" (i.e., a clear sign of commitment and future marriage). Cf. also Donne's "The Exstasie," "Love, these mixt souls, doth mixe againe, / And makes both one, each this, and that" (ll.35-36) and Thomas Overbury's "A Wife" (1622):

> Mariage; to all whose ioyes *two parties* be,
> And *doubled* are by being *parted* so,
> Wherein the very *Act* is Chastitie,
> Whereby *two Soules* into *one Body* goe.
>> Which make *two one*; while here they liuing be,
>> And after death in their *posteritie*. (ll. 31-36)

51   Lang-Graumann relates the speaker's efforts in "The Search" to Augustine's concept of *intentio*:

> In "The Search" scheint dem Menschen jedes Vermögen, Gott finden zu können, abgesprochen zu werden. Die Entscheidung liegt ganz bei Gott, und der Mensch vermag nichts. Aber dennoch sucht er mit aller Kraft, und der vertrauensvollen Erkenntnis der beiden letzten Strophen geht eine buchstäblich intensive Suche voraus, wie sie auch von Augustinus im Zusammenhang mit dem Bestreben, Gott zu erkennen, beschrieben wird. Er nennt sie *intentio*, das Aus- und Hinspannen der Seele auf Gott als alleiniges Ziel. (112)

Jeremiah's foretelling of the Israelites' march against Babylon provides a biblical parallel which illuminates the speaker's stance in "The Search" (where the speaker initially assumes too much power and autonomy) by showing the "right" devotional attitude (which then leads to the desired effect, ensuring God's support):

> They shall ask the way to Zion with their faces thitherward, saying, Come, and let us join ourselves to the LORD in a perpetual covenant that shall not be forgotten. In those days, and in that time, saith the LORD, the children of Israel shall come, they and the children of Judah together, going and weeping: they shall go, and seek the LORD their God (Jer 50.4-5)

Here, the enemies of Babylon will act at the command of God (and not on their own accord), and consequently, their arrows will not "return in vain":

> For, lo, I will raise and cause to come up against Babylon an assembly of great nations from the north country: and they shall set themselves in array against her; from thence she shall be taken: their arrows shall be as of a mighty expert man; none shall return in vain. (Jer 50.9)

The people of Israel will move because God wills it so, while the speaker in "The Search" seems to shoot and seek on his own (he does not consider God's will till the end of the eighth stanza) – at least, this is the impression the speaker has of his own actions (which is also implied in his perception that God has "fled" from him and that he must therefore pursue God).

In describing his search as "dumb," the speaker implies that the sigh may not have been loud enough for God to hear, and therefore turns it into a groan (this statement is also slightly ironic, since the search was obviously not "dumb" in the sense of silent or soundless; instead, the speaker has been talking constantly, beginning with the exclamations in ll.1-2, and he has been sighing, too).[52] But "dumb" can also mean devoid

---

A (musical) image of this she finds in the speaker's description of himself in the second stanza, which she sees as an implicit comparison with a taut string spanning over the whole cosmos.

52   Stein points out the recurrent relation of "groans" to music in Herbert's poems:

of meaning ("saying nothing to the understanding; inexpressive, mean-
ingless; stupid, senseless," OED, "dumb, *adj.* and *n.* A.7.a"), which
would imply that the speaker's appeal to God is unsuccessful because the
speaker's words do not have any (or do not have the right) meaning. In
addition, the statement that the search was dumb may refer not only to
the speaker but also to God's lack of response, which makes the search
soundless and the speaker's effort meaningless. Later on, "still" in line 30
can be read analogously to "dumb": either God is "yet" concealed, or
God is verbally "silent" (or both, God may be hidden and silent at the
same time).

The speaker's remedy of "tuning" his sigh into a groan remains unsuc-
cessful, because once again he is acting on his own authority ("I sent a
sigh," "I tun'd"). The speaker may tune his sighs (i.e. his vocal exclama-
tions), but this mere vocal tuning is not enough. The speaker requires
further tuning and a change of attitude.[53] Thus, although the speaker
thinks at this point that his attitude is the right one, it is not, and conse-
quently, there is no response from God (which leads him to the suspicion
that God may be paying attention to "some new fabrick," instead of ques-
tioning himself). The statement "all was one" in l. 24 shows the speak-
er's limited human perspective. From his own point of view, his efforts
are meaningless and irrelevant. The phrase also shows his loneliness – all
he perceives is himself, that is, "one." What is more, the speaker general-
ises and states that *all* is one (though he can, strictly speaking, only speak
for his own position in the world), which, too, shows his self-centred
perspective. "All was one" stands in contrast to God's "making two one"

In "The Search" the poet sends out a sigh [...], but nothing happens, His next move is to
alter the sigh [ll.21-22]. In "The Crosse" groans offer themselves [...] as a harmony, and
in "Grieve not the Holy Spirit" the mention of God's groans in one stanza brings in the
lute and a song of complaint in the next. [In] "Death," [...] "The sad effects of sadder
grones" is followed by "Thy mouth was open, but thou couldst not sing." [...] Finally,
"Sion" offers the most comprehensive example. There the groans are converted to a music
of praise [...] (116)

53   Cf. for example, "The Temper (I)," where the speaker describes his changing
      emotional states and finally resigns himself to God's power by stating "Stretch or
      contract me thy poore debtor: / This is but tuning of my breast, / To make the
      musick better." (ll. 22-24). Similar notions can be found, e.g., in Donne's poetry: in
      "Goodfriday," God "tune[s] all spheares" (l.22), that is, even the speaker's deviant
      soul-sphere; and in "Hymne to God my God in my Sicknesse," the speaker
      prepares for his imminent death (and meeting with God) and states, "I tune the
      Instrument here at the dore" (l.4).

in line 60, which the speaker perceives as both meaningful and desirable. Thus, stanzas one to six show the speaker in a state of profound loneliness: he is excluded from the community of herbs and stars (the former are "below" him, the latter are "above" him), and he does not get a response to his attempt at communicating with God.

There is, however, also some poetic irony in the speaker's statement that "all was one." While this phrase reflects the speaker's momentary despair, it also foreshadows the happy ending in l.60, "making two one," of which the speaker is not yet aware at this point of his journey, but which he "knows" already as the speaker of the completed poem. The similarity between both expressions also serves to make yet another point: although the speaker does not realise it in l.24, all *is* one already – God is listening, even though the speaker feels otherwise, and their union is predestined and known to God. Thus, the combination of both expressions also serves to comment implicitly on the speaker's ignorant and self-centred attitude and to underline the fact that the speaker needs to change his mindset.

3.4 Stanzas seven to twelve: God as the centre of attention

After the sixth stanza, the speaker moves away from a description of himself and his efforts to find God, and begins to focus on God, first by considering a rival creation, then by trying to describe God's will and the distance between them. The speaker tries to offer a possible explanation for God's absence by introducing the idea of a "new fabric" competing with the speaker for God's attention.

> 25 Lord, dost thou some new fabrick mould
> 26   Which favour winnes,
> 27 And keeps thee present, leaving th'old
> 28   Unto their sinnes?

Again, the speaker holds others responsible for God's perceived absence from his own life (the "new fabric" which may keep God away from him), as well as implying God's potential unfaithfulness (God may have left the speaker "unto his sinnes" in favour of the "new fabric").[54] Just as

---

54 Cf. also the similar setting in "Affliction (I)," where the speaker has the feeling that God has turned away from him. There, the speaker thinks about finding a new

"sphere and centre" denied God's presence to him, it is now the "new fabrick" that has caused God to turn away from the speaker. While "new fabric" is a fairly general and vacant expression, we can assume that it refers to some manlike, sentient creation, someone who competes with the speaker for God's attention and is preferred, while the speaker is "the old [fabrick] left "to their sinnes."[55] The use of "fabrick" is noteworthy here. "Fabric" may refer generally to "a product of skilled workmanship" (*OED*, "fabric, *n*. I.1."), and in particular to an "edifice or building" (*OED*, "fabric, *n*. I.1."), and or to the body (*OED*, "fabric, *n*. I.3.b").[56] It also stresses the process of making something and can refer to the "action or process of framing or constructing" and especially to the "construction and maintenance (of a church); = ecclesiastical Latin *fabrica ecclesiae*." (*OED*, "fabric, *n*. II.5.a.").[57]

The speaker's jealous sentiment also once more stresses the impression of the speaker as an amorous lover of God, as does the use of "favour" in l.26 and maybe even the allusion to the "old", presumably cast off for something "new."[58] Line 27 can be understood in two ways. In the first place, the "new fabric" keeps God present, while the speaker, with his lack of faith, has spiritually abandoned God and therefore needs to search for God now (although the speaker does not say so, and instead states

---

"master" (i.e. turning away from God) before he refutes this thought and asks God to make him love God truly.

55   Cf. also Herbert's "Sion," "And now thy Architecture meets with sinne; For all thy frame and fabrick is within" (ll.11-12): here, the fabric God has moulded (i.e., man's soul) is found inside man's body, and tainted by sin. This image ties in with the idea in "The Search," where the speaker fears that the old fabric is left "unto their sinnes" (and presumably *because* of their sins, which apart from "old" and "new" is the only feature mentioned to characterise this fabric).

56   The specific meaning of "fabric" as a piece of cloth does not exist till the 18th century (cf. *OED*, "fabric, *n*. I.4."), but it is of course included in the use of "fabric" as a product of skilled workmanship.

57   "Fabric" is related to "forge" (they both share the same root and the meaning "workmanship"). This is significant with regard the "The Temper (I)," and the notion of tempering metal in a forge (in a parallel way, "mould" can also be used for the shaping of metal in a forge). Thus, moulding fabric and forging metal are similar, creative processes. To some extent, the speaker also seems to claim creative power for himself: he "marks" (l.9) and "draws" (l.18).

58   Cf. also Donne's "A Litanie": "come/ and re-create mee, now growne ruinous: [...] Purge away / all vicious tinctures that new fashioned / I may rise up from death" (ll.3-9).

that God has "fled" (l.1), "leaving" (l.27) the speaker alone). But "keeps thee present" also evokes "keeps thee company," which focuses on God's imagined attitude towards this imagined creation in contrast to God's perceived abandonment of the speaker.

Returning to his stance at the beginning of the poem, the speaker then asks once more *where* God is, and, as in the first stanza, repeatedly uses interrogatives.

> 29 Where is my God? what hidden place
> 30   Conceals thee still?
> 31 What covert dare eclipse thy face?
> 32   Is it thy will?

While "where" is only used once, the speaker goes on with "what place" and "what covert," thus stressing again the spatiality of the search. Also, as in the first stanza, the speaker's exclamation "where is *my* God" shows once more his possessive attitude.

Stanza 8 ends with "Is it thy will," which, importantly, introduces the question of God's will, which the speaker had not considered before.[59] In the beginning, the speaker assumes that God had "fled" from him; in addition, nature seems to conspire against the speaker and his efforts to find God: sphere and centre deny God being there, herbs and stars have their own connection to God but provide no clue to the speaker how to attain such a connection, sighs and groans just return to him (without being sent back) and now the "hidden place" and "covert" are depicted as agents keeping God and God's face, respectively, away from the speaker. The "covert" is even credited with consciousness: it "dares" to eclipse God's face. However, the use of "conceal" and "ecplise" is also an important indication of the speaker's beginning change of mind: both presuppose not God's absence (which verbs like "fled" and "leaving" do), but merely God's invisibility to the speaker.

The consideration of God's will in l. 32 is an important step towards recognising that just searching for God is not sufficient; instead the speaker has to submit himself to God's will (which he is not yet willing to do). In the next stanza, he consequently tries to get around the (insur-

---

59 Cf. Strier 1983, 236: "With line 32 of "The Search," the whole framework which the poem has been employing is recognized to be an evasion."

mountable) obstacle of God's will, by offering alternative obstacles: "brasse, steel, or mountains."

> 33 O let not that of any thing;
> 34   Let rather brasse,
> 35 Or steel, or mountains be thy ring,
> 36   And I will passe.

These are material (i.e. graspable and understandable) and possess a spatial dimension, that is, they *can* be passed, and this elicits the speaker's confident statement "I will passe" – with a restriction, however: only provided that God will actually "let" the obstacle be "brasse, or steel, or mountains." While the speaker attributes to God the power to create obstacles and barriers which he *can* actually pass, he also implicitly acknowledges God's will as the decisive factor of his own success, since "let rather" assumes that the obstacle separating the speaker from God is *not* made of brass, steel or mountains.

The use of the word "ring" in l.35 may be a hint at their future union (suggesting not just a circular fortification but also a wedding ring) as well as an anticipation of the "bell" in l.59 ("ring" may also refer to a "ringing noise or sound, esp. of a bell" (*OED*, "ring, n.[2] I.1.a")) and thus indicate the approach of a harmonious state – in spite of the terrifying thought of God's will. However, the speaker does not yet fully want to accept the idea that it may be God's will which keeps God away. The reason for this is given in the next two stanzas, where the speaker approaches the idea of God's will again and shows how this idea overpowers him.

> 37 Thy will such an intrenching is,
> 38   As passeth thought:
> 39 To it all strength, all subtilties
> 40   Are things of nought.

> 41 Thy will such a strange distance is,
> 42   As that to it
> 43 East and West touch, the poles do kiss,
> 44   And parallels meet.

God's will is defined in terms of paradoxical spatial relations and seen in connection to "East and west touch, the poles do kiss, and parallels meet." This will itself is described as a "strange distance," which illuminates the metaphorical status of the speaker's descriptions (as God's will "passeth thought," he can only describe it in terms of metaphor) and the speaker's purpose. The speaker is concerned with being united to God, and the conceits he uses are central to his argumentation. The "strange distance" that is God's will is seen in comparison to other distances: the distance between East and West, between the two poles and between two parallels. The distance constituting God's will is so great that in comparison to it, East and West, the poles and parallels seem to meet.

"To it" in l.42 is ambiguous, and may either mean "in comparison to the strange distance that is thy will" or "(according) to thy will, East and West touch, etc.," that is, "your will is so powerful that it makes East and West touch." Thus, although the speaker perceives the distance between him and God as insurmountable, the notion of East and West, poles and parallels meeting is encouraging: if God can make parallels meet, He can also bridge the gap to the speaker. Significantly, the examples used all focus on joining two things that are most radically separated in space, and which can only be made to meet through God's power (while for human beings their actual union is impossible to imagine). At the same time the terms used, "East and West," "poles," and "parallels," are human expressions to denote natural spatial phenomena. Moreover, the vocabulary used, "touch," "kiss," "meet," suggests an intimate meeting (and not just an overcoming of natural laws). The speaker is able to acknowledge God's will as the cause of his perceived loneliness only because he simultaneously imagines it as the cause of their union.[60]

With the paradoxa in ll.43-44, the speaker takes up geographical as well as geometrical notions and presents God as maker and geometer,

---

60 Cf. Donne's "Goodfriday," where going westwards simultaneously takes the speaker further away from Christ (who is located in the East) but also closer towards Christ because going westwards means approaching death (and meeting Christ after death). The union of East and West is also depicted, quite explicitly, in "Hymne to God my God, in my sicknesse": "As West and East / In all flatt Maps (and I am one) are one, / So death doth touch the Resurrection" (ll.13-15). In both cases, the combination of East and West (and what it entails – the link between death and resurrection) gives hope to the speaker, as it does in "The Search," too.

and as a supreme master at whose will the laws of nature are redefined. In connection with the listing in stanza 9, the speaker also establishes a dichotomy between his (human, earthly) perspective and a much more extensive view. While "brasse, or steel, or mountains" are delimited and to some extent visible and graspable (because they are material), East and West, poles and parallels are, firstly, abstract notions (even though the speaker tried to make the palpable by having them "touch" and "kiss") and secondly, only perceptible on a much larger scale. When the speaker turns to consider God's will as the cause behind their separation, he also realises that this separation is as its most extreme – as extreme as only God's will can make it. In presenting his grief as extreme as his distance from God, he simultaneously points out the enormity of his grief and the fact that God has the power to change this distance.

The preparation for the speaker's turn from his own will to God's will is also shown in the repetitions of "will" and "passe." "I will passe" in l.36 is the last instance of an active verb applied to the speaker's action. The use of "will" instead of "shall" is significant, since it stresses the speaker's autonomy (which he needs to overcome) and implicitly brings in his own "will," which is then immediately opposed to God's will. The extensive dwelling on God's will, which takes up the whole of stanzas 10 and 11, serves to shift the focus from the speaker (and his attitude of self-reliance) to God. At the beginning of stanza 10, the speaker's militant attitude still shines through when he calls God's will an "intrenching" and states that "all strength" is insignificant to God's will, but it gives way to another view in stanza 11. The repetition of "will" from l.36 to 41 creates a smooth transition from a focus on the speaker's autonomy to focussing on the supremacy of God.

"Intrenching" is ambiguous, and can mean either "To place within a trench; to surround or fortify (a post, army, town, etc.) with trenches" (*OED*, "entrench/intrench, *v.* 1.a") or "to encroach or trespass upon; to infringe" (*OED*, "entrench/intrench, *v.* 4.a") and even "To make (a wound) by cutting" (*OED*, "entrench/intrench, *v.* 3"). Thus, God's action of "intrenching" indicates closure and impenetrability (the speaker can-not pass through the intrenching of God's will), but also permeability (God can reach and "intrench" the speaker). The spelling "in-trench" emphasises the existence of both options, and the possibility of God's will literally going *into* and through the speaker. Also, the gerund "in-trench-ing" suggests an ongoing, perpetual motion, similar to "making two one" in the last line.

These different meanings of "intrenching" tie in with the following line: the statement that God's will "passeth thought" is ambiguous, too, which hints at the reciprocity (and at the same time inequality) of the relation between God and speaker. In the first place, it means that the comprehension of God's will is beyond the speaker's thought and under-standing. Additionally, however, it can be read as "God's will passes thought," that is, it passes *through* the speaker's thought (which, in its self-centredness and melancholy actually obstructs the speaker's endeav-our to find God) and reaches the speaker himself. While the speaker is unable to pass through anything (either mentally or physically), God can pass through everything. Analogously, lines 39-40 can be read in two ways: either the speaker's strength and subtleties are not strong enough to get through the "intrenching" of God's will, or they are nothing to God, who goes through (i.e., intrenches) the speaker's strength and subtleties (which impede the speaker's search just as much as his thoughts) and reaches the speaker at his core.

The demonstration of God's power, which the speaker visualises in stanzas 10 and 11 (showing that the speaker is unable to reach God, while God is able to reach the speaker), incites him to change his attitude, so that in stanza 12 the speaker talks about "my grief," "my charge" and "my case" and instead of acting independently, he then asks God to "take these barres, these lengths away."

45 Since then my grief must be as large
46   As is thy space,
47 Thy distance from me; see my charge,
48   Lord, see my case.

The use of "since then" in 1.45 presents the statement following it as the logical conclusion from the previous stanza(s), which is enforced by the use of "must be." That is, if it is God's immeasurable and unfathomable will which keeps the speaker apart from God (which, subtly and gradual-ly, the speaker seems to have accepted as the cause for God's absence), then the speaker's grief will also be immeasurable, and the only option the speaker has is pleading instead of fighting.

The use of "charge" also serves to shift the speaker's attitude from an aggressive and combative stance to a more accepting and obedient one.[61] "Charge" refers in the first instance to the speaker's spiritual burden (*OED* "charge, *n.*[1] II.8."), but it can also refer to a military attack (*OED* III.18),[62] which corresponds to the speaker's earlier attempts to reach God. In combination with "see my case," legal connotations of both "charge" and case" suggest themselves. "Charge" as a legal term denotes "the duty or responsibility of taking care *of* (a person or thing); care, custody, superintendence" (*OED* II.13). It can also mean accusation, informally and legally (*OED* II.16.a), and while this is not the most prominent reading here, it echoes the speaker's implicit accusations of God's potential unfaithfulness and the speaker's abandonment in stanza seven. Equally "case" refers to the speaker's spiritual condition (*OED* "case, *n.*[1] 5.a"), but may also refer to "a legal action, *esp.* one to be decided in a court of law" (*OED* 7.a). By bringing in these legal connotations, the speaker makes God (who should "see" his charge and case) the supreme judge of his condition. Although the speaker talks about "my charge" and "my case," he wants them to become "your charge" and "your case" (i.e., God's responsibility).

The speaker's pleas to "see my charge" and "see my case" also contribute to the speaker's change of mind in two other ways. In the first instance, they show the speaker in a pleading stance (his attitude is still demanding, but less so than in ll.33-34, where with "let not" and "let rather" the speaker had asked for God's power in providing surmountable obstacles to the speaker. In addition, the emphasis on vision in ll. 47-48 is significant. Firstly, because it presupposes God's presence (just like the use of "hidden," "conceals" and "eclipse" in stanza eight presupposes that God is there but not visible): in order to literally "see" the speaker's

---

61 However, from 1653 on "charge" is also recorded as "[t]he quantity of [...] powder and shot, with which a firearm is loaded for one discharge" (*OED* "charge, *n.*1 II.3.a"), so the speaker may not have given up his combative attitude to the full extent.

62 Cf. also *OED*, III.19: "A signal for the attack sounded on a trumpet or other instrument," which can also be used figuratively. This meaning is not documented before 1650, though.

charge and case, God must be close enough to look upon them. Secondly, in ll. 47-48, the speaker reverses his previous attitude: whereas before *he* wanted to see God (searching for God and complaining that God was hidden from him), he now wants God to see *him*.[63]

While the speaker does not abandon his egocentric stance, and still focuses exclusively on his personal relation to God, he does abandon his own wilfulness. Stanzas 10 to 12 are therefore important as a preparation for the turn in stanza 13, since they readjust the speaker's role and attitude towards God.

3.5 Stanzas 13 to 15: convergence and prospective union

After the recognition that he has to resign himself to God's will, the speaker is able to talk explicitly about turning. The speaker now makes it clear that his final turn towards God (and his imagined prospective union with God) depend on God's turning towards the speaker, and that his own stance should be one of supplication and prayer: While in the beginning he had demanded to know "whither art thou fled," he now humbly prays to God, even asking for the ability to pray and address God in words, with "let me say" in l.51, and pleading to God to turn towards the speaker. Lines 50 to 52 are central in anticipating a change in the speaker's relationship to God, but the possibility of such a change and of getting close to God is already indicated in the previous stanzas – in the light of the previous stanzas, it is clear that God's "distance" from the speaker in l.47 can easily be annulled.

Stanza 13 describes the turning necessary for the speaker's peace of mind and salvation. Especially lines 50 to 52 are syntactically and semantically ambiguous in several ways:

> 49 O take these barres, these lengths, away;
> 50   Turn, and restore me:
> 51 Be not Almightie, let me say,
> 52   Against, but for me.

---

63   Cf. the similar development in "Goodfriday": the speaker does not want to see the crucifixion, and in looking towards Christ with his memory, he discovers that Christ is looking at him.

The verb "turn" in line 50 is ambiguous and can be read either as a transitive or intransitive verb. As an intransitive verb, it would refer to God, whom the speaker asks to turn in order to restore the speaker (that is "you turn yourself and restore me"), while as a transitive verb, it refers to the speaker himself, who asks God to turn and restore him (that is, "you turn me and restore me"). Similarly, "When thou dost turn" in line 53 is also ambiguous, keeping up the ambiguity of ll.50-51, and could mean either "when thou dost turn yourself towards me" or "when thou dost turn me towards you." Importantly, in either case, the turning is performed by God.[64] Nevertheless, the fact that both readings carry the same weight reflects the emphatic mutuality of their relationship.

Lines 51 to 52 are syntactically ambiguous, too. Either "Almighty" is an apposition, an insertion addressing God as "Almighty." The sentence, without the apposition, could then be paraphrased as "be not against me, but (be) for me," that is, "be not opposed to me, instead be favourable towards me." But "Almighty" could also be an adjective complementing the auxiliary verb "be." The object would in this case be "almighty against me" and the whole phrase would read, "be not almighty against me, instead be almighty in my favour." In both cases, the speaker asks God to cancel the opposition entailed in being "against" someone (either spatially set against someone or something, or emotionally opposed to someone or something).[65]

The plea "Be [...] for me" also points at a possible longing for an exclusive relationship with God (i.e., "be mine" or "be almighty for *me*, and not for others), which goes together with the allusions to love poetry found in "The Search" and the depiction of a relation to God in terms of an amorous relationship found in e.g. the Song of Songs.

There is yet another interpretation of line 51. The insertion "let me say" in line 51 interrupts the sentence, and when we read the stanza from top

---

64 The speaker's supplication in l.50 ("Turn, and restore me") is thus fundamentally different from Donne's similar expression in "Goodfriday" (ll.41f., "Restore thine image [...] / and I'll turn my face."), where the speaker is presented as the agent deciding about his own turning (though he clearly needs God's "corrections" in order to be able to turn).

65 Cf. also the end of "Justice (II)": "Against me there is none, but for me much" (l.24). Wilcox (Herbert 2007, 493) also points out Rom 8.31 "If God be for us, who can be against us."

to bottom, at first glance the initial meaning we get for the first part of line 51 is simply "be not almighty." The speaker would in this case ask God *not* to be an almighty God, that is, not be above the speaker but to come down to the speaker's (human) level. Although this interpretation is syntactically no longer tenable once we reach the end of line 52, it still resonates along the other interpretations. Since the speaker also asks God to take the "barres" and "lengths" away that separate him from God and considering that it is one of the speaker's aims to achieve a union with God towards the end of the poem, it does make sense to keep line 51 in mind as a plea for equality.

Moreover, "But for me" is acoustically close to "Before me" (and it is also close on the level of syntax, since "but for me" omits the verb from l. 51 and should actually read, "(be not […] against me, but be for me"), and this similarity adds "be not against me, instead be *be*fore me" as another connotation of lines 51 to 52. This additional meaning goes together with the speaker's role as a searcher, who is lacking and longing for God's guidance in his search. Once more, the potential of language opens up possibilities for connecting with God.

The potential approximation to God prepared in the 13th stanza allows the speaker to be more confident about achieving the union with God. There is still some degree of uncertainty: the speaker refers to an indefinite point in the future and to a turning that has not yet taken place (the ambiguity of l.50 with regard to who turns or is turned is kept up here), so that l.53 might also be understood as "*If* thou dost turn." However, the use of the simple present after l.53 and the speaker's detailed description of their union in the following lines show his newly won confidence in the fulfilment of this union.

Up to stanza 13, the speaker has dwelt extensively on the large space between him and God: God and God's will was described as "an intrenching," "a strange distance, a "large […] space," a "distance" again, as well as "barres" and "lengths." With the turn in the 13th stanza, the speaker can imagine (and describe) how this space is diminished, and the last two stanzas focus on the resulting nearness. Just as the distance from God was described as the most immense space possible, the closeness to God is described as the complete dissolution of space.

53 When thou dost turn, and wilt be neare,
54   What edge so keen,
55 What point so piercing can appeare
56   To come between?

57 For as thy absence doth excell
58   All distance known:
59 So doth thy nearenesse bear the bell,
60   Making two one.

"Wilt be neare" in l.53 is the last instance of "will" in the poem. While in the previous stanzas, God "willed" to be distant, He now explicitly "wills" to be near, and this nearness is stressed through its repetition in l.59. With the sharpness of a keen edge and a piercing point, the speaker takes up his earlier militant, combative imagery (and adds a separating force: both edge and point can be used to pierce but also to separate things, as they have been used to "come between" earlier in the poem), but this time opposing their violent forces to his divine union.

With the idiom "bear the bell," the speaker uses combative imagery one last time. "Bear the bell" means "to take the first place, to have foremost rank or position, to be the best" (*OED* "bell, *n.*[1] III.7.a"), marking God's nearness as the winner, and is used synonymously with "bear or carry away the bell" (meaning "to carry off the prize," which may refer a golden or silver bell sometimes given to the winner of races or contests). However, structurally, it is left open whether God's nearness wins over the smallest possible spatial extension (i.e., parallel to the excelling of God's absence), or whether it also wins over God's absence. "Bear the bell" is paralleled to "excell," and while "excell" is a (high-style) Latin loanword expressing distance and difference,[66] "bear the bell" seems humble and rustic, especially as it derives from the custom of attaching a bell to the leading cow or sheep of a flock (*OED* III.7.a). Thus, the use of this expression can also be seen as another allusion to the notion of a shepherd's search for his lost sheep (the speaker is searching for God's nearness, and God's nearness literally "bears the bell").

---

66 "Excell" derives from Latin "excellere," which means "to raise up, elevate" or "to rise, elevate itself." Cf. also the phrase and hymn "Gloria in excelsis Deo," where God is unreachable because far above human beings.

Of equal importance is the fact that "bear the bell" suggests sound. In stanzas five and six, the speaker tries to reach God with his sigh and groan, whose musical nature is made explicit with "I tun'd another." He is unsuccessful and complains that "the search was dumbe" (NB that this refers to acoustic communication – with regard to words, the whole poem is an attempt at verbal communication with God). In stanza 13, the speaker asks to "let me say," bringing in his own voice (which he attempted earlier with his sigh and groan, but without success so that the search remained "dumbe"). In the last stanza then, the speaker finally receives an acoustic response as God's nearness is associated with sound and the search becomes sonorous (and what is more, audible to the speaker). God's nearness may be seen not only as a guiding force, it also allows the speaker to hear God (something he was unable to do before). The bell thus serves a communicative function, as God's summons calling the speaker.[67] The reference to the bell as a musical instrument – bells are already tuned and thus in tune – might also hint at an harmonious union (this is also reflected in "making two one," which, musically, implies a progression from an interval to unison, and thus also from (potential) discord to (certain) concord).[68] Lastly, a ringing bell is also a sign of death (and although the speaker does not mention death in the poem, it

---

67 And inversely, bells can be used to call God. Cf. "Prayer (I)," "Church-bels beyond the starres heard" (l.13), which shows the bells' capacity to be heard by God (as well as men).

68 Musically, "bell" is also connected to "ring" in a second, more specific way: "A set *of* (esp. church) bells tuned to one another" is also called a "ring" (*OED*, "ring, n.2 I.2"). In the context of music and turning, the reference to bells in l.59 may also be an allusion to the practice of change ringing, which in England developed around the beginning of the 17th century (cf. Eisel 40). Change ringing (as the name already indicates) consists of slow, gradual changes in the order a number of tuned bells are rung. Though mostly secular (Cook 28-30, 36-38) and even seen as sinful (because it was used for pleasure, cf. Bunyan's giving up of bell ringing in "Grace Abounding" (13): "I had taken much delight in ringing, but my Conscience beginning to be tender: I thought such practice was but vain, and therefore forced my self to leave it," or Christopher Harvey's statement "ringing changes all our bells hath marr'd" ("The Sexton," l.19) in *The Synagogue*, Harvey 1874), the nature of change ringing (involving several bells and going on over a period of time) is certainly a powerful acoustic experience, "beyond the starres heard."

is a prerequisite for his final union with God): the nearness of death is simultaneously the nearness of God.[69]

Another effect of the last two stanzas is that of diminishing the spatial dimensions explored so far. The "edge so keen" and "point so piercing" have a very small spatial extension, yet they are still too big to come between the speaker and God. They are, however, imaginable and graspable, "touchable," while the space between speaker and God is not. The spatial construct that was unfolded at the beginning of the poem is now reduced – if the speaker and God unite in one point, then, from the speaker's perspective (to whom everything is only relevant with regard to his pursuit of God), movement (in the sense of shifting locations) stops and there is neither beginning nor ending. Accordingly, the very last line, "making two one," describes neither a completed (past) event nor an event happening in the future, but an ongoing process (without a specification of time), so that, on the one hand, disparate and separate movement disappears and, on the other, unifying and combining movement seems to continue forever.

The last two stanzas continue to show the speaker's strongly self-centred perspective – he sees God's nearness in relation to his own position just as he saw God's absence and vastness only in relation to himself, and he talks about "making two one," which continues the exclusivity he sees (or wishes for) in his relationship to God. Still, the speaker's attitude and perspective have changed fundamentally; and a double turn

---

69　Cf. also Donne's *Devotions*, "Who bends not his *eare* to any *bell* which upon any occasion rings? [...] Never send to know for whom the *bell* tolls; it tolls for *thee*. (17th Meditation, 87).

　　The reference to "bearing the bell" might also pick up the description of Aaron's robe, which is to be decorated with golden bells (Exod. 28.33-34; 39.25-26), so that "his sound shall be heard when he goeth in unto the holy place before the Lord, and when he cometh out, that he die not." (Exod. 28.35). Here, too, the bells assume a communicative function, as well as designating a leader. Herbert focuses on this imagery in "Aaron" (which contains musical tuning, as well as several kinds of turning). Here the bells have an explicitly musical function as well as a restoring power: "Harmonious bells below, raising the dead / To leade them unto life and rest" (ll.3-4) belong to "true Aarons" (l.5). The speaker contrasts these bells first to his own "noise of passions ringing me for dead" (l.8) and then to Christ's "onely musick," which enables him to become like Aaron and Christ, as well as giving him a "doctrine tun'd by Christ" (l.23).

has taken place that allows the speaker to turn towards God with the right devotional attitude and to perceive God's turn towards him.

4. The speaker's search as a pilgrimage

The title of the poem marks the speaker's activity as a search, which is then reinforced by l.3 ("My searches are my daily bread") and l.23 ("the search was dumbe before"). At the same time, it is characterised as a metaphorical search by the speaker's lack of physical movement – movement is emphasised in the poem (his mouth is shown to "send" and "tune," and his eyes and knees "pierce"), but the speaker's limbs seem to be immobile (the fact that his knees "pierce" the earth makes it literally impossible to move forward). Thus, "The Search" presents on a small scale what *The Temple* shows on a larger scale, namely a spiritual voyage with a certain goal.[70]

The setting of the poem (the depiction of the speaker's longing for spiritual comfort as a search and of his way to God as the departure from one place with the aim of arriving at another) is based on the notion of life as a voyage, man as a pilgrim and his way towards death and towards God as a pilgrimage.[71] The success of the speaker's pilgrimage in "The Search" is determined by his stance and conduct, so that the question of

---

70 In this regard, there is yet another important connection between Cusa's writings and "The Search." Cusa talks repeatedly of the believer as a "pilgrim" on his way through life, aiming at a union with God (*De Docta* 1981, 151ff., 158) – which is made possible through "maximum faith," which leads to mortification of the flesh (152). This "maximum faith" is also inextricably linked to love (151f.). This corresponds exactly to the speaker's aim in the poem: he is on a spiritual voyage in search of God, which, in turn, is characterised by the speaker's love for God.

71 The idea of life as a journey or pilgrimage is also a major topic in Donne's poems and sermons (see Schleiner 85-94). Cf. also Leimberg's discussion of the journey motif in Vaughan's *Silex Scintillans* (1996, 405-61), which, too, presents the speaker's spiritual progress in terms of an earthly pilgrimage and Vaughan's "The Search."

Herbert treats the topic explicitly in "The Pilgrimage," however, there is little personal development in the speaker of "The Pilgrimage." At the beginning of the poem, all obstacles are cleared: the speaker leaves "the gloomy cave of Desperation" (l.4) and "the rock of Pride" (l.6) behind and accepts his journey as a "long [...] and weary way" (l.3). He is initially mistaken in his destination, but quickly finds the "right way" towards death. Also, although the speaker does address God, the poem does not focus on their relationship.

how to approach God becomes just as important as the question of *where* to find God.

Herbert relies on a long tradition in presenting the speaker as a travelling searcher and seeker, beginning with the antique secular models of the *Odyssey* and *Aeneid* and continuing with Dante's *Divine Comedy*, medieval chivalric quests such as *Sir Gawain and the Green Knight*, and the allegorical framework of Spenser's *Faerie Queene*. Some of these texts present pilgrimage in the sense of a religiously motivated voyage, or merge secular and religious motifs.[72] What distinguishes Donne's and Herbert's poems from most of them, however – and at the same time links their poetry to secular love poetry – is the individual perspective created through a single first-person speaker and through this speaker's attitude of reflection and introspection (an attitude which is strengthened by the fact that these poems are comparatively short and therefore focussed on the speaker and desired goal).

The concept of pilgrimage is in many respects related to turning. In the first place, both turning and pilgrimage rely on the notion of life as a voyage (man's voyage from birth to death and beyond). More specifically, the concept of pilgrimage (in contrast to merely wandering through life) is mostly linked to Christianity – the pilgrim has to go through the hardships of life before he reaches his place in heaven, being always oriented towards God.[73]

---

72   Further secular examples include the *Roman de la Rose*, *Hypnerotomachia Poliphili* or *Don Quixote*; while other works present a mixture of amorous and religious plots, such as *Orlando Furioso*, *Gerusalemme Liberata*, and others are mostly or purely religious, such as *Everyman*, *The Passionate Man's Pilgrimage*, or *Pèlerinage de la vie humaine* (which Peters (140) calls a sacred contrafact ("Geistliche Kontrafaktur") to the *Roman de la Rose*). This tradition goes on with Bunyan's *The Pilgrim's Progress* and also Bunyan's *Grace Abounding to the Chief of Sinners*. Cf. also the reverse use of pilgrimage in Chaucer's *Canterbury Tales*, where the protagonists' journey to a place of devotion is an occasion for presenting secular narratives mostly without religious background.

73   Hahn points out that, although there are classical models that rely on the notion of life as a voyage, the notion of a pilgrimage ("the theme of wandering, alienation, and exile, combined with that of pious devotion," Hahn 1) is a specifically Christian one, based on seeing Christ as a stranger come to the world (and whom men can take as a model for imitation on their own pilgrimage, Hahn 22-29; cf. also Schleiner 85ff. and Dyas 12-65; cf. also Vaughan, who calls Christ a "Pilgrim-Sun" (1.3) in his poem "The Search"). Hahn divides pilgrimage ("*peregrinatio vitae*") into man's passage through life on the one hand, and the practice of

The notion of life as a journey or pilgrimage towards death is also found, for example, in Donne's sermon "Deaths Duell":

> Even the *Israel of God* hath no mansions; but journies, pilgrimages
> in this life. By that measure did *Iacob* measure his life to *Pharaoh*,
> *The daies of the years of my pilgrimage*. And though the *Apostle*
> would not say *morimur*, that, whilest wee *are in the body* wee *are
> dead*, yet hee sayes, *Peregrinamur*, whilest wee are *in the body*,
> wee are but in *a pilgrimage*, and wee are *absent from the Lord*
> ("Deaths Duell," Donne, *Sermons* X, no. 11, 234)

Donne stresses not only the transitory character of life, but also the absence from God as an important feature of the pilgrimage of life – which also motivates the speaker's lament and his search for God in Herbert's poem.[74] Donne here also stresses the goal of this voyage or pilgrimage: a transition through death towards eternal life:

> [T]his *exitus mortis* shall be *introitus in vitam*, our issue in death
> shall be an entrance into everlasting life. And these three considera-
> tions: our deliverance *à morte, in morte, per mortem*, from death, in
> death, and by death, will abundantly do all the offices of the foun-
> dations, of the buttresses, of the contignation, of this our building;
> that he that is our God is the God of all salvation, because *unto* this
> *God the Lord belong the issues of death*. (231)

---

asceticism on the other hand (that is, broadly, into a passive state, though full of hardships, and an active, meritorious state). The active, meritorious *peregrinatio* he sees as typically Catholic, rejected by Protestant teachings (especially Calvin) in favour of the Biblical, passive concept of *peregrinatio* as simply the journey through (the hardships of) life (156f.). He also differentiates between *peregrinatio vitae* and *peregrinatio mortem* (the transition to afterlife or heaven).

Schleiner points out the theological distinction between man's "*status viatoris*" (simply being "on the way") and his "*status comprehensoris*," having "apprehended, grasped, or reached" the divine (86). The speaker in "The Search" also changes from *viator* to *comprehensor* – he begins by aimlessly "wandering around" in search of God, and reaches a state where he accepts and acknowledges God's will, which gives him orientation and an aim for his voyage.

74 This description also corresponds to Augustine's view of man as a pilgrim "in exile from the Garden of Eden, yet on his way to the heavenly Jerusalem" (Bitton-Ashkelony 113). Cf. also Donne's Holy Sonnet, "O my black soule": "Thou art like a pilgrim, which abroad hath done / Treason, and durst not turne to whence hee is fled (ll.3-4)."

In searching for God's whereabouts and in anticipating a union with God, the speaker of "The Search" thus presents himself as a pilgrim, i.e., as a traveller on a journey to a sacred place (and, more generally, as a human being on his course through life).[75] As the speaker ponders how and where to find God, he goes through a process of transformation that takes place within a spatial framework, which he mentally traverses. The speaker stresses both the spatiality of his search and his own immobility – his voyage is a voyage of the mind, while his knees remain "piercing the earth." At the same time, he creates the impression of some kind of advancement, in describing his progress in spatial terms, with bars and lengths to be overcome (ll.49), and in attributing a spatial location to God, so that no "edge" or "point" (ll. 54f.) can come in between their union. What he achieves in this way is a spiritual advancement.[76] The ending may thus allude to a conversion experience that will help the speaker to live virtuously and in confidence of his salvation, but also a forecast of his own death and union with God in the afterlife.

5.   Progress towards God in Donne's "Thou hast made me"

Donne's Holy Sonnet "Thou hast made me" relies on spatial imagery to depict the speaker's pursuit of salvation, and opens up a an elaborate

---

75   From the 14th century on, "pilgrimage" is also applied generally to the course of life, albeit mostly in religious contexts (cf. OED, "pilgrimage, *n.* 3").

76   Cf. Strier, 1983, 238:

> We are clearly in another world here from that to which spatial and quantitative terms apply. The relevant conceptions of distance and closeness are emotional, not physical. Absence and nearness are themselves only inadequate and potentially misleading metaphors. The "search" is misguided from the beginning. The poem as a whole has been a critique and a *reductio* of its title conceit. The proper way of dealing with the sense of heaven's desertion is not through "The Search" but through "The Method" [...]. Sin, not space, is what keeps man from God.

> Cf. also Bauer (2004) on inward and outward space in Vaughan's "The Search" (301ff.) and Goldberg on the speaker's inner and outer journey in Donne's "Goodfriday, 1613" (481ff.).

> Tiffany argues that the Protestant notion of pilgrimage is ultimately that of an interior voyage, yet different from earlier spiritual pilgrimage as depicted in monastic writings, Augustine or Dante, in that it is based exclusively on the Bible and conceived as interior from the outset, not as a replacement for a "real" journey or depiction of such a journey (35-36). Cf. also Keeble, who stresses the detachment from the world as an ideal for the Protestant pilgrim, whose "true distinguishing marks" are "unworldliness and otherworldliness" (247).

three-dimensional framework within which the speaker then moves on his way to God, in a way similar to the one found in "The Search."[77]

> 01 Thou hast made me, And shall thy worke decay?
> 02 Repaire me now, for now mine end doth haste,
> 03 I runne to death, and death meets me as fast,
> 04 And all my pleasures are like yesterday.
> 05 I dare not move my dimme eyes any way,
> 06 Despaire behind, and death before doth cast
> 07 Such terrour, and my feebled flesh doth waste
> 08 By sinne in it, which it t'wards hell doth weigh;
> 09 Onely thou art above, and when towards thee
> 10 By thy leave I can looke, I rise againe;
> 11 But our old subtle foe so tempteth me,
> 12 That not one houre I can myself sustaine;
> 13 Thy Grace may winge me to prevent his art
> 14 And thou like Adamant draw mine iron heart.

Donne's sonnet appears like a condensed version of "The Search" (or rather, "The Search" seems like as an extended version of "Thou hast"). The speaker here describes the final stages of his journey through life and towards death ("for now mine end doth haste"), and the world around the speaker, visible in "The Search," is eclipsed by his fear of death ("I dare not move my dimme eyes any way"). The speaker's emphasis is thus on the direction of his movements and on the forces influencing his motions – and on his wish to "rise againe" towards God instead of being dragged down to hell. By omitting references to the world in which he (still) lives, and describing movements in a nondescript space, he foregrounds the nonliteral and metaphorical use of space.

While the speaker does not feel entirely deserted by God (instead of asking "whither art thou fled," he starts directly with "thou" and attributes the responsibility of his salvation to God), the initial situation is the same as in Herbert's poem: the speaker feels desolate and entreats God to help him. While the speaker in "The Search" does not specify *where* God is to be found, in "Thou hast made me" God is clearly situated above the speaker, and the speaker's journey is distinctly shown to be a journey

---

77 Another of Donne's poems which deals explicitly with travelling (and depicts the speaker's journey towards death (and towards God) in terms of a mundane voyage) is "Hymne to God my God in my sicknesse."

through life and towards death (as well as a quest for spiritual salvation). Space is constituted with explicit references to "behind," "before," and "above." "Below" is hinted at with "t'wards hell doth weigh" (i.e., the speaker's sin pulls him down) and "decay." In the sestet, the emphasis with regard to direction is on "above": the speaker "rises" and hopes to be "winged" and "drawn" to God.

The rhyme scheme marks the sonnet as a mixture of Italian and English form: there is a clear turn after l.8 (the rhyme changes and there is also a change of mood), but within the sestet ll.13-14 are separated by a new rhyme and thus form a kind of couplet confirming God's power. L.9 begins with "Onely," which is ambiguous: as an adverb, it stresses God's uniqueness, but as a conjunction it indicates an opposition (i.e., "but thou art above") – a turn from being pulled down to being drawn up (ll.11-12 then seem like a kind of drawback, bringing sin and hell back in, but they serve mainly to show the necessity of God's grace and power, which is then confirmed in the last two lines). The sudden realisation that God is indeed above him, helps the speaker to fight his terror of death and to replace it with confidence in God's grace.

The choice of words used to describe separation and approximation to God, resembles that of "The Search": the speaker "decays" in the absence of God and asks to be "repaired" and thus restored to a previous state free of sin (which also resonates in "I rise againe"). The opening reminder "thou hast made me" and "thy worke" stress the speaker's status as God's own creature. As does "The Search," "Thou hast made me" depicts a personal relation to God, stressing the individuality of the speaker and the exclusivity of their relation. The sonnet uses first person singular almost consistently, with a large number of personal pronouns referring to the speaker. The only exception to this is "our old subtle foe," which can be understood either as an expression with a general idiomatic character (avoiding the use of "devil," for which "foe" was a common replacement), or even as an attempt to establish a feeling of community (the devil is foe to the speaker and to God, who thus have something in common). The speaker also stresses the emotional aspect of this relationship in referring to his heart (which, though made of iron, can be moved and drawn to God).

Donne, too, emphasises the necessity of resignation to God's will. Without God, the speaker is helpless and erring ("I runne to death"), as well as blind (his "dimme eyes" resemble those of the speaker in "The Search," who complains that God is concealed and hidden, because he cannot see Him, as well as the situation in "Goodfriday, 1613," where the speaker is afraid to look East). In contrast to Herbert's speaker, the speaker in "Thou hast made me" readily gives up his apparent autonomy: he acts "by thy leave" and he stresses that he cannot "sustain" himself and wishes to be "drawn" to God as to a magnetic force. Even the bold claim "I rise againe" (hinting at the speaker's resurrection after death) is conditional and dependent on God's leave.

The speaker is on an inexorable journey towards death (he "runs" to death, and death meets him just "as fast") which will bring him closer to either heaven or hell. While "The Search" stresses the mutual turning of speaker and God and focuses mainly on their relationship (though it does pose the question of a potential rival competing for God's attention), in "Thou hast made me" the devil is brought in as another force influencing the speaker (comparable to "pleasure or businesse" in "Goodfriday, 1613"), as a rival to God, tempting the speaker with his "art." At the same time, the mutual attraction of speaker and death ("I runne to death, and death meets me as fast") is replaced by the (magnetlike) attraction of speaker and God. The last line of the sonnet thus hints at a union like the one made explicit in "The Search": it uses the image of magnetic force, which entails a reduction of all space between the two magnetic elements, as well as stressing mutual attraction.

6.   The written word as an approach to God in "Coloss. 3.3"

"Coloss. 3.3" shares with "The Search" and "Thou hast" the combination of a spatial and a spiritual way through life, as well as their emphasis on the speaker's movement, but it shows the speaker's approximation to God in a different way. In "The Search," the speaker tries to approach God (and establish a connection) by speaking to Him (and the same happens in "Thou hast"). In "Coloss. 3.3" the speaker approaches God through the process of writing – the written form of the poem is essential for "finding" the way to God.

Structurally, the poem consists of three elements, a biblical quotation preceding the text proper,[78] the ten lines of the poem, and an additional diagonal line created italicising a single word from each of the ten lines. Only the poem's written (and printed) form reveals the additional line "My life is hid in him that is my treasure," that provides half of Life's "double motion," so that the poem's iconic form becomes an essential part of the speaker's turn towards God.[79] At the same time, the additional, hidden, line is only revealed through the process of reading the poem.[80] The winding way through the poem's ten lines provides the basis

---

78   Bloch points out that Herbert modifies the biblical quotation in a double sense: In the preceding quotation, he changes "your life" to "our life," and within the poem, he changes the pronoun to "My life," making it more personal and directly related to the speaker (36).

79   "Coloss. 3.3," in its printed form in *The Temple*, is also a highly geometrical poem, presenting "an exact square of ten lines having ten syllables each [...]. The diagonal *intextus* divides this square into two equilateral triangles, each having three sides of nine units length" (Bauer 1999, 218).
    Song argues that the double motion in "Coloss. 3.3" resembles anamorphic pictures, that is, that there are two competing perspectives or interpretations (one clearly visible, one hidden) between which the reader switches while reading the poem: "'Coloss. 3.3' explores the anamorphic potential of poetry in order to enact a religious experience that transcends the individual reader's spatial and temporal limitations" (108). Such a process contributes to the iconicity of the poem's form: the poem's text forces the reader to combine two usually mutually exclusive viewpoints, and so does the poem's form.

80   Miller talks about a number of Herbert's poems (including "Coloss. 3.3") that are
    Metapoetical, emphasizing the *versus*, or winding of poetry over the line – or its meter or feet – and that associate such winding with the motions of the self in time. Poetic form and spiritual process comment on one another in [these poems]. (138)
    Cf. also Fish, 203f.:
    [T]he reader is himself involved in a double motion. For at whatever point [...] he becomes aware of the operation of the italicized words, he will be performing two (reading) actions, one linear ("straight") and sequential, the other vertical and episodic. Moreover, as the poem proceeds he will come more and more to regard the linear experience merely as a way of getting to the next component of the vertical experience.
    For poems that present an interplay of form and content like the one in "Coloss. 3.3" (that is, poems which are in some way pattern poems, though mostly less obviously so than "The Altar" and "Easter Wings"), Summers uses the term "hieroglyph," as the most inclusive term covering different occurrences of this kind of iconicity, defining it as "a figure, device, or sign having some hidden meaning; a secret or enigmatical symbol; an emblem" (123, quoting from *A New English Dictionary*, London 1702). Such a definition also emphasises a reader's involvement and the process of interpretation, as the "hidden meaning" needs to be discovered in the process of understanding the poem.

for the oblique and hidden line, which only becomes manifest through its interaction with all ten lines: The speaker (and also the reader) has to traverse the whole poem before can he discover the oblique reading (and thus the knowledge that his life has been *in* God all the time). Conversely, the oblique reading permeates all ten lines, that is, it is always present, even when it is not visible.[81]

Our life is hid with Christ in God.

01 *My* words & thoughts do both expresse this notion,
02 That *Life* hath with the sun a double motion.
03 The first *Is* straight, and our diurnall friend,
04 The other *Hid*, and doth obliquely bend.
05 One life is wrapt *In* flesh, and tends to earth.
06 The other winds towards *Him* whose happie birth
07 Taught me to live here so, *That* still one eye
08 Should aim and shoot at that which *Is* on high:
09 Quitting with daily labour all *My* pleasure,
10 To gain at harvest an eternall *Treasure*.

The beginning "My words & thoughts" already draws attention to the poem itself and its "words." The deictic "this" which follows can be seen as a reference to the "notion" expressed in l.2, but also as another reference to the poem itself.[82]

The speaker stresses the concealment and seclusion of the second movement of life, which draws attention to its special status and thus serves to make it actually *more* apparent and less hidden. In contrast to the speakers' inability to see in "The Search" and "Thou hast made me," being "hidden" here has a different function, strengthening the union

---

81 The to-and-fro movement from line to line resembles the motion of ploughing a field (progressing from furrow to furrow). Furthermore, a diligent and thorough reading is a requisite for discovering the oblique line, which is also similar to the hard work and diligence required in ploughing a field. Cf. also *Piers Plowman*, where Piers provides a model of virtuous and dutiful service to God, which is reflected in his diligent and untiring ploughing of the fields and Donne's "To Mr Tilman after he had taken orders," which uses the addressee's name to state "Thou, whose diviner soule hath caus'd thee now / To put thy hand unto the holy Plough" (ll.1f.). Cf. also Bauer (1999, 222-24) on the notion of ploughing in "Coloss. 3.3."

82 Bauer (1999) points out the closeness of "notion" and "notation" (219, 229), which further emphasises the self-referential, deictic nature of the poem's opening line.

between speaker and God as well as the indivisibility of both paraphrases of the biblical quotation. The speaker's life is "hid" *in* God, that is, close to God to such an extent that it can no longer be seen. The speaker also emphasises his personal relation to God. Although he starts out with a general statement about man's life, from l.7 on, he uses first person singular to describe this general experience. This coincides with a change of focus from "Life" to Christ: "Him, whose happie birth / taught me."[83] Consequently, the speaker gives up "My pleasure," but also creates the impression of his own personal "eternall Treasure." In addition, he marks the poem as a personal statement by beginning with "My words & thoughts."

The speaker's journey through life is thus determined by two different movements. The premise of life's double movement is linked to space, where these two movements are linked to each other. Although the movements are explicitly described with "straight," "obliquely," "bend," "tends," and "winds," the poem's italicised text represents an overall movement that is at once "straight" and "obliquely ben[t]", visually "tend[ing] to earth" as well as towards the "eternall Treasure," and thus combining characteristics of both lives.[84] Moreover, the complete text as well as the diagonal line created through italics lead towards and converge at the end of the poem.[85] Both movements taken together lead to a new interpretation of "eternall Treasure": it is defined as "My Treasure,"

---

83   Song argues that both the "straight" and the "winding" motion "refer to a split or
       fallen existence" (115), and that there is a "third motion" which provides
       orientation:

       The pronoun "*Him*" does indeed point the reader "on high" to the antecedent ("*Christ*") in
       the epigraph. This third motion allows the reader to escape the trap of temporal splitting
       that anamorphic art usually lays for its viewer. By orienting attention "on high," "*Him*"
       points the rader outside the bounds of the text image to the more stable, authoritative ref-
       erent of the unidirectional epigraph. (115)

84   McMahon sees the whole poem as "a microcosm of both nature and scripture,"
       "mim[ing] the solar movements and the history of salvation to reveal Christ in
       both" (67).

85   Cf. Veith, 143:

       Formally, in mathematical language, a "double motion" is resolved by an oblique vector.
       Theologically, the conflict of sin and grace is resolved in Christ. The oblique motto [...]
       signifies the doctrine of imputation, whereby the believer, engrafted into Christ, received
       the benefit of His righteousness, while Christ takes upon Himself all of the believer's sins.
       [...] The text [...] resolves the two contradictory "lives," the one sinful, the other godly,
       in terms of the assurance of salvation.

and moreover "My Treasure" is further specified as "Him," that is, Christ. The poem as a whole is thus a reinterpretation and personalisation of the biblical quote stressing not only the speaker's trust in God (just as his life "wrapt In flesh" will invariably "tend […] to earth," that is, lead to death, his "other" life will "wind" towards Christ), but also their personal relationship and inseparable union.

7. Conclusion

As we have seen, "The Search" sets up a spatial framework and shows a progress through this imagined space – the speaker's pilgrimage through life – in order to talk about a mental and spiritual process, the speaker's inner change from spiritual separation and loneliness to a complete union with God. Central to this turn is the speaker's change of attitude and his development towards resigning himself to God's will (a turn from "my will" to "your will" and from aggression to acceptance). Once he has accepted that it is God's will which keeps God concealed, he is able to plead for and imagine God's turn towards him and their eventual union. Thus, like "Goodfriday, 1613" the poem presents a double turn: the speaker's turn is made possible through his change, while God's turn is present all the time but only visible to the speaker after he has changed. At the same time, the poem stresses the speaker's personal and emotional relationship to God: right from the beginning, love is shown as the basis of this relationship with "My Lord, my Love," and underlined through the use of sacred parody.

In "Thou hast made me," the same kind of movement can be found in a more condensed and abstract space, while in "Coloss. 3.3" a similar movement (the winding way through the poem towards the insight that Christ is there all through life *and* at the end) takes place within the written text. Yet in these poems, too, the speaker's central aim is the union with God: like "The Search," they are characterised by the mutuality of "two becoming one." In all three poems, the idea of a journey is essential in reaching God, not just as the journey through life and towards death and eternal life, but as a means of imagining and expressing spiritual advancement.

IV. The transforming power of language
in "The Canonization"

We learned the Whole of Love –
The Alphabet – the Words –
A Chapter – then the mighty Book –
Then – Revelation closed –

But in Each Other's eyes
An Ignorance beheld –
Diviner than the Childhood's –
And each to each, a Child –

Attempted to expound
What Neither – understood –
Alas, that Wisdom is so large –
And Truth – so manifold!
(Emily Dickinson, J568)

1. Turning as transformation

Donne's "The Canonization" serves as an example to illustrate turning as a process of transformation, that is, as one thing "turning into" something else. In the poem, two lovers are transformed through their love, and this transformation is performed through the language of the poem. The change in the lovers' status (and its preservation in poetry) also changes their position in the world. While they are at first treated with scorn, they gain recognition and admiration and become a "patterne" for the world. The poem, too, can be seen as undergoing a transformation: starting as a defence of the lovers' relationship, it turns into a hymn in praise of the lovers. "Prayer (I)," like "The Canonization," deals with language and the impossibility to put something divine into words – and as in "The Canonization" this is achieved nonetheless (to the extent to which it *can* be expressed in words) through the text of the poem – which becomes transformed from a mere list of definitions of prayer into a meaningful whole.

"The Canonization" stands out from the other poems analysed in this thesis, since it is primarily a secular love poem. But it nevertheless has much in common with them, for although God is not mentioned explicitly in the poem, this love is also depicted in religious terms – religious imagery abounds, the lovers are portrayed as saints, and their transformation is a "canonization." In turn, several of the sacred poems under consideration allude to traditions of secular love poetry.

The aspect of transformation is also present in all other notions of turning discussed so far. The speaker's conversion depicted in "Goodfriday, 1613" contains an element of transformation, since it implies not only a change in the convert's perspective but also in the spiritual condition of his soul. In "The Search," the speaker likewise becomes converted and transformed from being in a state full of doubt and despair to being in union with God. In "The Temper (I)," the speaker's stretching and contracting is described as "tuning of my breast, / To make the musick better," which shows how the speaker himself becomes changed. And in the last chapter, the analysis of "La Corona" will show a transformation that is even more abstract, as the speaker seemingly "returns" to his starting point (that is, the beginning of the cycle), but has been changed along the way. In "The Canonization," the transformation of the lovers comprises a change of identity or essence: they become one being and they become saints. Simultaneously, the lovers' transformation in "The Canonization" goes together with a spatial turning. The lovers are turning towards each other, they turn away from the world and towards heaven (and at the same time, towards poetry), while the world in the end turns towards the lovers. In all the poems discussed, the process of transformation serves to bring the speaker closer to God. In "The Canonization," this outcome is brought about by the lovers turning into each other, while at the same time they become saints and go to heaven.

2.   The transformation of the lovers in "The Canonization"

Accordingly, "The Canonization" contains several processes of transformation. Literally, two lovers are changed by their love: the two distinct people are turned into one being, and the two ordinary human lovers are turned into saints. The lovers' transformation then also has an effect on other people, whose attitude towards the lovers changes from severe criticism into admiring imitation (that is, they are turned from critics to admirers), so that the lovers, initially scorned by the world before their transformation, will become a pattern for humanity after and because of their transformation. Starting from a state in which one loving speaker seems powerless and defensive, the lovers' position thus changes into one of supreme power and admirability. This transforming process is described in the poem, for example, in its vocabulary (stressing that the lovers can be everything ("we are...") and "are made such by love"), in its metaphors (e.g., using the image of the reborn phoenix in talking about the lovers' transformation), or in the use of grammar (e.g., changing the speaker from "I" to "we").

Thus, the speaker's words carry a strong transformative power. This power can be seen both as performative (i.e., the lovers' transformation seems to come about through the speaker's utterances), and it can be seen on the basis of a *de re/de dicto* distinction (i.e., there is a difference between what the speaker says and would like to be true, and the actual state of his world). Before looking at these two approaches, it is necessary to consider the speaker as speaker of a poem, i.e. as fictional characters within a fictional text. That is, it must be taken as a basic premise that the poem presents a fictional "reality," in which the fictional speaker's statements are presented as "real." Within this fictional world, a reader must decide whether the speaker's statements are just wishful thinking or a description of what actually happens to them. With this premise in mind, the text of the poem can, to begin with, be regarded in the same way as nonfictional utterances.[1]

If we use J. L. Austin's distinction between constative and performative utterances (Austin 1-7), for the utterances within this fictional world, many statements in "The Canonization" can be read either as constatives, merely describing something, or as performatives, changing an existing state of affairs. Austin's uses as examples of performative utterances, among others, "I do (sc. take this woman to be my lawful wedded wife)" and "I name this ship the *Queen Elizabeth*" (5); in the first case, the uttering of the words makes the marriage come about, in the second case, their utterance results in the fact that the ship bears the name "Queen Elizabeth."

Several of the transformations found in "The Canonization" are attributed to "love": the speaker states, "We are [flies]," "We're tapers, too," "We two being one are it," "we die and rise the same," and he claims that they are "made such by love" and "prove mysterious by this love." But the speaker in "The Canonization" also claims that their "leg-

---

1   Cf. also Bauer and Beck (2014).

end will be fit for verse" – while this "legend" is already expressed in the verses of the poem – and that they "shall be" approved and "canonized" – while he provides this approval within the poem. The act of canonization is most obviously performative: an act performed through language and changing an existing state of affairs. Though the speaker avoids any clear statements about who canonizes them and how exactly they become saints ("by these hymns" seems to be the closest approximation to an explanation), they do seem to become canonized in the course of the po-em.[2]

Another way of understanding the speaker's utterances (especially stanzas three to five) is by regarding them as an indirect expression of the speaker's wishes (that is, neither a description of facts nor a performative speech act). Although the speaker does not mark his statements as "wishful thinking" (which would considerably diminish his authority as speaker of the poem), it is conspicuous that the relationship between the (non-speaking) addressee and the lovers (expressed only in the speaker's words) drastically changes in favour of the lovers. Moreover, since the poem is fictional, the lovers' transformation and future invocation can neither be proven nor refuted; its potential truthfulness relies solely on the speaker's statements. Thus, these statements can also be understood by looking at the relation between what they state and these statements' relation to truth, that is, as a discrepancy between *de re* and *de dicto*. A *de dicto* reading is based on what the speaker says (i.e., what he claims or wants; the statement is true in all possible worlds which conform to the speaker's wishes, and while the actual world may be one of these worlds, the utterance alone does not substantiate this), while a *de re* reading conforms to actual facts and is true in the actual world (cf. Blume, n.p.; Von Fintel and Heim 83-86).[3] *De dicto*, the speaker *states* that they will be turned into saints and invoked by others; whether this is true in the world

---

2   The fact that the canonization seems to happen casually and "along the way," so to speak, may be due to the fact that it is not authorized nor official (cf. also Austin (26), who stresses the necessity of a "conventional procedure in order for the action to be felicitous and valid). While the act of canonization is a performative act when performed by the pope, creating saints by pronouncing them to be saints, the lovers' self-pronouncement does of course not fulfil the necessary requirements.

3   NB that it has to be kept in mind that the "actual world" is here the fictional world of the poem.

of the poem, however, cannot be substantiated. Assuming a *de dicto* reading, the whole poem could be seen as a nonliteral, ironical speech (i.e., claiming something like "*if* you don't acknowledge our love, we will become saints" or even "*if* you don't acknowledge our love, you will cause us to become saints"). *De re*, the poem merely offers a description of how the two lovers may be turned into saints, without any proof of whether this will truly happen in their fictional world. Of course, both options may merge when the speaker's wishes or beliefs do conform to the actual state of their world, that is, when what they describe does take place in the fictional world. Yet the poem offers no possibility for verification; firstly, because the speaker is subjective and potentially unreliable (he only presents his own point of view), and secondly, because he describes a state after the lovers' death that has not yet occurred at the time of speaking and cannot be proven.

Since the poem is not explicit about the speaker's wishes and desires, or about his state of mind (he may as well simply be crazy and hallucinating, or sarcastic about his and his beloved's unlucky position, though the earnestness of his assertions makes the latter case unlikely) it is difficult, if not impossible, to separate descriptions from actions, and wishful thinking from valid prophecies.

Everything looks like a fact (though consisting only of the lovers' unproven claims), since the speaker refrains from showing his attitude towards his own statements. While the speaker appears agitated in the first stanza and still emotionally affected in the second stanza, the last three stanzas of the poem (that is, the ones in which the speaker does claim the lovers' miraculous transformation) are devoid of words indicating personal emotion or the speaker's stance towards what he describes (for example, verbs such as "wish," "hope," "believe," or adverbs of probability). Moreover, since the speaker makes a prediction for the future, he claims something that cannot be confirmed. The change of addressee in the last stanza and the introduction of direct speech also contribute to blurring the distinction between possible future states and mere opinions: in stanza five, the lovers purport to present what "all" will say in the future. Thus the poem's assertions change from claims made by the speaker to claims made by "all" (which are, in turn, attributed to "all" by the speaker: he claims that "all" will claim that the lovers will be admired, etc."). This makes it even more difficult to determine what may be factual within the poem and what may be wishful thinking.

2.1 Title and form

The title of the poem reflects the transformation and sanctification described in the poem. The morphological form of the word, "canoniza-tion," highlights the fact that this is an ongoing process.[4] In the first place, the title "Canonization" refers to the theological procedure of being acknowledged as a saint by the Pope (listed in the calendar of saints) and being venerated accordingly. Although the Anglican Church retained or reinstalled numerous saints (mostly during Elizabeth I's reign), the process of canonization was abolished with the Reformation and never revived (cf. Buchanan 79, 402-04), so that canonization (in this sense) remained a purely Catholic practice. The noun "canonization" is only used with regard to this procedure (*OED* "canonization, *n.*"). The use of "canonization" has two consequences for the lovers in the poem. Firstly, it means that the lovers do not commit heresy in claiming to be canonized and become saints – if there is no official practice of canonization, there is no offense in not adhering to the rules of official canonization.[5] At the same time the lack of official canonization implies that the lovers cannot *really* be canonized, precisely because this practice is not acknowledged in Anglicanism.[6]

---

4   The title is present in most but not all manuscripts (see Gardner 73); even if the title is not originally from Donne, the verb "canonize" comes up explicitly in l.36 (albeit then referring to the completed process).

5   Cf. in contrast, Marlowe's *Doctor Faustus*, where Valdes states, "Faustus, these books, thy wit, and our experience / Shall make all nations to canonise us." (I.i., ll.121f. A-Text). The subsequent plot of the play shows this statement to be an empty promise, whereas "The Canonization" does not go beyond the description (and thus leaves no room for opposition). Equally, Lucifer promises to Faustus, "thou shalt turn thyself into what shape thou wilt" (II.iii, l.162f., A-Text) without a true change taking place – Faustus's substance does not alter. Here, too, being canonised and changing shape is linked to literature ("these books" and "this book").

6   This is valid only if one presupposes a Protestant, Anglican context for the poem. If one were to assume that the lovers are Catholic (and the unknown addressee as well, since the addressee's criticism extends only to their love and they seem to be socially acceptable otherwise) the situation would be quite different: the speaker would commit heresy in claiming the lovers' own canonization. However, there is

As a verb, however, "canonize" can also refer to the inclusion of a text in the scriptural canon (*OED*, "canonize, *v*.5") and also to a non-scriptural literary canon.[7] For example, William Covell advises in "England to her Three Daughters" to "Take the course to canonize your owne writers, that not euery bald ballader to the preiudice of Art, may passe currant with a Poets name" (Covell 1595, Q2ᵛ).[8] The idea of a literary canon strongly resonates in the poem and is largely expressed in the fourth stanza, which debates where the lovers' love will be chronicled. Lastly, a canon is also a musical form (vocal or instrumental) characterised by the strict imitation of one part by all other parts. The notion of imitation is also prominent in "The Canonization": people will ask for a "patterne of [their] love" in the future (that is, the lovers will be imitated and followed by other people), which corresponds to an imitational pattern in the form of the poem: "love" recurs at the end of the first and last line of each stanza, thus framing each stanza and everything that happens in the poem.

"The Canonization" is tightly structured, and the numbers found in the poem's structure may well carry a symbolic meaning. For example, the five stanzas establish a meaningful pattern since the number five was a symbol of marriage and chaste love, often used in epithalamia and other poems dealing with marriage (Riemer 26). According to Riemer, the 45 lines of the poem may be an allusion to Valentine's Day, the 45th day of the year (30). The tenfold recurrence of "love" may indicate perfection (Riemer 29), while the eleventh mentioning of "love" in l.39 is seen by Riemer as a negative sign, possibly standing for transgression, pride and

---

no reason to assume that Donne wrote a poem about two Catholic lovers (containing no denominational conflicts at all) amidst his collection of love poetry.

7   Cf. two examples given in the *OED*, one from Covell's *Polimanteia* given below and one from Thomas Nashe's *Christ's Tears over Jerusalem*, "Canonizing such a multifarious Genealogie of Comments" (1593, in *OED* "canonize, *v*.5"). More generally, "to canonize" can also refer to an approval by the church (*OED*, "canonize, *v*.6").

8   Covell's *Polimanteia* (in the same volume) begins with a reflection on "Divinations lawfull and unlawful" (defining "Divination" as a "foretelling of things to come, performing it in divers manners, as well artificially as naturally," Covell 1595, Br), which is also an important topic underlying "The Canonization": are the lovers in "The Canonization" divinely inspired saints foreseeing God's will, or are they common lovers and, with regard to their sanctification, even impostors?

death (which are all possible symbolic meanings of the number 11, Riemer 29f.). In any case, the frequent repetition of "love" makes it the most frequently used and therefore most prominent word in the poem.

The third stanza is placed in the middle of the poem, and in this stanza the lovers' transformation takes place. The central line of the poem is line 23, which mentions the phoenix, a symbol of renewal and regeneration. Line 23 is a turning point at which the lovers' condition changes just like that of a phoenix when it dies: the lovers die and are reborn at the same time. The third stanza, and line 23 in particular, thus also serves as an axis of reflection within the poem. There is a contrast in attitude and perspective, as well as in the lovers' condition, between the first two stanzas and the last two: whereas stanzas one and two deal with the world rather than with the lovers and show a rejecting and disapproving audience, stanzas four and five focus on the lovers and the world's reverence for them.[9]

2.2 Stanza 1: the lover(s)' low position in the present

The poem begins in an aggressive and simultaneously defensive mood. Speech and language are emphasised right from the beginning of the first stanza with the order "hold your tongue." This command is contrasted not with "let me speak" (the speaker *is* already speaking, and in a tone that suffers no opposition) but with "let me love," which emphasises the most powerful force in the poem. The addressee is prompted to criticise anything about the speaker (his appearance, his state of health, his failed career) except his love, and to mind his own business and career. Though the first stanza does not say explicitly that the addressee was chiding the speaker's love, this is implied by the alternatives given to the addressee – other occasions for taking offense and other possible occupations –, and that they are alternatives is made explicit by the "or" in l.2.

> 01 For Godsake hold your tongue, and let me love,
> 02 Or chide my palsie, or my gout,
> 03 My five gray haires, or ruin'd fortune flout,

---

9   Riemer suggests two possibilities for grouping the stanzas, either combining the first and last, as well as the second and fourth stanzas, all united by the middle stanza; or combining stanzas one and two, as well as stanzas three, four and five (Riemer 27).

04 With wealth your state, your mind with Arts improve,
05 Take you a course, get you a place,
06 Observe his honour, or his grace,
07 And the Kings reall, or his stamped face
08 Contemplate; what you will, approve,
09 So you will let me love.

The speaker's stance towards the implied addressee is made clear. The speaker gives a direct (and rude) order to the audience ("hold your tongue") and shows his displeasure by using the expressive "for God-sake."[10] This stands in contrast to the speaker's apparent position in the world; he is ostensibly old (having – at least or maybe no more than – "five[11] gray haires" and sicknesses typical of old age), sickly (suffering from "palsie" and "gout"), and poor (of "ruin'd fortune"), while the addressee seems to have plenty of possibilities to advance in the world: he may pursue "wealth" and "Arts," aspire to a career either secular (observing "his honour") or ecclesiastic (observing "his grace"), and strive for political power (getting close enough to contemplate "the Kings reall [...] face" or for money (contemplating the King's "stamped face" on coins).

While the language of the first two stanzas seems fairly simple in comparison to stanzas three to five, it is not without problems. In the first place, the use of "you" in the first stanza is ambiguous: The speaker may be addressing one specific adversary, he may be speaking to a specific group or he may be generalising and not mean anyone in particular. He may even be speaking to himself, imagining possible criticism from other people and enacting a defensive dialogue in his mind (if so, the lovers' transformation and future fame may not even exist beyond the speaker's imagination); this would be very much in accordance with a *de dicto* reading of the speaker's statements as a wishful fantasy).

---

10 Cf. also Potts (2007), who sees expressives as having a powerful impact on a conversation, as well as a performative power by directly influencing communication.

11 Apart from structural numbering, references to numbers are found in l.3 („five") and in ll.15, 24, 25, and possibly 38 ("one" and "two," see below). Although "gray haires" is not a positive attribute, the fact that there are exactly five may be another hint at the "married" state of the speaker. It is also conspicuous that the speaker, in spite of separating his love from matters of health, money or career, is very much aware of his physical state.

The idiomatic "What you will" in l.9 is vague and leaves it open what is covered by the term. Thus, lines 8-9 accord an apparent liberty to the addressee: ""what you will, approve, / So you will let me love." On closer inspection, however, "what you will" is restricted to everything *but* the speaker's love – of which the addressee clearly does *not* approve – and which seems to be the addressee's sole criticism. The phrase foreshadows "what you will" in l.19, which again seems to give the addressee a choice, which turns out to be insignificant, since the lovers are *everything* (so that it does not matter *what* they are called by the addressee). The liberty expressed in the third stanza (albeit not really the addressee's liberty), shows the lovers' ability to change and be transformed by love. And ironically, if the lovers are "what you will" (as they turn out to be in l.19), the addressee will necessarily approve of the lovers *as a pair of lovers*, if he approves of "what you will" in the first stanza.

There are two instances where the phrase "what you will" is used prominently in plays, which bear a relation to the use in "The Canonization." It is part of the title of Shakespeare's *Twelfth Night, or What You Will*, which focuses heavily on role-playing and changing identities. And *What You Will* is also the title of a comedy by Marston, in which the phrase's potential to mean anything and everything is explicitly discussed. Thus, the play opens with a metadramatic "Induction" during which the question whether the play is "commedy, tragedy, pastorall, morall, nocturnal, or historie?" is answered with "Faith, perfectly, neither, but even What You Will, – a slight toye, lightly composed, to swiftly finish, ill plotted, worse written, I feare me worst acted, and indeed What You Will" and its author (i.e., Marston) is described as, "your friend the author, the composer, the What You Will, seemes so faire in his owne glasse, so straight in his owne measure" (Marston 222). Thus, if alluding to Marston, Donne's use of the phrase here may well be a metapoetical comment on the nature of the "The Canonization," which is a poem, presenting the lovers' "legend," and thus "verse" that immortalises the lovers, and at the same time a means of transforming the lovers and thus part of their canonization. Interesting here is also Marston's description of the author as "composer" and the play as "composed" – the notion of "what you will" finds a musical counterpart in the Quodlibet (see below), which also presents an amalgamation of different genres.[12]

If we look at the possible meaning of the auxiliary "will" separately, there are two potential meanings resonating in the poem. It could either indicate a statement about the addressee's wants, habits or inclination (i.e., a volitional, habitual or dispositional reading, cf. Kissine 2008), that is, it would in this case be synonymous with "approve what you want" or "approve what you always/usually approve." This, however, only superficially concedes any liberties to the addressee, who is actually not given an opportunity to voice his opinion and whose words are determined by the speaker of the poem. Another relevant meaning of "will" is its use as an auxiliary verb for making predictions about the future, so that the notion "it is a matter of fact that you will approve in the future" also lingers. The possibilities of reading "will" as an auxiliary indicating either volition/habit/disposition or future acts are continued in l.9 with "so you will let me love" (where "will" is no longer part of an idiomatic expression). In the case of a future prediction, l.9 would gain an almost prophetic quality and show a knowledge that is beyond human comprehension (anticipating the lovers' destiny to become saints). The "so" at the beginning of l.9 can accordingly be read in two different ways. Either it is simply a conjunction indicating a condition: "you can do whatever you want to do, as long as you leave me alone and let me love" (which is the more prominent reading). Or, if l.9 is understood as a prediction about the future, "so" can be understood adverbially as "in this manner" (again showing the speaker's foresight) or as "thus" (implying that the addressee will let the speaker love as a logical consequence of his approval).

The first stanza does not say much about love; instead, it offers the addressee alternatives to concerning himself with the speaker's love: beauty, health, finance, politics or arts. The first stanza also introduces a distinction between the speaker and the addressee, and between their actions: the speaker's activity consists in loving, while the addressee is ordered to pursue worldly activities. In balancing his private emotions with

---

12 Another parallel can be found in Marston's *Antonio and Mellida*, where the boy Julio is killed by Antonio, whom he adores, and dying, says to him "So you will love me, doe even what you will" (Marston 111). Here, the situation found in "The Canonization" is reversed: "what you will" is not contrasted to love, but intimately joined to it: loving is a condition for doing "what you will."

important affairs of state (taking courses and getting places that would allow the addressee to get close to officials and even the king), the speaker assigns an enormous importance to his feelings and his relationship to his lover.

Although the speaker presents himself as insignificant here, neither young, healthy, wealthy nor influential and only distinguished by a love that the addressee condemns, the speaker's defence of his love is built on a literary tradition that justifies the speaker's attitude and weakens the addressee's stance by presenting it as a wrong one. Robbins cites as a precedent for the speaker's defence of pursuing love instead of worldly affairs Ovid's *Amores* 1.15 (cf. Donne 2010, 148), where Ovid introduces a number of topics which also can be found in "The Canonization." The speaker of *Amores* 1.15 contrasts his occupation as a poet with the refusal to "pursue the dusty prizes of a soldier's life, nor learn garrulous legal lore, nor set my voice for common case in the ungrateful forum" (377, later completed with references to political and financial power), similar to the speaker's list of alternative occupations in "The Canonization" (though Ovid's speaker places less emphasis on the separateness of love and career). The speaker also stresses the immortality he will gain through his poetry:

> [M]y quest is glory through all the years, to be ever known in song throughout the earth. [... S]ong is untouched by death. Before song let monarchs and monarchs' triumphs yield – yield, too, the bounteous banks of Targus bearing gold! [...] It is the living that Envy feeds upon; after doom it stirs no more, when each man's fame guards him as he deserves. I, too, when the final fires have eaten up my frame, shall still live on, and the great part of me survive my death. (377-79)

The speaker names a reason, missing in "The Canonization," for the addressee's scorn in addressing the chapter to "biting Envy" (377). The speaker also thinks about a possible future follower of his poetry in hoping that he may "[...] often be perused by anxious lovers" (379); in their anxiety, these future lovers bear similarity to the imagined speakers in stanza 5 for whom love "now is rage" and who invoke the canonized lovers.

And in Horace's *Ode* 3.30, the speaker describes his poetry as a "monument more lasting than bronze and loftier than the Pyramids' royal pile," which will lead to his eternal glory: "I shall not altogether die, but a mighty part of me shall escape the death-goddess. On and on shall I grow, ever fresh with the glory of after time [...] rise high from low estate" (Horace 279, cf. Hunt 80). This concern with lasting monuments is also found in the fourth stanza of "The Canonization."

In alluding implicitly to Ovid and the tradition following him (the same topics are also found, for example, in Shakespeare's sonnets – see the discussion of stanza four below), the speaker achieves two things. Firstly, he consolidates his position as a lover by placing himself in a tradition that celebrates and supports such a love. Secondly, he merges the power of love and the power of poetry. The lovers in "The Canonization" are transformed into immortal saints through love – they "die and rise the same, and prove / Mysterious by this love." But they also become immortal in Ovid's sense, because their love is preserved and transmitted in poetry. Thus, the first stanza, rather than merely presenting a ranting and raging speaker out of control, alludes to a literary model which supports and justifies the lovers' stance and thus strengthens their position and reasoning against the opposing addressee.

All other stanzas contain literary allusions, too. While in the first stanza the reference to Ovid is most prominent, in the second, the speaker refers more or less explicitly to Petrarchan stereotypes, the third stanza builds on the emblem tradition, the fourth treats the *exegi monumentum* topic of achieving immortality through poetry (already hinted at in the first stanza) and the last stanza shows how the lovers are verbally "invoked" by posterity (as in a prayer). These allusions, however, raise the question of who makes them and at whom they are directed; there are arguments in favour of the speaker and in favour of Donne as author. On the one hand, literary allusions in the poem are more likely to take place on the level of author-reader communication: Donne as author was certainly familiar with Ovid's works, and his readers could be expected to be as well. On the other hand, the speaker explicitly mentions "we'll build in sonnets pretty rooms" in l.32 and is thus well aware of the literariness and poetic merit of his statements (though this does not necessarily entail that the speaker *writes* the sonnets in which their love will be accommodated). A communication about literature on the level of speaker and implied addressee would also assume an understanding on the part of the addressee, and there is no evidence either for or against such an understanding in the poem. The speaker of the poem does not overtly mention any of these traditions, nor is there any indication that the addressee would understand such a reference.

In any case, these literary allusions characterise the one who makes them as a highly literate person and potential poet. At the same time, Donne plays with literary traditions by modifying and adding to them: At the beginning of the poem, the speaker appears emotional and inconsiderate and his speech sounds like a spontaneous outburst.[13] As the poem continues, however, it turns out to be a carefully crafted and sophisticated work of art building on several literary traditions.

2.3 Stanza 2: the lovers and poetry – a refutation of secular love poetry

In the second stanza, the speaker explicitly picks up stock conceits of Petrarchan love poetry,[14] that is, from a poetic tradition which is based on unrequited or at least unfulfilled love. The speaker implicitly demarcates his own emotions from those described by other poets (who do indeed attach to their emotions the importance of floods, illness and death,[15] just

---

13 Especially in the first stanza, the speaker bears considerable similarity to a dramatic protagonist's possible defence against criticism and interference by others – the addressee provides the role of a blocking figure arguing against the speaker's love (such as, for example, Lord Capulet in *Romeo and Juliet*, Malvolio in *Twelfth Night* or Angelo in *Measure for Measure*, cf. also Frye 155-61), and the speaker vehemently defends himself and his chosen path of live, excessively exaggerating its value and the benefits it will bring him – though it is not clear whether the "defence" here takes place in front of the opponent.

14 Cf. for example, Petrarch's hyperbolic use of tears in *Canzoniere* 17, 23, 30, 55, 135, 189, 228, 237, his use of sighs in 17, 23, 189, 301, 359, his descriptions of feeling hot and cold in 24, 52, 135, 66, 182, 134, 220 and his depiction of love as war in 36, 72, 88, 104, 127, 149, 164, 220, 274. Some examples closer to Donne would be Wyatt's "My galley chargèd with forgetfulness," Shakespeare's sonnet #147 "My love is as a fever," Sidney's *Astrophil and Stella* #45 (l.8, "from that sea deriv'd, teare's spring did flow") and #100 "O teares, no teares, but raine, from beautie's skies" as well as Donne's "Air and Angels" ll.15-18.

15 L.11 also brings to mind Bassanio's desire in *The Merchant of Venice*: Bassanio's sighs do cause harm in making Antonio speculate, so that mayor damage is caused when Antonio's ships are consequently drowned.

as he separates his own business, love, from the businesses of others in stanzas 1 and 2.

> 10 Alas, alas, who's injur'd by my love?
> 11 What merchants ships have my sighs drown'd?
> 12 Who saies my teares have overflow'd his ground?
> 13 When did my colds a forward spring remove?
> 14 When did the heats which my veines fill
> 15 Adde one man to the plaguie Bill?
> 16 Soldiers finde warres, and Lawyers finde out still
> 17 Litigious men, which quarrels move,
> 18 Though she and I do love.

The speaker stresses the privacy of his feelings, which have no impact on the world: "soldiers finde warres and Lawyers finde out still litigious men [...] though she and I do love."[16] The present tense and the use of "still" imply that wars and quarrels are ongoing, no matter what the lovers do, and no matter whether the lover's relationship is unhappy or harmonious, it will not influence the world (at least not in the negative way described in the second stanza). The "finde" in l.16 is contrasted in stanza 3 with "We in us finde th'Eagle and the Dove": soldiers and lawyers will only find war and strife, while the lovers will be able to find other (and presumably more significant) things in each other.[17]

The rejection of Petrarchan conceits (which are linked to the unattainability of the beloved) corresponds to the reciprocated love found in "The

---

16   The opposite attitude can be found, e.g., in "The Sunne Rising":
>   She'is all States, and all Princes, I,
>   Nothing else is.
>   Princes doe but play us; compar'd to this,
>   All honor's mimique; All wealth alchimie.
>   Thou sunne art halfe as happy'as wee,
>   In that the world's contracted thus;
>   Thine age askes ease, and since thy duties bee
>   To warme the world, that's done in warming us.
>   Shine here to us, and thou art every where;
>   This bed thy center is, these walls thy spheare. (ll.21-30)

17   According to Ficino,
>   Mutual love offers security by overcoming danger, peace by driving off dissension and happiness by avoiding misery, for where there is mutual regard, there are no plots; everything is in common; there controversy, deceit, homicide, and strife cease. (*Commentary on Plato's* Symposium V. ix., Ficino 1944, 178)

Canonization," which is made explicit in l.18, "she and I do love." It is noteworthy that in the first stanza there is only a single speaker, who mentions his emotions but not his beloved. In the second stanza, the presence of the speaker's beloved shows that he is also loved, which makes his love free from sighs and tears, colds and heats, wars and quarrels (which are all descriptions of a Petrarchan lover's *unrequited* love). This harmonious relationship is then stressed further, since from stanza 3 onwards the plural is used by the speaker and both lovers even become one in l.24. Thus, once more a literary tradition is used to define the speaker's position, in this case by contrasting the disastrous effects upon the world claimed by disproportionate, unrequited (Petrarchan) love with his own relationship.

By using rhetorical questions, he leaves open what exactly he has been accused of, but through the use of these questions he makes it clear that he does not believe himself to be guilty of the implied accusations. By contrasting the positive emotions of requited love with major catastrophes (ostensibly caused by unrequited love), the speaker not only plays with a literary tradition, he also makes the addressee's allegations seem ridiculous.

As in the first stanza, the speaker appears to be engaged in a kind of dialogue with the addressee, and here too, the exact relation between them is left open, since the addressee does not answer. Either the speaker is the floor holder in this dialogue, and the addressee is simply not given an opportunity to take the floor (Finegan 2012), or the addressee chooses not to answer or not to listen to what the speaker has to say, or the addressee may not even be present, and the speaker talking to himself. The same occurs in the last stanza: although there seems to be a talking audience, all the words are provided and determined by the speaker of the poem.[18]

---

18 There remains the question in how far the poem can be seen as a discourse between the speaker and the imaginary audience. One the one hand, the speaker seems to expect a reply here (or fear a reply, since he tells the addressee to hold his tongue and uses rhetorical questions to which the addressee does not have to reply), on the other hand, the written form of the poem excludes statements that are not already part of the poem (and in addition each stanza is very much closed and confined by its rhyme scheme).

2.4 Stanza 3: the lovers' mystical transformation

While the first two stanzas merely describe an existing state (the position of the two lovers with regard to the rest of the world), the rest of the poem focuses on the lovers' transformation into saints, which effectually takes place in the third stanza (no matter whether this transformation is "real" in the world of the poem or whether it only takes place in the speaker's imagination, and whether it is effected by love or by the power of words – at the end of stanza three, the lovers "prove / Mysterious"). This becomes visible in the poem's language, and especially in the use of certain verbs.

19 Call us what you will, wee'are made such by love;
20 Call her one, mee another flye,
21 We'are Tapers too, and at our owne cost die,
22 And wee in us finde th'Eagle and the Dove;
23 The Phoenix ridle hath more wit
24 By us, we two being one, are it,
25 So, to one neutrall thing both sexes fit.
26 Wee dye and rise the same, and prove
27 Mysterious by this love.

"Made" is used three times, in l. 19, in l.38 and in l. 42, and in ll. 19 and 38, "love" is named as the agent behind this "making." Line 19 is set in the simple present, which leaves it open whether the process described happens at the moment of speaking (i.e. "wee'are made such" right now), or happens continually whenever they are called "what you will" (which would suggest that the addressee has some power over the lovers) or whether the lovers can simply be called "what you will" because they *are* already made such by love, having been transformed through the power of love (i.e. reading "wee'are made such" as resultative, suggesting that this making happened already and that love is the cause of whatever the lovers may be or become). This openness contributes to the timelessness of love's transforming power and of the lovers' transformation.[19]

---

19 Lines 37-38, in contrast, use simple past, clearly indicating that this "making process" happened in the past (with reference to the speakers in stanza 5), while in l.42, the auxiliary verb is missing, which leaves it open whether the lovers' eyes were made mirrors and spies at some point in the past or are made mirrors and spies at the moment of speaking. "So" at the beginning of l.42 indicates a logical

"Make" and later "build" in the fourth stanza indicate that something new is created and that there will be a certain outcome that did not exist before. Other verbs in stanzas three to five indicate not the making of something but the direction into which an existing entity goes: "Finde (in)," "prove," "extract" and "drove (into)." While these are linked to processes of transformation (that is, to finding or proving something new, and to the actions of extracting and driving into as part of a transformation) they largely place focus on movement: "Find in" and "drive into" show a movement inwards, while "extract" show an outwards movement.

In l.19, an important step towards the lovers' union takes place: "we" is used for the first time. Strictly speaking, there is still only one speaker (which speaks for a group, in this case "she and I"). Yet he speaks with maximum assurance, and as we never get an opposing voice from "she" – instead we get assertions of their unity and equality – the speaker's authority in speaking for "she" cannot be scrutinised or questioned (that is *de dicto*, the speaker uses "we," but *de re* we cannot know if he really has the authority to speak for the beloved). Also, if the two lovers really become "one," their voices become one as well.[20] The use of "we" thus stresses their unity and status of belonging together. At the same time, "we" also serves to mark a separation of the lovers from the condemning addressee, who is clearly not a part of this community (i.e., an exclusive use of "we").

At the beginning of the third stanza, the speaker changes his strategy. Instead of continuing to refute the addressee's negative stance, he incorporates it into his own line of argumentation, thus turning it into something positive. This also changes the way in which the speaker describes their love: the first two stanzas stress the irrelevance of the lovers' feelings for the addressee and the world, now it is shown that the lovers are special because of their love.

---

consequence, however, and implies that the action happens after extracting the "whole worlds soule."

20   Cf. also the lovers' union in "The Exstasie": "We, then, who are this new soul" (l.45) resulting in a "dialogue of one." (l.74).

"Call us what you will" (which reflects the "what you will" in 1.8)[21] may be read either as "call us what *you* want" (similar to Marston's invitation to the audience to call his play and its author "What You Will"), or as "Call us anything/everything." Thus, when the addressee is encouraged to "call us what you will" (and the lovers seem to become exactly that), the speaker seems to include the addressee in the process of transformation (the addressee can name something and it will happen). Yet actually the addressee would only do what the speaker wants – he should call the lovers "what you will" so that the speaker can prove the power of love in becoming "what you will." "Such" refers to "what you will," but since it is not made explicit what the lovers will be called, it is also left unclear what is meant by "such," and the process from *being called* something to *being* something is not explicated. The following lines then provide an illustration of l.19, "Call us what you will, wee'are made such by love."

Calling someone a fly is in the first instance a negative description implying that the lovers are commonplace and insignificant, perishable and powerless, and maybe even parasitic. However, by combining flies and tapers, the speaker uses both images to his own advantage in evoking the emblem tradition: moths which are fatally attracted by candles and die in their flames can be found repeatedly in emblems as an image for the dangers of love.[22] The fatal condition depicted in these emblems is turned round by the speaker – to die for love becomes attractive and desirable. In addition, the lovers are shown not only as the moths dying in the fire, but also as the candles holding power over the moths. Thus, the addressee effectually becomes powerless, since his potential criticism is made out to be not only an accurate description of the lovers' state but also a positive description of this state. And although the addressee is prompted to act (that is, to call the lovers what he will), he is not actively doing

---

21 Again, the additional meanings of "will" (volitional will and future will) resonate.

22 Of course, moths and candles also occur separately in other emblems, however their joint appearance is much more frequent. Cf., for example, an emblem with the motto "En ma joye douleur" in Scève's *Délie*, accompanied by several epigrams about unhappy lovers (Scève 127f.), and another one with the motto "Amoris ingenui tormentum," in Junius' *Emblemata*, with a Latin epigram about a doomed lover (Junius, Emblema XLIX, 55f.).

anything – the power to make the lovers "what you will" is the trans-
forming power of love.

By adding "and at our owne cost die," the speaker makes explicit two
important points: the lovers' sexual relationship (i.e., "die" as experienc-
ing orgasm, *OED* "die, v.[1]7.d") and their closeness to death. Bringing in
their sexual relationship and fulfilment has several implications for the
poem. Firstly, it characterises their relationship as something personal
and private, not to be shared with the world: "at our owne cost die" indi-
cates that they spend themselves, but the phrase also emphasises that they
do it "at our own." Secondly, it contributes to underline that their rela-
tionship is not a typically Petrarchan, unfulfilled one (a notion that is
already present in he refutation of Petrarchan imagery in the second stan-
za and the statement "she and I do love") – the fulfilment of this relation-
ship is also made clear in l.26, "Wee dye and rise the same" which shows
their shared and equal sexual experience. Thirdly, the ambiguity of "die"
emphasises their closeness to death and the afterlife (again, this becomes
even more obvious in l.26). Their sexual experience is at the same time a
spiritual experience, which ties in with the other religious allusions
spread through the poem.[23]

The statement "We are Tapers" creates a semantic mismatch, i.e., a
conflicting combination of two words which due to certain properties do
not normally permit a combination (such as "The ham sandwich wants to
pay" a combination of an inanimate item with an activity performed by
animate beings, cf. De Swart 575-81): tapers are inanimate, while the
speaker is clearly human (being animate and able to talk). It is implausi-
ble to reconsider the speaker to be an inhuman object. It is much more
plausible to read the phrase metaphorically and to reinterpret the verb
phrase "are tapers" to mean "are like tapers in a certain respect." Howev-
er, considering the mysterious and supernatural quality of the lovers'
transformation, the possibility of a "real" transformation into tapers also
persists.

---

23 Cf. again, "The Extasie" which features the same connection between a fulfilled
relationship and a spiritual experience (though it describes a mental rather than
physical union, it hints at their sexual union with "T'our bodies turn we, then"
(l.69), and also an explicit connection to death: "We like sepulchral statues lay"
(l.18).

The adverb "too" in 1.21 continues the paradoxical description of the lovers. It presupposes that the lovers are something else as well, and in the context of the poem and particularly the third stanza it most likely refers to the statement made in 1.20, "Call her one, mee another flye." This would imply that the lovers are not just called "flies" but *are* flies as well as tapers. As with "wee'are tapers" the mismatch between human lovers and inhuman flies is more easily understood when assuming a metaphorical reading of "flies": the lovers are *like* flies in a certain respect. However, as in 1.21, it is also possible that the lovers are effectively transformed into flies, just as they can be made tapers through the power of love.

The use of "too" creates an equal status of both descriptions: the lovers seem to be flies and tapers at the same time (a simultaneity which evokes the emblem tradition, and the image of a moth attracted by a candle's flames, while being just as mysterious and supernatural as their transformation into tapers or flies). The description of the lovers' state is further extended in l. 22 with "wee in us finde the Eagle and the Dove." In the first place the use of two plurals ("we" and "Eagle and Dove") results in an ambiguity. Either *each* of the lovers finds *both* eagle and dove (a distributive reading of the line, Lasersohn 2011), or *each* of the lovers finds *one* of the animals (a cumulative reading), or *both* lovers *together* find *both* animals *together* (a collective reading).[24] This ambiguity disappears if it is considered possible that the two lovers are really transformed into one person: if the two lovers are one, it does not matter who finds what, since the lovers are inseparable anyway and will inevitably find eagle and dove together – the three possible readings of the sentence would then be identical. It is also not clear what it means that they "find" birds in themselves or each other. In the context of ll.20-21, it could mean that the lovers are *like* eagle and dove in some way, but it could also mean that they *are* eagle and dove (just as they are flies and tapers). Thus, again, a metaphorical and a literal reading are available, the latter of which re-

---

24   In the distributive reading, it cannot be distinguished whether the birds found by one lover are the same as those found by the other (i.e., whether one finds $eagle_1$ and $dove_1$ and the other finds $eagle_2$ and $dove_2$, or whether each finds $eagle_1$ and $dove_1$). There also remains the possibility that "the'Eagle" and "the Dove" are generic, in which case the number of eagles and doves becomes irrelevant anyway.

quires the acceptance of the possibility that the lovers are really capable of transformation.

The next statement, "The phoenix riddle has more wit by us," is left unexplained but is in principle not an impossible claim. However, it is also underspecified: it is left open what exactly "having more wit" means here, *why* it has more wit, *for whom* it has more wit, and, most important-ly, the comparative "more" lacks a standard of comparison. The speaker may be drawing a comparison to an earlier state (i.e., the phoenix riddle could have more wit "than before" their transformation), or he may be comparing it to a certain entity (i.e., "the phoenix riddle has more wit than X"), or he may be comparing the riddle's significance to the signifi-cance it has by/through someone else, i.e., maybe, "the phoenix riddle has more wit by us than by others." Since "we two being one" offers a kind of explanation for the riddle's increased wit (that is, "the phoenix riddle has more wit, because we two are one"), a combination of the first and third possibilities is likely: "the phoenix riddle has more wit *now than before* our transformation, since it got more wit *through* our trans-formation" – for example, because the lovers' mysterious dying and ris-ing provides the "evidence" for the phoenix's mythical dying and rising.

The statement "we two being one" poses problems similar to those of lines 19-22. Once again, it could be understood metaphorically, meaning that the lovers are so much in accord with one another that they are like one person, or it could be understood literally: the two lovers are trans-formed into one person.[25] In stressing the process of "two becoming one," the speaker can also rely on biblical authority, as stated for exam-ple in Gen 2.13, "Therefore shall a man leave his father and his mother, and shall cleave unto his wife: and they shall be one flesh" and in Eph 5.28-31, which is a passage also quoted in the marriage ceremony:

> He that loveth his wife loveth himself: for no man ever yet hated his own flesh, but nourisheth and cherisheth it, even as the Lord the Church: for we are members of his body, of his flesh, and of his bones. For this cause shall a man leave his father and mother, and shall be joined unto his wife; and they two shall be one flesh.

---

25 At the beginning of the poem, the speaker is singular; at the end of stanza 2 both lovers are mentioned and from l-19 "we" is used. In L. 24, the number is reversed again: the two become one.

Ephesians goes on with stating, "This is a great mystery; but I speak concerning Christ and the Church. Nevertheless, let every one of you in particular so love his wife, even as himself" (5.32-33). While St. Paul restricts the "mystery" to the relationship between Christ and the church, in "The Canonization" it is clearly applied to the lovers and the power of love: "we prove mysterious by this love" (ll.26-27). Thus, the lovers' relationship (including their physical relationship) may be seen not only as rightful and ordained by God but also implicitly as a marriage surpassing that of other people and providing a "pattern" for posterity.[26]

What it means that the lovers are "it" in l.24 is difficult to determine, since there are several possible referents for "it." It could refer to the phoenix, the phoenix riddle, wit, the eagle, the dove or "one neutrall thing." The "phoenix riddle" seems the most likely referent, since it is the closest preceding subject that can be found in the immediate context (cf. Järvikivi 2005). No matter which referent is chosen for "it," the resulting statement will be problematic, since it creates a mismatch by again equating the human lovers with something that is not human (and maybe not even material). If "it" would indeed refer indeed to "riddle," the sentence would be less problematic, meaning, "we are a riddle," i.e., "we are hard to understand" or "our union is hard to understand" (the use of "riddle" for human beings is documented from 1663 onwards, see OED "riddle, n.[1] 4"). Difficulties of interpretation arise precisely because the poem does not give a precise reference for "it." There is even the possibility that "it" is a noun, that is, that the lovers, once male and female, become a neutral "it." Such a reading would be supported by l.25, "So, to one neutrall thing both sexes fit."[27]

---

26 "The Canonization" can also be seen as a reference to and a (very bold) justification of Donne's own marriage to Anne More and its condemnation by others (cf. also Haskin 1993). In this case, the "more" in l.23 may also be an allusion to Anne More's name.

   Labriola points out that

   Trinitarian unity is interpreted traditionally as an amorous relationship among the Divine Persons. St. Augustine, for example, describes the Holy Spirit as the breath of love uniting the Father and the Son, and St. Bernard makes the metaphor more pointedly amorous when he likens the Holy Spirit to "a true kiss that is common to the one who kisses and to the one who is kissed" (1973, 329)

27 Leimberg (2012/13) points out a similar use of "it" in The Merchant of Venice and Shakespeare's sonnet #116. Here, too, "it" is used to describe something that

Eagle, dove and phoenix all have multiple symbolic meanings to which the speaker may be alluding in choosing these particular animals. If so, however, it is not specified which of these meanings the speaker refers to. It has been suggested that the eagle and the dove stand for masculinity and femininity, while the phoenix is asexual, and there are many other poems providing precedents for the use of eagle, dove and phoenix in love poetry (see Donne 2010, 151-52).[28] However, most of them show no conclusive similarity to the depiction in "The Canonization."

Donne himself offers a parallel to the phoenix, in the "Epithalamion, or Marriage Song on the Lady Elizabeth and Count Palatine being married on St. Valentine's Day," written between 1612 and 1613 (Donne 2010, 627). Here, Donne indeed applies the image of the phoenix and of two becoming one to an approved and socially accepted marriage.[29] Bride and bridegroom are described as "two phoenixes whose joined breasts / Are unto one another mutual nests" (ll.23f.). Like the phoenix's death and rebirth, the couple's sexual union results in their merging into one being and in their "death" in a sexual sense, and it leads to regeneration through the children resulting from this union. This marriage is further described as restoring the natural state of things (reverting from the existence of two phoenixes back to one):

> And by this act of these two phoenixes
> Nature again restorèd is,

---

cannot easily be expressed in precise words (sadness, love, mercy), and to leave open various possibilities of how exactly these emotional states can be pinned down. Leimberg also points out that the use of "all-the-world" in sonnet #112 is similar to that of "it." The expression "all-the world" is reminiscent of "what you will" in l.8 and especially in l. 19 of "The Canonization," which is both vague and full of potential: "*All-the-world* is a likely definition of *it*; for what is there that is not denoted by *it*" (2012/13, 71).

28   There are also counterexamples to this claim: For example, Deut 32:11 talks of a female eagle ("As an eagle stirreth up her nest, fluttereth over her young, spreadeth abroad her wings, taketh them, beareth them on her wings"), and in Shakespeare's "The Phoenix and the Turtle" the turtle is male while the phoenix is female.

29   That Donne had "The Canonization" in mind when writing this Epithalamion is also suggested by the reference to Valentine's Day (though this day was specified by the date of the wedding, Donne makes it a recurrent theme of the poem), and the mention of a "taper" in l.19f.: "Thou mak'st a taper see / What the sun never saw [...]."

> For since these two are two no more,
> There's but one phoenix still, as was before. (ll.99-103)

In contrast to the relationship described in "The Canonization," this is not a love condemned by the world or successful only in death. The marriage described in the "Epithalamion" is essentially a human marriage; it does not lead to sainthood or eternal adoration but to procreation: "Where motion kindles such fires as shall give / Young phoenixes, and yet the old shall live" (ll.25f.).

Eagle, dove and phoenix are also meaningful in the context of alchemical procedures (and an alchemical process is also implied in the last stanza, which describes how the "whole world's soul" is "driven" into the "glasses" of the lover's eyes (i.e., a distillation process), so that their eyes contain the epitome or essence of the world).[30] Des Harnais even goes so far as to argue that the whole text of "The Canonization" follows the symbolical description of creating the philosopher's stone (167-229), as depicted, for example in *Rosarium Philosophorum* (an alchemical treatise published in 1593, which Des Harnais takes as a model description): as the union and merging of man and woman (representing a cosmic marriage of opposites) which results in a hermaphrodite (67-166). While limiting the transformation described in "The Canonization" to *just* an account of alchemical transformation seems too restrictive, alchemy does provide an important background for understanding the poem. Alchemy is concerned primarily with transformation, with turning one thing into another, and is therefore an important subject matter in "The Canonization." Moreover, one of the main motivations in the pursuit of alchemy is the creation of the philosopher's stone, that is, a mystical process of transformation resulting in a substance that is superior to all others.

Linden points out that, even when restricted to the field of alchemy, all three birds have multiple meanings, though in general the dove is most often seen as feminine and the eagle as male (1996, 175-76). He sees the image of the phoenix as an image of the emergence of something new and unified out of existing and mutually opposing entities (eagle and dove are seen by Linden as images of "two-ness"), which "must be re-

---

30 Donne widely used alchemical imagery in his poems (cf. Duncan 1942 and Mazzeo 1957), including his religious poetry (cf. Linden 1984) and even in his sermons (cf. Keller 1992).

placed by 'one-ness'" (179). He also points to the fact that "alchemists commonly depicted the interaction of the opposing principles involved in making the philosopher's stone as a form of coition that brought death to the individual partners but birth to the product of their union." (176).[31] Thus, while there is no one-to-one alchemical symbolic meaning of the animals, they (and also the image of two lovers becoming one) can in alchemical terms be seen as a general reference to the union of different substances and subsequent creation of a new substance.[32]

At the same time, all three animals are also Christian symbols: the phoenix symbolises the resurrection of Christ (Ferguson points out that "[i]n Early Christian art, the phoenix constantly appears on funeral stones, its particular meaning being the resurrection of the dead and the triumph of eternal life over death," Ferguson 23); the eagle can variously be a symbol of the resurrection or of Christ; and the dove is a symbol of the Holy Ghost (Ferguson 15, 17, 23).[33] As mentioned above, the phoenix image is placed exactly in the middle of the whole poem and of the third stanza, and thus in the middle of the description of a mysterious transformation.

All three animals also feature prominently in Shakespeare's "The Phoenix and the Turtle," where phoenix and turtle are lovers, while the

---

31 Paracelsus describes the creation of the philosopher's stone with the image of the "Alchemical Phoenix" (i.e., the philosopher's stone) being carried by the "Flying Eagle" (another alchemical substance, Sulphur of Cinnabar) to

> the nest of the parent, where it is nourished by the element of fire, and the young ones dig out its eyes: from whence there emerges a whiteness, divided in its sphere, into a sphere and life out of its own heart. (Paracelsus 1894, 40; cf. also Duncan 270)

Linden points out that the dove as alchemical symbol is often associated with whiteness (1996, 176), so that all three animals would be present in some way in this image. However, the relation between dove, eagle and phoenix is neither clear in Paracelsus' description, nor does it conform with the relation in "The Canonization," where eagle and dove do not seem to be joined to the phoenix image.

32 Cf. also Des Harnais:

> The alchemic model, with its triple phase of Conjunction, Putrefaction, and Congelation matches the "Phoenix riddle" in its stages: the perfect Union of the pair, their mingling as Ashes in the urn, and finally their exaltation as Saints converting the world. (217)

33 The Eagle and the Dove may also be seen as attributes of (religious) literary inspiration: The eagle is the attribute of St. John Evangelist, while the dove is an attribute of St. Gregory, said to have been sitting on his shoulder while he was writing (Ferguson 16-17). Cf. also the discussion of the use of bird imagery (and the dove in particular) in the next chapter.

eagle is mentioned as the "featherd king" (l. 11). Not only is this a poem about perfect love (seen as sacred and lamented in an "anthem" (l. 21), which then begins in l. 22), the idea that the two lovers are one, die together and become a model for posterity is also a central feature of Shakespeare's poem, and – considering the peculiar use of the three birds – a possible source for "The Canonization."[34]

"We die and rise the same" in l.26 is syntactically underspecified in several ways. Firstly, the point in time when the lovers' dying and rising takes place is not made clear. One would assume that they die first and rise afterwards just like the phoenix (if two events are joined by "and," there is a conversational implicature to the effect that a temporal sequence is implied, Levinson 98-99, 108), however, if ll.20-24 are taken

---

34   Cf. lines 25-48:

> So they lovd, as love in twain,
> Had the essence but in one,
> Two distincts, division none:
> Number there in love was slain.

> Hearts remote, yet not asunder;
> Distance, and no space was seen
> 'Twixt this Turtle and his queen; [...]

> Property was thus appalld
> That the self was not the same:
> Single natures, double name,
> Neither two nor one was calld [...]

> That [reason] cried 'How true a twain
> Seemeth this concordant one:
> Love hath reason, Reason none,
> If what parts can so remain.' (Shakespeare 2002)

Although there are some obvious parallels between "The Canonization" and "The Phoenix and the Turtle," there is very little research on Shakespeare's potential influence on Donne's poem. Sherman discusses the impact of "The Phoenix and the Turtle" on "The Extasie" but not on "The Canonization" (182). Bednarz writes that "Donne seems to be echoing" "The Phoenix and the Turtle" in "The Canonization" (121). Milward sees in Donne's way of writing about "an ideal love between two human beings" a reference to the Phoenix riddle similar to Shakespeare's (62). Bauer and Zirker (2013) note that "in 'The Phoenix and the Turtle,' the poem appears as a funereal site and as 'this urn' [...] (comparable to Donne's 'well-wrought urn' in 'The Canonization') in which a metamorphosis into the life of poetic rhythm takes place" (27). McCoy points out that the love of phoenix and turtle is described only in the past tense (195) – parallel to last stanza of "The Canonization," in which the already deceased lovers are inaccessible for the – finally approving – audience.

literally to depict a state transcending human imagination, a simultaneity of dying and rising could also be accepted. "The same" refers to the lovers' state either in comparison to an earlier state (i.e., their state is the same no matter whether they are dying or rising), or in comparison to each other (i.e., they are the same person, "one neutrall thing"). Whether they are "the same" after dying and rising, or just after rising, or even before dying, is left open. By leaving the reference for "the same" unclear, a merging of both states it is possible.

The images the speaker provides in the third stanza to characterise their love evoke the emblem tradition; the stanza offers a series of emblem-like metaphors that make reference to traditions of love poetry and also enrich the poem by hinting at visual (and partly religious) analogues. The speaker provides just one motif (in this case, an image described verbally – flies and tapers, eagle and dove, phoenix), with which the reader will then be able to associate additional information (in an emblem, by combining pictura, inscriptio/motto above the picture and subscriptio/epigram below the picture, see Schöne 18-19). A contemporary reader would be able to associate the image of taper and fly not only with death but also with love, and the image of the phoenix not only with renewal but also with the resurrection of Christ, which contributes to the religious significance and justification of the speaker's love.[35]

The use of the word "mysterious" contributes to the religious significance of their transformation. It comes from the Greek μυστήριον, which was used to talk about divine truths (*OED*, "mystery, *n.*"). "Mystery" also denotes the sacraments (especially in the plural, it was used with

---

35   For example, in Paradin's *Devises Heroiques* (1551), the burning phoenix is accompanied by the motto "Unica revivisco" ("I alone come back to life"), i.e., seen as a reference to Christ. There is also an emblem combining the phoenix with religious martyrdom. It shows the phoenix being consumed by fire, with the epigram

   On dit que le Phoenix vie en mort va reprendre:
   Si qu'un mesme bucher est sa vie & sa mort.
   Bourreaux, bruslez les Saincts: vain sera votre effort.
   Ceux qu'estaindre voulez renaissent de leur cendre. (De Bèze, Embleme VI)

   [One says that the phoenix in death will take up life again, so that one pyre is his life and his death. Executioners, burn the saints: your effort is in vain, those who you want to extinguish will be born again from the cinders.]

reference to the Eucharist,[36] that is, it is also linked to a process of trans-formation and union), and the word "mystery" was also used for important incidents in the life of Christ or of saints (*OED*, "mystery, *n*."). The adjective "mysterious" is used not only for things that are beyond human comprehension, but also for speech or language that is hard to understand or obscure (*OED*, "mysterious, *adj*."). Thus, the complexity of the third stanza reflects the mystery of the lovers' change from ordinary human beings to saints. Since their divine transformation is hard or impossible to understand by men, it is expressed in a way which is hard or impossible to disentangle and understand by readers. And although the speaker talks *about* their transformation in different ways, he does not describe the exact nature of this transformation.

What the lovers present in this and the following two stanzas is the kind of religion of love which is already at hand in the Song of Songs and the tradition of medieval courtly love and perpetuated from there to the Early Modern period – showing a strong connection romantic and even erotic love on the one hand and religious elements on the other. The use of this tradition in the poem is connected to the impossibility of relying on the actual religious significance of the lovers' relationship (so the speaker cannot be blamed for heresy), through the possibility that what the speaker states is *de re* just a case of irony. Instead, there is a reliance on poetry and established literary genres following the same tradition.

2.5 Stanza 4: the lovers and poetry – their preservation as saints

Whereas in the second stanza a connection between the speaker's love and stereotypes of love poetry was rejected, in the fourth stanza poetry is represented as the appropriate medium to record their love as saints. The statement that the lovers "can dye by it, if not live by love" at the beginning of the fourth stanza again contains a mismatch, since the combination of the preposition "by" with "love" is peculiar.

> 28 Wee can dye by it, if not live by love,
> 29 And if unfit for tombes or hearse
> 30 Our legend bee, it will be fit for verse;

---

36 Incidentally, McCoy, in talking about "The Phoenix and the Turtle," describes the two birds' love as "a blend of death and sexual consummation taking the form of a perfect communion" (195).

31 And if no peece of Chronicle wee prove,
32 We'll build in sonnets pretty roomes;
33 As well a well wrought urne becomes
34 The greatest ashes, as halfe-acre tombes,
35 And by these hymnes, all shall approve
36 Us Canoniz'd for Love.

In l.19 "by love" is also used, and it is clear there that "love" is the agent causing the lovers' transformation. In l. 28 however, "by love" seems to have a triple function. In the first place, it evokes the idiom "to live by bread" (compare, e.g., Matt. 4.4). Secondly, it evokes the phrase "to die by (i.e., through) something, which cannot logically be combined with "live" – however, as dying leads to rising (as the third stanza has shown), "we die by love" may be expanded to "we die and rise by love." Thirdly, it may be seen parallel to the expression "by the book," that is, "we take love as our rule and guideline, and if we cannot live this way, we can at least die this way."[37]

"Can" may be interpreted in different ways, depending on which modal base is attributed to it (i.e., whether it has a deontic, epistemic or circumstantial reading, expressing, respectively, a conformity with rules and laws, with available knowledge or evidence, or with facts, cf. Kratzer 639-40). It could mean "We are allowed to die, even if we are not allowed to live" (a deontic reading) or, "We have the physical ability to die, even if we don't have the ability to live" (a circumstantial reading) or, "We have the physical ability to die even if we are not allowed to live" (the last interpretation involves a change of the modal base from circumstantial to deontic). Thus it remains unclear why and by whom the lovers' death is caused. It seems plausible to assume that love is the reason (since the lovers can "dye by it"), but it is not specified why love should cause death. Due to the religious overtones of the poem and especially the third stanza, it seems likely to assume God or divine love as the agent behind the lovers' transformation, but the poem does not say so explicitly.

The fourth stanza deals mainly with where to record the lovers' love for posterity. Similar to the rhetorical questions in the second stanza, the

---

37   Cf. also Juliet's statement to Romeo, "You kiss by th'book." (*Romeo and Juliet*, I.5.110).

conditional "if" in ll. 29-32 does not answer the question whether their love will be fit for one thing or another, but it strongly suggests a possible answer. Tombs, hearse and chronicles are unlikely to prove fit for their legend, while verse, sonnets and hymns will be suitable. "Tombs" is almost homophonous with "tomes," thus suggesting a larger prose work, Renaissance hearses were decorated with heraldic devices, eulogies and short memorial inscriptions (cf. Gardner 1965, 204; Donne 2010, 153), and chronicles again suggest a prose work of history. Verse, sonnets and hymns, in contrast, are all forms of poetry.[38] Thus, the speaker stresses that their love will be recorded not just in literature generally, but in poetry (in contrast to a traditional saint's "legend," which we would expect to find in a history or chronicle), and at the same time he emphasises that poetry is indeed capable of recording their love for posterity (thus referring again to the *exegi monumentum* tradition initiated by Horace and already hinted at in the first stanza). Though the use of "will" in l.30 and l.32 is in the first place a consequence of the use of if-clauses in l. 29 and l.31, "will" also seems to refer to the future here (the if-clause expressing both a conditional state and a future state), since the whole stanza makes predictions about the future, strengthening the impression that the speaker has superhuman foresight.

The speaker states that they will "build in sonnets pretty roomes," and their legend is compared to a "well-wrought" urn. The use of "build" and "wrought" stresses the handiwork involved in "making" poetry – the speaker here uses the image of the poet as an artisan creating something, that is poetry in the sense of ποίησις, as a piece of crafted, fabricated artisanship.[39] That the lovers will "build in sonnets pretty roomes" means

---

38   In addition, "verse" refers not only to poetry in general but is also a liturgical term usually used for psalm verses (a synonym of "versicle," see *OED* "verse, *n*. 2." and "versicle, *n*. 1.a"). Thus, the statement that the lovers' legend will be "fit for verse" is a statement about the poetic quality of their story, but also about its suitability for liturgical use.

39   The reference to a "well-wrought urn" finds a parallel in the Sidney Psalter, in which "wrought" is used to describe material and artistic processes of creation. In Mary Sidney's translation of psalm 139, "wrought" is also used in a technical, artisanal way:

> Each inmost piece in me is thine:
>   While yet I in my mother dwelt,
>   All that me clad
>   From thee I had.

either that they build their own "pretty rooms" within sonnets (i.e., reading "pretty roomes" as object of "build"), a reading which suggests that the lovers participate in the making of sonnets, that is, in the activity of the poet.[40] Or l. 32 can be interpreted as "we will build *in* the pretty rooms of sonnets" (i.e., reading "build" without object), that is, "we will settle in the pretty rooms" (cf. *OED* "build, *v.* I.2.a"). In this sense, "build" can also mean "to construct nests," and may be seen as a reference to the birds in the third stanza.

Stanza 4 also makes a distinction between a small, interior and a vast, exterior space. "The Canonization" thus presents two alternatives: life in the world and life (quickly followed by death and eternal life) outside the world. Since this world is one of decay ("grey hairs"), poverty ("ruined fortune"), ambition (ll.4-7), pursuit of money ("his stamped face"), drowned ships, floods, bad weather, plagues, wars and quarrels, the alternative (not living in this world) seems much better. Thus, the proper alternative is an otherworldly life in verse, sonnets, hymns or canons – in forms of art that are, in the first place, small and self-confined (the lovers are made "one another's hermitage" and their love will be recorded only

---

> Thou in my frame hast strangely dealt;
> Needs in my praise thy works must shine
>   So inly them my thoughts have felt.
>
> Thou how my back was beam-wise laid
>   And raft'ring of my ribs dost know:
>   Know'st every point
>   Of bone and joint,
>   How to this whole these parts did grow,
> In brave embroid'ry fair arrayed,
>   Though wrought in shop both dark and low. [...] (ll.43-56)

Although "wrought" in l. 56 primarily refers to God's creation of man, in the context of this stanza and of the preceding stanza, it can also refer to the speaker's act of writing and creating the text he speaks (the indexical "these parts" can be understood as the speaker's body parts or as the parts of the poem). "Wrought in shop" evokes the image of an artisan's workshop (and in l. 55, more specifically, of a weaver's workshop, where tapestries are manually woven and embroidered on a "frame"). An allusion to the Sidney Psalter would stress the status of the lovers' legend as a literary work (pointing at its materiality as a "textured," tangible text and at the process of writing and "making" poetry), and at the same time legitimate its status as religious work (i.e. a saints' legend) through a connection to the biblical psalms.

40   "Build" can also be used to refer to the creation of a literary works (see *OED* "build, *v.* I. 4.a").

in "pretty roomes" (evoking the near-homophonous "petty" and thus pointing once more at the smallness of their refuge), and secondly, more preserving than a tomb (while the tomb preserves a dead body for a limited time till both body and tomb decay, poetry preserves the lovers forever).[41]

Since "The Canonization" is a poem meant to be read (and hymns always have a text), the lovers' love, confined within the poem, is transmitted to the reader along with their essential "legend." Thus, the poem provides guidance to the survivors and future generations in where to turn and what to strive for in life. The lovers' transforming love is not just confined within a private space but made public, and indeed, as public as possible – within the poem, by being a legend and pattern, without the poem, precisely by being confined within the poem and accessible to readers. Only in this way is it possible to become an example and pattern to the world. Yet at the same time the exact nature of their love remains "mysterious" and is not mentioned at all, only circumscribed with the help of comparisons and paradox (which may be another reason why it is more fit for poetry than for a monument).

The lovers locate themselves within a minimum of confined space, which nonetheless holds all that is essential to them. Seen musically, the lovers are embedded in a canon or hymns, seen from other arts, they are embedded in a sonnet or in an urn; in all cases, inside a structure larger than themselves, but actually small (sonnets, hymns, canons are all small and limited forms, and so is the reduction of a human body to ashes

---

41   Cf. also Shakespeare's sonnets, where the perpetuity of verse and the superiority of a verbal "monument" is also a prominent topic, for example, in #18 "When in eternall lines to time thou grow'st, / So long as men can breath or eyes can see, / So long liues this, and this giues life to thee" (ll.12-14); in #19 "Yet do thy worst, old time; despite thy wrong, / My love shall in my verse ever live young" (ll.13-14); in #55 "Not marble, nor the guilded monument, / Of Princes shall out-liue this powrefull rime" (ll.1-2); in #81:

Your monument shall be my gentle verse,
Which eyes not yet created shall o'er-read,
And tongues to be, your being shall rehearse,
When all the breathers of this world are dead,
You still shall liue (such vertue hath my Pen)
Where breath most breaths, euen in the mouths of men. (ll.9-14)

and in #107 "And thou in this shalt finde thy monument, / When tyrants crests and tombs of brasse are spent" (ll.13-14).

stored in an urn – and even a tomb is little compared to the rest of the world). The lovers' relationship is contained in sonnets, in urns, in hymns, that is, in small vessels. The outer world, in contrast, is vast (encompassing sea and land) but not desirable to the lovers (and, the way it is presented, not desirable to the reader either).

The speaker then goes on with "and by these hymnes, all shall approve / Us Canoniz'd for Love." The meaning of "by" is underspecified: either, the lovers will be approved (and later invoked) *because of* these hymns (that is, because their love has been transformed and immortalised through love poetry in general and this poem in particular), or they will simply be approved *by* the singing of these hymns (the hymns expressing an already existing adoration). And similar to "will" in l. 9, "shall" is ambiguous and could be either a prediction of future events ("shall" being an auxiliary verb), or a command to the addressee. In the latter case, "shall" would have a deontic quality (i.e., express rules or laws), and one gets the impression that the events described follow laws that cannot be circumvented and that the speaker here predicts and pronounces a divine law.[42] By switching from "will" to "shall," the deontic quality seems to become more prominent than before. "All" is underspecified, too: it is not stated who exactly will approve of the lovers, whether it is just the present addressee(s), lovers in the future or all humankind, and this underspecification adds to the obscure speaker situation in the last stanza.

What it means to be "canonized *for* love" is also left open. Since there needs to be a reason for canonizing someone, "for love" could be read adverbially as "because of love" (parallel to, e.g., "for our sins"). But "love" could also be the object of "canonized," meaning that they are canonized in the service of love. Love could even be personified here, i.e.

---

42   The adoration of the lovers after their death finds a parallel in "The Relic" (ll.19-
      22):
         All women shall adore us, and some men;
         And, since at such times, miracles are sought,
         I would that age were by this paper taught
         What miracles wee harmlesse lovers wrought.
      As in "The Canonization," the lovers are the ones who have "wrought" something
      (here, miracles; in "The Canonization," their own "legend"). While the
      transformation in "The Canonization" is described as "mysterious," this passage
      from "The Relic" stresses the lovers' saintly status in a similar vein by pointing out
      their "miracles."

meaning "canonized to serve (the god of) Love." But "for love" might also refer not to "canonized" but to "approve" – meaning that people's approval in the future may be caused by love, or may serve love.

The fourth stanza is full of musical allusions: the references to hymns and being "canoniz'd" in this stanza allude not only to poetry and speech but also to singing and music. These musical allusions give a justification to the lovers' behaviour, as a hymn is an approved form of worship; at the same time they show order and harmony: both hymns and canons usually follow strict rules (usually four-part-harmony in the first case, strict imitation in the second). This order is contrasted to the chaos of the world, which, even though the pursuit of art is mentioned in line 4, is depicted as neither harmonious nor orderly in the second stanza. The lovers' union and unity thus find a musical parallel in the idea of musical concord and harmony (which governs all musical forms alike).[43]

The lover's legend is described as potentially "fit" (l. 30) or "unfit" (l. 29) for some purposes. "Fit" can also refer to "a part or section of a poem or song; a canto" (OED, "fit/fytte, n.[1] 1.") or to "a strain of music, stave" (OED "fit/fytte, n.[1] 2.") and thus stresses both the poetical aspects (resulting in "sonnets") and the musical aspects (resulting in "hymnes") of the lovers' legend. In the context of the poem, both the use of "hymnes" and the allusion to "canon" are fitting, since both terms in different ways reflect the fact that the two lovers are both multiple and one: the canon unites separate, independent parts into one piece of music; in the hymn several interdependent parts come together to create harmony.[44]

---

43   Cf. also section 2 in the next chapter. In addition, the description of the lovers' union as becoming "the same" also suggests the musical notion of the unison.

44   One could see the "canon" as an embodiment of polyphonic music in contrast to "hymn" as a prototypical homophonic style. Morley, for example, distinguishes between (homophonic) plainsongs and hymns on the one hand, and canons and fugues on the other (103, 114, 179). While this suggests a distinction into homophonic sacred music and polyphonic secular music, Morley does not generally equate church music with plainsong and hymn and secular music with canons and fugues. The best example of this is the motet, which he explicitly characterises as a polyphonic "song made for the church" (179). Still, in spite of being a very orderly and fixed form, the polyphonic character of a "canon" obscures the meaning of its words, and thus a "canon" would not have qualified as proper church music according to the council of Trent, which had condemned polyphonic music on the basis that the words were not understandable

The line "call us what you will" hints at yet another musical form, the quodlibet (cf. *OED*, "quodlibet, *n*.").[45] This musical form, is in principle not perfectly harmonious, since it consists of taking (and if necessary adapting or changing) various melodies and putting them together to follow harmonic rules (*OED*, "quodlibet, *n*."). An allusion to the quodlibet conveys two similarities between the musical form and the lovers' love in "The Canonization." It shows the union of disparate forms in one form (that is, it merges two different entities, which through this merging become inseparable from each other), and it shows a mixture of secular and sacred songs on the one hand, and secular and sacred love on the other hand (just as the – originally profane – lovers become holy through their love).[46]

2.6 Stanza 5: the lovers' elevated position in the future

The fifth stanza continues the outlook on the future began in the fourth stanza. The speaker situation in the last stanza is a point of much controversy in analyses of the poem.[47] In particular, the poem is not clear about who speaks which lines, about who is addressed and about the point in time when these lines are spoken.

> 37 And thus invoke us; You whom reverend love
> 38 Made one anothers hermitage;
> 39 You, to whom love was peace, that now is rage;
> 40 Who did the whole worlds soule extract, and drove
> 41 Into the glasses of your eyes

(contentwise, too, the fact that it is a poem about a secular love relationship would also disqualify "The Canonization").

45   The term quodlibet is also used in the context of philosophical debates, where it refers to an "academic exercise in which a master would discuss questions on any subject, which could be posed by any member of the audience." (*OED*, "quodlibet, *n*., etymology"; cf. also Krones 533-36). This is also applicable to "The Canonization," where the universal nature of love is disputed by an addressee and defended by the speaker, and where love can be described with reference to any expression and any subject.

46   Music also features prominently in "The Phoenix and the Turtle": the swan providing the funeral music is described as a "priest in surplice white" (l.13), the lovers' praise in the poem is called a "requiem" (l.16) and an "anthem" (l.21) and the two birds are described as a "concordant one" (l.46).

47   See, e.g., Slater (2006).

42 So made such mirrors, and such spies
43 That they did all to you epitomize,
44 Countries, Townes, Courts: Beg from above
45 A patterne of your love!

Since the last stanza begins with "and," l. 37 seems to continue the sentence begun in the fourth stanza. The phrase "and thus invoke us" is elliptical and lacks the "shall" from l.35, "and thus all shall invoke us" – still, the double meaning of "shall" is carried on (even though the deontic meaning becomes stronger). The adverb "thus" is indexical and could refer either to "these hymnes" ("and thus, by singing these hymns"), or to everything following "thus invoke us," which would then be a form of direct speech – or to both, indicating that "these hymnes" consist in what is said in stanza five (cf. also *OED* "thus, adv. 1.d": "referring either to a preceding or a subsequent speech"). "Thus" also implies a logical consequence, hinting at the inevitability of their invocation by others.

Since there is a change of perspective in l.37 (the pronoun "you" in l. 38 now seems to refer to the lovers and the tense changes to past tense in ll. 38-43), it seems plausible to assume that "you whom reverend love..." introduces a new (imagined) speaker, who addresses the lovers and talks to them after their death (i.e., invoking them) – since they will be saints, they can be addressed and expected to listen even though they will be dead at the time of the utterance). The punctuation of the poem gives little evidence to support this view; there is some evidence, though, that a semicolon could be used as an equivalent of a colon in Early Modern English (Blake 22), which would strongly back up a reading in which "and thus invoke us" introduces a direct speech. Such a reading of the poem would mean that, in contrast to the first two stanzas, in which an addressee (who is present in the speaker's time) was not allowed to speak, the lovers' imagined future admirers now "speak." But the words are predicted and predetermined: this speech consists only in what the speaker of the poem puts in the audience's mouth.

The lovers' peaceful love is contrasted with a love "that now is rage." "Now" is indexical, it refers to the speaker's time of utterance (that is, at some point after the lovers' death and canonization), but does not specify this time. "Rage" carries multiple meanings ranging from anger and ferocity to madness and passion (including sexual passion and desire) to sorrow and grief (*OED*, "rage, *n*."). The depiction of love as "rage" reminds one of the calamities listed in the second stanza, which, too, refer to other people's emotions and not to the lovers. To say that love "now" (i.e. in the imagined future) is rage creates a distinction between the lovers' time and the imagined future speakers' time (though it is left open for how long love has been considered as "rage" by the imagined speakers) and thus establishes a further separation between the lovers and the world as well as providing a positive description of the relationship that was condemned in the first two stanzas.

The speaker goes on with stating that the "whole world's soule" is extracted by the lovers. "Who did …" is elliptical, but it is plausible to assume the lovers as subject, especially since "your eyes" are mentioned in l.41. Analogously, "drove" lacks both subject and object, but it is plausible to assume the lovers as subject and the world's soul as object, assuming an ellipsis in l.40, which should then read "drove it." The lovers were up to this point characterised by their love (and by their self-sufficient and reclusive attitude), which implies that they are not looking at "Countries, Townes, Courts," which consequently cannot be reflected in their eyes. Still, the question arises how the "whole world's soule" is connected to their love. It seems plausible to see "love" as the "world's soule" then (or as the essence of the world's soul), since love is the lovers' only defining feature.

"Glasses" in l.41 refers to the depiction of the lover's eyes as flasks or vials used in the distillation process and thus introduces the image of an alchemical procedure used for the refinement of substances (to "epitomize" expresses the same process), but it is also a synonym of "mirrors." Thus, glasses, mirrors and spies[48] all present the same image: the lover's eyes become a mirror in which to see the "whole world's soule," that is, most likely "love" (however, the lovers are dead at this point, and though they can be invoked, they cannot be seen – the only evidence or epitomi-

---

48   In the 17th century, there is no other use of "spies" apart from that referring to someone who (usually secretly) spies on other people (*OED*, "spy, *n*."), which makes little sense in combination with "mirrors." "Spies" as a shorter form of "spy-glasses" or "spying-glasses" (i.e., an instrument, which, like mirrors and eyes, is used to perceive things) seems a more plausible reading, however, "spy-glasses" is not documented before 1707 and "spying-glass" not before 1682, while for none of them "spy" is used as a shorter form.

zation of their love is the poem itself). Furthermore, mirror can also mean "model or example" (*OED*, "mirror, *n*.1.a") and thus be seen as a synonym of "patterne."[49]

"They" in l.43 refers to the lovers' eyes: they are shown as distillation glasses in l.40f., capable to extract and therefore also to epitomize and as mirrors in l.42, capable to reflect something. Thus l. 43 can be read as "Your eyes epitomized everything to you," i.e., you see everything essential in your own eyes." "All" may be an anticipating reference to "Countries, Towns, Courts" in the next line, which would then specify "all the world," from big spaces to small spaces, and from low states to the highest social state.

Alternatively, the sentence may end after "epitomize" in l.43. Where the imagined speech ends also has consequences for the interpretation of the last line. If it goes on till the end of the poem, the last two lines would still be addressed to the lovers (i.e., reading "Countries, Towns, Courts" as detailing "all" from l.43), which means that that lovers should "beg from above" (i.e., a higher or truer pattern than themselves). If the imagined speech ends after l.43, in the last two lines the lovers would call on "Countries, Towns, Courts" to "beg from above" (i.e., seeing the lovers as a pattern for posterity after their death). The punctuation in ll.43-44, especially the colon in the middle of l.44, leaves it open how the lines are to be read. There is evidence that a colon could be used as an "emphatic pause," a "stronger form of the comma in the 16th century (Simpson 67f.),[50] which supports a reading in which there is no break between

---

49   Wilson points out that Donne uses mirror imagery mainly in his love poetry, and often to indicate a love that goes beyond a merely physical relationship:

> The intimately reciprocal reflections of the lovers in each other's eyes are, for example, a spiritual representation of unity far transcending the physical union that binds them together. Yet those reflections are, at the same time, but the visible manifestation of a far greater spiritual truth – the ideal love that exists in the celestial spheres. (1969, 120)

50   Simpson cites a passage from *Coriolanus* (5.3.70-72) in which the phrase clearly needs to go on: "The God of Soldiers: / With the consent of supreme Jove, inform / Thy thoughts with nobleness [...]" (the colon after Soldiers in l.70 is found in the Folio edition, see Shakespeare 2000, 255). There is also evidence in other editions of "The Canonization" that a colon could be used to express a longer pause, that is, similarly to a comma (just as the semicolon could be used for this purpose). The 1635 and 1669 editions of Donne's poetry both have a colon at the end of l.36, i.e., "Us Canoniz'd for Love: / And thus invoke us [...]," while the "And" at the beginning of l.37 clearly shows a continuation of the phrase.

"Countries, Townes, Courts" and "beg from above." Such a reading would mean, however, that there is another change of speaker and addressee in the last two lines, that is, ll. 36-43 would present a speech imagined by the speaker and "spoken" *by* the lovers' future admirers, while ll. 44-45 would be spoken again by the speaker and *directed at* their future followers.

The mention of "Countries, Townes, Courts" brings to mind the different occupations listed in the first stanza as alternatives to criticising the speaker's love – now people strive to follow the lovers, and the lovers become a "patterne" for "Countries, Townes, Courts."[51] The word "pattern" is derived from "patron" (*OED*, "pattern, *n*. and *adj*."), and the lovers as saints offer a model to the world at the same time as (and because) they *are* patron saints.[52] But the use of "pattern" in a religious context also has biblical precedents. For example, in 1 Tim 1.16 the speaker states that he is still alive so that "in me first Jesus Christ might shew forth all longsuffering, for a pattern to them which should hereafter believe on him to life everlasting," and Christ is described as a pattern by Donne in a sermon, where he says, "Christ is thy *Idœa*, thy Pattern, thine Original" ("Sermon Preached at the Spittle, Upon Easter-Monday 1622, on II Cor 4.6," Donne, *Sermons* IV, no. 3, 99), as well as in "Eclogue 1613. December 26," which is also a marriage poem: "Kings (as their patterne, God)" (l.44).

At the end of the "Second Anniversary," Elizabeth Drury is likewise seen as a pattern for humankind. In contrast to "The Canonization," God is made explicit as the initiator of her transformation:

> Since his will is, that to posterity,
> Thou shouldst for life and death a pattern be,
> And that the world should notice have of this,
> The purpose, and th'autority is his;
> Thou art the proclamation, and I am
> The trumpet, at whose voice the people came. (ll. 523-28)

---

51   In Shakespeare's Sonnet 19, the youth is "beauty's pattern to succeeding man" (l.12) and in sonnet 98, the addressee is described as a pattern for beautiful flowers: "you pattern of all those" (l.12).

52   Cf. Bauer 2015b, 280-81.

As in "The Canonization," becoming a pattern is a verbal process: Elizabeth becomes a "proclamation" which the speaker then makes public through the text of the poem.

"The Canonization" provides in many respects a constellation similar to that found in *Romeo and Juliet*.[53] First, the relationship in "The Canonization" seems to be frowned upon by the outside world but rightful in itself. Both couples are contrasted to the hatred and strife found in the world, and both see their relationship as saintly and sanctioned by God. Romeo and Juliet are self-sufficient and detached from society (which criticises their love). And finally, both couples find their only lasting retreat in a grave, separated from a world where their love is not permitted, but in the end recognised as "reverend love" and a pattern to others.[54] In "The Canonization," however, the lovers' fate is not seen as tragic, because the lovers are transformed and the poem depicts not only their death but also their transformation and "rising" – all from the perspective of the contented lovers themselves or that of an admiring and revering, not lamenting, posterity.

3. The transformation of language in "Prayer (I)"

Herbert's "Prayer (I)" focuses not on the transformation of a speaker (the speaker stays entirely in the background), but on language *per se*. Whereas "The Canonization" presents primarily a transformation *in* and *through* language, "Prayer (I)" presents a transformation *of* language itself. The poem thus shows the transformative power of language to a

---

53 Siegel compares the relation between secular love and religion in *Romeo and Juliet* and argues that the conflict presented in Romeo and Juliet is based on older ideas (notably shown and summarised in Barnaby Googe's *Zodiac of Life* and Spenser's *Faerie Queene*), the main features of which are the following. Firstly, the idea that, since God's creation and love are all-encompassing, they include everything found on earth, hence physical love, too, is good and legitimate – also because it ensures propagation and continuity on earth (Siegel 383). Secondly, that there is a division between opposing forces in the world, concord and discord, or chaos and order, which are both ruled and held together by love, in Googe's case, in the form of Cupid, in Spenser's case in the form of Venus (Siegel 384-85). Googe also includes the notion that love unites and knits together, just as the two lovers in "The Canonization" become one through love.

54 In *Romeo and Juliet* V.iii, the raising of Juliet's and Romeo's statues "in pure gold" (l.299ff.) provides a pattern to posterity. Cf. also Bauer and Zirker (2013) for a similar comparison of "The Exstasie" and *Romeo and Juliet*.

much stronger degree. In this way, the poem is also more self-referential. While "The Canonization" contains references to speech, talking, calling, writing, literary forms, invoking, "Prayer (I)" is both less specific (offering just a list of statements) and more focussed (since it is only and exclusively about prayer): The title and first word indicate that the topic of the poem is "prayer," and the ending "something understood" is another (if not the most fundamental and basic) definition of "prayer" and simultaneously points at the whole poem itself as "something understood."

The poem offers a series of apparently unrelated statements, and which are then transformed into a collective definition of prayer with the conclusion "something understood" (apparently without other any means than listing these statements). At the same time, the speaker establishes a relation to God both through his definitional attempts to understand what prayer is and through the final "something understood": incomprehension is turned into comprehension and, moreover, into a mutual understanding that goes both ways, from the speaker to God and from God to the speaker.

```
01   Prayer the Churches banquet, Angels age,
02              Gods breath in man returning to his birth,
03              The soul in paraphrase, heart in pilgrimage,
04   The Christian plummet sounding heav'n and earth;

05   Engine against th' Almightie, sinners towre,
06              Reversed thunder, Christ-side-piercing spear,
07              The six-daies world transposing in an houre,
08   A kinde of tune, which all things heare and fear;

09   Softnesse, and peace, and joy, and love, and blisse,
10              Exalted Manna, gladnesse of the best,
11              Heaven in ordinarie, man well drest,
12   The milkie way, the bird of Paradise,

13              Church-bels beyond the starres heard, the souls
                                                      bloud,
14              The land of spices; something understood.
```

This final sense of mutual understanding is achieved mainly through the consistent use of syntactic underspecification. The speaker simply lists different metaphors or images but leaves it open whether they are definitions, depictions or paraphrases of prayer – only the explicit title and the first word reveal that these are statements about or related to prayer.[55] By offering multiple options to understand what prayer is instead of defining it in a single statement, the speaker suggests that such a simple definition is impossible. The whole poem thus presents a kind of periphrasis. More precisely, Herbert uses systrophe, which is essential for leaving open several options and for enabling their convergence in "something understood."

Systrophe is described in detail by Henry Peacham:

> Systrophe of some called Conglobatio, of other convolutio, and it is when the Orator bringeth in many definitions of one thing, yet not such definitions as do declare the substance of a thing by the general kind (*The Garden of Eloquence*, 1593, 153, cf. also Hegnauer 28)

Salomon Hegnauer, in analysing "Prayer," considers Peacham's description as the only precise definition of the term, elaborating it as "a strict chain of asyndetically juxtaposed metaphors that translate a given term of reference [without a predicative verb]" (Hegnauer 27). Among others, Peacham gives as illustration a quote from Cicero: "historie [...] is the testimony of times, the light of veritie, the maintenance of memorie, the schoolemistresse of life, and messenger of antiquitie" (153). In contrast to Peacham's examples (which all follow the pattern of this quotation), Herbert does not use an auxiliary verb to determine that prayer *is* "the Churches banquet," that it *is* "Angels age" etc. He just provides "Prayer" as the title of the poem and first word, and (continuing without any punctuation marks) leaves it open how exactly prayer is related to the metaphors provided – not specifying whether this means that prayer *is* everything listed, that is *is like* everything listed, that it *feels like* everything listed, that, for different people, it *feels like one* of the descriptions given, and so on. Through the use of systrophe, it is also left open how these metaphors are connected to each other. Thus, it remains undefined *what* exactly prayer is, and every reader of the poem is given a number of op-

---

55   Also, the poem can be seen in relation to "Prayer (II)," sharing the same title. "Prayer (II)" likewise is *about* prayer but at the same time constitutes a kind of prayer.

tions for how to think about prayer and may or may not relate to each of the images offered.[56]

The speaker lists a wide choice of images, comprising physical and immaterial ideas and ranging from very small and mundane aspects ("man well drest") to the universe ("the milkie way"). Thus, the poem encompasses notions from all spheres of human perception and imagination and gives "prayer" a universal and at the same time very personal quality. Still, the metaphors used are telling with regard to the speaker's relation to God, since they show certain conceptions of prayer.[57]

As prayer is usually spoken (and when not spoken, explicitly characterised as "silent prayer"),[58] images related to sound are important: the depiction of prayer comprises a "sounding" plummet, there is "thunder," a "kinde of tune" which all things "heare," there are "Church-bels beyond the starres heard," the final something "understood" and even "Gods breath in man" can be seen as an allusion to sound production. "A kinde of tune" explicitly characterises prayer as music and brings in the notion of tuning discussed in the next chapter (prayer can easily be seen as a "kind of tuning"). There are also several references to food – "banquet", "manna," literally, the "milkie" way and the land of "spices" – which may serve to show the strengthening and invigorating force of prayer, but may also be seen as an allusion to the Eucharist and an eventual union of the praying speaker and God (the Eucharist is also reflected in the "souls bloud").[59]

---

56 Wilcox (Herbert 2007, 176) point out that the use of systrophe is common in mystical writing. Cf. also Greenwood, who points out the influence of Spanish Baroque poetry in the use of systrophe and cites a passage from St. John of the Cross, where systrophe is also used to convey a mystical experience (29-30).

57 Pruss argues that
    the overall metaphorical pattern of this poem resembles a spiral. While each quatrain present movement in four directions – upward, downward, inward, and outward – each stanza winds more closely towards the individual soul [...] In the final two words Herbert moves us from the temporal world to the eternal, and in this dramatic moment we enter the world of stillness. (22)

58 Harvey argues that the last phrase "functions as a coda and a volta simultaneously" and that it leads the poem from spoken prayer to the tradition of silent prayer; this is a tradition Harvey associates with Byzantine prayer in particular, where prayer is regarded as a sacrament (2013/14, 131).

59 Cf. also the ending of Herbert's "Love (III)": "You must sit down, sayes Love, and taste my meat: / So I did sit and eat," which also constitutes the ending of "The Church" and thus of the main part of The Temple.

It is emphasised that prayer is an emotional matter[60] that moves the soul and the heart: "The soul in paraphrase, heart in pilgrimage." Many images show the forceful and aggressive attitude of a speaker who feels that his prayers go unheard and unanswered: prayer is also depicted as an "Engine against th' Almightie" and a "sinners towre," "thunder" is dangerous, the "spear" harmful, "fear" is a negative emotion and "bloud" not always a positive sign. These notions (and the emotions they are associated with) are contrasted with the positive emotions caused by prayer: "Softnesse, and peace, and joy, and love, and blisse." Line 9 provides the only use of polysyndeton in the poem, which makes it all the more prominent. Most of the negative descriptions appear in the second quartet (the "souls bloud" is not a distinctly bad or good image) and are immediately followed and thus weakened by the abundance of positive descriptions in l.9.

While some of the descriptions (for example, the references to sound and food) are quite sensual, other images show prayer as something intangible and abstract. "A kinde of tune" and "something" are very general and vague descriptions, and prayer belongs to heart and soul, and is thus invisible and ungraspable, though linked to emotion. Prayer is usually voiced and expressed through language, however, and the sphere of heaven, the stars, the angels and God is brought closer to the speaker by including it in his description of prayer. Prayer can be both public and private, and the poem contains both aspects. On the one hand, prayer belongs to the (individual) soul and heart, on the other hand, prayer is an act of public worship involving "the Churches banquet," "Church-bels beyond the starres heard" and a "kinde of tune, which all things heare and fear." "Heaven in ordinarie," too can be read as an allusion to public worship and service in church. "Ordinarie" refers not only to an ordinary thing or person" (*OED*, "ordinary, *n.* III.15.a"), but also to an ecclesiastical person with power of jurisdiction in ecclesiastical cases, such as a bishop or archbishop (*OED*, "ordinary, *n.* I.1.a"). "Ordinarie" may also refer to the book prescribing the order and form of service (*OED*, "ordi-

---

60   Murphy argues that the poem embodies "private ejaculation" (in contrast to poems following more conventional forms), and bridges the gap between writing poetry and experiences that can never be fully expressed in words or written down (31-32).

nary, *n*. II.10."), which hints at prayer as a written form of communication. This sense of prayer as written communication is also present in yet another meaning of "ordinarie," namely, "a courier conveying dispatches or letters at regular intervals, freq. between different countries; (hence) post, mail." (*OED*, "ordinary, *n*. I.4").

The way towards which prayer is directed is made clear: there are references to "Angels," the plummet sounding "heav'n," "thunder," "exalted manna," "Heaven in ordinarie," the "milkie way, the bird of "Paradise" and the "Church-bels beyond the starres heard" all point at a location above the speaker, that is, heaven. The mention of the "bird of Paradise" and the "land of spices" further characterise this location as an unknown, exotic yet desirable place. While these expressions also show the distance to God, this distance is not seen as insurmountable. Several of the phrases used express a sense of permeability, creating the feeling that God can indeed be reached by the speaker: "the soul in paraphrase, heart in pilgrimage" and the "world transposing in an houre" show a movement and potential change that allows to approach God and anticipates the final turn of prayer into "something understood" – *para*phrase and *trans*posing explicitly contain the notion of change and transformation. Even the "Christ-side-piercing spear" reaches God in a very physical sense.[61]

What is more, some images contain the idea of reciprocity and "return" to a previous state, hinting at an existing connection to God and thus providing a basis for successful communication. "Gods breath in man returning to its birth" suggests the restoration of a previous state and the return or prayer to its "proper" place, while "heaven in ordinarie," too, shows the notion of something divine expressed in ordinary words as well as joining heaven and the "ordinarie" (heaven is already contained in "ordinarie"). The plummet sounds both "heav'n and earth," thus joining them. Manna falls down to earth but is at the same time "exalted," again expressing a double movement, just like "reversed thunder," which makes this doubleness explicit. Both "a kind of tune, which all things heare and fear" and "Church-bels beyond the starres heard" are inclusive and describe what can be heard by men as well as by God. These images

---

61   Cf. also the image of the spear in "The Search" and other of Herbert's poems, where it is likewise used as a means of communicating with God.

show also a vertical movement, from God down to man and from man up to God.

The different images presented in the poem do not follow a specific order, and the speaker is careful not to show a development and to keep the openness created through the use of systrophe. The sonnet form contributes to hold the various (largely unrelated) metaphors together and at the same time creates the expectation of a turn, some kind of summarising or contrasting statement, towards the end. This turn is given (though not where it might be expected, after line 8 or line 12) at the very end of the poem, in the second part of the last line. Its placement at the end of the poem, together with the sonnet form, gives "something understood" the character of a summary. In contrast to all previous descriptions, "something understood" is the only phrase without a noun describing some more or less specific idea or situation related to prayer. Because of its vagueness, "something understood" can summarise and gather in itself all other descriptions of prayer.

The construction "something understood" is ambiguous and does not specify *who* has understood something, whether man has understood something of God, or whether God has understood something of man. Also, both "understood" and "something" are ambiguous in themselves. "Something" may refer to a verbal statement that has been understood (i.e., heard and processed) or to something more abstract and immaterial that has been understood about the other or about each other. "Understood" may refer to a verbal message that has been "heard" and correctly processed by the hearer or to a circumstance or notion that has been "comprehended" or "grasped." In addition, it could also refer to something that is "understood" between two parties, that is "agreed upon," (*OED*, "understood, *adj.* 3") so that it is not necessary to state it explicitly, a reading which would stress the mutuality of prayer. In the context of the poem, "understanding" means successful communication (even if it does not refer to the transmission of a specific message), since prayer is always a form of communication.[62] Thus, without giving any precise

---

62 Cf. also Hammond 42. Hammond even sees "under-stood" as an English equivalent to the Latin "substantia" ("substance"), that is, as the essence and substance of something, and in this case prayer as the essence of life (42). Hammond also sees in the last phrase a description of prayer as "something which man stands under, his one protection in the world" (42).

definitions of "prayer," or of a praying person's relationship to God, the poem ends in a reassuring way by emphasising that prayer is "something understood" and therefore in some way successful. Simultaneously, the poem itself becomes "something understood," as the different unconnected phrases suddenly make sense through the ending of the poem. While systrophe provides primarily a way of circumscribing something, the poem is transformed from a mere enumeration of statements into a definition of "prayer" (or even into a prayer). This happens through the poem's form (the title marks it as "Prayer (I)" and the sonnet form provides unity), and through the poem's ending with "something understood," which as a whole is also ambiguous and may be read as part of the systrophe or (like the word "prayer" in l.1) as a summary and essence of the whole poem.

4. Conclusion

Both poems analysed show how one thing is turned into another through the power of language: In the first, two lovers are turned from mortal lovers into saints, in the second, a list of statements is turned into an understanding of prayer. In "The Canonization," the lovers are turned into saints "by love" but also by the language used. The poem offers several interpretative alternatives, and depending on the reading chosen, a reader is presented with a mere description of the lovers' states or with an active process of transformation which happens in the poem and through the poem. The speaker achieves this change by a number of strategies. Firstly, he uses the performative power of his statements for describing and simultaneously effecting his and his beloved's transformation from lovers to saints. As a consequence this also changes the audience's attitude towards them. In "Prayer (I)," language is used to effect a transformation from a simple listing of unconnected phrases to a definition and understanding of prayer, which simultaneously creates a sense of communication with God.

V. Turning and Tuning in Herbert's "The Temper (I)"

They leave us with the Infinite,
But He – is not a man –
His fingers are the size of fists –
His fists, the size of men –

And whom he foundeth, with his Arm
As Himmaleh, shall stand –
Gibraltar's Everlasting Shoe
Poised lightly on his Hand,

So trust him, Comrade –
You for you, and I, for you and me
Eternity is ample,
And quick enough, if true.
(Emily Dickinson, J350)

1. Turning and music

Three things are important when considering the relation between both concepts. Firstly, it is noticeable that there is a strong relation between the notion of turning and musical tuning. This argument will be illustrated presently. Secondly, it is conspicuous that ideas and terms relating to "real," instrumental or vocal music are often used to portray the concept of harmony and tuning in a more abstract sense (which is also what happens in the poems discussed in this chapter). The development of this connection will be traced in section 1.1. Thirdly, there is also a strong link between music and poetry (relevant here, because musical tuning is treated and shown within poetry – the speaker of a poem is tuned and turned within the text of the poem). This will be examined in section 1.2.

The notion of turning is inextricably linked to music, and to the musical notion of tuning. Turning generates music and harmony: according to classical and medieval notions, the circular turning of the planets leads to the music of the spheres, string instruments are tuned by turning a peg and a change in pitch implies an upwards or downwards movement of sound. Concurrently, tuning creates a change, a turn from untuned to tuned, from discord and dissonance to harmony and concord. Thus, at their most basic level, both turning and tuning depend on movement, either spatial (i.e., literal),[1] or metaphorical: music is created through

---

1   Thus movement is literally present, e.g., in the oscillation of chords, the flowing of channelled air or the beating of an elastic surface, and transmitted through movement (through the air to the ear). Musical composition also depends on

movement; turning is only possible through movement. Equally important is the fact that turning and tuning share a need for orientation: the question of where to turn, and a standard to which something or someone is tuned (such as a fixed pitch or the pitch of another instrument) are central aspects of turning and tuning.

This simultaneous turning-as-tuning (or tuning-as-turning) takes place on an individual level, in the tuning of a single instrument, and it also takes place within a larger, even universal context: the music of the spheres comes into existence through interdependent movement, and the interaction of musicians requires a common pitch (it also necessitates a turning towards each other and a listening to each other). In a metaphorical sense, too, this correlation can be found on an individual, private level (in the tuning or tempering of an individual human being), and a broader, public one: the integration of an individual into a larger group (such as, in a religious context, a whole congregation) requires an adherence to shared standards, according to which the whole community is tuned.

There is some evidence for the conceptual closeness of turning and tuning in the spelling variants found in Donne's "Goodfriday, 1613" (either "tune all spheares" or "turne all spheres" in l.22, cf. chapter 2), and in Herbert's "The Search ("I tun'd another [sigh] into a grone" or, in the 1656 edition, "I turned another [sigh] into a grone" in l.21f., cf. chapter 3). In these examples, it can be seen that *both* readings equally make sense and that they can even be used interchangeably.

Herbert's "The Temper (I)" will be used as an example to explore how musical imagery is employed in generating turning and to show how closely related (and correlated) both concepts are. In this poem, the speaker feels out of balance; he is either downcast or overly excited (that is, either too high or too low), but never in the "right" mood and complains about his condition, for which he holds God responsible. The speaker finds a way to describe his emotional states by recurring to various metaphors related to space and music. Only by accepting his varying emotional states as willed by God, and by resigning himself to God, is he

---

movement: intervals and consonances are created by notes going up and down, i.e., vertical movement; rhythm is defined by different and changing durations; melodies and harmony are created by the interaction of both. Written music is read from left to right, creating a movement across the page (in the same way that words on a page can only be read dynamically).

able to reinterpret them as a prerequisite for salvation willed by God and a sign of God's attention (instead of a lack of the same). He actively chooses to consider his torment as a musical tuning instead of a torture, that is, he chooses an image with positive connotations and thus pictures for himself a way out of his misery and towards salvation. This reinterpretation enables the speaker to turn away from his discomforts to focus on his personal relation to God, which he is now able to perceive as positive and reciprocal. This change of attitude also leads to the perceived cancellation of all difference (which is a state the speaker prefers even to the elevation he sometimes feels): whether the speaker feels high or low does not matter anymore, as long as he feels connected to God.

While in "The Temper (I)," the speaker's emphasis is on his emotional state, on *feeling* in or out of tune and in need of tempering till he can accept his state, in Donne's "Hymne to God my God, in my sicknesse," notions of turning and tuning are combined in a mental exercise, which the speaker goes through in order to prepare and "tune" himself for his death. Both poems show different stages in the same struggle for accepting God's will: At the beginning of "The Temper (I)," the speaker does not yet accept his inner turmoil as God-given and seeks another way out, while the speaker of "Hymne to God," aware of his inevitable condition and expecting his imminent death, interprets his state in the only way allowing him to keep up his hopes. In addition, "The Temper (I)" is more straightforwardly about music, while "Hymne to God" uses the fields of geography and illness to the same extent; this is why the relation between turning and tuning will first be illustrated on the basis of Herbert's poem.

1.1 Turning, tuning and movement: man as a musical instrument

The central premise underlying "The Temper (I)" and "Hymne to God" is that man *can* be tuned similarly to a musical instrument. This is based on the notion of a universal harmony, reflected on a smaller scale in the world and in human beings. The idea of universal harmony comes from Pythagoras (cf. James 20-40), and was taken up and preserved by Plato, who imagined a construction of the cosmos based on musical proportions, and the construction of body and soul as an imitation of the order and harmony of this cosmos (cf. *Timaeus* 60-75, James 41-59).

Boethius expanded this idea within a Christian context. In *De Institutione Musica*, Boethius distinguishes three kinds of music, relating everything in existence to music: cosmic music (*musica mundana*), the music of the spheres and of the world (governing, for example, the combination of elements or the changing seasons), human music (*musica humana*), the harmony of the human body and soul, and the music belonging to instruments (*musica instrumentalis*) (Boethius 9-10).

Through Ficino's *Commentary* on Plato's *Timaeus*, the idea of a connection between musical harmony and the harmony of the human soul was spread through Europe during the Renaissance,[2] as Ficino saw a connection between music and soul based on motion and thus a strong influence of music on the soul (an influence which the other senses do not have, since they lack the element of motion):[3]

> Musical consonance occurs in the element which is the mean of all [i.e., the air, Walker 9] and reaches the ears through motion, spherical motion: so that it is not surprising that it should be fitting to the soul, which is both the mean of things, and the origin of circular motion. In addition, musical sound, more than anything else perceived by the senses, conveys, as if animated, the emotions and thoughts of the singer's or player's soul to the listeners' souls; thus it preeminently corresponds with the soul. [...] [M]usical sound by the movement of the air moves the body: by purified air it excites

---

2 Finney argues that "[f]or two centuries this Ficinian formula – musical sound by movement of the air moves the body and spirits – was used by many philosophers and scientists to explain a variety of musical effects" (139).

3 John Davies' "Orchestra" (1596) provides a good illustration of this connection between large-scale harmonic and musical principles and spatial movement. It depicts this interplay as dancing and thus as an action that is defined through its combination of music and spatial movement:

   The turning vault of heaven formed was:
   Whose starrie wheeles he hath so made to passe,
   As that their movings doe a musick frame,
   And they themselves, still daunce unto the same (st.19, Davies 1975, 95)

   This "daunce" is performed by the spheres, but also by men, in imitation of the planets' movement, thus characterising it as a universal harmonic principle, which also (in Davies' account) presupposes order and measure. The imitation of heavenly motion on earth comes from Love (st. 96, Davies 1975, 115); love teaches men to dance and in this way makes them imitate the motion of the spheres. Although the speaker refers mostly to earthly Love, it is also described as "sacred" (st.111, Davies 1975, 119).

the aerial spirit which is the bond of body and soul: by emotion it affects the senses and at the same time the soul: by meaning it works on the mind: finally, by the very movement of the subtle air it penetrates strongly: by its contemperation it flows smoothly: by the conformity of its quality it floods us with a wonderful pleasure: by its nature, both spiritual and material, it at once seizes, and claims as its own, man in his entirety. (Opera Omnia, Basel 1576, 1453, translation Walker 1958, 8f.)

Ficino presents the soul's responsiveness to music as a reason for the soul's inner consonance. Thus, while he does not mention it explicitly here, he assumes an outer principle of harmony that is mirrored within the soul. Kepler later picked up Plato's idea of universal harmony again, and even tried to depict planetary motions as musical scales and intervals (Kepler 431-48, cf. also Finney 37), thus spreading and perpetuating the idea of spherical harmony.[4] The conception of the music of the spheres, and of a corresponding harmony in man, serves to explain the choice of metaphor in both "The Temper" and "Hymne to God." While the speakers in "The Temper" and "Hymne to God" are not moved or changed *by* music, they become *like* a musical instrument and are tuned due to their souls' likeness to music.[5]

Being in tune is essential to achieve harmony and concord with other voices and instruments. In the same way, the speaker of a poem seeks

---

4   The notion of the music of the spheres was well-established in poetry even before Donne. Philip Sidney, for example, mentions the "the planet-like music of Poetry" (2002, 117), thereby linking the idea of planetary music and universal harmony to poetry. Cf. also Shakespeare's sonnet #8, where music is described as marriage, which in turn serves as a model for the addressee:

   If the true concord of well-tunèd sounds,
   By unions married, do offend thine ear,
   They do but sweetly chide thee, who confounds
   In singleness the parts that thou shouldst bear.
   Mark how one string, sweet husband to another,
   Strikes each in each by mutual ordering,
   Resembling sire and child, and happy mother,
   Who all in one, one pleasing note do sing:
     Whose speechless song, being many, seeming one,
     Sings this to thee: "Thou single wilt prove none." (ll.5-14)

5   Boethius already includes this idea, when he writes, "For what unites the incorporeal nature of reason with the body if not a certain harmony and, as it were, careful tuning of low and high pitches as though producing one consonance?" (Boethius 10).

harmony and concord with God or a beloved. The notion of concord is also one of unity, as concord is created by being in tune and sounding together. It stands in contrast to discord (which musically means either being out of tune, or not playing together).[6]

Davies relates the harmony of the body to that of the soul (which should "tune the body"). In *Microcosmos*, he writes,

> And yet the *body's* but the *Instrument*
> Whereon the *soule* doth play what she doth please;
> But if the *stringes* thereof doe not content,
> The *harmony* doth but the *soule* displease;
> Then tune the *body Soule*, or playing cease. (Davies 1603, 60f.)

It is quite telling that Davies calls this poem *Microcosmos*, which assumes the existence of a larger macrocosmos comprising heaven and earth, whose workings are reflected in man, that is, the tuning and attunement of body and soul finds a correspondence in the tuning and attunement of the cosmos: the external harmony of the world is mirrored in the harmony of the human body and soul.[7] In his sermons, Donne makes this

---

6   However, discord is not entirely negative; it can be seen as a path towards concord, as, for example, described by Francis Bacon: "Is not the precept of a musician, to fall from a discord or harsh accord upon a concord or sweet accord, alike true in affection?" (Bacon 134). With regard to the use of "sweet," Richard Hooker describes David as "adding unto poetry melody in public prayer, melody both vocal and instrumental, for the raising up of men's hearts, and the sweetening of their affections towards God" (169). Hollander points out that "[…] in the sixteenth century, "sweet" also means "well-tuned," and argues that Hooker implies here that the singing of prayers will "tune" or "temper" the affections or feelings of the singers." (Hollander 253, cf. also *OED*, "sweet, *adj*. and *adv*. A.4.a"). This meaning of "sweet" can also be seen in the compounds "sweet-tuned" and "sweet-tempered" (*OED*, "sweet, *adj*. and *adv*."). Wilcox points out the extensive use of "sweet" in *The Temple* (Herbert 2007, xliv-xlv), to "convey the intense experience of God" with "the full range of meanings from sensual pleasure and artistic beauty to moral virtuousness and redemptive love" (xliv).

7   Davies also makes explicit that while God commands everything, men are required to "know and doe":

> The *Heau'ns*, and *Earth*, and all the *Elements*,
> (And what besides *Man*, is of them compos'd)
> Doo GOD obey in his *commandements*,
> For, as *Hee* wils, so are they al dispos'd;
> Yet never he himselfe to them disclos'd;
> Then not from *knowlegde* their obedience springs,

relation explicit in several instances. For example, by pointing out, when he writes about the world before the fall (which then gets out of tune) that, "God made this whole world in such an uniformity, such a correspondency, such a concinnity of parts, as that it was an Instrument, perfectly in tune." ("Lent-Sermon Preached at White-hall, February 12, 1618, on Ezek 33.32," Donne, *Sermons* II, no. 7, 170). About the place of man in this world, he writes, "Is the world a great and harmonious Organ, where all parts are play'd, and all play parts; and must thou only sit idle and hear it?" ("Sermon Preached at Pauls Cross, 24 March 1616, on Prov 22.11," Donne, *Sermons* I, no. 3, 207). He also brings spatial turning and musical tuning together: God's providence during humanity's journey is "to Tune us, to Compose and give us a Harmonie and Concord of affections, in all perturbations and passions, and discords in the passages of this life" ("Sermon upon the XX. Verse of the V. Chapter of the Booke of Judges, Preached at the Crosse the 15th of September 1622," Donne, *Sermons* IV, no. 7, 180).

The numerical proportions found in music also lend themselves to a comparison with symbolic uses of numbers and proportions. In *The Schoole of Musicke* (1603), Thomas Robinson, by interpreting tonal and harmonic proportions accordingly, creates an analogy between musical harmony and the relation between God and man:

> [...] hee [the musician] must read the scriptures, for it is the fountaine of all knowledge, & it teacheth the divine harmonie of the soule of man: for Musicke is none other then a perfect harmonie, whose divinitie is seene in the perfectnesse of his proportions, as, his unison showeth the unitie [...] his third, [...] the Trinitie, his fift, [...] representeth the perfection of that most perfect number of five, which made the perfect atonement, betweene God and man; His eight [...] representeth his *Alpha* and *Omega*; & as what is above his eight is but as a repetition, as from his unison, as it were a new beginning; so it sheweth our returne from whence we came. (Robinson, n.p.)

But from the *nature* in their *kinds* inclos'd;
Yet *Men* he made to know and doe the things
That be of *him*, which *grace* and *Knowledge* bringes. (Davies 1603, 44f.)

By stressing the "perfect atonement, betweene God and man" and "our returne from whence we came," Robinson characterises harmony as a way of thinking about spiritual "(re)turning" and salvation.

The instruments most frequently used for metaphorical comparisons to the human soul or body are the organ and the lute or lyre. The organ, because of its name, allows for an association with human organs, as well as with the human voice as "organ of speech" (instrument and voice also share their mode of producing sound from a flow of air directed through a pipe). The lute or lyre produces music with the help of strings or chords, and "chord" (in an old spelling also "cord," see *OED* "cord, *n*.1") suggests a relation to Latin cor/cordis – the heart (as does the word "concord," which comes from Latin "con" (together) plus "cor" (heart), cf. *OED*, "concord, *n*.") – an etymology which emphasises the connection between musical and spiritual harmony: the heart was also compared to an instrument with strings or chords, which could be "tuned." Wind instruments in general, by making use of the human breath, were be used for comparisons with human beings.

Furthermore, the crucifixion was also seen in analogy to musical tuning and Christ's body was compared to a psaltery, lyre or harp by Augustine (2001, 117-18) and Cassiodorus (43-44), based on their exegesis of psalm 57.8, "Awake up, my glory; awake, psaltery and harp," which provides the basis for seeing the crucifixion as a tuning of Christ's body.[8] This is important for "The Temper" as well as for "Hymne to God," since in both poems, the speakers hint at their own painful tuning as an imitation of the crucifixion.[9]

---

8   Cf. also Sutherland 196 and Pickering 285-301. Herbert explicitly takes up this
     idea in "Easter" (cf. also Tuve 1952, 144-45 and Fiddes 373-74):
          Awake, my lute, and struggle for thy part
                         With all thy art.
          The crosse taught all wood to resound his name,
                         Who bore the same.
          His stretched sinews taught all strings, what key
          Is best to celebrate this most high day. (ll.7-12)

9   Cf. Steele (71-74) and Tuve (1952, 144-45), who see the speaker's stretching and
     contracting as an allusion to the crucifixion and therefore as an imitation of Christ.
     Westerweel argues that l.23 picks up a tradition popular in emblem books, the
     "tuning of the heart," which is placed in relation to the Passion (1984, 101-106);
     such an allusion thus supports the depiction of the speaker's suffering as an
     imitation of Christ's suffering.

1.2 Music and poetry: the poet as God's instrument and musician

If man can be compared to an instrument played by God, the god-pleasing poet can be seen as God's mouthpiece, uttering only what has been inspired by God.[10] This notion is important for the two poems discussed, because in both cases the speaker shows himself as God's instrument, while he is at the same time the speaker of a poem, whose concerns about his spiritual welfare ostensibly provide the cause for the poem's existence. Moreover, each of these poems makes an implicit statement about what (religious) poetry should be, as the speakers' concerns are presented in the form of well-written and accomplished poetry.

Plato already points out the "higher purpose" of musical harmony – under which he subsumes speech as well – as "restoring [the Soul] to order and concord:

> And harmony, which has motions akin to the revolutions of the Soul within us, was given by the Muses to him who makes intelligent use of the Muses, not as an aid to irrational pleasure, as is now supposed, but as an auxiliary to the inner revolution of the Soul, when it has lost its harmony, to assist in restoring it to order and concord with itself (*Timaeus* 109)

Clement of Alexandria placed this notion in a Christian context:

> "Praise Him on the Psaltery"; for the tongue is the psaltery of the Lord. "And praise Him on the lyre." By the lyre is meant the mouth struck by the Spirit, as it were by a plectrum. [...] "Praise Him on the chords (strings) and organ." Our body He calls an organ, and its nerves are the strings, by which it has received harmonious tension, and when struck by the Spirit, it gives forth human voices. ("The Instructor," 216; book II, chap. IV)

Not only does Clement put music and poetry on the same level by combining tongue and psaltery, lyre and mouth, he characterises those who praise God as "struck by the Spirit," like an instrument is struck by a musician.

---

10   On divine inspiration and its reflection in a poet's work, discussed in this paragraph, see also Niefer (2017), especially the chapters on Wither's *A Preparation to the Psalter* and on the *Sidney Psalter*.

Similarly, Puttenham calls poets "the first philosophers ethic and the first artificial [i.e., artistic] musicians" (99), attributing to them not only music but also the power to move people towards "good manners" and "call the people together by admiration to a plausible and virtuous conversation" (99).[11] Philip Sidney, too, in his *Apology for Poetry*, combines poetry and music in his description of the psalms, stressing the status of the psalms as "divine poem" and "heavenly poesy":

> And may not I presume a little further, to show the reasonableness of this word *vates*, and say that the holy David's Psalms are a divine poem? If I do, I shall not do it without the testimony of great learned men, both ancient and modern. But even the name psalms will speak for me, which, being interpreted, is nothing but songs; then, that it is fully written in metre, as all learned hebricians agree, although the rules be not yet fully found; lastly and principally, his handling his prophecy, which is merely poetical. For what else is the awaking his musical instruments, the often and free changing of persons, his notable *prosopopoeias*, when he maketh you, as it were, see God coming in His majesty, his telling of the beasts' joyfulness, and hills leaping, but a heavenly poesy, wherein almost he showeth himself a passionate lover of that unspeakable and everlasting beauty to be seen by the eyes of the mind, only cleared by faith? (2002, 84)

Sidney argues that the psalms, because they are poetical, move people towards God.[12] In a similar vein, Donne praises the Sidneys' translation of the psalms (and the psalms themselves) precisely because they combine music and text:

> A Brother and a Sister, made by thee
> The Organ, where thou art the Harmony [...]
> Make all this All, three Quires, heaven, earth, and sphears;
> The first, Heaven, hath a song, but no man heares,

---

11 This seems to contradict his statement that the sounds of poetry are less exquisite than those made by "artificial music." It does make sense, however, if one bears in mind that Puttenham here refers to Greek musicians who were also poets, like Orpheus.

12 Sidney also notes the improving influence of poetry in general:

> Truly, I have known men, that even with reading *Amadis de Gaule*, which, God knoweth, wanteth much of a perfect poesy, have found their hearts moved to the exercise of courtesy, liberality, and especially courage. (2002, 95)

> The Spheares have Musick, but they have no tongue,
> Their harmony is rather danc'd than sung;
> But our third Quire, to which the first gives eare,
> (For, Angels learne by what the Church does here)
> This Quire hath all. (ll.15-29)
> […] may
> These their sweet learned labours, all the way
> Be as our tuning, that, when hence we part,
> We may fall in with them, and sing our part. (ll. 53-56)

The title of Donne's collection "Songs and Sonnets" also shows a link between both kinds of art. Each word unites in itself music and language. A "Song" is of course a piece of music, but it is also distinguished by having a (lyrical) text to be sung. A "Sonnet" is in the first place a poem, but the word goes back to the Italian "sonetto" coming from "suono," "sound" (*OED*, "sonnet, *n*.1"). In addition, French sonnets were frequently set to music in 17th-century France, creating another tie between text and music. The title is not originally from Donne but from the editor of the second edition (1635) of Donne's poems (Gardner xlvii). Nevertheless, it shows that the connection was a matter of course in the minds of lettered people at Donne's time.[13]

According to Renaissance theorists, the qualities that distinguish good poetry are comparable to the qualities of well-composed music. Samuel Daniel, for example, writes, "English verse then hath number, measure, and harmonie in the best porportion of Musicke" (*A Defence of Rhyme*), and George Puttenham states that "poesy is a skill to speak and write harmonically; and verses or rhyme be a kind of musical utterance, by reason of a certain congruity in sounds pleasing, though not perchance so exquisitely as the harmonical concents of the artificial music" (154), and that the poet "by his measures and concords of sundry proportions doth counterfait the harmonical tunes of the vocal and instrumental musics."

---

13   This connection can also be found in the use of the word "poetic." In the 16th century, the expression "musica poetica" was used to refer to the process of composing a piece of music and was found as the title of theories of theoretical works on music and composition. Here, "poetical" does not refer to writing poetry, but quite generally to something "relating to artistic creation or composition" (*OED*, "poetic, *adj*. and *n*. 6"), i.e., to the Greek concept of "poiesis," artistic creation or making. Cf. also Sidney's *Apology*, where he stresses the notion of the poet as maker (2002, 84-86).

(174). Thomas Campion says, "The world is made by Symmetry and proportion, and is in that respect compared to Musick, and Musick to Poetry. [...] What musick can there be where there is no proportion obserued?" (*Observations in the Art of English Poesie*). In these examples, the *tertium comparationis* between music and poetry lies in the ordered and proportioned nature of both, and in the harmony and symmetry that can be present in both.[14]

Order was linked both to virtue, and to well-written poetry (and to well-composed music). The virtue of order is pointed out, for example, by Donne in a sermon:

> God hath ordered all things in measure, and number, and waight; *Let all things be done decently and in order: for God, is the God of order, and not of confusion.* [...] There is no order in the Author of sin; and therfore the God of order cannot, directly nor indirectly, positively nor consecutively, be the Author of sin. There is no order in sin it selfe. The nature, the definition of sin, is disorder. ("Sermon Preached upon Whitsunday, on John 16.8-11," Donne, *Sermons* VII, no. 8, 229-30)

In the same sermon, Donne explicitly links discord to sinfulness and harmony to God:

> When a naturall man comes to be displeased with his own actions, and to discerne sin in them, though his natural faculties be the Instruments in these actions, yet the Holy Ghost sets this Instrument in tune, and makes all that is musique and harmony in the faculties of this naturall man (222)
>
> So they disordered God's purpose; and when they had once broke that chaine, when they had once put that harmony out of tune, then came in disorder, discord, confusion, and that is sin. (230-31)

In "The Temper," the speaker goes from a state of confusion to order and harmony (the same happens in "Hymne to God," there the speaker is aware of this tuning and ordering process from the beginning). At the same time, at the end of a poem, the text turns out to be orderly and well-

---

14   Cf. also Heninger (3-18, 287-397), who points out the influence of Pythagoras's conception of the cosmos (based on numberical proportions and their harmonic correspondence) on Early Modern Poetics, and the notion of a poet as the "maker" of a "literary microcosm."

proportioned and adequate for its subject matter, so that its harmony and order reflect the speaker's spiritual state.

2.   The speaker's tuning in "The Temper (I)"

The significance of music in "The Temper" is established by the title, and further elaborated throughout the poem. Musical imagery is one way for the speaker to describe his emotional states, and his final choice of musical imagery over other images enables him to reinterpret his state of emotional disruption from a negative to a positive one, and to overcome his dissatisfied and aggressive stance in favour of a resigned and peaceful attitude. In addition, the poem also has the poetic praise of God as a subject, as the speaker begins with the question of how to praise God, and, after exploring his own condition, ends with a praise of God. The poem is therefore concerned with aspects of poetic composition, with finding the right measure and balance, and the right level of adequacy for the speaker's purposes.

Within *The Temple*, "The Temper (I)" is preceded by "Love (I)" and "Love (II)" and followed by "The Temper (II)" and "Jordan (I)." "Love (I)" is concerned with the rejection of worldly love and its praise in favour of heavenly love, and "Love (II) continues this theme while focussing more on praising God. It ends with "All knees shall bow to thee; all wits shall rise, / And praise him who did make and mend our eies," introducing the subject of contrary movements (albeit seen in a positive light here), which "The Temper (I)" then continues. "The Temper (I)" then begins with the question of *how* to praise God and continues to explore spatial movement. While "The Temper (I) ends on a positive note, "The Temper (II)" shows a sudden decline of hope (i.e., it reverts once more to intemperance) and presents again a plea for more constancy and trust in God. Notably, the two Temper poems are followed by "Jordan (I)," that is, by a poem which is, like "The Temper (I)," to some extent poetological and like "Love (I)" and "Love (II)" concerned with discarding secular love poetry in favour of sacred poetry. The two Temper poems are thus embedded in a context of poems about divine love and praise, and about how to express it. This interest also shines through in "The Temper (I)," which is mostly concerned with the speaker's personal feelings and relation to God, while at the same time broaching the issue of divine praise, and ending in fact with a praise of God, made possible through the speaker's change of attitude (and mood) along the poem.

2.1 The title

The title of the poem is rich in meaning and already indicates the main concerns of the poem. The poem was originally called "The Christian Temper" (Herbert 2007, 194), which, while placing more emphasis on the speaker's specifically religious attitude, leaves less room for ambiguity. "The Temper" is ambiguous and allows for manifold interpretations.[15] In general, "temper" refers to "the constitution or character of something or someone (OED, "temper, n.II.4.a.") and thus to a "universal temperament or characteristic nature" (OED, "temperament, n.II.3."). It can refer to a mental state and to a bodily state. Related to this is the notion of the four cardinal humours, as the term "temper" was sometimes used for "the various proportions in which the four humours are combined" (OED, "temper, n. II.8.). The idea of mental balance also resonates in the poem,[16] as well as the notion of general temperance and moderation (OED, "temper, n.I.3.") as a morally desirable mode of conduct (i.e., this is what the title "The Christian Temper" focuses on). "Temper" thus implies the existence of different qualities (either physical or mental) and a certain relation between them, which is characterised by a potential for change: On several levels, the speaker depicts himself as out of temper, being tempered and, in the end, in temper.

In addition to all these meanings, the choice of "temper" also opens the way for two other thematic fields that are essential to the poem. It is a term used also with reference to metalwork, where it refers to "the particular degree of hardness and elasticity or resiliency imparted to steel by tempering (OED, "temper, n. II.5."), that is, through heating it up and then immersing it in water (OED, "temper, v. III.14.a."), which in turn

---

15 Cf. also Bowers (1962), who exlores the different connotations of the title.

16 Bowers also sees in the title an allusion to restoring (physical and mental) health through Christ as physician: "The chief medicine of Christ the physician is, of course, the blood and water that issued from his pierced side" (208). He also sees the title as an allusion to the Eucharist as an action of healing through Christ's blood (208) and as an allusion to "the tempered mixture of mortal water and divine blood in the Eucharist cup" (211). Cf. also Groves, who argues for a "eucharistic nuance" in the meaning of "temper" (329-30).

leads from a dilation to a contraction of the steel. And last but not least, "temper" is also a musical term for the tuning of a musical instrument, that is, either generally bringing it in tune or, more specifically, to tune an instrument according to a particular musical temperament (*OED*, "temper, *v*.III.15.*").

Thus, all the main topics are laid out already in the title and are then developed in the poem, as is the speaker's turn from interpreting his state as painful and undesirable to seeing it as a tempering or tuning bringing him closer to God.[17] The speaker presents an exploration of his different states of mind, while at the same time pursuing a persuasive strategy in presenting his woes in so much detail (all the time addressing and imploring God to change his state). In the last two stanzas, the speaker's attitude changes – while his emotional instability remains the same, he now evaluates it differently. Whereas in the beginning he interprets his changing states as a punishment and as a sign of God's indifference or even displeasure, he later sees it as a procedure to make him better (and as a sign of God's attention and love.[18]

2.2 The first stanza: conditions for praise

The poem begins with the general question of how to praise God. While this question is not related to the problem of the speaker's varying moods, it serves a purpose in the speaker's approach to God. The beginning "How should I" could initially be read as a poetological question about the right way to praise God. The continuation of the second sentence "how should my rymes" marks the question as a rhetorical one, however: the speaker *would* praise God if his soul always felt what it sometimes feels. Thus, the speaker indirectly makes his praise condition-

---

17 This correlation between title and poem, and the importance of the title for an interpretation of the whole poem, is characteristic of *The Temple* (cf. Bauer 1995a, Bauer 1994/95 and Ferry 1993), where most titles are "the germ as well as the quintessence of the poem" (Bauer 1995a, 103).

18 Doerksen argues that the stanza form

aids in the process of human-divine accommodation of which the poem speaks. In almost every stanza a particular significance may be found in the contrast between the opening pentameter line and the closing trimeter. (206)

While it is perhaps too much to assign a distinct meaning to the first and last line of each stanza, as Doerksen tries to do, the form in general can be seen as a reflection of the speaker's stretching and contracting.

al: only if God makes him feel in a certain way will he speaker praise God.[19] While the speaker does not specify what it is that his soul sometimes feels and which he desires to feel "always" (and the second stanza describes the speaker's varying states without making explicit that peering above all heavens is what the speaker desires) he makes clear that it is a positive and desirable state, which will enable him to duly praise God.

01 How should I praise thee, Lord! How should my rymes
02   Gladly engrave thy love in steel,
03   If what my soul doth feel sometimes,
04   My soul might ever feel!

The manner of the speaker's praise is further specified: his "rymes" will "engrave thy love in steel." This wording is significant in several ways. Firstly, the speaker explicitly characterises himself as a poet, praising God in "rymes." The use of "engrave," on the other hand, evokes primarily a visual, graphic representation of God's love – i.e., a copperplate engraving like the ones forming part of an emblem.[20] In addition, printed music was also engraved, so that right from the beginning, both the speaker's "rymes" and God's love are also associated with music. Regardless of whether the act of engraving refers primarily to illustrations or to music, this engraving happens through the speaker's rhymes (which is a clear reference to his status as a poet), and is thus always linked to poetry.

On another note, the mention of "steel" also hints more generally at the field of metalwork (and the tempering of metal) as well as to the speaker's militant attitude, that becomes manifest later in the poem – "steel" may refer to the material a weapon is made of, and also directly to a weapon made of steel (*OED*, "steel, *n.*[1] 3.a"), and "engrave" is not only a technical process related to printing but also generally refers to cutting something or someone (*OED*, "engrave, *v.* 3.b.") as well as literally

---

19   Bowers sees the allusion to musical tuning in the context of praising God: "As man is stretched by his afflictions to promote repentance, so a lute string is tuned to produced harmonious chords of praise and thankfulness" (207).

20   Colie argues that *The Temple* as a whole, as a collection of poems resisting a fixed ordering, has "something of the emblem-technique of immediacy" (50), and also functions similarly to an emblem book, to teach and educate the reader (67).

evoking the act of sending someone to his grave. Thus, the phrase combines the promise of lavish praise with an undertone of insubordination.

There is yet another hint at the speaker's not quite so disinterested attitude: he talks not about his own love for God, but about "thy love," which he will record in his rhymes. This focus on God's love looks less self-centred than focussing directly on the speaker's feelings, but is in fact more so and shows the speaker's concern for his own peace of mind and salvation, since the poem treats God's love for the speaker alone. "Thy love" also avoids the question of the speaker's unconditional love of God. The speaker is clearly unsatisfied with his state: in the first stanza he wishes for a reason to praise God, and in the third and fourth stanza he becomes aggressive and argumentative, talking about a contest of power and mentioning combat and torture.

The poem's focus on a personal relationship is also evident in the use of pronouns: there is a single speaker, and the whole poem is addressed to God. Personal pronouns are used abundantly, as the speaker over and over again refers to himself and directly addresses God – although the speaker's situation is neither exclusive nor uncommon, other people and their feelings are not taken into consideration. This focus is made clear from the beginning: the speaker talks about his own praise of God, and about "my" soul, which is mentioned twice, in l.3 and 4.

Another important point the speaker makes from the start, even before he begins to use spatial imagery, is that he focuses on his feelings, and on a metaphorical description of them. This is emphasised through the repetitive mention of "my soul doth feel" and "my soul might ever feel" in ll.3 and 4, respectively. What the speaker describes is abstract in a double sense: his soul is neither visible nor perceptible with the senses, and the "feelings" of his soul are equally invisible and imperceptible. There is thus a stark contrast between these immaterial and imperceptible emotional states and the strong physical and sensuous images that are used to depict these states.

Ll.1-4 seem repetitive and paradoxical at first glance: literally, the speaker seems to wonder whether he might (at some point in the future) feel forever what he (already) sometimes feels. This is due to an underspecification of "feel," which sounds almost tautological, since the speaker leaves it open what kind of feelings he refers to. However, by opening up the distinction between "what my soul doth feel sometimes" and what "my soul might ever feel," he shows that the former state must be something special, a special way of feeling (i.e., *not* how his soul usually or normally feels) which is so desirable that he want to feel this way forever (in the second stanza he then specifies how he feels "sometimes," without determining how his soul "might ever feel" – though being above the heavens seems more desirable than falling to hell – while in the third stanza he complains about that fact that his states *change* at all, which leads to a general wish for equanimity).

The crucial difference between lines 3 and 4 lies in the contrast between "sometimes" and "ever": the speaker is dissatisfied with the short-lived nature of his positive feelings (later, in the last two stanzas, he moves away from desiring *any* changeable state, and instead prefers tempering and equality). "Ever" is ambiguous and leaves it open whether he refers to his life on earth (i.e., he wants to feel this way "continually throughout his life") or to his afterlife (he literally wants to feel this way "forever/evermore, i.e., in all eternity"), since "ever" allows for both options. In addition, the sentence combines what he feels sometimes, i.e., what he has felt before, as part of his life on earth and what he *might* ever feel (a phrase which does not specify when it will happen). Both spaces can be combined, however, through the speaker's immortal soul, whose perpetuity allows him to imagine the continuity of his feelings till death and beyond, and this transition is facilitated by the ambiguous use of "ever." As mentioned, the speaker's wish for positive emotions changes through the poem, and makes way for the desire of being united to God. The more worldly attitude shown in the beginning provides a requisite starting point for the speaker's later turn – he starts with his actual emotions (present dissatisfaction and occasional elation), and the poem's progress allows him to reach a more serene state of equanimity and an outlook on life after death.

The matter of the speaker's praise of God thus becomes a rhetorical question, with two main purposes. Firstly, it serves to "convince" God by presenting an impediment for due praise (the speaker's unstable mood) and a solution, almost an attempt a bribery (since the speaker can only duly praise God when he feels a certain way, and only when he "ever" feels this way, God must make the speaker permanently happy). Secondly, "writing" the poem and exploring his emotional states makes the speaker change his attitude about his initial request: from demanding happiness and elation, he goes on to resignation and acceptance of *all* his moods. At the same time, the question of praising God remains a serious one, since the poem *does* constitute a praise of God, especially in its hopeful and confident ending. The poem thus follows a logical structure: the matter of praise provides an occasion for writing the poem; this quickly passes on to an exploration of the speaker's different emotional states, which in turn leads the speaker to a state of resignation and contentment with all his emotional states, and the confidence in God's presence in all circumstances and beyond death.[21]

2.3 The second stanza: establishing space

The second stanza jumps straight to a description of the speaker's emotional disruption, without getting significantly more specific, however.

> 05 Although there were some fourtie heav'ns, or more,
> 06   Sometimes I peere above them all;
> 07   Sometimes I hardly reach a score,
> 08   Sometimes to hell I fall.

The immaterial notion of the first stanza, the feeling soul, is replaced by a more physical and material image: the speaker peers, reaches and falls, all within a distinct space. Yet, while the speaker's movements are described in active voice, his own activity is rather undefined. "Peere" may refer to the speaker actively looking above the heavens or just to the fact that he is visible there (*OED*, "peer, *v.*[3] 1.a") – though even if the speaker actively looks, this is not an activity that can alter his situation and his changing moods in any way. "Reaching" and "falling" are likewise active but do not necessarily involve any cooperation or volition on the part of the speaker. So, in spite of showing various movements of the speaker, ll. 6-8 attribute very little autonomy to him (nor is another agent mentioned at this point). The emphasis is instead on "sometimes" (which appears at

---

21 Stein sees the first stanza as a declarative sentence, and at the same time as an incentive for change: the poem "begins with a declaration [namely ll.1-4]. And ends with a declaration [ll.25-28]. The 'plain intention' of the poem is to transform its initial attitude into its concluding one" (27-28).

the beginning of ll.6-8, where we would expect the subject of the sentence, i.e., in this case the speaker), which contributes to this lack of autonomy and creates an atmosphere of unpredictability: It seems a matter of chance how the speaker feels, not to be influenced by his actions or behaviour. The different meanings of "reach" hint at other topics that are important to the speaker. "Reach" introduces the notion of stretching and contracting, which is then further elaborated in the next stanza, as it can also mean "To undergo stretching; to become stretched" or "to stretch oneself" (*OED*, "reach, *v*.[1] I.6.b."). With this meaning, "reach" is also used to describe Christ's posture on the cross.[22]

The introduction of heaven and hell as reference points has several effects on the speaker's depiction of his feelings. In the first place, the speaker creates a vertical axis that comprises heaven (or rather, all imaginable heavens) and hell as the furthest points of the speaker's experience. As the speaker mentions "fourtie heav'ns, or more," the "score" which the speaker sometimes hardly reaches constitutes roughly the middle on the way to the top. In addition, on a smaller scale, the speaker's reaching and falling (and later on in the poem, his explicit stretching and contracting) presupposes a spatial perception of himself. In this way, the second stanza introduces a spatial construction which opens the way for further spatial imagery, including torture, the tempering of metal and musical tuning.

A model for the kind of spatial movement can be found in psalm 139:[23]

> O lord, thou hast searched me, and known me.
> Thou knowest my downsitting and mine uprising, thou understandest my thought afar off.
> [...]

---

22   Cf. some examples for "reach, *v*.1., I.6.a.": "Crist [...] on rode wes rauht" (Richard Morris, *An Old English Miscellany*) and "Drawing and retching out thy body to the length and breadth of the cross" (*Book of Christian Prayers*). The speaker's choice of words thus opens the way for a potential comparison of himself to Christ. The up-and-down movement found in stanza two, reminiscent of Christ being raised on the cross and taken down, likewise contributes to suggest this comparison. However, this is a state the speaker does not endure voluntarily, and of which he complains in stanzas two to four (even though what he endures is "just" emotional turmoil and no actual crucifixion) – thus showing that he is *not* Christlike.

23   Cf. also Wilcox, who sees l.7 of this psalm as "underl[ying] the experiences described" (Herbert 2007, 192) in "The Temper (I)."

Whither shall I go from thy spirit? or whither shall I flee from thy presence?

If I ascend up into heaven, thou art there: if I make my bed in hell, behold, thou art there.

If I take the wings of the morning, and dwell in the uttermost parts of the sea;

Even there shall thy hand lead me, and thy right hand shall hold me. (verses 1-2, 7-10)

Psalm 139 also contains the image of a bird ("wings of the morning" is a metaphorical paraphrase for the rising sun as well as depicting to the speaker as a bird), and the image of God's protecting hands. In contrast to psalm 139, however, in which the speaker can confidently go everywhere and even make his bed in hell, because he is assured of God's presence, the speaker in "The Temper" feels that he is not "going" anywhere of his own accord, but stretched and contacted against his will, and is therefore in need of turning.

Conspicuously, the speaker in "The Temper" excludes the world in his spatial setup, which would in a "real-world" setting be located between heaven and hell and also mark the place where the speaker's body (and therefore also his soul) is situated. The absence of the world from the spatial construction found in stanza two contributes to mark it as a metaphorical space: a mental space in which the speaker locates his feelings (and not his body) in order to describe and order them, and which leads to a change of perspective: his inner, invisible state is shown in terms of an outward representation.

The speaker even characterises his description as unreal, in beginning the stanza with the hypothetical "although there were," which, however, is vague, and may just refer to the doubtful existence of forty heavens. He then goes on in simple present, and presents his changing states as habitual. That the speaker does not refer to the "real" world may also be seen in the fact that he talks about "fourtie heav'ns, or more." However, it corresponds well to the speaker's mood swings – when he is elated, he feels like peering above forty heavens, when he is desperate, he feels like falling towards hell.[24]

---

24 Wilcox points out that "the idea of multiple heavens is biblical," and gives 2 Cor 12.2 as an example for the mention of a "third heaven" (Herbert 2007, 194). The Williams manuscript of *The Temple* even mentions "a hundred" heavens (Herbert

At the same time, an evaluation of the speaker's different states takes place through the use of heaven and hell as reference points – reaching heaven (or the heavens) is of course more desirable than falling towards hell. In this way, although the speaker does not make explicit which of these states he prefers (i.e., what he means by "what my soul doth feel sometimes" in the first stanza), there is nevertheless a clear distinction of a positive and a negative state (complemented by an unsatisfactory state in the middle, whose deficiency is underlined by "I hardly reach").

The use of heaven and hell has yet another connotation which is relevant to the poem and the speaker's situation. Heaven and hell present the two options for the speaker's afterlife, and the speaker's attitude on his journey through life determines where he will arrive after death. The second stanza therefore also introduces the question of salvation, and may be seen as a prospect on the speaker's options. In combination with God as exclusive addressee, and the emphasis on the speaker's soul in the first stanza, the second stanza thus also characterises the speaker's emotions as religious feelings. They are deficient, however, in their intemperate extent and in their lack of complete confidence and resignation to God's will: only when the speaker is elated does he think of heaven, whereas when he is in despair he pictures himself falling to hell (thereby showing doubt and a lack of trust in God).[25]

2007, 194), so that the final choice of "forty" seems to point at more than just the speaker's elation. "Forty" as a symbolic number may point to a "period of probation or trial," denoting, for example, the years in which the Israelites wandered in the wilderness, the days Moses remained on Mount Sinai, the days and nights of the Flood, Christ's forty days in the wilderness and the forty days of Lent (Ferguson 154-55). In all these instances, "forty" indicates a temporary, non-permanent state leading towards a significant event, which corresponds to the speaker's situation in "The Temper (I)": he wishes to replace his unstable, temporary moods with a "love and trust" (l.27) that lasts "ever."

Incidentally, "to reach" can also mean "to exaggerate," i.e., "to stretch (the truth)" (*OED*, "reach, v.1 I.6.a."), which can be seen in relation to the speaker's exaggerated mention of forty heavens.

25 Cf. also Donne's Holy Sonnet "Thou hast made me," which depicts the speaker's feelings of hope and despair in a similar way: the speaker is "weighed" towards hell, while he hopes to rise towards God. Rising is linked to vision: "when towards thee / By thy leave I can looke, I rise againe." Here, too, the speaker's rising is depicted as active ("I rise againe"), but is actually instigated by God, who is ask to "draw" up the speaker. Similarly to "The Temper," where the speaker wants to "roost and nestle" under God's roof, the speaker here asks God to "wing" him.

The three different emotional states shown in stanza two are all introduced by "sometimes." The anaphoric repetition of "sometimes" serves several purposes. In the first place, it refers back to the "sometimes" in the first stanza and shows possible options for how the speaker's soul "doth feel sometimes." In the second place, it indicates habitual states, without indicating any of them as more probable, more frequent or more desirable (although being lifted up to heaven is of course more desirable than falling to hell). The order of the three states is important, however: even though the neutral use of "sometimes" does not favour a chronological ranking of the speaker's different emotions, they are described in a certain order, beginning with elation and ending with despair. The last impression a reader gets is thus one of despair, and the speaker continues in this vein (therefore also creating a necessity for a poem addressed to God and asking for more confidence). If the speaker's condition is seen in analogy to the crucifixion, then the order in stanza two presents him, temporarily, without a hope of resurrection.

2.4 The third and fourth stanzas: fighting God

While the second stanza merely presents the speaker's different emotional states, without an explicit assessment, the next stanza evaluates these states. It names God as the cause of the speaker's troubles and stresses the speaker's discomfort at his changing moods, presenting God as the speaker's torturer. The use of "too little" and "too big" is also evaluative and characterises the speaker's state as out of proportion. In the third stanza, his tone thus becomes accusing and implies a certain inappropriateness in letting him suffer.

```
09  O rack me not to such a vast extent;
10     Those distances belong to thee:
11     The world's too little for thy tent,
12        A grave too big for me.
```

The speaker's plea in l.9, "O rack me not" points at physical torture, so that, once again, the immaterial sphere of the soul is mixed with a physical, corporeal presentation in order to adequately describe what the speaker feels within his soul. To "rack" can simply mean "To inflict mental pain or torture on (a person); to torment (the mind, soul, etc.)"

(*OED*, "rack, *v.*¹.2.c."), which is what the speaker actually experiences. Still, by adding "to such a vast extent" (which is primarily a spatial expression, though it can of course also be read metaphorically) and later referring explicitly to the speaker being stretched and contracted, the physical meaning of "rack" becomes more prominent. While "rack" can be used neutrally to simply describe the action of stretching (*OED*, "rack, *v.*¹.1."), what the speaker has in mind is clearly an unpleasant and undesirable procedure, which refers to an act of torture, that is, to the stretching of the body on the rack (*OED*, "rack, *v.*¹.2.a.") – which is quite literally achieved through a motion of circular turning.

Furthermore, to "rack" insinuates (forceful) separation, as it also means "To pull or tear apart, separate by force, break up" (*OED*, "rack, *v.*¹.1.c.") and thus counters not only the speaker's wish for inner peace and uniformity (he wants to be whole instead of being torn apart by his conflicting emotions) but may also hint at his later goal of getting closer to and becoming united to God, that is, of becoming whole (a goal which, although not yet explicit at this stage in the poem, becomes apparent later on). And in spite of its negative connotations with regard to torture, the mention of "rack" in the second stanza, and the notion of stretching it introduces (as well as the complementary notion of contracting, which, while it is not yet mentioned in stanza two, is hinted at in the extremes "too little" and "too big"), provides the basis for the later reinterpretation of the speaker's emotional disruption from torturing to tuning: The act of "stretching" the speaker (as on a rack – that is, a decidedly negative state) is in itself similar to the act of tuning a string instrument by stretching or loosening a string (a positive action). The torture image thus paves the way for the later tuning image. Fittingly, the word order in l.9 and the way negation is used here ("O rack me not" instead of "Do not rack me") lead to an *apo koinou* construction (that is, "O rack me (not)" and "not to such a vast extent" are combined in one phrase, which thus leads to ambiguity), which also allows for a quite different reading: Line 9 could be seen as a plea to be racked ("O rack me"), which is then followed by a restriction ("not to such a vast extent").[26] This does not work, of course,

---

26 In this positive context, "O rack me" may also evoke the phonetically close "O rock me," that is, a plea to be held and rocked by God like a little child (cf. also

since "rack" already implies "too much" – the speaker cannot be racked only a little bit. The possibility of this reading, however, hints at the speaker's later willingness to be stretched and contracted.

The phrase "to such a vast extent" characterises the dimension of the speaker's being racked as extremely large (also, it may either refer literally to spatial elongation, or be used metaphorically), and the same holds for "those distances," that is, the distances between reaching above forty heavens and falling towards hell that the speaker has to endure. The speaker tries to dissociate himself from them, using the more distant "those" instead of "these," and assigning them to God by making clear that they "belong to thee." This characterises the distances as potentially immense and unfathomable (if they belong to God and not to the speaker), and at the same time, the speaker presents his state as an unnatural state for a human being.

In the next two lines, the speaker goes even further in his judgement by using the expressions "too little" and "too big." He also sets up a dichotomy between "the world" and "a grave," as well as between "thy tent" and "for me." Within this dichotomy, he allocates the world to God and the grave to himself, only to refute this distribution immediately. This dichotomy has several effects. In using a negation, the speaker strengthens his stance of denial and refusal of his unstable moods. Simultaneously, he continues to pursue the notion of stretching and implicitly adds contracting, and marks both as inappropriate.

In mentioning the grave, the speaker also keeps up the thought of his own death and life after death. Moreover, 1.12 is ambiguous. It may refer generally to the fact that a grave is too big for the speaker, that is, that he is too little for a grave and should not die (yet), omitting "is" (i.e., a grave is too big for me). Or, referring "a grave" back to "the world," 1.12 may be omitting "the world is," and the complete phrase would be "the world is a grave too big for me" (which seems more plausible considering the speaker's persuasive strategy). In both cases, the speaker characterises something as "too big" for him (either the world, or a grave), and thus creates an impression of being little in some way (which he expands in the next stanza, when he calls himself a "crumme of dust").

1.13, "Wilt thou meet arms with man" and 1.26, "Thy hands made both, and I am there," which both contain the notion of being held in God's arms).

Lines 11-12 look parallel because they contain the parallel expressions "too little" and "too big," and they are syntactically almost parallel – l.12 even relies on l.11 (with either omission, it refers back to l.11). However, they express different things. The remark, "The world's too little for thy tent" seems odd in a poem concerned mainly with the speaker's condition. If the world is too little for God's tent, this implies that God should not be there (but in a larger or grander place, i.e., in heaven). Also, by attributing God's presence to his "tent" (i.e., to the tabernacle), the speaker attributes it to a place that is distant from the speaker (both in space and in time).

In marking "the world" and "a grave" as too little and too big, respectively, the speaker attributes an inappropriate size to spaces that cannot be changed easily, while elsewhere in the poem he talks about himself being stretched and contracted, and God being able to fit everywhere. The speaker might have stated instead that God (or God's tent) is too big for the world, and that he himself is too little for a grave, hence that both must change to achieve the right measure – or that he alone must change and accept God's ability to fit everywhere. Yet what he argues for is different: Compared to God, the world is very little, and the speaker (for whom the world as a grave would be too big) even more so. If the world is too little for God, this implies that God should not be there; if the world is a grave too big for the speaker, it implies that it should not be a grave (especially not for the speaker). Thus, the speaker tries to persuade God not to come to him (on earth), and not to make the world a grave – to stay away from all these matters which are too small and insignificant and do not merit God's attention and stick to the "distances" that actually befit God.

After this attempt at persuading God to leave him alone, the speaker changes his tone and seems to challenge God (in yet another attempt to stop God from inflicting pain on the speaker). Although his exclamation in l.9 is phrased as a plea, through stanzas three and four he becomes increasingly judgemental and accusing. He attributes an aggressive intention to God in using "rack" (an aggression which actually comes from the speaker, who perceives his states as torture), he rejects his state by assigning "those distances" to God (i.e. refusing them as proper states for the speaker), and he makes judgements by using "too little" and "too big." The fourth stanza continues the argumentative vein of stanza three and the speaker introduces a combative element.

As in the beginning of the poem, the speaker uses rhetorical questions, this time addressed to God. In the previous stanza the speaker used evaluative expressions ("rack," "vast extent," "too little" and "too big") to describe his emotional disruption as an act of violence as well as disproportionate. The rhetorical questions in the fourth stanza serve the same purpose. They assign a combative stance to God (again, a stance that is actually displayed by the speaker) and they exaggerate the inequality of such a power struggle.

13 Wilt thou meet arms with man, that thou dost stretch
14   A crumme of dust from heav'n to hell?
15   Will great God measure with a wretch?
16   Shall he thy stature spell?

Although the idea is not entirely absurd (recalling, for example, Jacob's wrestling with the angel in Gen 32), the speaker presents it as unfeasible. Firstly, by using rhetorical questions, to which the obvious answer seems to be "no": God will not "meet arms with man" nor will he "measure with a wretch" (or rather, God will not "meet arms" nor "measure" with the speaker). However, while God Almighty will not or should not, Christ on the cross will "meet arms" and "measure" with the speaker in a positive sense, by becoming human and sacrificing himself. Secondly, by pointing out the unequal power relations, contrasting "great God" with a "crumme of dust" and "wretch" – which also tacitly presupposes an unjust God who attacks those that are smaller and more vulnerable. Ll. 13-14 are ambiguous: either stretching a "crumme of dust" is instrumental in order to "meet arms with man" (making man big enough to confront God and meet arms), or stretching a "crumme of dust" (i.,e., inflicting pain on the speaker) already constitutes "meet[ing] arms." In both cases, however, a sense of disproportion and incongruity remains. Furthermore, this is the only stanza where the speaker uses third person and talks about "man," even though he still describes his own struggle with God. The change from first to third person, and the generalisation it implies, makes his exaggerated description even more disproportionate, since it implies that God generally fights those that are beneath him. Thus, the rhetorical questions point out the speaker's dependency and inferiority to God and thus serve as an implicit allusion to God's responsibility for humankind.

At the same time, the stanza continues several of the poem's main themes. The phrase "meet arms" offers a whole range of meanings, not all of them indicating strife and opposition. In the first place, it refers to the touching of weapons, that is, to actual fighting. At the same time, "meet arms" very literally means the touching of limbs, and thus an approaching, joining movement. The question in l.13 can thus also be read as a serious plea for God's closeness, i.e., "wilt thou join arms with me, wilt thou embrace me," and the use of the preposition "with" strengthens this notion of communion. Here, too, both readings of ll.13-14 are at play. Stretching (in the positive sense of tempering and tuning) is a necessary requirement to meet arms with (i.e., be united to) God, and at the same time stretching as tempering and tuning is a sign of God's attention on the speaker and thus already implies a closeness to God.

L.13, "Wilt thou meet arms with man, that thou dost stretch" evokes the image of Christ's outstretched arms on the cross, and thus of Christ "meeting arms" with humankind through his incarnation. The phrase also evokes the iconographic tradition of the "arma Christi," that is, of the depiction of the symbols and instruments of the Passion (in the first place, the cross itself), as instruments which led to Christ's triumph over death, i.e., as Christ's weapons against death and Satan (cf. Schiller 198-200). Such an allusion continues the themes of combat and torture, as well as presenting Christ's "arms"/"arma" – both as weapons and as limbs – as the instruments which "temper" the speaker.[27]

"Stretch" is mentioned for the first time in l.13, taking up "rack" from the previous stanza (which describes the same expanding movement), and leading over to "stretch or contract" in l.22. The speaker self-deprecatingly calls himself a "crumme of dust" and a "wretch," thus insisting on his smallness and pitiable state. Also, by referring to himself as a "crumme of dust," the speaker once more brings in his own death, recalling Gen 3.19, "In the sweat of thy face shalt thou eat bread, till thou

---

27   Gayk argues that with the Reformation, the depiction of the "arma Christi" passed from visual representations to written texts (273-75). Newhauser and Russell relate the "arma Christi" to the notion of spiritual pilgrimage, seeing them as devices for meditation and devotion facilitating an imaginary journey (99-108).

return unto the ground; for out of it wast thou taken: for dust thou art, and unto dust shalt thou return," as well as Gen 2.7, "And the Lord God formed man of the dust of the ground, and breathed into his nostrils the breath of life; and man became a living soul."[28] The speaker talks about a stretching "from heav'n to hell," which refers back to the second stanza and, again, leaves out the world in between (which is indeed irrelevant here, since the speaker is only concerned with the maximum extension implied by "from heav'n to hell").

"Measure" in the following line likewise allows for different interpretations. It can be used in a militant sense, that is, "to measure swords [...] (with) [...]: to meet in a contest or battle, or to try one's strength (with)." In this sense it was originally used "with reference to the practice of ensuring that duellists' swords were of the same length" (*OED*, "measure, v. I.2.g"), and taking this sense of "measure" into consideration adds yet another element of irony to the speaker's question: since God is of course always superior to the speaker, there is no point in ensuring a fair fight by measuring swords. In this sense, "measure" also simply means to "bring into comparison or competition" (*OED*, "measure, v. III.12," l.15 of "The Temper" is actually listed as an example of this use).

More generally, and in a less competitive sense, "measure" simply means to "ascertain or determine the magnitude or quantity of (something)" (*OED*, "measure, v. I.2.a") and to "make proportional to or commensurate with something else; to regulate or moderate according to a standard" (*OED*, "measure, v. II.11.a), a meaning which is also relevant in "The Temper," as the speaker asks for a moderation of his changing moods.

As "measure" is also a musical (and poetological) term, meaning "To set down in musical measures; to put into metre; to divide into metrical units" (*OED*, "measure, v. IV.16."), its use constitutes another slight hint towards the "tuning of my breast" and the resulting better music in stanza

---

28 Especially with regard to Gen 2, which describes the creation of man, but also in alluding to Gen 3, where God tells Adam and Eve that they have to fend for themselves on leaving Paradise, and which also makes mention of man's creation, the speaker may also implicitly appeal to God's responsibility, as the speaker's creator, for his creation. Cf. also stanza 7 of "The Search," "Lord, dost thou some new fabrick mould [...] leaving th'old / Unto their sinnes?" and the beginning of Donne's Holy Sonnet "Thou hast made me, And shall thy worke decay?"

six. Finally, "measure" can also mean "encircle" or "encompass" (*OED*, "measure, *v*. I.5.a."), which is something the speaker wishes for (and envisions) when he compares himself to a bird roosting and nestling under God's roof and pictures himself in God's hands in the last stanza. Similarly to ll.13-14, the speaker's question in l.15 can also be read as a plea, "Wilt thou put me in proportion, wilt thou encircle me." And, parallel to l.13, just as "meet arms" was followed by "with," "measure" is followed by "with," suggesting union rather than distance. Thus, even when the speaker protests that he does not want this kind of tempering, there is an undertone indicating the opposite, creating a kind of inadvertent irony (as if he subconsciously already knew his pains as "tuning"), till in l.23 the speaker explicitly arrives at the insight "this is but tuning of my breast."

The mention of "measure" also introduces the notion of balance and stability. While the speaker has still not yet clarified what exactly it is that his "soul doth feel sometimes" (although he has provided an implicit evaluation in giving heaven and hell as possible options, and in rejecting a grave or the world as a grave), he has made clear that he suffers from his changing moods. Wilcox (Herbert 2007, 194) points out a parallel passage in Isa 40.12, "Who hath measured the waters in the hollow of his hand, and meted out heaven with the span, and comprehended the dust of the earth in a measure, and weighed the mountains in scales, and the hills in a balance?" This passage stresses the reassuring balance created by God through measuring, meting out and weighing, a balance which the speaker wants in "The Temper" but still lacks at the point when he makes mention of "meet/mete" and "measure" and needs to acquire through tempering.[29]

As mentioned above, stretching and contracting can also be seen as a reference to the tempering of metal, which is heated up and cooled down (and expands and contracts during this process), in order to improve its consistency and make it more resilient. While this notion evokes weaponry (that is, meeting arms and measuring swords with God), it also leads to

---

29   That Herbert might have had Isaiah 40 in mind, is also visible from the thematic parallels in verse 22, "It is he that sitteth upon the circle of the earth, and the inhabitants thereof are as grasshoppers; that stretcheth out the heavens as a curtain, and spreadeth them out as a tent to dwell in," and verse 31, "But they that wait upon the Lord shall renew their strength; they shall mount up with wings as eagles; they shall run, and not be weary; and they shall walk, and not faint."

an improved, more even and balanced state, thus presenting a positive result of "stretching and contracting,"

The next line, "Shall he thy stature spell?" concludes the set of questions challenging God's intention. While it can be read as a rhetorical question, and thus as a continuation of the previous, challenging tone, like the previous questions it can also be read seriously, as a consideration of the implications of the speaker's stretching and contracting on his relation to God, and moreover, on his role as a religious poet.

Wilcox points out the significance of the word "spell" for Herbert's poetry:

> Spelling is a human activity of great significance in *The Temple*, associated with interpreting the Bible, and understanding mortality and eternity, as well as with writing poetry. To spell is fundamental to reading ('Go spell and reade', 157 *A Dialogue-Antheme* 4) and to writing or expressing what has been read. One of H.'s most important lines, 'Thy word is all, if we could spell' (152 *The Flower* 21), implies that spelling is not only understanding God (the 'word' both written and incarnate) but also imitating him and putting his teachings into practice [...] (Herbert 2007, xliv)

The several meanings of "spell" are also significant in "The Temper." The primary meaning is "to read (a book, etc.) letter by letter; to peruse, or make out, slowly or with difficulty" (*OED*, "spell, *v.*^{2} I.1.a") and, complementary, "to form words by means of letters; to repeat or set down the letters of words; to read off the separate letters forming a word or words (*OED*, "spell, *v.*^{2} II.6.a"). This slow, step-by-step process can lead to a more careful and attentive way of reading and writing, so that figuratively "spell" can also mean "to discover or find out, to guess or suspect, by close study or observation" (*OED*, "spell, *v.*^{2} I.2.a") and "to consider, contemplate, scan intently" (*OED*, "spell, *v.*^{2} I.2.c." for which "The Temper" is listed as an example).[30]

"Stature" refers in the first instance to height or size (*OED*, "stature, *n.*1") or to physical appearance (*OED*, "stature, *n.* 2"), but can also be

---

30 Two slightly later uses of "spell" make this process of study and comprehension even more explicit: "To make out, understand, decipher, or comprehend, by study" (*OED*, "spell, *v*.2 I.2.b," documented from 1635) and "to engage in study or contemplation *of* something" (*OED*, "spell, *v*.2 II.6.b," documented from 1645).

used figuratively to denote "high rank, status, or importance" (*OED*, "stature, *n*. 5"), and is, with reference to God, inevitably great (the speaker also attributes "those distances" from heaven to hell to God in l.10). With regard to "The Temper," l.16 can thus be interpreted as "Shall man express thy stature" or as "Shall man contemplate and study (and maybe understand) thy stature." Taken literally, the first interpretation must be answered with "yes," since God's greatness and power is, in any case, expressed *through* the speaker's stretching and contracting (whether it is perceived as torture or tuning) – the speaker becomes a sign of God's glory. Similar to Job, the speaker may have to suffer to demonstrate God's ability to stretch and contract him. The second interpretation gives another reason for the speaker's suffering: his stretching and contracting may be necessary to make him contemplate God (if, just like Job, he accepts his fate as willed by God) and resign to God's will (a process that is part of the speaker's reinterpretation from torture to tuning). Thus, l.16 provides two possible approaches for the speaker's suffering.

In addition, the use of "spell" draws attention to the fact that this question is uttered in the context of a poem (i.e., an elaborate, carefully written text), and, moreover, a poem which begins with the question of God's praise. L. 16 can thus also be read literally as "Shall he express thy stature in (written) words," behind which lies the assumption that God makes the speaker suffer so that the speaker *can* contemplate and write about God's stature (i.e., "Are you making me suffer, so I can write about your greatness?").[31] Here, too, the speaker's inadvertent irony shines through. While the apparently obvious answer to l.16 is "no," it is quite possible to answer this question with "yes": man shall "spell" God's "stature" and is doing so through the poem itself. The reasoning from the first stanza is thus turned round: In the beginning of the poem, the speaker complains that he can only praise God if his soul always feels what it sometimes feels, that is, elated and not moving from heaven to hell. In l.16, the speaker now takes into consideration that his sufferings may be the motivation for praising God (i.e. spelling God's stature). Line 16 thus

---

31   In a similar vein, Sherwood (1989, 135, 177n18), in analysing "Employment (I)" ("If as a flowre doth spread and die, / Thou wouldst extend me to some good," ll.1-2) points out that one meaning of "extend" is "to write out in full" (cf. *OED*, "extend, *v*. I.2.b").

also provides a transition to the more conciliatory attitude of the next stanza, since it moves the speaker's reasoning away from the semantic fields of torture and combat to the more peaceful notions of writing and understanding.[32]

2.5 Stanzas five and six: finding peace

In the fifth stanza, the tone and rhetorical strategy change. The speaker turns from a demanding and challenging attitude to a peaceful and plead-ing one, which is the first step towards his resignation to God's will and sets the course for the later reinterpretation of stretching and contracting from torture to tuning. The fifth stanza begins with "O let me," which parallels the beginning of the third stanza, "O rack me," and is even pho-netically similar. While "O rack me" is followed by "not," and thus re-fused, "O let me" is actually repeated in the next line; also, while "rack" is full of negative connotations, "O let me" is a plea to "roost and nestle."

> 17 O let me, when thy roof my soul hath hid,
> 18   O let me roost and nestle there:
> 19   Then of a sinner thou art rid,
> 20   And I of hope and fear.

Although "roost" and "nestle" can both be used figuratively, the prima-ry association is that of a bird coming to rest and making a nest. When "roost" is used with reference to people, it either has a more permanent sense, meaning, "to lodge oneself, have one's abode or quarters," or re-fers specifically to "pass[ing] the night (*OED*, "roost, *v.*[1]2").[33] The same holds for "nestle," which when used for people means "to live, settle, take up residence, or encamp in a place (*OED*, "nestle, *v.*[1].2."), and can

---

32 Cf. also the ending of Donne's "Upon the translation of the Psalmes": "may / These their sweet learned labours, all the way / Be as our tuning, that, when hence we part / We may fall in with them, and sing our part" (ll.53-56). Here, the psalms, which in the poem are described as special because they combine music *and* words, are the means of tuning men during their life on earth.

33 Cf. also *OED*, "roost, *n.*1.2.d": "a resting place; *spec.* a place to sleep in, a bed." As a noun, "roost" denotes not only a henhouse but also quite generally "the internal framework of a roof, formed by the rafters and joists." (*OED*, "roost, *n.*1.1.a"), which would link it to the idea of nestling under the rafters of a roof. However, this meaning does not seem to have been in use at Herbert's time – the *OED* only lists examples significantly earlier or later than Herbert's poems.

also mean "to lie, esp. snugly or half-hidden or embedded" (*OED*, "nestle, *v.*[1]4.a."). Both senses of "roost" and "nestle," respectively, can be seen as a wish to come to rest, to stay in one place instead of being stretched and undergoing emotional turmoil.

The whole stanza can also be seen as another allusion to the speaker's death. "Roost" and "nestle" connote a (peaceful and permanent) sleeping or dwelling place, at a time "when thy roof my soul hath hid." A roof is high up, implying that the speaker will go up (to heaven), and the implicit comparison with a bird likewise suggests an upward movement (i.e., flying into the sky). There the speaker will be "under God's roof," that is, enclosed and sheltered by God. The reference to God's roof could also be seen as an allusion to a church, denoting a place where God can be encountered as well as a place where funeral services are performed. At the speaker's death, God will be rid of a sinner, since the mortal, sinning part of the speaker will be dead, and the speaker will be rid of "hope and fear," since he will be with God, no longer fearing and no longer in need of hope. The image of the speaker resting under God's roof also anticipates the last poem of *The Temple*, "Love (III)," where the speaker's soul is welcomed into Love's abode.

The association with birds created through the use of "roost" and "nestle" is also significant for the speaker's turning away from a stance of strife and confrontation towards peace and resignation. While there are several birds with a symbolic religious meaning, the bird that immediately comes to mind here is the dove as a symbol of peace and reconciliation. More precisely, the dove stands for peace between God and man and precedes the covenant between them: the dove Noah sends out heralds the end of the flood and of Noah's journey and introduces a period of rest and stability. In addition, a dove is a small bird that can be held in hands, an image which anticipates the speaker's being held in God's hands in the last stanza.[34]

---

34   The same holds for the eagle, which is the attribute of St. John Evangelist. Cf. also the use of phoenix, eagle and dove in "The Canonization," discussed in the last chapter. The dove also stands for purity, which accords with the speaker's statement "then of a sinner thou art rid" in l.19. Ferguson also notes that the pelican, a symbol for Christ's sacrifice on the cross, "is sometimes shown nesting on the top of the Cross" (23). If the speaker is seen as an imitator of Christ, there

Ferguson points out that "in the earliest days of Christian art, birds were used as symbols of the 'winged soul.' Long before any attempt was made by the artist to identify birds according to species, the bird form was employed to suggest the spiritual, as opposed to the material." (Ferguson 12). This symbolic use is also prominent in the Psalms, where the image of the dove is used several times as a reference to the speaker, and to describe the speaker's soul or state of mind. In addition, the dove can also be interpreted as a symbol of literary inspiration (being an attribute of St. Gregory, said to have been sitting on his shoulder when he was writing (Ferguson 16)), which continues the idea of "spelling" rather than "meeting arms" and "measuring" with God.

The speaker underlines his plea by trying to convince God and showing the advantages of being accepted under God's roof: "then of a sinner thou art rid." He immediately continues with an advantage to himself, however: "And I of hope and fear." The speaker has not yet reached the complete resignation necessary to accept both stretching and contracting as "but tuning of my breast," and would rather get rid of all extremes. Also, the state he imagines for himself is one of confidence and fulfilment, where he is no longer fearing and therefore no longer in need of hope.[35]

The fifth stanza describes a prospect of the speaker's salvation, "when thy roof my soul hath hid." Even though the fifth stanza shows a harmonic and peaceful picture, the speaker's stance is still demanding. In the sixth stanza, the speaker goes back to his present state and gives up his demands.

---

may well be an allusion to the pelican in the speaker's plea to "roost and nestle"; however, the image of the dove as symbol of peace is much stronger in stanza five.

35 Strier sees a development from thinking in terms of space to thinking in terms of emotional states: the second stanza "translates times into places. It correlates emotions with cosmological locations" (1983, 228). The fifth stanza displays a shift from emphasizing ascent to emphasizing enclosure. [...] God's "roof" is conceived of in cottage rather than cosmological terms. And something has begun to happen to the spatial vocabulary. Despite the persistence of this language, "there" in line 18 seems to be less a place than a state of mind or soul, an imagined state of complete security and protectedness. [...] the second half of the stanza, with its focus on named emotions, reminds us that the actual context of the poem is psychological rather than ontological. What the speaker wishes to escape from is not life in space but life in time. Hope and fear are both future-oriented emotions and they are both responses to the possibility of change. (1983, 230)

> 21 Yet take thy way; for sure thy way is best:
> 22   Stretch or contract me thy poore debter:
> 23   This is but tuning of my breast,
> 24   To make the musick better.

The stanza begins with "yet," which explicitly and formally indicates some sort of change – in this case, the speaker's turn to real resignation and his complete acceptance of God's way. "Take thy way" and "stretch or contract me" are the poem's last demands, and they attribute power to God. "Thy way" is repeated and explicitly marked as the "best." The speaker describes himself as "thy poor debter," explicitly assigning blame to himself and admitting an obligation towards God.[36] At the same time, the speaker is poor – he is unable to pay his debts, which leads to a necessity of imprisonment but also to his dependence on God's mercy. This characterisation also shows the speaker's wish to be "imprisoned" by God, to be enclosed, encircled, and held by God.[37]

The speaker now brings in the field of music, already present in the poem's title, which has important consequences for the speaker's attitude. Lines 23-24 finally give an explicit definition of the speaker's stretching and contracting, "This is but tuning of my breast," and a reason why he must suffer: "To make the musick better."[38] They thus present the most important turn in the speaker's attitude: stretching and contracting is reinterpreted from a violent act of torture and combat to an act of creating

---

36   Wilcox sees here an additional meaning of "contract": the use of "poore debter" creates a legal contract between the speaker as debtor and God as creditor (Herbert 2007, 195).

37   Cf. the speaker's plea in Donne's Holy Sonnet "Batter my Heart": "Take me to you, imprison me, for I, / Except you enthrall me, never shall be free."

38   Cf. also Herbert's "Providence":
> Nothing escapes them both; all must appeare,
> And be dispos'd, and dress'd, and tun'd by thee,
> Who sweetly temper'st all. If we could heare
> Thy skill and art, what musick would it be! (ll. 37-40)

The next stanza shows the pervasiveness of God in a similar way as the last stanza of "The Temper":
> Thou art in small things great, not small in any:
> Thy even praise can neither rise, nor fall.
> Thou art in all things one, in each thing many:
> For thou art infinite in one and all. (ll. 41-44)

harmony, showing God's well-meaning attention and love.[39] The speaker compares himself to a musical instrument in need of tuning, and the action of stretching or contracting to the tuning of this (string) instrument: the strings can be tuned by being tightened or loosened. More precisely, he talks about a tuning of his "breast," insinuating that the tuning takes place in his heart. As mentioned above, "concord" comes from Latin "con" (together) plus "cor" (heart), which makes the heart a fitting place for tuning (in addition, the heart is seen as the seat of the emotions, and, in using the image of tuning, the speaker changes his emotions).

This turn towards music (that is, the reinterpretation from suffering to tuning) has been anticipated throughout the poem. It is present from the outset, in the poem's title, and also in the vacillation between upward and downward movements (i.e. musically, high and low, raising and falling) and the reference to "distance" (which can likewise be seen as the distance between two notes of different pitch). There are several musical meanings of "measure": it can refer to "metrical or rhythmical sound or movement," also referring to a tune or melody (*OED*, "measure, *n.* III.14"), it can denote musical rhythm on a small scale (referring to the relation between single notes (*OED*, "measure, *n.* III.17.a) or with reference to a larger piece of music (*OED*, "measure, *n.* III.18). And it can also refer to dancing (*OED*, "measure, *n.* III.15.a"). Thus "Will great God measure with a wretch?" can now be understood in a different sense, meaning something like "Will great God make music with me" or even "be music with me."

The speaker's "falling" ("to hell I fall" and "fall with dust") can also be seen in a different light now, as it has a musical equivalent in the idea of

---

39 Harman sees the varying states in "The Temper" as descriptions of the speaker's different perceptions of his self, which he can accept in the end because he is surrounded and held by God, with the introduction of the notion of tuning providing the central turning point towards acceptance of his various states of self:

> The tuning metaphor [...] transforms the hope that the speaker might avoid being an unstable self (stanza one), or a set of discrete selves (stanza two), or a fragmented self (stanza three), or a hidden self (stanza four), into a notion that these are all versions of the self – however discontinuous the self might therefore be. This solution recovers the idea that there is a self [...] but it sacrifices the hope expressed in the first stanza, that the self might be stable, that the experience of being many might be reduced to the experience of being one. In fact that hope is not only relinquished (in stanza six), but is reversed (in stanza seven) as the speaker actually gives thanks for being many instead of being one. (153-54)

the cadence at the end of a musical piece. "Cadence" comes from Latin cadere, "to fall," and the poem describes several kinds of "falling." It evokes the speaker's state after *the* Fall, that is, theologically, after man's expulsion from paradise and the appearance of original sin, which leads to the speaker's experience of "falling" to hell and "falling" with dust in the poem. Musically, it indicates the end: the end of his life, and literally, the end of his verses and the poem. Cadence is also a poetical concept referring to "'The flow of verses or periods' [...]; rhythm, rhythmical construction, measure" (*OED*, "cadence, *n.* I.1.a). Puttenham likewise links "cadence" both to music and to poetry (and especially to the ending of rhymes) when he writes,

> [...] a rhyme of good symphony should not conclude his concords with one and the same terminant syllable, as *less, less, less*, but with divers and like terminants, as *les, pres, mes*, as was before declared in the chapter of your cadences. And your clauses in prose should neither finish with the same nor with the like terminants, but with the contrary as hath been showed before in the book of proportions, yet many use it otherwise, neglecting the poetical harmony and skill. And the Earl of *Surrey* with Sir *Thomas Wyatt*, the most excellent makers of their time, more peradventure respecting the fitness and ponderosity of their words then the true cadence or symphony, were very licentious in this point. (Puttenham 258)

Thus, in Puttenham's notion of cadence, elements of music and speech are combined and musical terms are used interchangeably for both. As an alternative to picturing the speaker's emotional despair, his falling can also be seen in a positive light: as a way of indicating the "end" of the speaker, becoming "dust" and approaching death (but therefore also getting closer to God), and as an harmonious, measured and ordered way of coming to the end. Musical imagery provides the speaker with a mode of thought that changes his whole outlook on his situation. It not only takes his negative feelings away, but turns them into completely positive emotions. At the same time his resistance to God becomes resignation and acceptance.

2.6 Stanza seven: prospective union

The speaker's internal change in stanzas six, and his resignation to God's will, allow the speaker to imagine his final turn towards God and God's turn towards him, resulting in their union.

> 25   Whether I fly with angels, fall with dust,
> 26   Thy hands made both, and I am there:
> 27   Thy power and love, my love and trust
> 28   Make one place ev'ry where.

As the speaker has now resigned himself to God's will, he can take his fate with equanimity and it does not matter any longer whether he flies with angels, or falls with dust. Again, both activities refer to the speaker's emotions (and thus to the "hope" and "fear" expressed in l.20), but also to his death, to which he can now look forward with confidence, as it enables his union with God.[40] This union is described in the last three lines of the poem. While the speaker is not yet dead, and not yet united to God, he now feels God's presence. Consequently, he uses the present tense: "I am there" and "Make one place ev'ry where." The statement of being in God's hands may be seen as a sign of the speaker's resignedness and trust (cf. Psalm 31.5, "Into thine hand I commit my spirit: thou hast redeemed me, O Lord God of truth") but also as a reference to death (cf. Luke 23.46, "And when Jesus had cried with a loud voice, he said, Father, into thy hands I commend my spirit: and having said thus, he gave up the ghost.").

There is a strong sense of reciprocity. "There" is ambiguous – it may refer either to flying with angels, or to falling with dust, or to being in God's hands.[41] There are also two possible ways of emphasis: either the

---

40   Nuttall sees l. 25 as an allusion to the speaker's hope and fear *about* his afterlife (which causes his present emotional turmoil: "'flie with angels' is an image of aspiration rather than of triumphant achievement" expressing hope (rather than certainty) of salvation (34), while "fall with dust" expresses the speaker's fear of damnation:

> 'Dust' implies mortality, and mortality, especially when joined with the idea of falling, implies damnation. No Protestant reader, with the consequences of a 'fall from grace' still ringing in his ears from the last sermon he heard, could avoid this inference. (35)

41   Cf. Fish 161. Cf. also Vendler: "The compact use of the one adverb, "there," to stand for two places, heaven and earth, because both were made by God's hands, seems yet another final resolution of the distances in the poem" (40).

speaker stresses "I am *there*" or he stresses "*I am* there" – which would contribute to shift the focus from the speaker's changing states indicated by "sometimes ..." in the second stanza to his present state.[42] Yet, since spatial difference no longer matters in the last stanza, it also becomes insignificant what "there" refers to, as *all* space becomes "one place ev'ry where" in which God's presence is felt. The next line, "Thy power and love, my love and trust" shows this union to an even greater extent by using chiasmus to link the speaker's and God's emotions.[43] Significantly, the speaker and God are joined through "love": "thy love" and "my love" become one.[44] This union of the speaker and God in the next stanza can also be seen in musical terms: instead of thinking about himself as vacillating up and down, as being out of tune and either too high or too low, the speaker now accepts his human state regardless of whether it means going up or going down, and thus reaches a feeling of being

---

42   Cf. Strier:

> Stanza 7 responds to stanza 5; "there" appears in the same position in both. The final paradoxical use of the term answers the earlier prayer ("O let me roost and nestle there") by freeing the idea of security from any connection with times or places. The realities to which this final stanza points are independent of times and places. They are also [...] independent of "feelings" in the sense of responses to immediate stimuli – sensations. "Love and "trust" [...] are distinguished in the poem from "what my soul doth feel sometimes." The final equilibrium of the poem, the "Christian temper" [...] is precisely "that firm and steadfast constancy of heart which is the chief part of faith [quoting Calvin's *Institutes of the Christian Religion*, III.ii.33, cf. Calvin 581]" (1983, 233).

43   Fish points out the ambiguity of "make" in l.27, which also strengthens the close relationship between the speaker and God expressed in the last stanza:

> What this [ambiguity] does is give the poet a part in the action of the concluding line – making one place everywhere ("make" has a multiple subject). God's power and love, His continuing presence in the world, are of course the final cause of this effect, but the poet's love and trust in that other love are necessary for its perception since the perceiving consciousness he was born with suggests something else altogether (that "this" or "that" is). (162)

Cf. also Vendler:

> Herbert first rewrites racking as union, then rewrites distance as unity ("there"), and finally rewrites unity ("one place") as immensity ("everywhere"). We should not forget that he is at the same time rewriting the cause of this transformation: at first everything was his God's doing, but at the penultimate line the change becomes a cooperative act in which two loves intersect, and God's power is conjoined with man's trust. (41)

44   Cf. also Donne, "The Good-Morrow": "one little roome, an everywhere." Here, too, the equation of "one little roome" and "everywhere" is made possible by (worldly) love. Strier sees two opposite developments in these poems:

> Donne's [lines work] to include everything in one place; Herbert's to eliminate the significance of places by making them all functionally the same. "One place" in Herbert means "the same place," that is, not in a "place" at all. (1983, 233n36)

in harmony and concord with God. The perceived discord between speaker and God has been turned into a sort of unison.

The last line, "make one place ev'ry where" marks the cancellation of space and thus of all difference and instability (cf. also the similar ending of "The Search," "making two one"). The speaker pictures himself united to and encircled by God, in God's hands and one with God. As the speaker and God meet, there is no more space and thus no more movement, yet at the same time the very last word of the poem is "everywhere," which lets God's presence seem pervasive and all-encompassing.[45]

3. Spiritual attunement in "Hymne to God my God, in my sicknesse"

In "The Temper (I)," the speaker finds a musical metaphor to define his suffering as tuning and thus as an approach towards God. In "Hymne to God" this train of thought is there from the beginning, whereas in "The Temper (I)," the speaker has to explore it by first trying out different ways of interpreting his situation and relation to God. The speaker in "The Temper" is thus tuned more or less passively and gradually: While he describes how he feels, a change of attitude takes place that makes him arrive at the statement "This is but tuning of my breast." The speaker in "Hymne to God" to some extent tunes himself, and he emphasises his own involvement: "*I* tune the Instrument here at the dore, / And what *I* must doe then, [*I*] thinke now before" (ll.4-5).[46]

The speaker distinguishes what he "must *do* then" (before he can enter God's "holy room") from what he will "*think* now before." The poem does not specify what the speaker's action will consist of (and cannot do

---

45   Cf. also Fish (161):
       The reader who negotiates the distance between "Whether" and "there" passes from a (syntactical) world where everything is in its time and place to a world where specification of either is impossible, to a *uni*verse. This same movement is compressed into an even smaller space in the final line, where "one place" actually does become "ev'ry where" in the twinkling of a reading eye.

46   However, the clause "think here before" leaves it open whether the thinking refers to the speaker or to the reader of the poem. Line 21 begins with "*we* think," so that at least at this point the reader is involved in the speaker's reasoning. And although the last line is a "sermon" to mine own," it is still a sermon and can be read by the reader.

so, since the speaker will *do* only when he is in heaven). Since the speaker is bedridden, he cannot do more than "think" in his present condition. The speaker's tuning can consist only in creating the right attitude and state of mind (which is what he attempts in the poem). However, this "thinking" is essential, since it prepares the speaker's mind, making the poem a kind of meditation or preparatory exercise before the speaker's anticipated death.

As in "The Temper," in Donne's "Hymne to God" the speaker tries out different ways of picturing his way to God. Although the outset is a different one – the speaker in "Hymne to God" interprets his illness as a form of tuning right from the beginning – the development and the outcome are similar: the speaker presupposes as the central metaphor the tuning of himself. He then adds to this idea the field of geography and cartography: the notion of himself as a map and of going through his illness as a progress through the world. In the last two stanzas, the speaker changes this setting: he narrows down the vast space established in stanzas two to four and focuses on the location of the cross, which in turn leads to an identification with Christ.

3.1 The title

As in "the Temper," the title is already programmatic.[47] It is marked by three things. Firstly, there is the generic labelling of the poem as "hymn." Secondly, the address "*to* God *my* God, in *my* sicknesse" already indicates the speaker's upward orientation and personal striving towards heaven. Thirdly, there is the repetition "to God my God."

That the poem is presented as a "hymn" marks it as a poem that is likely to be musical in some way, as a hymn combines music and poetry. A hymn does not have a specific poetic form, and it is usually addressed to a deity ("A song of praise to God; any composition in praise of God," *OED* "hymn, *n.* 1"). The word "hymn" was originally used for a variety of classical Greek poems, such as epic narratives, marriage songs or laments, but mostly written in praise of ancient divinities (*New Grove* "Hymn," 18). Three things are particularly interesting in this context.

---

47   This title is also found in some manuscripts (see Gardner 1978, 50). While it is not completely certain that the title comes directly from Donne, Gardner strongly argues in favour of it (1978, 132-35).

Firstly, though the origin of the word "hymn" is not known, "Pindar and Bacchylides connected the term *humnos* with *huphainein*, meaning "to weave" or "to combine artfully" (*New Grove*, "Hymn," 18). This derivation links the hymn as a musical genre to the word "text," which comes from Latin "textum" and also means "that which is woven, web, texture" (*OED*, "text, *n.*") and strengthens the ties between music and word which are combined in the genre of the hymn. Furthermore, the performance of ancient hymns was often accompanied by dancing (*New Grove*, "Hymn, 18"), which adds a dynamic quality and a spatial dimension to the character of a "hymn." Lastly, in addition to being musical, a hymn is usually also public. Greek hymns were sung by a chorus, not by an individual, and later, Christian hymns, were sung by the congregation. The Greek hymn was followed by the Latin hymn, which was already strophic and mostly used in services (*New Grove*, "Hymn, 19"). The Protestant hymn emerging in the Renaissance is distinguished from the Latin (and the modern) hymn in that its text is an original composition and does not come from the Bible (*New Grove*, "Hymn, 29").[48]

The second feature of the title, the address "to God my God, in my sicknesse" shows not only the speaker's orientation upwards to heaven but also the personal character of this hymn. "To God" is still neutral and a form of address that can be expected in a hymn. "My God" however, makes this a poem about the personal, individual relationship of the speaker to God, which runs counter to the task of a hymn as congregational song. "In my sicknesse" further personalises this poem in applying it to the speaker's personal situation and reason of speaking to God. However, there is a precedence for such a personal setting in the Psalms, which, too, are both public and intimate.[49]

The third characteristic is the addition of "my God," leading to a repetition of "God." In the first place, this is a reminder of Christ's last words, "My God, my God, why hast thou forsaken me?" (Matt. 27.46). It also links the "Hymne to God" to Donne's *Devotions*, where "my God, my

---

48   A blending of the hymn as classical and Renaissance genre can be found in Edmund Spenser's strongly neoplatonic "Four Hymns."

49   See Wilson 1993, 81 and Gottwald 535.

God" appears in most Expostulations, as well as some Prayers.[50] Repetition is found not only in the title but throughout the poem: "I am coming" and "I come" in lines 1/3, "here" in lines 4/5, "flat" in lines 8/14, "my west" in 11/13, "one" in line 14, "straits" in lines 10 and 19 (twice), "think" in lines 5/29, "other" in lines 27/28, "Adam" four times in lines 22-25. These repetitions stand in contrast to the flow of reading created by the many enjambments and long sentences found in the poem. Most noticeable are the repetitions of the first person pronoun and its declensions: "I" appears ten times, "my" appears nine times, "me" four times, and "mine" once. Like the possessive pronoun in the title, this emphasis on the speaker and his concerns disagrees with the public and congregational character of a generic hymn.

The dichotomy between public and private which becomes apparent in the title, the many repetitions and variations of "I" and the poem's treatment of the speaker's individual sickness and longing for salvation is evocative of the subtitle of Herbert's *The Temple*: "Sacred Poems and Private Ejaculations." However, the "Hymne to God" does not differentiate between public and private matters. Rather, Donne takes a sacred genre that is conventionally public (hymns were intended to be sung by a congregation, not by one individual) and turns it into a private ejaculation. This is further developed in the combination of the possessive pronoun with items that should either be attributed to another individual or cannot belong to an individual at all. Thus, the speaker mentions "*my* South-west discovery" (presumably referring to the Magellan Strait discovered in 1520 and named after its discoverer (cf. Donne 2010, 611), of "*my* West" (twice), and of the Pacific as "*my* home," personalising not only the genre of the hymn but making himself in his thoughts the focus of the whole world.[51] In the last stanza, he also talks of "my Text" and "my Sermon," although the Text (in the sense of "Scripture") is a common property and sermons are public speeches.

---

50 The "Hymne to God" is likely to have been written after Donne suffered from a serious illness in 1623 (Gardner 132-35) and thus at the same time and on the same occasion as his *Devotions Upon Emergent Occasions*.

51 Cf. also Donne's Holy Sonnet "I am a little world made cunningly."

3.2 The first stanza: the speaker as music

The first stanza begins with the speaker's continuous movement: "I am comming." This is the only instance of present progressive in the poem (the ensuing descriptions of the speaker's state use the simple present), but it is enough (together with references to time and place) to locate this movement as one that is happening at the moment of speaking, already begun and not yet concluded.

> 01 Since I am comming to that Holy roome,
> 02   Where, with thy Quire of Saints for evermore,
> 03 I shall be made thy Musique; As I come
> 04   I tune the Instrument here at the dore,
> 05   And what I must doe then, thinke now before.

The direction of the speaker's movement is also clear: "to" heaven. Just as in the title – "*to* God" – the preposition indicates the addressee, the way towards whom the poem's words are directed, the "to" in line 1 indicates the way towards which at least the spiritual part of the speaker is directed. "Since" is ambiguous; it can be either causal or temporal. That is, either the speaker states that *while* he is coming, he tunes the instrument, or that *because* he is coming he tunes the instrument. Both meanings merge, as the speaker, by his own account, *is* coming and *is* tuning the instrument.

The speaker's goal is depicted as "that" holy room." "Holy" reminds one of the homophones "whole"/ "wholly," indicating completeness – the speaker's journey and the circle of his life will be completed and whole once he has reached the holy room (this sense of conclusion, and the speaker's wish for conclusion, runs along the central idea of raising and lowering that is brought in at the end of the third stanza, "So death doth touch the Resurrection," 1.15).[52]

"For evermore" in the second line contrasts with the movement found in the first line; it refers to eternity and allows no temporal change. "For evermore" is ambiguous: either, the speaker will be with the Quire of Saints "for evermore" and, as a result, be made God's music, or, being

---

52   "Holy" is also rather similar to "halo," anticipating the holy state of the choir of saints in the next line, and also containing the image of the circle in the shape of the halo).

with the Quire of Saints, he shall be made God's music "for evermore" (i.e., presenting the process of becoming God's music as going on through eternity). While the latter reading is less salient than the first, it finds a parallel in the ending of "The Search," where the process of "two becoming one" is likewise presented without temporal restriction, i.e., potentially going on for all eternity.

    L.5, "And what I must doe then, thinke now before," links doing and thinking. The poem is about what the speaker "think[s] now," which is presented in active terms: he is "coming" to the Holy Room, he tunes the instrument, he "must doe" what he thinks now. Yet the speaker also describes himself as physically passive and lying on his bed, which is not made apparent till the next stanza. The activity he describes in the first stanza is a mental activity, characterised by thinking "now" (and doing "then," that is, only after death). The interplay between the speaker's mental activity and corporeal passivity, which is developed from the second stanza onwards, reflects the conflict between the extremes of a *vita activa* and a *vita contemplativa*. The speaker has been active in his life at least to the point of preaching to others (in l.28 he states that "to others soules I preach'd thy word"). In his present state, he has turned towards himself and God, and is in a state of spiritual contemplation.

3.3 Stanzas two to four: the speaker as map

The second stanza sets the time and location for this poem (since the speaker is *not yet* dead). The semantic field changes from music to geography and cartography (although musical allusions continue throughout the poem).

> 06 Whilst my Physicians by their love are growne
> 07   Cosmographers, and I their Mapp, who lie
> 08 Flat on this bed, that by them may be showne
> 09   That this is my South-west discoverie
> 10   *Per fretum febris,* by these streights to die,

The adverbial at the beginning of this stanza, "whilst," gives the time of speaking, while "flat on this bed" provides the place of the speaker's body, but also an assessment of the speaker's situation (which is both a musical description (see below) and a medical one).[53] "Lie," a static verb, is in opposition to the coming, tuning and doing announced in the first stanza. These activities involve movement and change, while "lie" shows a complete absence of motion. At the same time, the connotation of "lie" as "not being truthful" might even give such an activity a sinful character. However, the state of lying around provides an ideal basis for thinking, and the poem is as much about what the speaker thinks as about what he does (or rather, what is done to him). In fact, since the speaker is forced to lie down due to his illness, he cannot do anything but think: coming, tuning and doing are not performed physically but within his mind.[54] Thanks to his illness, he thus goes further than his physicians: while they, as cosmographers, can only observe, the speaker not only becomes their "map" but also a traveller (mentally) visiting different places on the map while travelling towards death.[55]

Since the speaker's mind (his *think*ing) is more active than his body in this poem, the description of his physical state is found only in a subordinate clause (which covers the whole of stanza two). "I joy" at the beginning of the third stanza, initiating the main clause, again stresses the non-physical level as the main place of movement and development. However, the dichotomy between "*that* [...] room" and "*this* bed" in lines 1 and 8 also shows that the bed is still nearer to the speaker than the heavenly room.

The physicians are described as "cosmographers," which includes working in the fields of both geography and astronomy. Thus, the speaker also implicitly presents himself as a "cosmos," the world to be studied

---

53   Robinson notes, "Now that a Musition should bee a Phisition, I see no such necessitie, But that Musicke is Phisical, it is plainlie seene by those maladies it cureth" (Robinson, n.p.).

54   While the speaker in "The Temper" is not ill, he shares with the speaker of Donne's "Hymne" the condition of being out of temper, i.e., in an unbalanced state and in need of tempering (a literal allusion to the four temperaments is implied in the title "The Temper"). Herbert's speaker is emotionally out of temper, which causes him physical pain comparable to torture, while Donne's speaker is physically out of temper (his humours are unbalanced, thus causing a fever), which – on the contrary – causes some degree of emotional serenity and assurance.

55   Cf. also the use of maps in assisting interior pilgrimage discussed in the context of "The Search."

by these "cosmographers."[56] In presenting himself as a "Mapp" contemplated by the physicians, the speaker introduces yet another allegorical level.[57] In the third stanza, the speaker then talks about east and west becoming one (in a map such as him), so that, when east and west are seen as the directions of life and death, the allegory no longer refers just to the body of the speaker, but also to his soul. In addition, the physicians' studies also include the field of music, since cosmographers will also deal with the music of the spheres. Nonetheless, the speaker is not the physicians' instrument but God's. Not the physicians will heal the speaker – like cosmographers, they can only observe but not act –, but God, through tempering and tuning, assists the speaker in his mental preparation. The frequent emphasis on the first person shows that it is the speaker who actively needs to prepare for death. He must tune the instrument; he must preach to himself. He has taken over the role of the physicians, since they can only help to heal the body, which in the case of the speaker seems already beyond repair. The physicians' motivation is left open: they become cosmographer's "by their love," but whether this is their love for the speaker, their love of God or simply their love of examination and thirst for knowledge (i.e., whether they act out of charity or curiosity) is not specified. The speaker talks about "his" "south-west-discovery," even though his physicians are presented as cosmographers. Also, he needs his fever in order to be cleansed and prepared for heaven: he must die "per fretum febris," i.e., "by the 'raging heat' *(fretum)* of fever, or [must] travel by the 'strait' *(fretum)* of fever" (Gardner 107). However, "fretum" is reminiscent of "fret," i.e., the rings or bars placed

---

56 This goes along with the idea of man as a microcosm reflecting the larger macrocosm of universe and earth, a notion which is also inherent in the idea of a universal harmony being mirrored in the human soul.

57 Anderson argues that many statements in "Hymne to God" can be explained by considering the medieval T-O-map as the model behind the map imagery in the poem (in addition to a modern map representing geography more accurately): On some T-O maps, the three parts of the map (Asia, Europe and Africa) are assigned to the sons of Noah and accordingly labelled with their names (466-67), and the base of the "T" division is the strait of Gibraltar, which would explain why it is mentioned by name in the poem (while the straits of Anyan and Magellan correspond to the boundaries of a modern map including America, cf. 467-69). Anderson also sees the shape of the "T" reflected in the poem's reference to the cross, "Adam's tree" and the speaker stretched out on the bed (470-71).

on the fingerboard of plucked instruments in order to indicate the place for each single note. Therefore, in musical terms, the "fret" of the fever is very much a means of tuning the speaker. Thirdly, a "fret" is also a "breach or passage made by the sea" (*OED*, "fret, n.[4]"), and, integrating this meaning into the allegory of going through straits, the fever thus helps to open a way through the ocean for the speaker. His fever, creating physical and mental turmoil, may be compared to the speaker's ups and downs in "The Temper." In both cases, the state is unpleasant and the respective speaker is incapable of changing it – however, he can reinterpret it into a tuning.

"Joy" and "see" at the beginning of the third stanza are again active (though not physical) activities. They go together with the speaker's thinking, which makes him "see" his death and feel "joy" at his anticipated salvation.

> 11 I joy, that in these straits, I see my West;
> 12   For, though theire currants yeeld returne to none,
> 13 What shall my West hurt me? As West and East
> 14   In all flatt Maps (and I am one) are one,
> 15   So death doth touch the Resurrection.

"Current" is associated with the passing of time (*OED*, "current, *n.* 2.5") and thus has a chronological component: the speaker not only moves literally from sick body to dead body, and figuratively from sinful to contrite disposition, he also moves from an earthly past and present to a heavenly future. "Current" is also directional, making this course of events irreversible.

L.12, "theire currants yeeld returne to none," evokes music in a double sense. Firstly, the use of "current" is reminiscent of the Early Modern "courante," a "running" dance (cf. *OED*, "courante/courant, *n.* etymology" and Strahle 97, who points out "Curranto" as alternative name).[58]

---

58   Cf. also stanza 69 of Davies' *Orchestra*, which presents the courante as a dance characterised by "traversing" and "turning":
> What shall I name those currant travases,
> That on a triple *Dactyle* foote doe run
> Close by the ground with slyding passages,
> Wherein that Dauncer greatest prayse hath won
> Which with best order can all orders shun:
>   For every where he wantonly must range,

Secondly, "returne" in this context is reminiscent of "ritornello," which, as a musical term, usually refers to an element of repetition or a refrain (cf. *OED*, "ritornello, *n.*" and Strahle 309-10) but can also be used to denote the tuning peg of a string instrument and the action of tuning an instrument by turning a peg: "a twirle or turning about as of a pin or peg of a Lute" (Florio 447, cf. also Strahle 310).[59]

"Current" can also mean "circulation of money" or "currency" (*OED*, "current, *n.* 4"), introducing the idea of financial wealth gained through overseas trade. In this sense, the currents yield "return to none," i.e., they yield no profit to anyone. Still, they are profitable to the speaker (the word order also suggests this: the phrase begins with "theire currants yeeld returne" – before the meaning is reversed by "to none"), even more profitable by not yielding return, since the Bible teaches, "Blessed are the poor in spirit: for theirs is the kingdom of heaven" (Matt 5:3). This is in accordance with the speaker's choice of the "straight and narrow path." Since the speaker's journey on the world's oceans is a spiritual one, he can neither expect any profit from it, nor can he be physically hurt ("What shall my West hurt me?").[60]

The idea of a flat map in which east and west touch is central to the speaker's envisioning of his resurrection, as it provides a simple and graspable image to depict something inconceivable. Technically, the touching of East and West is only possible in "flat" maps representing the world in two hemispheres (each showing one half of the world), touching each other on the middle of the map. Yet, the map can also be imagined as three-dimensional: "[…] east and west in a flat map are one only after the map is no longer flat but has been fitted over a globe so that the east and west edges touch each other" (Campbell 194; cf. also the maps of Waldseemüller mentioned in the discussion of geography in the second chapter – printed on paper, i.e., two-dimensional, and designed for the construction of three-dimensional globes).

And turne and wind, with unexpected change.
Morley likewise describes the courante as "trauising and running" (181).

59   The irresistible movement expressed in l.12, together with its allusion to dancing, also evokes the Dance of Death tradition – paradoxically, the speaker stresses his immobility (lying flat on his bed) while continually moving towards death.

60   In the next stanza, the speaker alludes to the profit he will gain: the "Easterne riches" in l.17 promise his salvation through the crucifixion.

Topographically, the idea of uniting east and west not only implies infinity (there is no point where one could determine the beginning or ending of east and west), but can also be understood as bundling all places on earth in one point (if east and west really coincide in one point, there is no more space around them). However, the map is imperfect while it is flattened and spread out like the speaker on his bed; only when it is rolled up it its ends touch each other, creating a circle and uniting beginning and end. In his sermons, Donne also plays with the idea of a flat map becoming round:[61]

> Take a flat Map, A Globe *in plano*, and here is East, and there is West, as far asunder as two points can be put: but reduce this flat Map to roundnesse, which is the true form, and then East and West touch one another, and are all one: So consider mans life aright, to be a Circle, *Pulvis es, & in pulverem reverteris, Dust thou art, and to Dust thou must return; Nudus egressus, Nudus revertar, Naked I came, and naked I must go.* ("Sermon Preached to the Lords upon Easter-day, on Ps. 89.48," Donne, *Sermons* II, no. 9, 199)

> In a flat Map, there goes no more, to make West East, though they be distant in an extremity, but to paste that flat Map upon a round body, and then West and East are all one. In a flat soule, in a dejected conscience, in a troubled spirit, there goes no more to the making of that trouble, peace, then to apply that trouble to the body of the Merits, to the body of the Gospel of Christ Jesus, and conforme thee to him, and thy West is East, thy Trouble of spirit is Tranquillity of spirit. The name of Christ is *Oriens, The East* ("Sermon Preached upon the Penitentiall Psalmes, 1623, on Ps. 6.8-10," Donne, *Sermons* VI, no. 1, 59)

While the first example depicts man's circle of life by focussing on his transience, the second explicitly adds to this the hope of resurrection, which is also present in "Hymne to God." Just like Herbert in "The Temper," Donne here refers to man becoming dust again as a positive notion raising hope: in returning to "dust," man will also return to God. The second excerpt shows another important image, the "flat" soul, which

---

61   This idea also forms the basis for the speaker's movement in "Goodfriday, 1613": the speaker rides westwards, away from Christ on the cross and towards his own death, but, as east and west are one, he simultaneously gets closer to heaven and thus to a union with Christ.

links the map (first flat, then rolled up), the speaker's body (lying "flat on this bed") and the speaker's soul (being "flat" and "dejected"). At the same time, "flat" has musical connotations (cf. *OED*, "flat, *adj.*, *adv.*, and *n.*³ II.11.b"): a note may be too high or too low, in the latter case being too "flat." "Flat" may also refer to an accidental indicating that a note *should* be sung or played a semitone lower. In the first case, being too low and therefore "flat" implies a need for "raising."

Stanza four then gives a short survey of the world at Donne's time and the main routes for navigating and voyaging in this world.

16 Is the Pacifique Sea my home? Or are
17   The Easterne riches? Is *Jerusalem?*
18 *Anyan,* and *Magellan,* and *Gibraltare,*
19   All streights, and none but streights, are wayes to them,
20   Whether where *Japhet* dwelt, or *Cham,* or *Sem.*

The list of locations presented here encompasses the whole world. First, it mentions the three major oceanic passages of Donne's time and thus, the means of travelling around the world. Second, Noah's sons were said to be the ancestors of all population on earth. Thus, the combination of "sea" and "home" does not seem fitting at first glance (though the poem makes use of a maritime allegory, it is not about sailors or "living" at sea). Usually, an ocean is a place of transition, while "home" is a place of stability and stasis. Consequently, the speaker questions his long stay on the sea. However, the name "Pacific" sea is related to "pax," which the speaker will not find while he is still in transit, but towards which traversing sea and straits will lead him. Straits, too, are places of transition, not permanence. The reference to "pax" is thus not misplaced – the speaker is already at peace, since he sees his illness as a possibility for contrition and the very stage of transition as one that secures his "home" in heaven and his permanent peace. The three sons of Noah, by contrast, are not located at places of transition; they "dwell" in different corners of the world. Like the straits of Anyan, Magellan and Gibraltar, they serve to sketch Donne's known world: the speaker uses geographical and personal names as cornerstones for the world that can be found on maps and globes.

In addition to the metaphors and thematic fields used explicitly, there are a number of "covert" allusions found in the poem. These types of hidden allusions or "secret wordplay" are not unusual in Early Modern poetry, [62] and they play an important role in "Hymne to God." In the first stanza, the speaker states that he is coming "to that Holy roome" (1.1) and that he tunes "the Instrument here at the dore" (1.4). The first stanza thus joins the spatial notion of entering a room, and the musical (as well as spatial) notion of tuning an instrument. Both are united through the idea of a "key," which, although it is not mentioned explicitly in the poem, is a notion that resonates in the poem and is central to the speaker's turning. In the first place, the "Holy roome" where the speaker wants to join the "Quire of saints," as an allusion to heaven, can be imagined as one with a door for which St. Peter possesses the keys. Secondly, musical tuning is also related to the notion of "key", as the tonality of a piece of music is determined by its key, and consonance depends on being in the right key. In addition, "key" is a synonym for "tuning-key" (*OED*, "key, *n.*[1] and *adj*. A.III.14.a).[63] This is an important notion in "Hymne to God," since being tuned is presented as a prerequisite for entering the "Holy roome" and thus, as a "key" to heaven.

The allegory of the speaker's voyage to death as compared to a (maritime) voyage on earth leading to a certain destination, particularly in the fourth stanza, can also be linked implicitly to the notion of "key." Firstly, heaven is phonetically very similar to haven (although the two words are not etymologically related). Secondly, the image of a safe haven entails that of a "quay" – pronounced exactly like "key" and sometimes even

---

62   Cf. Bauer (1995b) and (2015b).

63   Cf. also *The Tempest*, 1.2.77-85: "Thy false uncle [...], having both the key / Of office and office, set all hearts i'th'state / To what tune pleased his ear" (176f.). Peacham compares Britain to a harp tuned by James I:

> While I lay bathed in my native blood,
> And yeelded nought save harsh, & hellish soundes:
> And save from Heaven, I had no hope of good,
> Thou pittiedst (Dread Soveraigne) my woundes,
>   Repair'dst my ruine, and with Ivorie key,
>   Didst tune my stringes, that slackt or broken lay.

> Now since I breathed by thy Royall hand,
> And found my concord, by so smooth a tuch,
> I give the world abroade to understand,
> Ne're was the musick of old Orpheus such,
>   As that I make, by meane (Deare Lord) of thee,
>   From discord drawne, to sweetest unitie. (*Minerva Britanna* 1612, 45)

spelled like it – "a man-made bank or landing-stage" (*OED*, "quay, *n.*") and with the spelling "key," synonymous to "quay" or a "low island, sand-bank, or reef, such as those common in the West Indies or off the coast of Florida" (*OED*, "key, *n. 3*") which a ship can aim at. There is at least one instance in which "key" was used as a synonym for "harbour" (from F. Quarles' *Argalus & Parthenia*: "That thou mast safely slide Into the bosome of thy quiet Key, And quite thee fairely of th'iniurious Sea," *OED*, "key, *n.2*"). Thus, the harbour that is sought is at the same time the "key" to heaven. This harbour is located in the west – in the direction of death and decay (from Latin de+cadere – "fall down") and decline. Musically, a key determines a composition's harmony and final direction (the piece will normally end in this key) and is a decisive aspect of the piece's formal structure.[64] Although the "key" to the "holy room" is not mentioned, the poem makes clear what it is made of: the speaker's tempering and tuning. Illness and death function as a key to God's "holy room," since the fever is the means of "tuning" the speaker, necessary to enter heaven, while only death can ultimately bring him from earth to heaven. The phrase "Easterne riches," especially in combination with the immediately following "Jerusalem" indicates a spiritual point of orientation: the riches of "Easter," that is, of the passion, are found in Jerusalem. Thus, l.17 points at the speaker's destiny (a painful death) as well as his subsequent reward (i.e., they "yield returne" in the form of redemption and salvation).

In this respect, the speaker's emphasis on "straits" is important, since it indicates not only his orientation but also that this orientation is "right" and "virtuous." The use of "straits" – "by these streights to die" (l.10), "in these straits, I see my West" (l.11) and "All streights, and none but streights, are wayes to them" (l.19), supported by the various spellings used, carries several connotations. In the first place, it refers to geological, oceanic straits, i.e., to defined and narrow "ways" in and across the seas. It also alludes to Matt. 7.14, "Because strait is the gate, and narrow is the way, which leadeth unto life, and few there be that find it," showing that these straits are the right way (as well as a narrow way). "Strait" also stands in opposition to being bent or crooked (and in this sense can

---

64   Cf. also the speaker's envious description of the stars in "The Search," "As having keyes unto thy love" (l.15).

also mean "extended at full length, cf. *OED*, "straight, *adj.*, *n.* and *adv.* A.1.a.").[65] "Strait" may also mean "Pressing hardly, severe, rigorous." (OED, "strait, *adj.*, *n.* and *adv.* A.II.5.a") and may in this sense refer to the speaker's death throws. Lastly, it may also be a self-referential allusion to poetic style, to *oratio astricta*, i.e., metrically bound, lyrical style (in contrast to *oratio soluta*, i.e., "free" and "unbound" prose style, cf. Cicero's *Orator* 352, 355, 462f.; §64, §67, §187, respectively), and therefore to the poem itself as a way of moving towards God.

The fact that the straits yield "return to none" and that the speaker will be singing "for evermore" show an orientation towards a (final) goal – the movement described goes in one specific direction, towards death and beyond. The emphasis on "straits" ("all straits, and none but straits, are ways to them") adds to this sense of order and orientation (the speaker's voyage not only goes through straits but also seems to advance in a strait/straight line). Not only does the speaker's illness facilitate his coming to God by (as he expects in the present situation) leading him straight to death ("by these straits to die"), it also chastises his body and prepares the speaker as a whole – he will already be "tune[d]" before he comes to God. The speaker states, "Therfore that he may raise the Lord throws down": the speaker has already been thrown down and "lie[s] Flat on this bed," waiting to be "raised." Since he is *in* the straits ("and none but straits"), there is no possibility to go astray and he is on the way to death and heaven and can be confident to go to Paradise (if he goes the "strait" way).[66]

The poem also stresses the fact that the speaker has almost reached his goal: after his journey through life, there is only the last strait or straight, death, which he has to pass on his way to God. However, going through this strait is painful and laborious for the speaker. In *Death's Duell* (see also the chapter on "The Search," section 4, Donne compares the way through death towards eternal life to a birth:

> [T]his *exitus mortis* shall be *introitus in vitam*, our issue in death shall be an entrance into everlasting life. [...] our deliverance *à*

---

65 Cf. also the "straight" (l.3) motion in "Coloss. 3.3" as one way to reach God.

66 Labriola (1995) sees the geographical description in the fourth stanza as a reference to the shape of the cross, and therefore the speaker's description of himself as a map as an imitation of Christ.

> *morte, in morte, per mortem*, from death, in death, and by death"
> ("Deaths Duell," Donne, *Sermons* X, no. 11, 231)

This notion resonates in "Hymne to God": in the literally narrow (i.e., "strait and narrow") way and the speaker's painful illness, but also in the concurrence of life and death, Adam's Paradise and Christ's Calvary, and the joining of "raise" and "throw down" in the last line: the speaker goes not only from earthly life towards fleshly death, but also from a life span passed "in death" towards eternal life.

3.4 Stanzas five and six: approaching Christ

After presenting a very large and comprehensive space in stanzas two to four, in line 21 the speaker leads over to a much smaller and confined space, the location of "*Paradise* and *Calvarie*." At the same time he moves from contemporary locations to past, biblical locations, a movement which is already initiated in the fourth stanza. In lines 16 and 17, the speaker gradually shortens the parallel structures "Is the Pacific sea my home?" – "Or are / The eastern riches [my home]?" – "Is Jerusalem [my home]?" Thus, we get the impression that the speaker gradually gets nearer to Jerusalem, which is both an existing place in Donne's time and a biblical location. In line 21 the speaker also comes back to "thinking," that is, to a nonphysical activity.

> 21 We thinke that *Paradise* and *Calvarie*,
> 22   *Christs* Crosse, and *Adams* tree, stood in one place;
> 23 Looke Lord, and finde both *Adams* met in me;
> 24   As the first *Adams* sweat surrounds my face,
> 25   May the last *Adams* blood my soule embrace.

God *looks* (or is asked to look) – which is more active than the speaker's vision – he merely *sees*. On the one hand, "see" is a verb that can also be used for God's omniscience: "God sees everything." On the other hand, the use of "look" (and of the imperative form) as a plea to God to look (or more precisely, to look *down*) at a speaker is found, for example, in many of the psalms.

If we look back at the "flat" body and "flat map" in lines 8 and 14, line 22 provides the opposite and complementary movement. Being flat is associated with a human and material condition; being raised is associated with Christ and God.[67] The references to being "flat" and being "raised" (in the last line) correspond to the topographic distinction between the earth as human realm and heaven as a divine place. What is still missing is a reference to what is *below* the earth, hell, which is, however, already hinted at in the "flat" condition of the human speaker (i.e., in musical terms, he is lowered slightly). "Lie" is also contrasted with "stand": the frail human speaker cannot do more than "lie," while the cross and the tree "stand" independently. Yet it is not Christ (nor Adam) who stand up, but the locations and "landmarks" associated with them (Paradise and Calvary; cross and tree). [68] The speaker asks God to "finde both *Adams* met in me" (1.23), that is, to see him not only as a fallen human being but also as a man redeemed by Christ ("May the last *Adams* blood my soule embrace," 1.25) and imitating Christ ("in his purple wrapp'd" in the next stanza).

The poem contains several references to temporal order. In line 5, the speaker states, "And what I must do then, think here before." In stanza five he makes reference to the "first" and "last" Adam, which also indicates a temporal order: Adam, foreshadowing Christ in traditional typological exegesis, *will* be followed by Christ.[69] The chronological order of events thus leads from Adam to Christ and from "his thorns" to "his other crown": from the Fall to redemption and salvation. The speaker stands in between, he is "coming" towards heaven as he speaks. This means not only that he has not yet reached his goal, but also that he is in flux, moving at the same time as he is speaking – that is, moving with his mind while his body "lies flat on this bed" (similarly, in the "Hymne to God the Father," the speaker "runs" through sin, but at the same time he is "still").

In the last stanza, the speaker explicitly turns from musical imagery to the spoken word: the "text" and the "sermon."

---

67   As mentioned above, being "flat" can also be seen in a musical context: it refers to being out of tune, at a lower pitch than necessary, so that a raising of the "instrument's" pitch is needed to bring it into tune.

68   Cf. also the placement of Christ "as thou hang'st upon the tree" in "Goodfriday, 1613" – here, the tree is likewise used to provide a geographical "landmark" and to place Christ in a mental landscape.

69   King David, as another important precursor of Christ, is not mentioned in the poem, but present implicitly in the speaker's role as a (religious) poet.

26 So, in his purple wrapp'd receive mee Lord,
27   By these his thornes give me his other Crowne;
28 And as to others soules I preach'd thy word,
29   Be this my Text, my Sermon to mine owne,
30   Therfore that he may raise the Lord throws down.

The speaker describes himself as "in his [i.e., Christ's] purple wrapp'd," which is a reference to the bloody body of Christ, and, by imitation, to the speaker's body – the speaker thus presents himself as an imitator of Christ, and the pains of his illness and death as an imitation of the passion. At the same time, it may refer to the garments of a clergyman (also keeping in mind Donne's calling as minister and later Dean of St. Paul's), part of whose duties is the preaching of sermons. It thus describes an intimate and private state as well as a garment associated with a public function.

The last line of the hymn, "Therfore that He may raise, the Lord throws down," syntactically reverts the order established in the rest of the poem. Although "throwing down" must come before the "rising," the clause containing the raising is put first, so that the poem ends with the speaker still being "down." Since the speaker is not yet dead, he cannot yet be raised, even though his raising will be the logical consequence of his statements.[70]

The poem thus ends by emphasising two points: the union of "raising" and "throwing down", actions that have constituted a main topic throughout the poem, and the "text" itself. This "text," though it refers primarily to the last line, "Therfore that he may raise the Lord throws down," may also be seen as a reference to the whole poem, which is also a "text" and closer in length to a sermon than just the last line – l.29, "Be this my Text," and especially the deictic "this," includes both options.

In "Hymne to God," flatness is also contrasted with roundness and wholeness. Sweat *surrounds* the speaker's face; his soul is *embraced* by blood. "Death doth touch the resurrection," creating a full circle. The speaker compares himself to a "flat" map but at the same time presup-

---

70   In musical terms going back to the beginning (without a "return") means also going back to the tonic and thus concluding a piece of music (just as the speaker's life must be concluded in order for him to ascend to heaven).

poses the circularity necessary to make east and west meet. He asks for a (circular) "Crowne," and the movement described in the very last line, "Therfore that he may raise the Lord throws down" is also circular: only what is down can be raised; only what is raised can be thrown down.[71]

Donne uses the image of the flat map in yet another sermon, already quoted at the beginning of this chapter, where it is linked to biblical interpretation:

> You shal have but two parts out of these words; And to make these two parts, I consider the Text, as the two *Hemispheres* of the world, laid open in a flat, in a plaine Map. All those parts of the world, which the Ancients have used to consider, are in one of these Hemispheres; [...] but yet the other *Hemisphere*, that of America is as big as it; though, but by occasion of new, and late discoveries, we had had nothing to say of *America*. So the first part of our Text, will bee as that first *Hemisphere*; [...] but by the new discoveries of some humors of men, and rumors of men, we shall have occasion to say somewhat of a second part to. The parts are, first, the Literall, the Historicall sense of the words; And then an emergent, a collaterall, an occasionall sense of them. [...] How the words were spoken then, How they may be applied now, will be our two parts. ("Sermon upon the XX. Verse of the V. Chapter of the Booke of Judges, Preached at the Crosse the 15th of September 1622," Donne, *Sermons* IV, no. 7, 181)

Here, the two hemispheres are compared to two ways of interpreting the Bible. Although the text does not state it explicitly, here, too, the two hemispheres must be considered to be joined in some way, since the biblical exegesis does differentiate but not separate its two components. The speaker in "Hymne to God" performs both a historical and an "emergent, occasional" interpretation (the choice of words bearing a notable similarity to the *Devotions upon Emergent Occasions*) of the Scriptures: He talks about the crucifixion and the dwelling places of biblical figures from an historical perspective, but he also applies them to further his personal hope of salvation. The sermon "to mine own" therefore does exactly

---

71   This last line of the poem reminds one of the Latin motto "Oriens morior, moriens orior," that contains exactly this circularity in its formal structure. Donne also exploits this notion in "A Valediction Forbidding Mourning"; cf. Bauer 1995b, 110f.

what a sermon should do: it provides scriptural examples and it also expounds them.

In the *Devotions*, Donne states,

> Thy first breath breathed a *Soule* into mee, and shall thy breath
> blow it out? Thy breath in the *Congregation,* thy *Word* in the
> *Church,* breathes *communion,* and *consolation* here, and *consummation* heereafter; shall thy breath in this Chamber breathe *dissolution,* and *destruction, divorce,* and *separation*? (II. Expostulation,
> *Devotions* 13)

The speaker here asserts the right to God's consolation in solitude (and
not just in public church-going). The same can be found in "Hymne to
God": the speaker preaches a sermon to himself. The speaker's "sermon
to my own" can be seen not only as an exhortation to tune himself in
preparation for heaven, but also as consolation in approaching his death.

While the hymn is directed "to God," the "sermon" is directed "to" the
speaker. This marks a distinction between music as something divine,
intended for God, and word or text as something intended for man.
Words can be fully understood, while music cannot (or, to go back to the
beginning of the poem, words can be *thought*, while music can be *done*).
The very last line of the poem thus combines music and word. In another
one of the sermons quoted at the beginning of this chapter, Donne also
states,

> [...] as *S. Basil* says, *Corpus Hominis, Organum Dei,* when the person acts that which the song says; when the words become works,
> this is a song to an instrument: for, as *S. Augustine* pursues the same
> purpose, *Psallere est ex perceptis Dei agere*; to sing, and to sing to
> an instrument, is to perform that holy duty in action, which we
> speak of in discourse ("Lent-Sermon Preached at White-hall, February 12, 1618, on Ezek 33.32," Donne, *Sermons* II, no. 7, 167)

And he concludes this sermon with addressing God: "We may not onely
be to you, *as a lovely song,* sung to an Instrument; nor you only *heare
our words* but *doe them*" (178).

4. Conclusion

If we look at both poems in comparison, we see that, although the speaker's point of departure is different, they both combine and interweave tuning and turning in a similar way: musical notions are used to imagine and describe the speaker's process of turning. In "The Temper," the speaker tries out different ways of describing his emotions and his relation to God. From an aggressive and challenging stance, he finally finds a metaphor that allows him to accept his state as it is: as "tuning of my breast." With this final interpretation of his stretching and contracting, he is able to accept God's will and reach a state of resignation. This acceptance now enables him to picture his union to God as a double turning of himself and of God towards him, made possible through mutual love. In "Hymne to God my God, in my sicknesse," the speaker likewise sees his suffering as a tuning which prepares him to meet God after his death.

VI. Circular turning in "La Corona"

The Day that I was crowned
Was like the other Days –
Until the Coronation came –
And then – 'twas Otherwise –

As Carbon in the Coal
And Carbon in the Gem
Are One – and yet the former
Were dull for Diadem –

I rose, and all was plain –
But when the Day declined
Myself and It, in Majesty
Were equally – adorned –

The Grace that I – was chose –
To Me – surpassed the Crown
That was the Witness for the Grace –
'Twas even that 'twas Mine –
(Emily Dickinson, J356)

1. Turning in "La Corona"

The concluding chapter is concerned with Donne's "La Corona," which employs the form of a crown of sonnets and is thus a fitting example to illustrate circular turning. This aspect of turning is on the one hand more concrete than in the poems discussed till now – circularity and a final turn to the beginning can be seen immediately in the poem's form. On the other hand, due to its form, the poem ends in the same way it begins, apparently resulting in an unchanged state of affairs. The poem thus presents a more abstract form of turning than the other occurrences of turning discussed so far, since progress and change, both spatial and spiritual, are less obvious than in the other poems. Nevertheless, there is a development through the poem, as well as an element of linear, evolving change, so that the concluding line of the cycle does not merely carry the same meaning as the opening line. Like "La Corona," "A Wreath" exploits poetic form as a way to approach God. In "La Corona" the crown is already there but only becomes a true crown by going through it poem by poem and completing the circle (which makes the form of the crown of sonnets indispensable for the speaker's claims), thereby turning to God. "A Wreath" does not present a crown and makes this explicit in content and form, yet in offering only "a poore wreath" – and meditating on the conditions for making this wreath – achieves the same goal: getting closer to God.

1.1 Title and form

The formal arrangement of the cycle combines a circular form (the end of the last sonnet is linked back to the beginning of the first sonnet) with a linear progress (each sonnet is tied to the next and to the preceding one, creating a chain, so that the order cannot be altered), creating a paradoxical movement that is linear and circular at the same time.[1] Circularity and linearity are thus essential features of this form, and essential for the kind of turning found in "La Corona." A change takes place through an advancement that happens not on the level of narrative (which could be repeated ad infinitum), but through a progress in the speaker's state of mind and in the state of his poetic work. And although in theory the cycle could be read again and again, there is a break at the end of the whole cycle: the last line is not simply a repetition and return to the first, it also gains a different, richer meaning by having read through the whole poem – as if the speaker (and the reader, too), after a journey following the life of Christ, comes back to the place of departure, and having been changed by the experiences of the journey, sees things in a different light.[2] Litur-

---

1   Cf. also the similarly contrary movements in Herbert's "Coloss. 3.3."
2   The circular form in itself does not guarantee this kind of transforming progress. On the contrary, it may also further a going round in circles from which there is no escape. Such a conception can be found, for example, in Herbert's "Sinnes Round" or in a stanza 113 of Southwell's "Saint Peter's Complaint." In "Saint Peter's Complaint," the speaker blames "bewitching evill, that hides death in deceites" (1.667): "Thou hast made me to myselfe a hell" (l. 672). He is able to see his sins, but cannot escape from them:

> My eye, reades mournfull lessons to my hart,
> My hart, doth to my thought the griefes expound,
> My thought, the same doth to my toungue impart,
> My toungue, the message in the eares doth sound.
> My eares, back to my hart their sorrowes send:
> Thus circkling griefes runne round without an end. (ll. 673-78)

Through the use of anadiplosis, the single lines are linked to each other, creating a sense of constant, forward motion – yet without spiritual progress. The speaker feels entrapped by his "circkling grief," and line 678 can be read in two ways: either the speaker's griefs run round in circles, without orientation and without moving forwards, or his griefs encircle and entrap the speaker, so that he cannot escape from them.

gically, "La Corona" is both self-contained and repeatable: The life of Christ has been narrated from Annunciation to Ascension, and although it can be repeated (and will be repeated through the church year), one cycle is finished at the end of the seventh sonnet.[3]

The narrative of Christ's life and death is linked to the speaker's state as a human being and as a poet. The speaker's position changes from "low" and "devout" (l.1.2) to "raise[d]" (l.7.14); his relation to Christ changes from distant to intimate, from an "All-changing unchang'd Antient of dayes" to a personal Christ whom the speaker perceives to act "for mee." The speaker's vision changes from darkness to light (from a dark-humoured state of melancholy to the vision of Christ as a "bright torch" marking a path for the speaker), and his poetic achievement changes from "this crown" in l.1.1 (at this point there is no clear reference for the indexical "this" – it could refer to an existing "crown" out-

---

"Sinnes Round" uses the same formal device as "La Corona, i.e., the last line of a stanza is also the first line of the next stanza), but the poem only has three stanzas with six lines each, so that the crown of sonnets is hinted at but not put into effect. The poem begins with, "Sorrie I am, my God, sorrie I am, / That my offences course it in a ring," and it ends again with "Sorrie I am, my God, sorrie I am." As in "Saint Peter's Complaint," the speaker's sins go round in circles (they "course it in a ring," i.e. they dance in a circle, cf. Herbert 2007, 430), and the speaker sees no escape: his circling only leads to "New thoughts of sinning," (l.17), and not to a mental state which might bring him closer to God or to any hope of salvation. In both "Saint Peter's Complaint" and "Sinnes Round," the speaker lacks a perspective: he is unable to see beyond himself and his thoughts only turn around himself. (Cf. also the first six stanzas of Herbert's "The Search," where the speaker is searching for God but unable to see beyond himself).

3   Chambers argues that the cycle reflects both the liturgical year (presenting all its major events, 1977, 160-64) and the liturgical day (as a reflection of the liturgical year in small, and with the seven sonnets as a reminiscence of the seven canonical hours in the medieval church (1977, 167-68).

Baumgaertner sees the seven sonnets as an allusion to the seven notes in a musical scale, where the eighth note is a repetition of the first and the scale begins again on a higher pitch, just as the continuation of sonnet seven is the first sonnet again, but with a significant change in the speaker (1984, 147-50).

Johnson, too, sees a musical element in the poem's formal arrangement. In analysing repetition and variation in musical compositions, she considers the phenomenon of a series of repetitive elements or variations that are concluded with a final repetition which contains a significant change and therefore receives special emphasis (a process she calls "terminal heightening"), and she finds the same phenomenon in the changing meaning of the repeated first and last lines of "La Corona" (1972, 66).

side the poem, or to the poem itself, that has only just begun and is not yet a completed "crown") to "this crowne" in l.7.14, which has just been presented to Christ.

The title "La Corona" alludes to several meanings at once, some of which are explicitly taken up by the speaker, mostly in the opening sonnet.[4] In the first place, it refers to the poetic form which is used in the cycle, the crown of sonnets (or in Italian "corona di sonnetti," Martz 1955, 105f.), that is, to an especially elaborate arrangement of sonnets (which in themselves present a skilful form of poetry). This poetic form literally combines turning in the sense of moving from one line to the next and from one sonnet to the next (that is, turning in the sense of winding), which is common to all poems, with turning as a return back to the beginning, which is unique to this form and thus creates circularity. Throughout the sequence and especially in the first stanza, this paradoxical movement is also stressed by the use of similarly paradoxical expressions: "All-changing, unchanged" (1.4), "At our end begins our endless rest" (1.10) and "This first last end now" (1.11).

This circular form contributes to make the poem both iconic (the form reflects the content) and self-referential (the form points at the content, and the speaker points at "this crown of prayer and praise"). Self-referentiality simultaneously contributes to reinforce circularity (in turning back to the poem itself) and, since the first sonnet also touches on the process of writing the "Corona," it shows progress as the poem develops and unfolds.

Secondly, the circular form, the name "La Corona" and the cycle's content (an account of the different stages of the life of Christ) allude to the rosary. There is a variant of reciting the rosary called the "Corona of our Lady," divided into seven parts, which focuses on Mary's life, and which goes through the different steps of Mary's life from the time before she was born to her assumption and coronation (Martz 1955, 105-07, cf. also Patterson 72-79), that is, in a way very similar to Donne's divi-

---

4   Although it is uncertain whether the title "La Corona" is originally by Donne (manuscripts differ between "La Corona" and "The Crowne," Gardner 57), the crown form, the treatment of the word "crown" and the recounting of events from the life of Christ make it sufficiently clear that the poem *is* a crown of sonnets and also that it alludes to the rosary.

sion of the life of Christ.[5] Donne thus combines an existing devotional practice with an existing poetical form in order to create a poem where both devotion and formal expression are joined inseparably. The link to the rosary also marks Donne's sequence as an expression of prayer, meditation and praise. Like the rosary, "La Corona" is characterised by repetition (though in the rosary, the prayers used are repeated several times and in identical form, and the subjects for meditation are always the same) and an anticipated change or progress in the speaker or reciter (in both cases, the prayers or poems are intended to improve the speaker's state of mind and his relationship to God).[6]

2. The first sonnet: a proem

The opening sonnet can be seen as a kind of proem and meta-sonnet *about* the "Corona"; it is connected to the other sonnets through its form and self-referential treatment of the crown of sonnets, but at the same time stands apart from the depiction of Christ that begins in the second sonnet (in line with this, it does not have a programmatic title, but is simply numbered "I"). Donne's speaker is aware of the corona form (and its implications), which are discussed in the opening sonnet, and presents himself as a poet. In describing his sequence as "a crown of prayer and praise," the speaker alludes to the poetic form and at the same time characterises "La Corona" as religious poetry directed to God. Thus, there is a strong emphasis on the sequence's quality as poetry and at the same time on its quality as religious poetry (i.e., "prayer and praise").[7]

---

5   There is also a form called the "Corona of our Lord," consisting of 33 Ave Marias (Martz 1955, 107).

6   Because of its closeness to the rosary, there has been some speculation about the extent to which "La Corona" is Catholic or Protestant. Sabine argues that the cycle (with its allusion to the rosary and Marian worship) "betrays traces of Catholic devotional stealth" (7). She also sees the second sonnet as a as a reference to the hardships and imprisonment Donne's mother had to endure as a Catholic (2-7) and the "little roome" as a reference to secret worship and in particular to Donne's collection of "Catholic" paintings, which he kept in his private rooms (7-8, cf. also Gilman 71).

7   Cf. Chambers: "The liturgical nature of *La Corona* is announced by the first line of the first sonnet, for this particular *corona*, or crown, is to be one of 'prayer and praise,' one whose purposes are precisely those of the rite" (1977, 160). However, "prayer and praise" may also refer to private devotion, and as the use of pronouns shows, the speaker sometimes focuses on himself and sometimes includes other

I
01 Deigne at my hands this crown of prayer and praise,
02 Weav'd in my low devout melancholie,
03 Thou which of good, hast, yea art treasury,
04 All changing unchang'd Antient of dayes,
05 But doe not, with a vile crowne of fraile bayes,
06 Reward my muses white sincerity,
07 But what thy thorny crowne gain'd, that give mee,
08 A crowne of Glory, which doth flower alwayes;
09 The ends crowne our workes, but thou crown'st our ends,
10 For, at our end begins our endlesse rest,
11 This first last end, now zealously possest,
12 With a strong sober thirst, my soul attends.
13 'Tis time that heart and voice be lifted high,
14 Salvation to all that will is nigh.

2.1 The different crowns found in "La Corona"

The fact that the speaker uses the formal arrangement of a "crown of sonnets" implicitly shows his status as a sophisticated and thoughtful poet. The speaker also emphasises his creativity and craftsmanship as a poet: he refers to his muse in the first and last sonnet, he stresses that the poems come "at my hands," and he talks about "our workes" (which, in his case, are his poems). Furthermore, he describes his crown as "weav'd,"[8] that is, he compares his poetic production to a manual process involving the crossing and combining of different layers (the texture in

---

believers. Chambers (1977, 167-68) also points at one of Donne's sermons, where Donne (speaking about the Lord's Prayer) links prayer and praise, as well as highlighting the importance of the number seven and the circularity of the Lord's Prayer:

> Prayer and Praise [...] not onely consist together, but constitute one another [...] As that Prayer consists of seven petitions, and seven is infinite, so by being at first begun with glory and acknowledgement of his [God's] raigning in heaven, and then shut up in the same manner, with acclamations of power and glory, it is made a circle of praise and a circle is infinite, too, the Prayer, and the Praise is equally infinite. ("Sermon Preached at S. Pauls, on Ps. 90.14," Donne, *Sermons* V, no. 14, 270-71).

8   Accoustically, "weave" is close to "wreath" or "wreathe," and a "wreath" can also be a synonym of "crown" (cf. *OED*, "wreath, *n*. II.11"). Donne hints at this when he mentions the "crowne of fraile bayes," which is actually a laurel wreath, and the "wreath" is an important concept in Herbert's poem of the same name.

textile weaving, of several stems in a crown of thorns or roses, and of different textual elements in poetry).

The "vile crowne of fraile bayes" may refer to a victor's laurel wreath (i.e., gained on grounds of physical superiority) but also to a poet's laurel wreath.[9] The speaker rejects the prospect of this crown in favour of a "crowne of Glory." Although the imperative "give mee" in l.1.7 can be understood as a plea or request rather than a command, asking for a "crowne of Glory, which doth flower always" is not a matter of course, and the confidence expressed in such a plea (the confidence that he will be successful in writing a corona worth the crown of glory, as well as the confidence that he will be granted what he asks for) stands in contrast to the speaker's professed "low" and "devout" stance.[10]

The speaker's listing of different crowns in l.1.5-8 provides two alternatives, separated by Christ's death (which also enables the second alternative): The "crowne of fraile bayes" is that of earthly fame, rejected by the speaker, the "thorny crowne" refers directly to the crucifixion, and the "crowne of Glory" refers to heaven and salvation. Christ's death is a connecting link between earth and heaven: at his death, he passes from earth to heaven, and in dying enables the same for humankind. In addition, "crown" may also refer to the "circular ornament for the head conceived as gained in heaven by a saint, martyr, virgin, or Doctor of the

9   The laurel crown worn by victors and poets in classical Greece was reinstated in Italy in 1315 for Albertino Mussato and later for Petrarch (Weiss 20-32).

10   Kronenfeld states that "The central quandary between the desire to praise and the felt imperfections of the praiser is more deeply and immediately realized in the poem than commentary has suggested (295)." However, the speakers in both Donne's and Herbert's poems ultimately do not seem to be very much troubled by their poetic imperfections. In the first place, each speaker has a certain conception of himself as a poet (inferior to God and God's creations but not generally inferior as a poet), which he instantiates in creating an elaborate work of art. In the second place, in "La Corona," the speaker does create a crown which he himself finds worthy to be presented to God, and in "A Wreath" the speaker anticipates a "crown of praise" he will give to God (while he has in fact already presented God with a sophisticated "crown of praise"). The speakers may fully perceive their *moral* imperfections, but in "La Corona" the speaker is confident enough to ask for an eternal reward in exchange for his poem, while in "A Wreath" the speaker's protestation of his artistic imperfections looks more like a rhetorical device (especially at the end, the poem looks like an instance of recusatio) than like true distress over a badly written poem.

Church, or as conferred on any soul received into heaven; the reward or glory represented by this" (*OED*, "crown, *n.*I.2.a").[11]

An allusion to the literal meaning of "rosary" (which comes from Latin "rosarium," rose bush or rose garden) may also be found in the speaker's distinctions between a "vile crowne of fraile bayes" (roses, by contrast, are often perceived as noble flowers), a "thorny crowne" (i.e., one which has thorns like roses, but no flowers), and a "crowne of Glory, which doth *flower* always."[12] The last crown may be seen in contrast to the perennial but eventually withering bay leaves; also, bay leaves do not "flower," while roses do.

The emphasis on circularity inherent in the use of "crown" (as well as the double focus on writing poetry and attaining salvation) is continued with the expression "a crowne of glory." Although this is a set phrase, both "crown" (see above) and "glory" carry multiple connotations. "Glory" may refer to "the splendour and bliss of heaven (*OED*, "glory, *n.*7.a"), which is the primary meaning here. In addition, "glory" once again stresses the sequence's circularity, since it may also refer generally to a circle of light (cf. *OED* "glory, *n.* 9.c") and, more specifically, to a halo: "the circle of light represented as surrounding the head, or the whole figure, of the Saviour, the Virgin, or one of the Saints; an aureole or nimbus" (*OED* "glory, *n.* 9.a"). In characterising the crown of glory as one "which doth flower always," the speaker also alludes to 1 Pet 5.4, "ye shall receive a crown of glory that fadeth not away," and especially to Isa 28.1-5, which contrasts a "crown of pride [...] whose glorious beauty is a fading flower" (Isa 28.1) to "the Lord of hosts" who shall "be for a crown of glory, and for a diadem of beauty" (Isa 28.5). This implicit reference (and the rejection of pride contained in it) again underlines the speaker's stance of "low" and "devout" humility.[13]

---

11   Cf. also 1 Cor 9.24-25: "Know ye not that those who run in a race all run, but one receiveth the prize? [...] Now they do it to obtain a corruptible crown, but we an incorruptible." Here, the corruptible crown would be precisely the laurel wreath rejected by the speaker in "La Corona."

12   Another allusion can be seen in the speaker's concern with moisture and drought in the fifth and sixth sonnets, where Christ's blood is perceived as life-giving in the same way that water is life-giving for plants.

13   "Glory" may also refer to earthly fame (cf. *OED* "glory, *n.* 2.a": "Exalted [...] praise, honour, or admiration accorded by common consent to a person or thing; honourable fame, renown" and 3.: "Something that brings honour and renown"),

The speaker also makes sure to locate his own poetic creation below God's creation in stating that "the ends crowne our workes, but thou crown'st our ends." "The ends crown our works" is proverbial (cf. *Oxford Dictionary of English Proverbs* 220) and 1.1.9 may be seen as an allusion to the good deeds and industrious employment expected from a virtuous Christian. At the same time, there is one visible "work" here, which is the poem itself, and the speaker's "manual" labour is further emphasised by "at my hands" and "weav'd."

"End" is ambiguous and may refer either to "ending" or to "aim," and both meanings are present in l. 9. If the speaker's work consists in the "Corona," then the "end" is quite clear: prayer and praise. The speaker emphasises the "end" and by using "crown" explicitly creates a connection to the crown of sonnets – which, however, is characterised by its circularity and, formally, does not have a proper "end." The speaker thus plays with both meanings and with the poetic form used, and he highlights the fact that there is an "outcome" to the "Corona." His poetic achievements (though created with "white sincerity") are set below Christ's achievement of saving humankind, and the speaker makes this clear from the beginning in describing his state of mind not only as a "low [...] melancholie" but also as a "devout" one.

Even though the speaker creates a poetic crown for Christ, it is ultimately Christ who will crown the speaker. The speaker's concern with the form of "La Corona" is thus interlinked with his concern for his own afterlife. When he discusses the implications of "crown," he asks for one "which doth flower alwayes," and his thoughts about his work ("The ends crowne our works") are turned into thoughts about his death and salvation ("Thou crown'st our ends). At the same time, lines 9-11 indicate that (in spite of the circularity created by the crown of sonnets) there *is* a concrete end towards which the speaker is looking, namely his own death. The connection between creating poetry and attaining salvation is also visible in the speaker's references to his muse and his soul. Although the primary focus of "La Corona" is a spiritual one, the speaker seems

---

but the speaker excludes this meaning by contrasting the "vile crowne of fraile bayes" with the "crowne of glory." Yet, even if the speaker is not thirsting for earthly fame, the poetic accomplishment he aims at is one that would bring him fame as a consummate artist (i.e., "a crowne of glory," but not one that would "flower alwayes").

almost as much concerned with poetic success. His muse is only mentioned twice (in 1.1.6 and in 1.7.13), but each time in prominent positions: in the opening sonnet and at the end of the sequence. His soul is mentioned four times, in 1.1.12, 1.3.9, 1.5.14 and, consequently, 1.6.1. Yet the soul is *not* mentioned in the seventh sonnet, whose last six lines deal explicitly with the speaker's salvation; instead it is the muse that is stressed again in the end. Muse and soul are thus linked to each other, and the speaker's poetic endeavours build a kind of frame within which he presents the life of Christ and reflects on his own salvation. The depictions of muse and soul thus lead to a merging of both entities, of the speaker's creative part and of his spiritual part, so that the speaker as poet and the speaker as a sinner in need of redemption become inseparable through the course of the sequence.

Furthermore, the muse is characterised as possessing "white sincerity" and the speaker implores the Holy Spirit to raise his muse (not his soul) in the end. In both cases the muse is associated with attributes we would expect in relation to the speaker's soul. "White sincerity" is an unusual trait for a "muse," since "white" as a colour of "innocence of soul, of purity, and of holiness of life" (Ferguson 152) is usually associated with spiritual qualities and often attributed to Christ or the Virgin Mary.[14] In Donne's Holy Sonnet "If faithfull soules," a similar expression is found: "my mindes white truth," and in two instances Donne uses "white integrity." In "To Mr Henry Wotton," "white integrity" is attributed to those who do not sin (in this case, only beasts): "Angels sinned first, then devils, and then man. / Only, perchance, beasts sin not; wretched we /Are beasts in all but white integrity" (ll.40-42), and in "A Funeral Elegy," Elizabeth Drury is described as "Clothed in her virgin white integrity"

---

14   On the other hand, stressing the sincerity of a poet-lover's feelings is also a topos found in love poetry, for example, in the opening sonnet of *Astrophil and Stella*, which begins with "Loving in truth" and ends with the Muse's prompt to "looke in thy heart and write," which can also be seen as indicating sincerity (i.e., the speaker should simply write down his true emotions). Cf. also O'Connell (1986, 121-23), who sees the first sonnet as an attempt to imitate love poetry: the crown of prayer and praise is

> a religious analogue to the crown of posies, both flowers and poems, that a love poet presents to his mistress to honor her and win her favour. Yet this shift from secular to sacred is radically unsuccessful. Even as he presents his crown, the speaker senses his audacity in offering his own creation to the Creator of all reality (1986, 121)

(l.75), that is, "white" is attributed to the virginity of a decidedly virtuous woman.[15] Hotson, in discussing a portrait by Hilliard, analyses the symbolism of white hands (50-51), and in addition to Donne's examples, he mentions Joseph Hall's *Characters of Vertues and Vices* (1608), where "The Faithful Man" "hath white hands, and a cleane soule" (21) and a poem from Robert Tofte's sequence *Laura* which contains the line "White as thy hands, so white thy faith shall bee" (Part I, #30, l.10). He also looks at white hands in heraldry and concludes that "[t]he white of joined hands [...] exhibits the 'true faith' or 'true love'" as sound, sincere, and spotless" (51).[16]

The Muse's "white sincerity" stands in contrast to the speaker's "melancholie." "Melancholy" derives from the Greek μελαγχολία (from "μελαν," indicating blackness, and "χολή," meaning "bile", cf. *OED* "melancholy, *n*.[1]"), and thus points directly at the darkness or blackness of his state: white sincerity is attributed to the Muse, while black "low devout melancholie" belongs to the speaker.[17] The Muse is presented as an exterior agent, and the speaker's melancholy describes an interior state (a physical state, through an imbalance of tempers, as well as an emotional state). With the help of his Muse, the speaker can address Christ, who (in the last stanza) is shown to bring the speaker out of his "dark" state by proving light for him.[18]

---

15 In "Child-hood," Vaughan uses "white designs" (l.4) for the innocence of children's intentions.

16 With "true love," Hotson refers to worldly love and the depiction of a marital union in heraldry.

17 The combination of "white sincerity" and "melancholie" results in black and white, which is the colour of the Dominicans, distinguished by their black-and-white robes. The main attribute of St. Dominic is the rosary (Ferguson 115), since he was credited with introducing the practice of praying the rosary.

18 Cf. the Holy Sonnet "Oh my blacke soule," which ends with

   Oh make thy selfe with holy mourning blacke,
   And red with blushing, as thou art with sinne;
   Or wash thee in Christs blood, which hath this might
   That being red, it dyes red soules to white. (ll.11-14)

   Here, the alternatives to sinful blackness are "holy mourning" (comparable to the speaker's melancholy in "La Corona") and becoming white through Christ's blood (similarly, in the last sonnet of "La Corona," "drossie clay" is "purely washt, or burnt"). Cf. also Zirker (2018).

In addition, the invocation of the muse(s) follows classical traditions (cf., for example, the beginning of the *Iliad* and *Odyssey*, the *Aneid* and *Metamorphoses*, and of later Renaissance texts such as Spenser's *Faerie Queene* or Drayton's *Poly-Olbion*). The speaker's address to Christ, to whom the speaker's muse is subordinated, resembles the classical invocation of the muses and thus marks the "Corona" simultaneously as a serious work of art and as a religions text. The connection between muse and soul also becomes apparent in the statement, "'Tis time that heart and voice be lifted high." The division into "heart and voice" (and their combination into one subject) reflects the connection of muse and soul – the speaker's heart can be allocated to his soul, while his voice is that of a poet (driven by his muse and his religious zeal), which he raises to God.

The change of address within the first sonnet indicates a "public" in addition to a "private" intention. The first eight lines are addressed to God and express the speaker's very own desire. In l.1.9, the speaker changes to the collective "our" (which does of course include the individual speaker) and reflects generally on "ends." In l.1.12 he switches again to "my soul" and in l.1.11 the demonstrative "this" in "this first last end" is again singular and shows closeness to the speaker. The phrase refers back to "our end" in l.1.10 (i.e., to death), and makes this end more specific and individual through the use of singular and indexical. "'Tis time that heart and voice be lifted high" is in turn a general statement again and can be understood as a calling to all people, to "all that will" (again including the speaker). Moreover, the "voice [...] lifted high" implies raising one's voice, that is, speaking (or even singing) with a loud voice and therefore also evokes a public rather than private setting.[19]

---

19 In one of Donne's sermons the image of the crown is also used in a decidedly "public" way, to illustrate the proliferation of God's word (and of good moral behaviour) from the preacher to his congregation:

Saint Paul [not only] calls those whom he had converted, his Crown, his Crown, in the Church; but he cals them his Crown in heaven. [...] you, to whom God sends us, doe as well make up our Crown, as we doe yours, since your being wrought upon, and our working upon you conduce to both our Crowns [...]. If when we have begot you in Christ, by our preaching, you also beget others by your holy life and conversation, you have added another generation unto us, and you have preached over our Sermons again, as fruitfully as we our selves; you shall be our Crown, and they shall be your Crowns, and Christ Jesus a Crown of everlasting glory to us all. ("Sermon Preached at Lincolns Inne, on Col. 1.24," Donne, *Sermons* III, no. 16, 346-47).

2.2 Thirst and salvation

In the first sonnet, the speaker introduces another image that is important for the whole poem, the "strong sober thirst" of his soul. The speaker states that he "attends" "this first last end" with a "strong sober thirst." This can be read as his thirsting *for* death, but it can also be read as a description of his state *while* he waits for death. In the latter case, his thirst provides a motivation for writing a devotional poem, since only God can allay the thirst of his soul, and the speaker later makes this explicit in 1.5.14 and in 11.6.1-4, where he explains who his "dry" soul will be saved by Christ's blood.

By introducing his soul's thirst, the speaker adds another motivation for writing the poem, and makes it a matter of urgency that his pleas be answered: thirst is a strong and vital human need, and the speaker thus not merely asks for a reward for his Muse's effort, he also shows himself to act from urgent necessity. In addition, in describing himself as thirsty, the speaker imitates Christ: especially in the context of the "thorny crowne" in 1.1.7, the mention of "thirst" brings to mind Christ's thirst on the cross (cf. John 19.28). This thirst is satisfied by Christ's blood in the sixth stanza, a fact which marks the allaying of the speaker's thirst as a Eucharistic action. Lastly, thirst is recurrent, so that the moistening of his soul is not a final action but one that needs to be repeated (at least as long as the speaker is alive and has not yet reached "this first last end") – like the reading of the Corona itself.

By characterising this thirst as "sober," the speaker immediately makes clear that his desire is virtuous. It is an earnest thirst (cf. *OED*, "sober, adj.* II.4"), not just a greedy lusting, like a thirst for alcohol (cf. *OED*, "sober, *adj*. I.2.b"), and, though strong, his thirst is not excessive (cf.

Although the speaker in "La Corona" focuses on his own salvation rather than on that of other people, the use of the crown image in Donne's sermon shares several aspects of the "crown" in "La Corona." In the first place, the sermon provides another instance of a crown (or crowns) coming into existence through words: people become a "crown" through the preacher's sermons to his congregation and the congregation's subsequent "holy life and conversation." Secondly, the proliferation from preacher to congregation to others, and from one generation to another resembles both a circular movement (creating larger and larger circles) and a regenerative process (adding another "generation" and being "fruitful"), which fits in with the image of the "dry soule" being restored to new life through Christ's moistening blood found in "La Corona."

OED, "sober, *adj*.I.1.b"). In describing his longing for God as a thirst of his soul, the speaker uses a phrase that also appears in several psalms, which adds to his emphasis that his is a "sober" thirst. Line 1.12 also echoes Matt. 5.6, "Blessed are they which do hunger and thirst after righteousness: for they shall be filled," which contains the promise that makes the speaker confident in his "strong sober thirst." At the same time, to thirst is a sensual, bodily experience (and even the characterisation as "sober" cannot change that), which is here ascribed to the soul, that is, to the speaker's immaterial part.

The image of the "thirsty" soul is explicitly picked up again in the fifth and sixth stanzas, when "at [Christ's] death," the speaker asks Christ to *"Moyst, with one drop of thy blood, my dry soule"* (and the repetition of this line in 1.6.1, with a change of meaning for "moyst" from imperative to participial adjective, indicates that the speaker's wish will be granted in the future and his soul will be moist(ened)). The soul is called "too stony hard, and yet too fleshly" (6.3), and the blood's effect on the soul is one of invigoration and restoration: the soul will be "freed by that drop, from being starv'd, hard, or foule" (6.4). The power of the blood is three-fold: it feeds what is starving, it softens what is hard and it cleanses or heals what is foul. When the soul receives this drop, it will be spiritually nourished, and its obstinacy and sinfulness will be taken away. In being "freed," the soul will be redeemed and restored to everlasting life. Once more, the speaker describes his soul in terms of physical, bodily qualities, especially in using "fleshly" and "being starv'd." This tension between material and immaterial qualities underlines the metaphorical level of the descriptions used (which is of course already present in describing the soul as "dry," "stony hard" and "fleshly"), and at the same time the speaker introduces additional connotations, showing the soul as something that is alive and dynamic and in need of nourishment.

A similar image is found in the last sonnet, where the addressee's tears are described as a cleansing liquid ("Yee whose just teares, or tribulation / Have purely washt, or burnt your drossie clay"), while Christ's blood serves to "mark the path" to the speaker's salvation. In line 12, the moistening blood is mentioned again: "Oh, with thine owne blood quench thine owne just wrath." Here, the blood has the function of extinguishing fire, equally live-saving, but different from the nourishing force in stanzas 5-6, where the speaker asks for just "one drop of thy blood," to "moyst […] my dry soule." In the last sonnet he then talks about a large quantity of tears (enough to "wash" the clay) and about "thine owne blood" in general (enough to mark the path and to heaven and to "quench" God's wrath). Also, in stanza five, the speaker addresses Christ crucified, while ll. 7.3-4 seem to be addressed to other men (those who actually possess "drossie clay"), and in l.7.12 the reference to "thine owne just wrath" suggests that the speaker addresses God in general (or at least merges the conception of Christ giving his blood to redeem humanity and God Almighty possessing "just wrath").

3. Sonnets two to four: the speaker's different perspectives

From the second sonnet on, all sonnets are titled to indicate the episodes from Christ's life and death they refer to. While the first sonnet is largely addressed to God, in the following sonnets the speaker changes between different perspectives and also between different addressees. Sonnets two to four describe the annunciation, nativity and presentation at the temple, i.e., they are concerned with Jesus yet unborn and as a child. The speaker presents himself as part of the scenes he describes in sonnets two to four, and directly addresses Mary and Joseph.

3.1 The second sonnet: from heaven to earth – God becomes human

The title "Annunciation" of the second sonnet evokes the traditional annunciation scene, that is, a set tableau with the angel Gabriel announcing the conception and birth of Jesus to Mary. The speaker takes up this traditional image, but he makes himself the messenger: he directly addresses Mary and "announces" Jesus' coming into the world to her (and thus, indirectly, also to the reader). In speaking to Mary and participating in the annunciation, the speaker of the sonnet brings himself closer to the events he describes (and in this way also closer to Christ) by becoming part of them. At the same time, the speaker stays omniscient and refers to points in time and space long before and after the annunciation. Although the sonnet is about the annunciation, the speaker incorporates the incarnation into this and the following sonnet.

2. Annunciation
01 *Salvation to all that will is nigh,*
02 That All, which alwayes is All every where,
03 Which cannot sinne, and yet all sinnes must beare,
04 Which cannot die, yet cannot chuse but die,
05 Loe, faithfull Virgin, yeelds himselfe to lye
06 In prison, in thy wombe; and though he there
07 Can take no sinne, nor thou give, yet he'will weare
08 Taken from thence, flesh, which deaths force may trie.
09 Ere by the spheares time was created, thou
10 Wast in his minde, who is thy Sonne, and Brother,
11 Whom thou conceiv'st, conceiv'd; yea thou art now
12 Thy Makers maker, and thy Fathers mother,
13 Thou' hast light in darke; and shut'st in little roome,
14 *Immensity cloysterd in thy deare wombe.*

Here, too, the speaker emphasises circularity and circular motion. The sonnet stresses the "inwardness" of Christ in the womb, and simultaneously the all-encompassing immensity of God. Hence, although most of the action in this sonnet consists of "proclaiming," the speaker oscillates between several temporal and spatial dimensions. The sonnet begins by repeating l.1.14, "*Salvation to all that will is nigh.*" The "all" from l.2.1 is taken up in the next line and the focus switches from the salvation of humankind to God in his different shapes. Ll.2.2-8 form a complex sentence: to the subject of this sentence, "That All" in l.2.2, several subordinate clauses and insertions are added, till the main verb "yeelds" appears in l.2.5, followed by a complex predicate ("yeelds himself to lye / In prison") and another insertion ("in thy wombe"). The continuation of l.2.6, "and though he there" (which, strictly speaking, continues the sentence begun in l.2.2) introduces another equally complex sentence.

Donne's use of "All" to refer to the cosmos (a meaning which he makes explicit with "which always is All every where") was still novel at the time (cf. *OED*, "all, *adj., pron.,* and *n., adv.,* and *conj.*B.II.7.a": "The universe, the macrocosm; the whole of nature or existence"), as the first documented use dates from 1598 (found in Thomas Bastard's collection of epigrams *Chrestoleros*):[20]

---

20 "La Corona" was presumably written around 1607-1608 (Donne 2010, 475). There is also the phrase "all of all," used to refer to God and even as an address of God, also documented for the first time in 1598 (*OED*, "all, *adj., pron.,* and *n., adv.,* and

> Man is a little world and beares the face,
> And picture of the Universitie:
> All but resembleth God, all but his glasse,
> All but the picture of his majestie.
>   Man is the little world (so we him call,)
>   The world the little God, God the great All.
> (Liber Primus, No.4, "De Microcosmo")

The way in which "All" is presented in this quotation shows two things that are relevant in "La Corona," too. Firstly, God is equated with the cosmos, and thus shown as omnipresent. At the same time, the notion of spheres is brought in (in the notion of the round earth and the celestial spheres).[21] Secondly, the "All" is here immediately related to the world and to man and shown as pervasive and encompassing: man is a little world and situated *in* the world which surrounds him, the world is a "little God" (i.e. in this sense a "little All") surrounded by the cosmos, and God is the "great All" after which there is nothing greater.[22] In Donne's poem, man and cosmos are connected through God's pervasiveness as well as through Christ's incarnation, *"Immensity cloysterd in thy deare wombe"* (1.2.14): the womb is a small, human, earthly sphere, a "little roome" (1.2.13), into which the "All" "yeelds himselfe to lye" (1.2.5).[23]

---

conj. P22"). The *OED* ("all, *adj.*, *pron.*, and *n.*, *adv.*, and *conj.*II.6.b.) also lists another quote, from Daniel's *Musophilus* (1599, Daniel 1963), which bears so much similarity to Donne's poem that is seems to have been a direct influence:

> Short-breath'd Mortalitie would yet extend
>   That spanne of life so farre forth as it may,
>   And robbe her Fate; seeke to beguile her end
>   Of some few lingring dayes of after-stay,
>   That all this little All, might not descend
>   Into the dark, a universall pray.
>   And give our labours yet this poore delight,
>   That when our daies doe end, they are not done:
>   And though we die, we shall not perish quite,
>   But live two lives, where other have but one. (ll.33-42)

21 Cf. also the beginning of "Goodfriday, 1613" again: "Let mans Soule be a Spheare."

22 Cf. also Cusa's emphasis on everything being enfolded "in" God, in the discussion of "The Search."

23 The ambiguous "Sonne" in 1.2.10, in its meaning as "sun," providing "light in darke" (1.2.13), is also spherical.

The whole line "[t]hat All, which alwayes is All every where," which echoes the "All changing unchang'd Antient of dayes" from the first stanza, emphasises God's eternity and infinity ("always" can be read as "forever" and as "everywhere," and "All every where" underlines this endlessness), which is then contrasted to Christ's mortality and confinement in a human body, and further, in Mary's womb. Ll.2.3-4 anticipate the crucifixion, that is, Christ "which [...] all sinnes must beare" and "which [...] cannot chuse but die." In l.5 the speaker refers back to l.2, "that All," i.e., to God's immensity, which is followed by stressing the weakness and limitation of Christ: he "yeelds," he "lye[s]," he is "in prison" and "in thy wombe." The speaker then stresses sin and death again: mortal and weak "flesh" and "deaths force."

On the one hand, the autonomy of God is repeatedly shown, he yields "himself," he "will" wear flesh (which is ambiguous and shows either futurity or volition), and l. 2.8, "flesh, which deaths force may trie" is syntactically ambiguous: either God made flesh may try (i.e., taste) death's force, or death's force may try (i.e., (unsuccessfully) struggle with) God made flesh. The reciprocity implied in this double reading already shows Christ deliberately seeking out death (as well as death "coming towards" Christ) and the future battle between them. On the other hand, God "must beare" all sins and "lye[s]" "in prison." The tension between God's power and Christ's deliberate powerlessness is made most explicit in the expression "cannot chuse but die": while it implies a lack of choice, it also mentions choice explicitly. "Chuse" is ambiguous, and can refer either to choosing between alternative options (*OED*, "choose, *v*.1.a and 2"), or to a strong inclination, "to will, to wish" something (*OED*, "choose, *v*. 3"). Both meanings merge here: the "All" cannot choose between dying and living, it must necessarily choose dying (as predestined); at the same time, the "All" willingly wants and chooses to die for the sins of humankind.

In l.2.9 the temporal perspective changes and the speaker again assumes a broader view by referring to a point before the creation of time and space: "Ere by the spheares time was created" not only contains a temporal component, it also implies that the time-creating spheres did not exist before, and hence, no space at all that can be conceived by men (what did exist before, however, is "his minde"). The speaker merges different time frames and different causal relations to create circularity. The "All" is spherical, containing the circular "spheares," and so is their movement. The temporal paradox of Mary being conceived by God before giving birth to God is expanded over ll.2.9-12 and contemplated in different ways. Mary is conceived by God before she conceives Jesus, Jesus is her "Sonne, and Brother," she is her "Makers maker" and her "Fathers mother."

The last two lines go back to the spatial paradox of God becoming flesh and stress spatial aspects: "shut'st," "little roome," cloysterd" and, again, "thy deare wombe" all express a confinement and limitation within which "immensity" is enclosed.[24] The statement "thou' hast light in darke" may refer either to Christ (the "light") lying in the darkness of Mary's womb, or it may refer to Mary's enlightenment and certain knowledge of salvation in contrast to the speaker, who seems to remain in darkness till the seventh sonnet, where he stresses the light brought by Christ: the "everlasting day" (l.7.1), the "uprising of this Sunne, and Sonne" (l.7.2) and the "Bright torch, which shin'st, that I the way may see" (l.7.11). Thus, in this sonnet the speaker merges cause and effect, different time frames and apparently incompatible spaces, which come together in an "All" that permeates everything from infinity to minuteness.

3.2 The third sonnet: the speaker looks down on Christ in the crib

The third sonnet describes the "Nativitie." The speaker continues to address Mary as if he were present, and he now becomes much more descriptive in his display of "Inne," "stall," "starres" and "wisemen." However, the description of the nativity with a focus on Mary only comprises the first eight lines, then the speaker turns to addressing his soul, which is shown to be looking at Jesus in the crib. He thus makes his account of the nativity more vivid and dramatic by presenting his soul as a distinct character that can be addressed (or, alternatively, by talking to his soul in a kind of soliloquy), and he again incorporates himself into the scene he

---

24 In depicting Mary's womb as a cloister, Donne picks up a traditional image: the use of "cloysterd" may also hint at the traditional idea of Mary as a "hortus conclusus."

describes: his soul takes part in the activity of the magi and shepherds in contemplating Jesus.[25]

> 3. Nativitie
> 01 *Immensitie cloysterd in thy deare wombe,*
> 02 Now leaves his welbelov'd imprisonment,
> 03 There he hath made himself to his intent
> 04 Weake enough, now into our world to come;
> 05 But Oh, for thee, for him, hath th' Inne no roome?
> 06 Yet lay him in this stall, and from th'Orient,
> 07 Starres, and wisemen will travell to prevent
> 08 Th'effect of *Herods* jealous generall doome.
> 09 Seest thou, my Soule, with thy faiths eyes, how he
> 10 Which fils all place, yet none holds him, doth lye?
> 11 Was not his pity towards thee wondrous high,
> 12 That would have need to be pittied by thee?
> 13 Kisse him, and with him into Egypt goe,
> 14 *With his kinde mother, who partakes thy woe.*

Once more, the speaker focuses on space and different spatial dimensions. In the first eight lines, the speaker's view constantly changes from one place to another. He begins by repeating that "immensitie" is "cloysterd in thy deare wombe," that is, he once more stresses the merging of endless, divine space with a very small, confined and human space (it is "cloysterd," the womb is closed, and the womb is human). "Immensitie" is now personified and refers to Christ himself, thus showing again the contrast between God's all-encompassing dimension and infinity and the confined, "well-belov'd imprisonment."[26] Christ's enclosure and his weakness are shown as intentional: he "leaves" his "imprisonment" and "hath made himself to his intent /Weake enough." The *apo koinou* construction in l.3.3-4 allows to read l.3.3 separately, as "He hath made himself, to his intent" (i.e., God has created himself, in the form of Christ) thus stressing God's deliberate act of creation, as well as referring back

---

25   Cf. also Zirker (2018) on Donne's exploration of the soul through the use of dramatic elements, especially on the direct address of the soul.

26   In stanzas 2 and 3, the speaker describes two kinds of (human) space with the same terms: the inn has "no roome," while Mary, through the power of God, can accommodate "immensity" and the "All, which alwayes is All every where" "in little roome," which shows the contrast between human limitation and divine omnipotence.

to the paradox originating from the unity of Christ and God, expressed in ll. 2.9-12 (God is both maker and son, and was there before Mary as well as through Mary, because he "hath made himself" as Christ).

In l.3.4 the speaker talks about "our world," and thus briefly includes humanity in general, before he addresses Mary again. L.3.2 emphasises the moment of speaking: "now leaves," as does l.3.4: "now into our world to come." The speaker's exclamation, "But Oh, for thee, for him, hath th' Inne no roome? / Yet lay him in this stall," once more shows the speaker's apparent attendance at the nativity (which is also stressed by the use of "this stall," as if the speaker could really see and point at the stable).[27] In the continuation of l.3.6, however, the speaker changes his perspective and becomes an omniscient narrator looking forward to the future: to the more immediate future of the adoration of the magi, and further on, to the massacre of the innocents. "Wisemen will travel to prevent" is ambiguous: it may mean they come before (i.e., earlier than) "Herods jealous generall doome" (which is underlined by the fact that "Starres" travel in the same way, to appear over Bethlehem), and the use of "prevent" also suggests that they hindered Herod's actions, which they did to some extent by not reporting back to Herod on their way home (cf. Donne 1978, 60 and Donne 2010, 480). L.3.7-8 refers to the future in a triple way: to the coming of the magi in the near future, shortly after Jesus's birth, to "Herods generall doome," that is, the massacre of the innocents, and to the flight to Egypt (which is the "effect" of "Herods generall doome") in the more distant future. Thus, in ll.3.6-8 the speaker once more mixes different time frames: the placing of Jesus in the crib, the voyage of the magi (which he describes as a future event, they "will travel" from the "Orient," although their voyage is mostly over when Jesus is born), Herod's massacre (which will not yet take place for a while) and the flight into Egypt (taking place shortly before the massacre) are all

---

27 The concreteness and immediacy of this setting resembles the "composition of place" as the first step of a devotional meditation (i.e., in Loyolan style). However, unlike that of a traditional meditation, the "place" changes from sonnet to sonnet in "La Corona"; these changes of topic and place rather suggest the practice of praying the rosary and evoking some of the mysteries of the rosary. Cf. also Martz (1955, 107), who argues for the cycle as a meditation following the devotional "Corona of our Lady" structure, though with a shift in emphasis from Mary to Christ.

joined to each other and temporally connected by the speaker, in his hindsight as a later-born narrator of the story of Christ.

After l.3.8, there is another change of perspective, and the speaker now turns back to the present moment of speaking. In ll. 3.9-13, the addressee is at first ambiguous: the speaker might still be addressing Mary (calling her "my Soule" just as he exclaimed in l.3.5f. "for thee, for him, hath th' Inne no roome? / Yet lay him in this stall") or his own soul. Ll. 3.11-12, "Was not his pity towards thee wondrous high, / That would have need to be pittied by thee?" ties in with the notion of Mary being her "Makers maker" and her "Fathers mother" expressed in the previous sonnet. In l.3.14, the ambiguity disappears when the speaker urges the soul to go to Egypt "with his kinde mother."

The speaker stresses the soul's ability to see the nativity: "Seest thou, my Soule, with thy faiths eyes." If this refers to the speaker's soul, the emphasis on seeing with "faiths eyes" is very similar to the speaker's insistence on "seeing" the crucifixion in "Goodfriday, 1613," where references to the speaker's vision abound: "there I should see a Sunne," "I do not see / That spectacle," "Who sees Gods face," "to see God dye," "Could I behold those hands," "Could I behold that endlesse height," "durst I / [...] cast mine eye," "these things [...] be from mine eye," and finally (and most importantly), "[my memory] looks towards them; and thou look'st towards me." In "La Corona," too, the speaker "sees" events with his memory that were passed down to him as cultural and religious knowledge, and here, too, the immediacy inherent in "seeing" is used to meditate on the life of Christ and to create a stronger connection to God (even if the lines are read as an address to Mary, it is still the speaker who evokes the nativity scene and the impact of Jesus lying in the crib).[28]

---

28   Throughout "La Corona", the visibility and invisibility of what the speaker describes is important: The speaker uses "loe" three times, explicitly appealing to his addressee's vision and stressing that what he describes is "visible" in some sense, as well as several other explicit references to "seeing." However, Mary cannot see Jesus before his birth, Joseph cannot see how Jesus "speakes wonders," nor can he "see" Jesus at the temple before turning back. And neither the speaker nor a general contemporary reader can "see" any of these events, because they live in a different time. The speaker thus simultaneously points at the visibility of what he describes and makes clear that he is not talking about "real" vision, but about events taking place within the poem and within the speaker's imagination (which

In "Goodfriday," seeing Christ enables the speaker to talk to Christ; in "La Corona," the speaker addresses God Almighty (the "All changing unchang'd Antient of dayes," l.1.4), he talks to Christ ("But what thy thorny crowne gain'd, that give mee," l.1.7 and especially in sonnets five to seven), he addresses Mary ("Loe, faithfull Virgin," l.2.5) and, later on, Joseph ("*Joseph* turne backe," l.4.2). The speaker goes even further and tells his soul to kiss Jesus and to go with him into Egypt. The soul is thus personified and made physical and material, and the speaker imagines a maximum of physical closeness between his soul and Jesus. The shared woe of Mary and the speaker's soul in l.3.14 adds another element of communion.

L.3.10 again makes reference to God's all-encompassing greatness, God "fils all place, yet none holds him."[29] This stands in contrast to the smallness and passivity of the baby lying in the crib. The passive state of a newborn baby, however, is contrasted with the active and conscious way in which this "laying" is described: in l.3.6 Mary is called to "lay him in this stall," which takes Jesus as passive object, whereas in l.3.10 he simply "doth lye" (which is quite neutral with regard to his own involvement. And both actions echo l.2.5, where Jesus "yeelds himselfe to lye," which presents it as an active and conscious action.

Once more, the speaker also merges different time frames. God's pity towards the speaker's soul "was wondrous high" at a time when God had "need to be pittied by thee," which, in this stanza, may refer to Christ as a babe but can also be read as an anticipation of the crucifixion, especially when considering the crucifixion and consequent absolution as an instance of God's pity for humankind, and keeping in mind that the soul shares Mary's "woe." That is, the speaker combines an event taking place at a certain point in time (either adoration or crucifixion) with a general and timeless act (God's pity for men). He uses using the past tense for this general act and a conditional for the speaker's potential pity for Christ – we would expect either present or past tense to describe the soul's emotions, and present for God's pity. The general statement in

---

ties in with the notion of the "Corona" as a meditation, in which places and events from Christ's life and death are vividly imagined).

29   Cf. also the Second Definition from the *Liber XXIV Philosophorum*, "Deus est sphaera infinita cuius centrum est ubique, circumferentia vero nusquam," in the discussion of "The Search."

ll.3.11-12, in the past tense, is embedded into the present of "seeing" Christ in the manger and the demand to kiss and follow Jesus, which entails an orientation towards the future, or rather, towards two future events of different dimension, a short (and probably immediate) kiss and a longer journey that has not yet taken place (if the need to pity Christ refers to the crucifixion, this also means an orientation towards an even more distant future).

3.3 The fourth sonnet: Christ turns from child into saviour

The title of the fourth sonnet differs from the others in describing a specific location, the Temple, instead of an action or state.[30] This sonnet is the last one to present Jesus' childhood, before the speaker turns straight to the crucifixion.

> 4. Temple
> 01 *With his kinde mother, who partakes thy woe,*
> 02 *Joseph* turne backe; see where your child doth sit,
> 03 Blowing, yea blowing out those sparks of wit,
> 04 Which himselfe on those Doctors did bestow;
> 05 The Word but lately could not speake, and loe
> 06 It sodenly speakes wonders, whence comes it,
> 07 That all which was, and all which should be writ,
> 08 A shallow seeming child, should deeply know?
> 09 His Godhead was not soule to his manhood,
> 10 Nor had time mellow'd him to this ripenesse,
> 11 But as for one which hath a long taske, 'tis good,
> 12 With the Sunne to beginne his businesse,

---

30   Chambers offers an explanation why Donne chose exactly this part of Christ's life, which is distinguished from the topics of the other sonnets by its episodic character. He argues that the Temple scene is emblematic of the double nature of Christ (1960, 213-14 and 216) and that

> The subject matter of the fourth sonnet looks back to the human frailty of the birth of Jesus, signifies the first manifestation of his divinity, marks his entrance into the ministry, and forecasts the end for which he came. [...] the "Temple" appears in a poem of prayer and praise upon the life of Christ not as an extraneous element but as a thematic part which is in effect a précis of the whole. (1960, 217)

Thus, the Temple scene provides a turning point in the life of Christ from his role as frail child to adult saviour, as well as containing the essence of Christ as both human and divine (which is also reflected in its position right at the centre of "La Corona").

13 He in his ages morning thus began
14 *By miracles exceeding power of man.*

In the transition from sonnet three to four, the speaker repeats l.3.14, but changes the addressee. In l.3.14, it is the speaker's soul which should accompany Mary and Jesus into Egypt, while in l.4.1, it is Joseph who should turn back to the Temple with Mary. The speaker's change of addressee allows him to connect to Joseph as well, so that in sonnets two to four there are three addressees: Mary, Joseph and the speaker's soul. Christ as a child is never directly addressed by the speaker and (in sonnets two to four) only described in the third person, until l.5.12, where he talks to Christ on the cross: "Now thou art lifted up."

Again, the speaker merges different temporal levels, combining past, present and future: "all which was, and all which should be writ, / A shallow seeming child, should deeply know," and, as in the previous stanzas, the speaker also alludes to God's greatness (who "should deeply know" "all which was, and all which should be writ") in comparison to the confinement of a human body ("a shallow seeming child"). The speaker makes it clear that Jesus's wisdom was not developed by life experience (he is still "in his ages morning" and not yet "mellow'd" to "ripenesse"), but is part of his "miracles exceeding power of man" so that he "sodenly speaks wonders." The speaker tells Joseph to "turne backe," which here means to turn towards Christ and to "see where your child doth sit" (l.4.2). This appeal is parallel to the speaker's address of his own soul in ll.3.9-10: "Seest thou [...] how he / [...] doth lye." At the same time, the explicit call to "turne backe" adds to the multiple turns within the sequence: the turning from one event to another, the circular turning made explicit again and again, the speaker's turn from sinfulness to salvation and from darkness to light, and in the end, the sequence's structural turn back to the first line (a most prominent turning back).

Ll. 4.7-8 provide the centre of the whole poem, and also constitute a turning point, from Christ as a child to Christ as a mature person. The "all" is repeated, "all which was" and "all which should be writ," and thus encompasses past and future. In the present (at this point in the poem and the narrative) stands the "shallow seeming child" which "should deeply know." This description emphasises that the knowledge and wisdom Christ shows as a child is divine: it only "seems" shallow, at the same time, "shallow" also contains "all" in its middle.

The speaker shifts the focus of this episode as recounted in Luke 2.41-52 from Jesus' teaching and the people's marvel at his wisdom to focus on the "Word" – combining speech, text and knowledge – in contrast to merely human knowledge. The Doctors' meagre "sparks of wit" stand in opposition to the "deep" knowledge of Jesus, which comprises all past and future knowledge. At the same time, "deeply" stresses the inwardness of his knowledge and "know" itself describes an "inner" quality: knowledge is not visible from the outside (the use of "sparks" also leads to an implicit comparison with the description of Christ as a "bright torch" in l.7.11).

Jesus does not need to be "mellow'd" because he is already in a state of "ripenesse," though he begins "in his ages morning." This, too, stresses that his wisdom is not one that developed over time through age and experience, but a wisdom and knowledge that was already "in" him from the beginning: what is "in" Christ now comes "out" and is taught (and thus made visible) to others.

4.   Sonnets five to seven: the speaker's relation to Christ

After spending three stanzas describing Christ's conception, birth and childhood (i.e. with the beginning of Christ's life), the speaker jumps directly to the end: the next three stanzas are concerned with Christ's death and resurrection. While the speaker has only spoken about Jesus in the third person in stanzas two to four, he now frequently addresses Christ directly.

4.1 The fifth sonnet: the speaker looks up to Christ Crucified

The title of the fifth sonnet is even more conspicuous than the topographic "Temple" from the previous one: The gerund "crucifying" describes a specified action and refers to the actual moment of Christ being crucified. The speaker thus stresses the immediacy of the crucifixion. Through the use of active instead of passive voice, there is also a focus on the people performing the crucifixion – and on the fact that something is "being done" to Christ (which culminates in ll.5.6-9, where God is prescribed a fate and reduced to an inch).

5. Crucifying
01 *By miracles exceeding power of man,*
02 He faith in some, envie in some begat,
03 For, what meek[31] spirits admire, ambitious, hate;
04 In both affections many to him ran,
05 But Oh! the worst are most, they will and can,
06 Alas, and do, unto th'immaculate,
07 Whose creature Fate is, now prescribe a Fate,
08 Measuring selfe-lifes infinity to'a span,
09 Nay to an inch. Loe, where condemned hee
10 Beares his own crosse, with paine, yet by and by
11 When it beares him, he must beare more and die.
12 Now thou art lifted up, draw mee to thee,
13 And at thy death giving such liberall dole,
14 *Moyst, with one drop of thy blood, my dry soule.*

All of Christ's adult years in between are summed up in lines 5.1-4 of the fifth sonnet, which thus span the period between Jesus' adolescence and the crucifixion. Again, the transition between the sonnets is reinterpreted, and the "miracles exceeding power of man," that in 1.4.14 referred to Jesus' mental maturity as an adolescent, now summarise all miracles performed during his lifetime (which had an impact on other people – leading to faith and envy). The speaker attributes this faith and envy to meek and ambitious spirits respectively; that is, faith goes together with meekness, and envy goes together with ambition. In referring to a faithful and meek spirit, he may also hint back at his own state of "low devout melancholy," which is a decidedly meek state, and thus implicitly identify himself with the faithful. This would also mean that he rejects ambition and, keeping in mind that in 1.1.8 the speaker had asked for a "crowne of Glory," which does seem a rather ambitious demand, his reference to "meek spirits" in the fifth sonnet may be another step on the way towards a truer and deeper state of devotion.

---

31   There are two variants for 1.5.3. Gardner, whose text is otherwise followed for "La Corona," has chosen "weake" here, on the grounds that "Donne may have felt that 'meeke' was too obvious an antithesis to 'ambitious' and altered it to make the contrast between the Christian and worldly assessments of weakness and strength" (Donne 1978, 61). Robbins argues that "meeke" is to be preferred, since it creates a parallel to the contrast of faith and envy in 1.5.2, contrasting meekness (as a Christian virtue) with ambition (Donne 2010, 483).

Ll.5.1-4 are set in past tense; while in l.5.5, the speaker changes to the present tense. Even though the speaker frequently changes tenses throughout the sequence, the simple present used from l.5.5 onwards looks very much like a dramatic present: the speaker shows his personal agitation with the exclamation "But Oh!," which echoes the same exclamation in l.3.5. In the third sonnet, the speaker addresses Mary, making himself part of the scene and showing sympathy through his exclamation, while in sonnet five, the speaker (up to l.5.12) voices his feelings as a sympathetic and commiserative though impotent observer of the crucifixion (his feelings are reinforced by "alas" in l.5.6). The climactic "they will, and can, [...] and do" raises the expectation of an immediate action, only to be followed by the long-winded "[they] do, unto th'immaculate, / Whose creature Fate is, now prescribe a Fate, / Measuring selfe-lifes infinity to'a span, / Nay to an inch." These lines, however, are central in showing the consequences of confining divinity to a human body (which is mentioned so often in sonnets two to four): human weakness and powerlessness. Temporal dimensions ("Fate") and spatial dimensions ("to'a span, / Nay to an inch") are, firstly, merged and, secondly, contracted and diminished. "Infinity" is ambiguous and can refer either to time or to space, as does the action of "measuring." "Span" and even "inch" (*OED*, "inch, n.[1]. 2.a") can likewise be used with reference to time and space. Infinity thus becomes minute, and God's autonomy and self-containedness changes to being controlled by others.[32]

The speaker also stresses the action of "bearing" in its different shapes: Jesus "beares his own crosse, with paine, yet by and by / When it beares him, he must beare more and die." This emphasis on "bear" is important to the speaker, since it is a prerequisite for his own salvation. "He must beare more" is ambiguous: Jesus must bear more pain, and he must bear more than the cross (i.e., become crucified), and through this, he must bear even more, namely men's (and the speaker's) sins. Consequently, Christ's "bearing more" is immediately followed by the speaker's plea, "Now thou art lifted up, draw mee to thee." "Now" stresses not only the temporal order of events (Jesus first bears his cross, then is lifted up on

---

32   Cf. also Herbert's "The Search," where the speaker is unable to "seek thee out" and "The Temper (I)," where the speaker states, "Will great God measure with a wretch?", attributing the action of measuring to God.

the cross), but also the speaker's "presence" at the crucifixion as well as including the wish to be drawn to Christ immediately (that is, "right now").

L.5.12 is the first instance of the speaker directly addressing Jesus, after the numerous invocations of God in the first sonnet. Two of the sequence's four references to the speaker's soul are found at the transition from sonnet five to six, and the speaker's soul is thus brought to the fore at this point. As in 1.1.11-12, "This first last end [...] my soul attends" and 1.3.9-14, "Seest thou, my Soule, [...] Was not his pity towards thee wondrous high," the speaker refers to his soul only in connection to his salvation (the remaining mention of the soul, "His Godhead was not soule to his manhood" is the only instance of "soul" not referring to the speaker, and attributes a "human" soul to Jesus).

The speaker's plea in 1.5.12 contains a twofold movement. Firstly, he wants to be drawn up (to where Christ is "lifted up"). That is, he wants to move upwards from his location on earth, either to Christ on the cross (which suggests his own crucifixion as an action of penitence, and thus presents an imitation of Christ as a way to salvation) or to heaven (which suggests his own resurrection). Secondly, he simply wants to be closer to Christ ("draw mee to thee"), that is, he wants to be where Christ is. "Drawn" is ambiguous, and refers to being moved either spatially or emotionally (the spatial meaning is in itself twofold and may refer to the speaker's body or soul). Considering the speaker's description of his soul in the next sonnet, as well as 1.1.13, "'Tis time that heart and voice be lifted high," it becomes clear that he wishes to be drawn in both senses. The speaker's wish to be "drawn" to Christ is evocative of the use of "draw" in Donne's Holy Sonnet "Thou hast made me," which ends with "Thy Grace may winge me to prevent his art / And thou like Adamant draw mine iron heart." (ll.13-14). Here, God is imagined as a strong magnetic force, attracting the "iron" speaker and lifting him up to heaven – similarly, in "La Corona" the passive speaker relies on God's force to lift him up.[33]

---

33   Cf. also the speaker's independent (and therefore unsuccessful) drawing of a sigh in "The Search": "I sent a sigh to seek thee out, / Deep drawn in pain, / Wing'd like an arrow: but my scout / Returns in vain" (ll. 17-20). The speaker is the one who "draws" the sigh-arrow, and he is also the one who "wings" it – both actions are merely human and lack God's divine force. Only after giving up his own will and

In ll.5.12-14, the speaker places his own situation in relation to Christ's by contrasting both: Christ is "lifted up," while the speaker is still below, and Christ may spare "one drop of blood," while the speaker's soul is dry. Through this contrast, the speaker also creates a connection to Christ: because Christ is high up and he is down below, he can ask to be drawn up, and because Christ has a drop of blood and his soul is dry, he can ask for it to be moistened. "Draw mee to thee" shows a clear direction, from "mee" to "thee," as well as a separating and distancing element between "mee" and "thee": "to" literally stands between both pronouns, and it indicates a distance that needs to be bridged. Because of the word order in l.5.14 (the main verb "moyst" is followed by the adverbial "with one drop of thy blood," while the object "my dry soule" is postponed), there is nothing between "thy blood" and "my dry soule" – and thus nothing between "thy blood" and "my soul" except the dryness of the speaker's soul (a state which he wants to change). In addition, what the speaker describes in l. 5.14 is a close physical contact, comparable to that of his soul kissing Jesus in stanza three. While in the third stanza the speaker's soul seemed superior to Jesus as a baby (in the double sense of being above and being more powerful), suggesting a stooping down movement towards the baby in the crib, it is now the speaker who looks up to Jesus on the cross, and Jesus' blood that comes down on the speaker's soul. This shows that a turn has taken place on several levels, a reversal of perspective, position and power. As a consequence of this turn, now that Christ is superior, the speaker can ask for (and even presuppose) a "liberall dole" from Christ.[34] The speaker here picks up the image of life-giving liquid, which was first introduced in the opening sonnet with the reference to a "strong sober thirst," und is then explored in detail in the sixth sonnet.[35]

---

accepting God's supreme and unsurmountable will, the speaker realises that God will come to him (i.e. that God must "draw" him) and not viceversa. Cf. also the speaker's plea to God at the end of "Thou hast made me": "draw mine iron heart."

34   The use of "liberall" in l.5.13, and its closeness to "liberty" and "liberating," may already hint at the liberation of the speaker's soul through Christ's drop of blood in l.6.1-4.

35   This union of Christ's blood and the speaker's soul, moistening the soul and allaying its thirst, can also be seen as a hint at the Eucharist (cf. also DiPasquale 82f.).

4.2 The sixth sonnet: the speaker goes with Christ from death to life

The sixth sonnet contains a sudden change of perspective from Christ's fate to the speaker's fate. Sonnets two to five had shown episodes from the life of Jesus, and the title "Resurrection" naturally leads to the expectation that this sonnet deals with Christ's resurrection. However, the speaker in sonnet six talks almost exclusively about his own resurrection.

> 6. Resurrection
> 01 *Moyst with one drop of thy blood, my dry soule*
> 02 Shall (though she now be in extreme degree
> 03 Too stony hard, and yet too fleshly,) bee
> 04 Freed by that drop, from being starv'd, hard, or foule,
> 05 And life, by this death abled, shall controule
> 06 Death, whom thy death slue; nor shall to mee
> 07 Feare of first or last death, bring miserie,
> 08 If in thy little booke my name thou'enroule,
> 09 Flesh in that long sleep is not putrified,
> 10 But made that there, of which, and for which 'twas;
> 11 Nor can by other meanes be glorified.
> 12 May then sinnes sleep, and deaths soone from me passe,
> 13 That wak't from both, I againe risen may
> 14 *Salute the last, and everlasting day.*

As before, there is a reinterpretation of the connecting line: while l.5.14 is a plea to Christ to moisten the speaker's soul, in l.6.1 "moyst" is a participle used as adjective (cf. *OED*, "moist, *v.* forms") and describes the speaker's soul after it has already been moistened (the result of this moistening is shown in ll.6.2-4).[36] The speaker thus presents a (positive) outlook on his future: his soul "shall [...] bee / freed" – even though he also dwells extensively on the present, deteriorate state of his soul. Syntactically, even though it will be achieved by just one drop of blood, the way to salvation is presented as long and winding: an enjambment links "my dry soule" and "shall," this is followed by a lengthy insertion about the soul's flaws covering almost two lines, till the statement continues with "bee" at the end of l.6.3 and, after another enjambment, ends with

---

36   Robbins argues that "[t]he change of parts of speech from verb to adjective has enacted the granting of his prayer" (Donne 2010, 484). However, there is a caveat: the speaker here makes a statement about the future (his soul "Shall [...] be [...] freed"), imagined by the speaker but not yet fulfilled.

"freed" in 1.6.4 (only to be followed by another description of the soul's present condition). In this way, the predicate "shall – be – freed" is protracted over three lines.

The speaker's soul is at the moment of speaking "too stony hard, and yet too fleshly," and will be freed "from being starv'd, hard, or foule" by "one drop of blood." The extent of the soul's sinfulness is emphasised by four different adjectives, opposed to which stands a single drop of Christ's blood. The singleness of this drop is highlighted by the repetition of "one drop" in ll. 5.14 and 5.1 and the equally singular "that drop" in 1.6.4; moreover, the use of "drop" stresses its smallness and minuteness. The life-giving power of the single drop thus appears even more miraculous. At the same time, the drop is also circular, and its spherical nature can be seen as a sign of divine harmonious proportion, on a small scale, just as the spherical all is divinely proportioned on a large scale (cf. Leimberg 1996, 321-23).[37]

The speaker then continues to focus on salvation and life after death. In ll.6.5-8, even though the speaker addresses Christ again (with "thy death" and "thy little booke"), it is not entirely clear whose life and whose triumph over death is referred to. "This death" in 1.6.5 clearly refers to Christ's death mentioned at the end of the fifth sonnet (which is supported by the choice of words: "abled" means "enabled" but it also contains "a-bled," which may be read as a participial adjective pointing at Christ's bleeding on the cross), just as "thy death" in 1.6.6 can be identified as Christ's death by the pronoun. But the lack of a determiner for "life" in 1.6.5 makes it difficult to decide what it refers to. The first and most obvious option is to read "life" as a reference to Christ (i.e., Christ *is* the life, following, e.g., John 11.25, John 14.11 and Coloss. 3.4), i.e., Christ is the one who "shall controule / Death," because his death slew Death (cf. Hos. 13.14, Heb 2.14, 2Tim 1.10 and the Easter Preface in the *Book of Common Prayer*, "Who by his death hath destroyed death" (see Donne (2010, 484) and Donne (1978, 62)). In this case, the switch to direct ad-

---

37 Robbins (Donne 2010, 483) points out Aquinas's hymn "Adoro Te Devote," which is about the Eucharist and which contains the stanza "Pie Pelicane, Jesu Domine, / Me immundum munda tuo Sanguine, / Cujus una stilla salvum facere / Totum mundum quit ab omni scelere." (Aquinas 68-71, ll. 21-24), i.e., "Devout pelican, Jesus Christ, / clean my uncleanness with your blood / One drop of which can save / the whole world of all its sins."

dress in l.6.6 seems rather abrupt. Secondly, it could also be seen as a reference to the life of men (including the speaker's life) or life in general, that will be resurrected (that is "controule / Death") *because* Christ's death slew Death. Consequently, "death" at the beginning of l.6.6 is either Death slain by Christ, or the speaker's/humankind's death (overcome because Christ slew Death altogether). The speaker then turns to the consequences Christ's conquest over death has for him personally: he will not fear death if his name is enrolled in the "little booke" (which is only possible because death has been conquered).

"First or last death" in l.6.7 likewise lacks a referent, which makes it harder to understand. The "first death" is likely to be physical death ("first" brought into the world through the Fall, and the "first" death that the speaker will go through), while "last death" may refer to the Second Death mentioned in Rev 2.11, 20.14 and 21.8 (cf. Donne 1978, 62), to be expected by sinners at the resurrection (if their name is not in the book of life, 20.15). These sinners are detailed as "the fearful, and unbelieving, and the abominable, and murderers, and whoremongers, and sorcerers, and idolaters, and all liars" (21.8)," from which the speaker distances himself by *not* fearing the last death (and this list of the damned includes liars, which implicitly stresses again the speaker's professed sincerity). By mentioning the book of life, and calling it a "little booke" the speaker points towards Revelation as a biblical context (see below). Yet instead of using "second death," which occurs in all three Revelation passages, Donne choses "last death", which not only gives a smoother rhythm but also underlines that this is indeed the last (and for some, lasting) death, while the faithful and just will receive everlasting life. At the same time, it foreshadows the "last, and everlasting day" in l.6.14 and echoes the "first last end" in ll.1.11.

The understanding of ll.6.5-7 is further complicated by the several repetitions of "death": within three lines, "death" is mentioned four times and there is a fifth reference in the omission after "first" (i.e., "first death or last death"). One thing seems to be clear, however: "life" in l.6.5 refers to an everlasting life that comes *after* death and has mastery over death, and the dominion of life over death is shown to have a personal impact on the speaker. The repetitions in ll.6.5-7 also emphasise this dominion: death is both controlled and slain, and there is no fear of either "first or last death" – which is in line with the topic of the sonnet, resurrection, that is, with the overcoming of death. The speaker thus mixes his anticipated death and triumph over death with Christ's, just as the combination of title and text in this sonnet mixes Christ's and the speaker's resurrection.

In addition to Christ's sacrifice, in ll.6.6-8, the speaker states another reason for overcoming death: "nor shall to mee / Feare of first or last death, bring miserie, / If in thy little booke my name thou'enroule." Although this condition is linked to the previous lines – it continues the sentence begun in l.6.1 and "nor" also indicates a connection to the previous phrase – it now presents a different perspective. The mention of the "little booke" (which alludes to the "book of life" mentioned several times in the Bible and frequently in Rev 3.5 and Rev 20.12-15)[38] brings in the prospect of the Last Judgement: if the speaker's name is listed in the book, he will be saved on the Last Day of Judgement. His salvation is presented as conditional in l.6.8 "If [...] my name thou'enroule" (just as the raising of the muse in l.7.13 is introduced by "if"). Moreover, "if" may refer to the previous or to the following lines, so that both the enrolment and the resurrection dependent on the enrolment are conditional.

Whereas before it was Christ's death that ensured salvation, it is now the act of writing down the speaker's name, that is, a literary and verbal activity. The choice of words is significant here: "enroule" contains both "roule" (i.e. "roll") and "en-" (i.e. "in-"), so that "enrolling" the speaker's name (and thus ensuring his salvation) becomes linked to a circular motion and to the act of enclosing and surrounding. Analogously, "controule" in l.6.5 hints at the same notion of circularity inherent to "enroule." In both cases, the "rolling," circular force is more powerful: life "controls" death and "enrolling" the speaker's name saves him from damnation. By referring to God's "little booke," and the enrolment of his name in this book, the speaker introduces writing as a powerful instrument and a means of salvation. The use of "enroule" suggests that the "little booke" literally is a scroll, a book in the shape of a (round) roll, and the circular nature of the crown of sonnets makes the poem a roll, too. Although in l.6.8 the power of saving the speaker through writing is attributed to God,

---

38   The term "little booke" may come from the "little book" mentioned in Rev 10.2-
      10, though the book there is distinct from the book of life.

the speaker's approach in "La Corona" is quite similar: he writes down a sequence of poems, through which he accompanies (and to some extent re-enacts) Christ's journey, and along which his mindset ("low" in the beginning) changes, giving him a hopeful outlook on his salvation. As the first stanza has shown, the speaker is aware of his own literary activity and of writing the "Corona." In the sixth sonnet, Christ is now depicted as "writing," providing another characteristic that the speaker appears to share with Christ. Ll.6.9-11 are rather general again and apply to all of humanity. They describe the transformation of the flesh that will happen after death ("in that long sleep"). In l.l.6.12, however, the speaker turns back to his own condition, and (as in l.6.6 with "nor to mee") marks ll.6.9-11 as relevant for his own salvation.

As in the previous stanzas, this sonnet, too, merges different time spheres and in part shows a temporal or causal reversal of events. As mentioned above, the reference for the speaker's "first or last death" is ambiguous; the speaker may either refer to "Death" generally in contrast to Christ's death, or to death in the sense of sleep vs. death as dying. The combination with "or" suggests that it does not matter which one is meant, and since the sonnet is about the resurrection it suggests that in fact any death will be overcome.

LL. 6.9-11 describe a general event that will take place in the future, after the speaker's death and in fact any man's death: the use of "that" shows that it is not yet close to him. Also, "then" in l.6.12 can refer to the result of the glorification of the flesh described in ll.6.9-11, or it may refer simply to a point in the future. In l.6.12, he makes his description personal again with "may [they] soone from me passe." The auxiliary "may" in l.6.12 and l.6.12 also underlines the conditional and future character of his description. In any case, the transformation of the flesh is again a circular process, it goes back to its origin, which is simultaneously its future purpose.

The speaker states that he will be woken from "sinnes sleep, and deaths," to the "last and everlasting day," which means that sin and death will end definitely and never recur. He describes this future state as "againe risen," which reflects the literal meaning of re-surrection. In addition, "againe" indicates both a repetition (his body rises again and he is "alive" again) and a return (to the state of being risen and upright, and to a previous state of perfection, "of which and for which" his flesh was made), and thus shows another circular movement.

While in l.6.7 the speaker talks about his "first or last death," in l.6.14 he mentions the "last and everlasting day." A "day" usually implies repetition and a linear (one day is followed by another as time goes on) as well as a circular progress (a single day day is marked by lasting from sunrise to sunset, i.e. the sun's circular rising and setting); the "day" in l.6.14, however, is explicitly characterised as "last and everlasting" and not followed by another day. Thus linear, temporal and repetitive progress is abolished, as is the "night" (associated with "sinnes sleep, and deaths") in between the days. The speaker thus plays with the notions of circular and linear movement, and with the finiteness and infinity of time, which are changed and transformed through God's power: "death" becomes a temporary and repetitive state, while a "day" becomes endless and unique. Both "first or last death" and "last and everlasting day" bring to mind ll.1.10-11 from the opening sonnet: "at our end begins our endlesse rest, / This first last end." While "rest" is neutral (though associated with night rather than day), "end" explicitly implies finiteness. In the first stanza, too, the notion of temporal continuity is thus reversed: "first last end" implies a repetitiveness instead of an ending, while "endless rest" is a permanent state (of everlasting life) that begins at the "end" (the word "endless" explicitly distinguishes this state from one with an "end").

4.3 The seventh sonnet: Christ shows the way from earth to heaven

The seventh and last sonnet has a double function: it continues (and brings to a close) the narrative of Christ's life and death, and it links back to the sequence's beginning, thus closing the crown of sonnets. In this sonnet, the speaker combines the different topics of "La Corona" as well as the changing perspectives he had adopted through the sequence, and which had also become apparent through the changing addressees: he addresses Christ, he addresses a general (Christian) public and he addresses himself. He thus connects the history of salvation, its relevance for Christians in general and its relevance for himself (which includes not only the overcoming of sin and death but also poetic success).

7. Ascention
01 *Salute the last and everlasting day,*
02 Joy at th'uprising of this Sunne, and Sonne,
03 Yee whose just teares, or tribulation
04 Have purely washt, or burnt your drossie clay;
05 Behold the Highest, parting hence away,
06 Lightens the darke clouds, which hee treads upon,
07 Nor doth hee by ascending, show alone,
08 But first hee, and hee first enters the way.
09 O strong Ramme, which hast batter'd heaven for mee,
10 Mild lambe, which with thy blood, hast mark'd the path;
11 Bright torch, which shin'st, that I the way may see,
12 Oh, with thine owne blood quench thine owne just wrath,
13 And if thy holy Spirit, my Muse did raise,
14 *Deigne at my hands this crowne of prayer and praise.*

The first eight lines of the last sonnet are addressed to a general public, which is made clear in 1.7.3, "Yee whose just teares, or tribulation."[39] While "yee" may be either singular or plural, and could in theory also refer to the speaker himself, all conventional uses of "ye" hint at an addressee different from the speaker (i.e., "ye" is either used in the plural, or with imperatives, with a deferential attitude, or in object position, cf. *OED*, "ye, *pron.* and *n.*"). "Ye whose just teares" thus seems to refer back to "all that will" from the first sonnet. The address in 1.7.3 also marks "salute" in 1.7.1, "joy" in 1.7.2 and "behold" in 1.7.5 as imperatives. The change from "I may salute the last and everlasting day" to "ye (shall) salute the last and everlasting day" shows once more a reinterpretation of the connecting line, which entails a double change of perspective: the speaker's view changes from the depiction of a personal, private action to a public call, as well as from a hypothetical outlook on the future ("I may salute") to a depiction of this future as a present state and a promise come true.

Ll.7.5-8 describe Christ's ascension, which is another scene in the life and death of Christ witnessed by the speaker and presented as a "public" view of God, beheld not only by the speaker but also by those he calls to salute, joy and behold. Noticeably, in these lines, God is mentioned only in the third person – while the speaker "beholds" with the others, he is

---

39 Cf. also the change of addressee in the last stanza of "The Canonization," where the lovers imagine a future audience addressing the lovers.

still addressing "yee" and describes what others might "see," not focus-
sing on his personal relation to God. Hence, the remoteness of God is
brought to the fore: he is called the "Highest" and depicted "parting
away" and treading on clouds, that is, high above and distant from the
speaker and all other observers.

While previously the speaker had stressed first *and* last, beginning *and*
ending, the expression "first hee, and hee first" in l.7.8 (and the circulari-
ty created through its chiastic structure) highlights simultaneously the all-
encompassing nature and the primacy of God: God is first and – where
we would expect "last" – first again (and, as God is all-encompassing, he
includes the "end"). But the use of "first" also creates an expectation of
what comes next: Christ enters the way "first," and the speaker comes
second. The speaker emphasises that Christ not only "shows" but also
"enters the way." This statement appears redundant at first glance, since
Christ shows "by ascending" (which already includes "entering the
way"); however, it creates another shared characteristic between the
speaker and Christ: the speaker, too, hopes to "enter the way," as he
makes clear in the next three lines, and to follow in Christ's footsteps.
The "way" and the action of "entering the way" (albeit successively and
not at the same time), thus create a common ground, in a literal and met-
aphorical sense, between the speaker and Christ: Christ leads the way to
heaven and the speaker follows, and this joined activity links them to
each other (in addition, the whole sequence can be seen as a "way" to
Christ preceding and facilitating the speaker's way to heaven" described
in ll.7.9-11).

In l.7.9, the speaker turns back to the personal relation to God estab-
lished in the fifth sonnet and addresses Christ again. Although ll.7.9-11
present general images and actions of Christ, and the titles used for Christ
introduce a certain degree of indirectness (Christ is not named directly
but called "strong Ramme," "Mild lambe" and "bright torch"), the speak-
er immediately interprets all shapes and actions of Christ as adopted and
performed for his own personal salvation. Thus, Christ has "batter'd
heaven for mee" and "mark'd the path [...] that I the way may see." The
emphasis is on providing a way for the speaker's journey to heaven,
Christ "first enters the way," but the speaker hopes to follow. Although
in the previous lines Christ was shown to move upwards ("uprising," "the

Highest," "ascending"), the use of "enter the way" stresses an inward movement ("battering" heaven also suggests a way to go in, not up). The upward movement is not abandoned, however, and in l.7.13, the speaker then talks about the "raising" of his Muse again

As with the resurrection in the previous sonnet, Christ's ascension and the speaker's ascension are merged through their common actions: they both enter heaven on the same way. The speaker states that Christ has battered heaven, marked the path and made the way visible for the speaker, and although it is left open in how far he has progressed on this path, the speaker thus emphasises that Christ has personally made it possible for him to progress to heaven.

In the last sonnet, the speaker also takes up the metaphor of his soul's "thirst" and God's live-giving blood introduced in the first sonnet and expanded in the fifth one. In ll.7.3-4, he mentions the addressee's "just teares, or tribulation" that "have purely washt, or burnt your drossie clay" (and, as the audience may include himself, these are potentially his own "just teares, or tribulation"). He thus refers back to the power of Christ's blood to moisten his soul and to free it "from being starv'd, hard, or foule" (l.5.4). In offering the alternatives "have purely washt" and "burnt your drossie clay," the speaker continues the metaphor of life-giving liquid, and adds the cleansing (and thus equally life-giving) quality of fire. In l.7.12, "Oh, with thine owne blood quench thine owne just wrath," the image of Christ's life-giving blood is taken up once more. After "quench" we would expect a reference to the speaker's "strong, sober thirst" that is finally quenched. Instead it is God's wrath that is assuaged. In addition, the preceding line characterises God as "bright torch," i.e., as made of fire, so that the use of "quench" also leads to the expectation of extinguishing fire, which ties in with the notion of wrath, often perceived as fiery and "kindled." The effect of quenching God's wrath is the same as that of moistening the speaker's soul: in both cases, Christ's blood enables the speaker's salvation.[40]

---

40 Quenching a fire implies a loss of light, and therefore of vision, and "quench" itself could be used to refer to the loss of sight (*OED*, "quench, *v*. 1.d"). In ll.7.10-11, however, the speaker explicitly states, "Mild lambe, which with thy blood, hast mark'd the path / Bright torch, which shin'st, that I the way may see," and thus ensures that "quench" in l.7.12 is not associated with a loss of vision.

The last two lines return back to the sequence's beginning, to the question of poetic inspiration and the speaker's muse, and of course to the opening line of "La Corona." They are joined to the previous line by "and if," and thus seem to continue the list of images detailing the speaker's way to salvation. The existence of the finished crown of sonnets seems to indicate that the Muse *was* raised by the holy spirit (i.e., that the sequence is the result of the speaker's divine inspiration), yet the speaker cannot be sure of this: the conditional "and if" indicates a lack of certainty, a state that the speaker wishes or hopes for, but of which he cannot be sure. And *if* his muse has indeed been raised, he hopes that God will "deigne" his "crowne of prayer and praise" – which adds another level of uncertainty, since God's acceptance of the crown now depends on the poet's divine inspiration. The speaker's stance at the end of the last sonnet is thus considerably less demanding than his request "give mee / a crowne of Glory" in l.1.7-8 and indicates a change in the speaker's attitude from a professed state of "low devout melancholy" towards a more sincere state of devotion.

The last two lines also show the merging of muse and soul. L.7.13 begins with "And if thy holy Spirit," and the most likely continuation – in association with the Holy Spirit and following four lines about the speaker's salvation – would be a reference to the speaker's soul. The fact that the speaker continues with "my Muse did raise" instead of the expected "my Soul did raise" is thus highly significant. Firstly, in linking the muse to the Holy Spirit, and in depicting it as potentially "raised" (while the speaker before talked about his spiritual raising and his way to heaven), a close connection and even a union of soul and muse is suggested; they share important characteristics and to some extent appear interchangeable (l.1.13, "'Tis time that heart and voice be lifted high," also hints at this union). Secondly, the reference to the speaker's muse links the last sonnet back to the first one (where the speaker asks God to "reward my muses white sincerity" – the only other mention of the speaker's muse) and this change of topic contributes to close the circle and end the crown of sonnets. In addition, l.7.13 also displays a structural ambiguity that points back at the sequence itself and strengthens the connection between speaker and God. "And if thy holy Spirit, my Muse did raise" refers, in the first place, to a raising of the Muse by the Holy Spirit. Yet, it can also be read reversely as "And if my Muse did raise thy holy Spirit" (a reading supported by the comma separating both phrases and the word order of "my Muse did raise").The latter interpretation points again at "La Corona" as a poem of "prayer and praise" which "praises" and thus "elevates" God (and the word "praise" literally contains "raise"), and at the same time creates a sense of reciprocity between the Holy Spirit providing inspiration and the speaker offering the crown of sonnets.

A formal return to the beginning of "La Corona," literally closing the circle and letting the crown of sonnets come into existence, is of course most visible in the last line, whose wording repeats the first line of the sequence. Up to now, almost all of the connecting lines between the single sonnets contained a change of meaning in their repetition (and even in the transition from sonnet one to two, "Salvation to all that will is nigh," one could argue that "nigh" refers in l.1.14 to "salvation" in general, and in l.2.1 to God's imminent incarnation). Thus, as in the previous sonnets, we would expect a reinterpretation in the last line, and not just a simple repetition of the opening line, and, indeed, "deigne at my hands this crowne of prayer and praise" has gained a new meaning now that a crown of sonnets has come into existence and "this crowne" has a clear reference.

The meaning of the indexical demonstrative "this" from the opening line is turned round in the last line. In l.1.1, "this" refers to the sequence that has just begun (i.e., "this crown, which lies ahead of the reader"), while in l.7.14 "this" refers to a poem that has just been finished and read (i.e., "this crown, which lies behind the reader"). This change in meaning is accompanied by an ambiguity of "deigne" that allows for two different readings. "To deigne" may mean either "to condescend to bestow or grant, to vouchsafe" (*OED* "deign, *v.* 2.a") or "to condescend or vouchsafe to accept; to take or accept graciously (*OED* "deign, *v.* 2.b"). A consideration of both meanings of "deigne" is only possible because "at my hands" implies either giving or receiving (it may mean "from my hands" or "to my hands"), and because "weav'd" is likewise open and may mean "was weaved" or "is (being) weaved right now."

While the latter meaning of "deigne," "to accept," is more prominent in both opening and closing line (that is, the speaker offers his crown to God: in l.1.1, the crown he is about to begin; in l.7.14, the crown that has just been finished), the first meaning, "to bestow," as a plea for the poetic inspiration, is also present in l.1.1. This meaning becomes even more significant when considering that the speaker deals with the problem of poetic inspiration several times in the first sonnet: he begs a reward for his "muse" in l.1.5, he talks about his "thirst" in l.1.12 and about the lifting of "heart and voice" in l.1.13. This pleading is shown to be successful through the completion of the "Corona" itself, and this success is also explicitly stated in l.7.13, where the muse has been raised. So, in the first sonnet, "deign at my hands" may be seen as a plea to God to give the speaker the ability to write such a crown at all, while in the last sonnet it is a plea to God to accept the finished crown from the speaker (which is simultaneously a beginning crown again). The ending is thus not simply a repetition of the beginning but also the presentation of the accomplished poetic work. And although the text returns to its beginning, several changes have taken place, which indicate not regression or turning back, but development and progress.

5. Circularity and progress in "La Corona"

The whole sequence displays a tension and interplay between a circular, repetitive movement and a linear, progressive movement, and only both motions taken together lead to Christ: the speaker's relationship to Christ is characterised by re-thinking, re-considering, going back to the narrative of Christ, and in doing so, he comes closer to Christ and his own salvation.

The interplay between circularity and linearity also becomes visible in the treatment of "first" and "last," of finiteness and infinity ("last and everlasting") and the "end" (there is no "end" in a circle) throughout the sequence. The importance of circularity is evident, first and foremost, in the use of the crown of sonnets and the consequent emphasis on "crown" especially in the first sonnet. The transitions from one sonnet to another create repetition (since the previous line is repeated), and at the same time the lines are "turned round" through changes of addressee and syntactic form, resulting in each case in a kind of large-scale *apo koinou* construction. These frequent apo kouinou constructions are like the links of a chain simultaneously strengthening the connection between the single sonnets (when they form the last and first line of two sonnets, through their identity) and creating flexibility and development (through the possibility of multiple interpretations).[41]

In addition, the speaker often uses rhetorical figures indicating circularity and repetition. Thus, simple repetitions appear several times (such as "Blowing, yea blowing," "yet by and by," "with thine owne blood quench thine owne just wrath"), as well as the oxymoron "This first last end" (l.11) and figurae etymologicae ("All-changing, unchanged," "That All, which alwayes is all," "at our end begins our endlesse rest," "Which cannot sinne, and yet all sinnes must beare," "Whom thou conceiv'st, conceived" and "Thy maker's maker"). Polysemy is also used to create repetitions (e.g., "Whose creature Fate is, now prescribe a fate," "When it bears him, he must bear more," "Death, whom thy death slew"). The figure of chiasmus is particularly fitting to present circularity and reversal, since it displays an enclosing structure resembling a circular one and turns round its syntactic elements (e.g., "The ends crown our works, but thou crown'st our ends," "But first he, and he first"). Thus, the formal devices go hand in hand with the poem's content: the crown of sonnets, the progress from one sonnet to the next and the rhetorical devices used contribute to create circularity and reversal.[42]

At the same time, through the course of the sequence, the speaker also recounts the linear, chronological story of Christ. The development in the

---

41   Cf. Wroth's "Crown of Sonnets" in *Pamphilia to Amphilanthus*, which also uses *apo koinou* constructions in the linking lines, and the similarly tight structure of "The Pearl," achieved through using the same words and phrases in the first and last line of each stanza.

42   Maurer points out the ambivalence of the circle as symbol (and the appropriateness of its use in "La Corona": The matter of the poem admits the full wealth of the circle's symbolic potential (54)):

> The circle as shape and as motion is an emblem of the paradoxes of Christianity. God is beginning and end; and the story of the Redemption is replete with incidents in which the God-man is raised by being cast down. [...] In human terms, however, these paradoxes encompass deep ambivalence. The circle not only symbolizes perfection; it stands in mathematics for nothing. The self-sustaining motion of the sun [...] is, from the vantage point of earth, a rising and setting. (54).

> Sullivan sees "La Corona," "A Wreath" and other wreath poems (as which she also lists Vaughan's "The Garland," Marvell's "The Coronet" and even Herbert's "Jordan (II)") in the tradition of medieval florilegia, imitating the process of compiling phrases and quotations from notable works (1995/96, 96-98), as well as the process of self-correction advised in creating a florilegium (which in the wreath poems she sees reflected in the use of rhetorical figures creating reversal and changes of meaning, 1995/96, 98-100).

chronological advancement of the events described, leading from the annunciation to Christ's ascension also becomes evident in the sonnets' titles, especially in the last three, "Crucifying," "Resurrection" and "Ascention," which indicate movement and change. Further, the connecting lines between the sonnets, while they formally repeat themselves, also contain a change of meaning in their repetition. And to some extent, even the poetical form, the crown of sonnets, presupposes progress, because, although it is an essentially circular form, it can only come into existence through the progression of several sonnets.

Simultaneously, the speaker depicts his own raising from a state of "low devout melancholie" to seeing his way to heaven. Thus, the circular form of the sequence (reinforced through word meanings and rhetorical figures that stress circularity and repetition) becomes a medium of change and progress. This progress is visible on several levels. L.1.2 makes the speaker's "low" state explicit, while l.7.13 describes the muse as "raised." With the exception of the opening and closing lines, l.1.2 and l.7.13 are the outermost lines of the poem, so that "low" and "raise" denote two extremes right at the limits of the text.

"First", "last" and "end" presuppose some kind of order and progress, even though their meanings change: the "last" day becomes "everlasting" and the "end" becomes "endlesse" – a "day" thus signifies the end of time, and the "end" becomes a permanent and lasting state. The speaker also uses several metaphors that show motion and progress. The change from "low" to "raise" is the most obvious one, but the speaker also talks about being "lifted," Christ "leaves," the wisemen "travell," the holy family and the speaker's soul "goe," and Joseph is called to "turne back." The speaker states that "our endless rest" "begins" and that Jesus "in his ages morning thus began." Christ is "lifted up" and the speaker wants to be "drawn" to Christ, and he imagines how death will "passe" from him and he will have "risen." In the last stanza, the number of expressions indicating movement increases. The speaker talks of Christ's "uprising," Christ "treads" and after "ascending" "enters" into heaven. This movement culminates in "raise," which applies to the speaker. Furthermore, especially in the last sonnet he stresses the "way" that lies ahead of him and his ability to "see" this way. Thus, the whole sequence is pervaded with expressions indicating direction and movement (both vertical and horizontal) and thus progress and change.

The end of "la Corona" thus presents two results. In the first place, it shows the successful completion of a sequence of poems, a finished "crowne of prayer and praise." In addition, the speaker has changed through the poem, he has established a spiritual connection to Christ, and may even be divinely inspired (if his muse has been raised by the Holy Spirit, as he hopes in l.7.13). This goes along with the apparent merging of Christ's resurrection and the speaker's resurrection in the sixth sonnet, which also brings them closer together, and this connection makes him confident of his salvation and it also makes him interpret Christ's sacrifice as a sacrifice for his own benefit, which becomes evident in ll.7.9-11.

Another kind of development which takes place during the sequence is the implicit merging of the speaker's spiritual and creative parts. By shifting the initial emphasis on the speaker's "muse" to his soul, and, in the last stanza, back to his muse (to be raised by – and thus connected to – the holy spirit), by placing "heart and voice" on one level, and by applying verbs which are nearly synonymous in their meaning – "lifted," "draw" and "raised" all indicate an upwards movement brought about by God – to his muse as well as his soul, the speaker assumes an inseparability of his state as a human being and his identity as a poet.

Thus, the end of "La Corona" is not only a return back to the beginning, it also offers a more positive outlook on the speaker's salvation (for which the process of developing and "writing" the sequence has been crucial) and on the beginning of a heavenly life after death. Even if the sequence is to be read again from the beginning, this assurance will be carried back by the speaker. Yet this assurance is not final, the conditional character of the speaker's success means that he cannot be certain that his muse has been raised, and though heaven has been "batter'd" for him, the path has been "mark'd" and he "may see" the "way," these statements do not indicate that the speaker has already walked the way to heaven: he has to continue on his way through life and he has to continue to strive for salvation, and therefore he has to go back to the beginning and repeat his meditation time and again.

5.1 The speaker's turn to Christ

The speaker's alternating perspectives through "La Corona" also express his changing relationship to Christ. As mentioned above, while recounting the story of Christ from annunciation to ascension (which in itself contains a turn from a downward movement to an upward movement), the speaker often switches between different temporal and spatial frames, between past, present and future as well as between smaller and larger spaces, and these changes all contribute to create a motion of spatial and temporal meandering.

At the same time, in spite of these frequent changes, there is a development visible through the sequence. The changing use of pronouns, especially the use of direct address, is central in depicting the speaker's distance from God and the proximity evolving along the poem (at the same time, using these pronouns not only depicts but also contributes to create distance and proximity): direct address creates the impression of direct communication with the addressee and is telling with regard to the speaker's development. In addressing Mary and Joseph, the speaker makes himself part of the scene he describes and becomes a "witness" of the childhood of Jesus. His address of a general audience ("all that will," "yee whose just teares") also shows him as part of this audience (he is one of those "that will," and he tells others to "salute," "joy" and "behold" while he does the same), though his commanding voice also sets him apart from his addressees (giving him the role of a preacher who admonishes others without excluding himself).

With regard to his address of God, an important change takes place during the sequence, which is part of the speaker's turn towards a prospect of salvation. In the first sonnet, God Almighty is addressed as "Thou which of good, hast, yea art treasury, / All changing unchang'd Antient of days" (ll.1.3-4). After the direct address in the first sonnet, God is not addressed again for the next three sonnets. In a more distant manner, the speaker talks about "that All, which alwayes is All every where" (1.2.2), and Jesus as a child is never addressed directly – in spite of the speaker's communication with Mary and Joseph. In l.5.12, however, the speaker's stance changes, and he finally speaks to Christ on the cross: "Now thou art lifted up, draw mee to thee."

The turn to directly addressing God at the end of stanza five is very similar to the turn in "Goodfriday, 1613," where the speaker (who before averted his eyes and searched for possible reasons not to look at Christ) suddenly addresses Christ on the cross with "and thou look'st towards mee" (l.35). In both cases, the respective lines present the first instance of direct communication with Christ and thus a crucial step in the speaker's relation to Christ. It is also noticeable that in both cases, the sentence structure itself creates a relation between both. In "thou look'st towards mee," the pronouns "thou" and "mee" are joined by "look'st towards," which creates a movement from Christ "towards" the speaker. In "La Corona," "thou art lifted up, draw mee to thee" shows a similar structure: in "[thou] draw mee to thee," the pronouns "mee" and "thee" are joined in their function as objects to "draw," while the verb "draw" creates a movement outstretching from Christ to the speaker.

From l.5.12 on, the speaker then frequently addresses Christ directly, and although in ll.7.1-8 the speaker interrupts this personal communication to address a larger audience, he then goes back to his personal relation to Christ, which is continued till the end of the cycle. At the end of the sequence, the offering of the "Corona" can thus also be seen as the offering of personal and private "prayer and praise."

The impersonal God (God Almighty and Jesus as a child) is characterised as "all" in l.2.2, associated with "all" in l.1.4 and ll.3.9-19 ("he / Which fils all place") and knows "all which was, and all which should be writ" (l.4.7). The use of "all" also creates a connection to the larger audience, that is, to the "all that will" from l.1.14. Before the crucifixion, Jesus is seen in terms of unfathomable infinity: as "immensity" and "he / Which fils all place," as "selfe-life's infinity," and in ll.7.1-8, as "this Sunne and Sonne" and "the Highest." Christ on the cross in contrast is only addressed as "thou" and "thee," and described with the help of graspable, material images ("strong Ramme," "mild lambe," "bright torch"). It is also noticeable that throughout the sequence the speaker very frequently refers to himself ("at my hands," "give mee," "draw mee to thee," "to mee," "my name," "from me passe," "I againe risen," "for mee," "I the way may see"), to his soul ("my Soule," "my soul attends," "thy faiths eyes," "towards thee," "by thee," "thy woe," "my dry soule"), or to his muse ("my muses white sincerity," "my Muse"). Thus, throughout the sequence the speaker stresses the fact that this is a poem about himself and his own salvation as much as about the history of salvation.

6. "A Wreath": a miniature corona

Herbert's "A Wreath" shares a number of characteristics with Donne's "Corona," both with regard to its formal structure and its main topics, and obviously takes "La Corona" as a model. "A Wreath" presents a circular form, which is also broached within the poem, and it joins the concern for poetic success to a concern for the speaker's spiritual salvation. Like "La Corona," "A Wreath" expresses a kind of circularity which not only connects beginning and end but also contains a significant change. The "wreath" comes into existence in writing or reading the poem: the twelve lines become a wreath, firstly, because they are named as such ("a wreathed garland," "this poore wreath") and secondly, because they are bound together by anadiplosis and chiasmus. The transformation into a wreath of words thus happens not through the outward form of the crown of sonnets ("A Wreath" does not follow an established form, lacking even the 14 lines that would have made it into a sonnet), but inside the poem. And another transformation takes place as well: the recognition that this "poore wreath" is actually already a "crowne of praise" and, like "La Corona," shows the way of living necessary to obtain a more precious crown. Whereas "La Corona" merges elements of public devotion (recounting the narrative of Christ and including other participants in Christ's life as well as other believers), with the speaker's personal relation to Christ, "A Wreath," shorter and more condensed, is immediately personal and focuses exclusively on the speaker and God. This becomes evident in the use of a less representative and "public" form (a "poore wreath" instead of a crown of sonnets).[43]

---

43 Walker takes the opposite view and considers "La Corona" as an essentially inward, exclusively private and individual expression of the speaker's relation to God (1987, 41-42). She sees the main difference between "La Corona" and "A Wreath" in the latter poem's more public character, which emerges primarily in ll. 5-8 of "A Wreath" (1987, 42-43). However, such a reading neglects the equally general statements found in Donne's poem (e.g., in ll.1.9-10 or ll. 6.9-11), and the use of pronouns including a larger audience such as "our workes" and "our ends" in l.1.9 and "to all that will" in l.2.1, as well as the more representative form of Donne's poem, which is precisely *not* a "poore wreath."

01 A wreathed garland of deserved praise,
02 Of praise deserved, unto thee I give,
03 I give to thee, who knowest all my wayes,
04 My crooked winding wayes, wherein I live,
05 Wherein I die, not live: for life is straight,
06 Straight as a line, and ever tends to thee,
07 To thee, who art more farre above deceit,
08 Than deceit seems above simplicitie.
09 Give me simplicitie, that I may live,
10 So live and like, that I may know thy wayes,
11 Know them and practise them: then shall I give
12 For this poore wreath, give thee a crown of praise.

The title "A Wreath" indicates its circular nature and offers similar ambiguities as Donne's use of "Corona" and "crown." In the first place, "wreath" indicates a circular shape, that is, "Something wound, wreathed, or coiled into a circular shape or form; a twisted or wreathed band, fillet, or the like" (*OED* "wreath, *n.* I.1.a"). "Wreath" also denotes a "fold, crease, or wrinkle" (*OED* "wreath, *n.* I.4.a") and a "twist, coil, or winding (of some material thing or natural growth); a sinuosity; a winding motion" (*OED* "wreath, *n.* I.6.a"), the word can be used to describe a form or a process (leading up to this form) and thus refers back to the process of creating a "wreathed" poem.

In a more specific sense, "wreath" denotes a "chaplet or garland of flowers, leaves, or the like, esp. worn or awarded as a mark of distinction, honour, etc." (*OED* "wreath, *n.* II.11.a"), and the importance of this meaning of "wreath" is made explicit in the first line with a "wreathed garland." "Garland" likewise has multiple meanings that play a role in the poem. A "garland" may refer to a "wreath made of flowers, leaves, etc., worn on the head like a crown, or hung about an object for decoration" (*OED* "garland, *n.* 1.a"), or for a "wreath, crown, etc. worn as a mark of distinction" (*OED* "garland, *n.* 3").[44] "Wreath" and "garland" are thus very similar in use and meaning, which makes "wreathed garland" a pleonasm that like Donne's "weav'd" crown enforces the notions of in-

---

44 "Garland" was also used for Christ's crown of thorns (*OED* "garland, *n.* 1.b"), and although this use is only documented up to 1460, the similar meaning and use of "crown" and "garland" suggest that a reference to the crown of thorns is also present here.

tertwining and circularity. Notably, "garland" was also a common title for anthologies (and from 1753 on "wreath" was used in the same manner, cf. *OED* "garland, *n.* 4" and "wreath, *n.* II.11.e"), to that the use of "garland" is to some extent self-referential and also serves to stress the literary character of the poem.

The several meanings and associations of "wreath" and "garland" thus allow for similar ambiguities as Donne's use of "crown." Both words refer to the poem as a whole as well as to the poem's structure, and they introduce the notions of circularity and "winding" which are then contrasted to "straightness." The speaker presents the poem as "A Wreath" and a "wreathed garland," and in the end contrasts "this poore wreath" with a "crown of praise." He thus introduces the notion of poetic quality and implicitly plays with the idea of a poet's laurel wreath. While neither "wreath" nor crown" is used with regard to a perpetual crown in the poem, the speaker also raises the topic of his salvation ("that I may live, / So live and like, that I may know thy ways") and links this topic to the poem's structure by opposing his "crooked winding ways" to a life "straight as a line."

Circularity and winding (entailing repetition) are also reflected in the poem, through the uses of various rhetorical figures and linguistic devices. In the first place, the ending refers back to the opening line. Although l.1. and l.12 are not identical, l.12 again mentions "this poore wreath" and the purpose of the wreath, "praise." As in "La Corona," the indexical demonstrative "this" is used to point directly at the poem (the beginning of the poem is less direct and uses the indefinite article, "A wreathed garland." Likewise, in l.12 the not-yet-existing "crown of praise" is qualified by the indefinite article and "this" is used only for the existing "wreath").

The rhyme scheme of the whole poem also has a circular character, it is symmetrical and almost mirrored in the middle: abab cdcd baba. What is more, ll.1-4 and ll.7-10 have the same full rhymes in reverse order (praise-praise, give-give, wayes-wayes, live-live), so that, with regard to rhyme, in the third there is a return to the first quartet and to the poem's beginning – centred around the middle quartet (whose rhyme scheme is not symmetrical). The first and last line end with "praise," which is another allusion to Donne's poem.

In addition, Herbert uses anadiplosis to link each line to the next. The last word or phrase in a line is repeated at the beginning of the next line (either literally or integrated into another phrase). In this way, Herbert creates a chainlike linking (in this case of single lines) that resembles the connecting lines of "La Corona." The key words are thus repeated: "praise," "give," "wayes," "live," "straight," "to thee," "deceit," "simplicitie," "live," "wayes" (and "them," respectively), "give." "Praise" in l.12 is be repeated by returning again to the first line. These repetitions interact with the repetitions required by the rhyme scheme, so that "praise," "give," "ways" and "live" each appear several times in the poem. Further, there is a caesura in the middle of almost all lines (except in the first line and in l.8), which adds to the repetitive, small-structured and winding character of the poem.[45]

This anadiplosis is interrupted in only one place: in l.5, the speaker, instead of repeating "live," corrects himself to "Wherein I die, not live." The ongoing flow of the poem (ll.5-8 also deviate with regard to the rhyme scheme) is thus stopped at a point where a change in the speaker is required. The speaker recognises that he does not really "live" but "dies" in his "crooked winding ways," and that he must pursue "straightness" and "simplicitie." He thus opens up a dichotomy between different kinds of life and death: his earthly life (when crooked and winding) is death, while a life determined by straightness and simplicity and tending towards God will lead to everlasting life: in the course of the poem, the speaker turns from a life following "my wayes" (which equals spiritual death) to a life following "thy wayes" (which signifies true life after physical death). At the same time, while the speaker implies that a "winding" way leads away from God, the poem offered contains a lot of deliberately and carefully composed "winding" offered to God (in addition "death" is a necessary requirement to reach eternal life), so that there is a tension between "straight" and "winding" ways similar to the one in

---

45   In addition to circularity, Kronenfeld sees self-correction as a main characteristic of "The Wreath," which distinguishes it from other poems employing reduplicatio/anadiplosis (such as "Saint Peter's Complaint" and "Sinnes Round") and leads to progress and improvement (299).

"Coloss. 3.3.": one life is "straight," while the other does "obliquely bend" – however, it is the latter which "winds towards *Him*."[46]

"A Wreath" also expands a topic that is only touched briefly in "La Corona," the question of sincerity (which is here linked to simplicity, and opposed to "deceit"). In 1.1.6 of "La Corona," the speaker talks about "my muses white sincerity," a characterisation which appears strange in relation to the "muse," but may be seen as an expression of the speaker's moral state (that is, his honesty) or his sincere intentions (including his intentions as a poet). Similarly, in "A Wreath," the speaker's plea for simplicity may refer either to his moral constitution (that is, he wants to be free of deceit), or to his poetic style (he wants to write in a "true" and "simple" way).[47]

Considering the speaker's status as a poet, the self-referential nature of "A Wreath" and the pun contained in "straight as a line" (the poem consists of lines that are both written "straight" and winding across line breaks), we can see that the speaker here talks about his way of writing: firstly, about the "truth" of what he writes (or more precisely, about the absence of "deceit"), and secondly, about his "simple" and "straight" style.[48]

The speaker explicitly refers to the "wreathed" poem in the first and last lines (which stresses the lack of straightness in the poem), and within the poem he mentions his "crooked winding ways," which he wants to discard. Structurally, however, one line always presses on to the next one (with the exception of 1.5 just mentioned). The chiasmus "of deserved praise" / "of praise deserved" in ll.1-2 also seems to briefly interrupt the

---

46 With regard to the last three lines of "A Wreath" cf. also ll. 9-10 of "Coloss. 3.3" and their emphasis on "daily labour" and the "eternall *Treasure*" gained in heaven for this earthly life.

47 As mentioned above, the colour white is a symbol of innocence, purity and holiness. As a symbol of innocence and purity, and in connection with the absence of deceit, the speaker's plea for simplicity may also be read as the wish to become like a child (keeping in mind Matt. 18.3 "Except ye be converted, and become as little children, ye shall not enter into the kingdom of heaven").

48 The poem also reflects other statements about how to write poetry, for example, "Jordan (I)," "[I,] who plainly say, My God, My King," and "Jordan (II)," "There is in love a sweetnesse readie penn'd; / Copie out onely that, and save expense," as well as Donne's Holy Sonnet "If faithfull soules" and the first sonnet of Sidney's *Astrophil and Stella* mentioned above.

chain-like linking of one line to another (even if the pattern of anadiplosis is still adhered to). If "deserved" refers to Christ, it should be a matter of course that Christ deserves praise, and there is no need to stress this by repeating it. However, "of praise deserved" may also hint at "of praise deserving" and allude to the wreath's poetic quality (that is, "deserving of praise"). The chiasmus makes the phrase appear closed and self-contained, like a miniature "wreath" consisting of just two lines, which the speaker offers to God with "unto thee I give." Then, however, he goes on with "I give to thee, who knowest all my wayes," which necessitates a continuation and exploration of the speaker's ways and thus leads to the completion of the full twelve lines forming the actual wreath.

As with Donne's poem, there is a progress towards the end of the sequence, and a changed state in the end. The "wreath" has been finished and read, and "this poore wreath" refers to the poem that has just been read. Although the poem alludes to Donne's "Corona," exploits the circularity that is also inherent to a "crown" and already praises God, the speaker in l.12 opposes the "poore wreath" to a "crown of praise," which he hopes to attain (in "La Corona," too, the speaker discards the "vile crowne of fraile bayes" in favour of a "crowne of Glory, which doth flower always"). Though the speaker leaves it open why exactly the wreath is "poore," this description may refer to several negative characteristics. The wreath may be "poore" because of its winding irregularity and lack of perfect symmetry, presenting poorly composed poetry (maybe even in comparison to Donne's longer and fully elaborated crown of sonnets).[49] Or it may be "poore" because written by a sinful (and spiritually poor) speaker who still lacks the simplicity he is asking for in the poem. In characterising his work as "poore," the speaker may also allude to Matt 5.3, "Blessed are the poor in spirit: for theirs is the kingdom of heaven," and thus indirectly ask for salvation. Furthermore, the association of "wreath" and "garland" with perishable flowers and leaves also makes it seem "poore" compared to a lasting crown. The "crown of praise" in contrast, finds a model in "La Corona," and is a divine symbol

---

49 Considering that the poem has twelve lines, "poore" may also allude to the fact that it lacks another two lines to become a sonnet. Fabb even considers "A Wreath" as a "weak" sonnet, which although it does not fully adhere to the sonnet form, strongly suggests it (77-78).

(a sign of divine perfection and eternity). The desired turn from "poore wreath" to crown of praise" can thus be read either as a plea for poetic inspiration, or as a plea for salvation (the speaker will give the "crowne of praise" only after he knows and practises God's ways). Thus, as in "La Corona" the speaker's conception of himself as a poet becomes joined to his conception as a mortal and sinner, and God is shown simultaneously as the source of inspiration and of salvation.

7. Conclusion

"La Corona" shows a combination of circular and linear elements, which is essential for the speaker's development and progress through the sequence. Although the text returns to its beginning, there is a development through the sequence: the speaker's relation to God has changed and become more personal, and he is "raised" from his state of "low devout melancholy" to confidently seeing his way to salvation. Turning back thus becomes part of turning forward to God – by going through the devotional exercise of writing sacred poetry again and again. The same interplay of circular and linear devices can be seen in Herbert's "A Wreath," and here, too (though less obviously than in "La Corona"), the speaker has changed at the end of the poem and looks forward to giving a "crown of praise."

We can see in "La Corona" a number of issues that we have seen repeatedly in previous analyses: the speaker's personal relation to God (or in the case of "The Canonization," a relationship to a beloved human being which embodies a divine relationship), the merging of the personal and general importance of the speaker's experience, the combination of linear (turning away from or towards someone) and circular (turning back) movements, the use of several recurring conceptual fields and above all the exploitation of the possibilities of language in order to realise all these aspects within poetry.

The poems' speakers move in space and time, they move "bodily" as well as spiritually, as they move towards God and spiritual salvation. They imagine themselves as spheres, maps, alchemical substances, musical instruments, birds, lovers and fighters, and as imitators of Christ. They are defined by their striving towards God, as much as by their role as poets, as human beings in search of God who employ language artfully and skilfully in this search. Their ways are manifold, but the speakers of the poems are always driven by their relation to God, by their own motivation to turn and by the mutuality of turning itself and the vision of God's turning towards them.

By analysing a variety of poems in detail, I hope to have shown *that* the notion of turning is widely present in Metaphysical Poetry and *how* it is present – how turning is conceptualised by using the various possibilities language offers and by recurring to a number of thematic fields that are closely linked to the notion of turning. I hope to have shown that the notion of turning provides more than a number of metaphors or conceits – it offers a paradigm and pattern of thought in order to express and conceptualise a central concern of the seventeenth century: where to turn and how to turn in order to save one's soul. I also hope to have shown the pervasiveness of the notion of turning in Metaphysical Poetry, as well as the variety and diversity in which turning is expressed and conveyed, the various fields and topics which are employed to conceptualise turning, as well as the rich and elaborate use of language through which turning becomes visible in Metaphysical Poetry. The pervasiveness of the notion of turning in Metaphysical Poetry is indicative of its importance in the Early Modern period; the scope and diversity with which turning is expressed is indicative of the poets' creative talent as well as of the suitability of the particular style of Metaphysical Poetry.

The poetical treatment of the notion of turning is of course not restricted to the poems of Donne and Herbert. It can also be found in their contemporaries and successors, in the poems of, for example, Vaughan, Marvell, Crashaw or Traherne, who to various degrees and in different shapes, all take up the diverse expressions of turning analysed here. The pervasiveness of the notion of turning in Metaphysical Poetry, and the language employed by Donne and Herbert to write about this phenomenon was influential beyond their immediate successors. It is also visible, for example, in Bunyan's *The Pilgrim's Progress*, which is based in its entirety on the notion of life as a (spiritual) journey, and presents a different yet similar way of dealing with the question of how to turn towards God: While the main character Christian has little choice and the direction in which he must go is mostly clear and prescribed for him, his adventures show many possibilities of "right" and "wrong" turns (i.e. away from or towards God) as well as the consequences of such wrong turns (God turning away from those making the wrong decisions). The notion of turning becomes even more apparent in Bunyan's *Grace Abounding to the Chief of Sinners*, which recounts a personal conversion experience and the narrator's turning towards God as well as God's perceived turning towards him. Thus, it presents a setting and spiritual development that is very similar to the situations found in the poems analysed here.

The influence not only of Metaphysical Poetry but also of the way the notion of turning appears in Metaphysical Poetry extends into the nineteenth century. The same patterns of thought we find in Donne's and Herbert's poetry allow Christina Rossetti some centuries later to let her speaker exclaim, at the beginning of a poem, "Tune me, O Lord, into one harmony / With Thee, one full responsive vibrant chord" (ll. 1-2). And it is certainly the influence of Donne and Herbert that enables Emily Dickinson to write a poem like "The face I carry with me – last," quoted above as a motto for the analysis of "Goodfriday, 1613" (and which would be equally suitable for "La Corona").[50] And while the direct influence of Donne and Herbert is less obvious in contemporary poetry, the individual's search for truth and orientation has lost nothing of its topicality, or, as Donne puts it in another one of his sermons that deals explicitly with the notion of turning:

> *Pray*, and *Stay*, are two blessed Monosyllables; To ascend to God, To attend Gods descent to us, is the Motion, and the Rest of a Christian; And as all Motion is for Rest, so let all the Motions of our soule in our prayers to God be, that our wills may rest in his, and that all that pleases him, may please us, therefore because it pleases him; for therefore, because it pleases him, it becomes good for us, and then, when it pleases him, it becomes seasonable unto us, and expedient for us. ("Sermon preached upon the Penitential Psalms, on Ps. 6.2 and 3," Donne, *Sermons* V, no. 17, 363)

---

50   See Haskin (2007) on the gradual discovery of Donne in the 19th century. Rossetti was likely to have known Donne and was certainly influenced by Herbert (cf. Marsh 1994, Kent 250-73). Cf. Banzer (417-33) on the influence of Donne and Herbert on Dickinson's writing.

VII. Bibliography

A. Works by Donne and Herbert

Donne, John. *The Complete Poems of John Donne*. Ed. Robin Robbins. Harlow: Longman, 2010.

Donne, John. *Devotions Upon Emergent Occasions*. Ed. Anthony Raspa. Montreal: McGill-Queen's UP, 1975.

Donne, John. *John Donne: The Divine Poems*. Ed. Helen Gardner. Oxford: OUP, 1978.

Donne, John. *Essays in Divinity*. Ed. Evelyn M. Simpson. Oxford: OUP, 1952.

Donne, John. *The Sermons of John Donne*. 10 vols. Ed. George R. Potter and Evelyn M. Simpson. Berkeley: U of California P, 1962.

Donne, John. *John Donne: The Elegies and The Songs and Sonnets*. Ed. Helen Gardner. Oxford: OUP, 1965.

Herbert, George. *The English Poems of George Herbert*. Ed. Helen Wilcox. Cambridge: CUP, 2007.

Herbert, George. *The Temple: Sacred Poems and Private Ejaculations*. Transl. Inge Leimberg. Münster: Waxmann, 2002.

Herbert, George. *The English Poems of George Herbert*. Ed. C. A. Patrides. London: Dent, 1974.

Herbert, George. *The Temple and A Priest to the Temple*. Ed. A. R. Waller. London: Dent, 1902.

B. Other Texts

Aquinas, Thomas. *The Aquinas Prayer Book: The Prayers and Hymns of St. Thomas Aquinas*. Ed. and transl. Robert Anderson and Johann Moser. Manchester, NH: Sophia Institute Press, 2000.

Augustine. *Selbstgespräche*. Ed. and transl. Peter Remark. München: Heimeren, 1965.

Augustine. *St. Augustine's Confessions*. 2 vols. Transl. William Watts. Loeb Classical Library. London: Heinemann, 1912.

Augustine. *The Works of Saint Augustine. Vol.III.17. Expositions of the Psalms, 51-72*. Ed. John E. Rotelle. Transl. Maria Boulding. New York: New City P, 2001.

Bacon, Francis. *Of the Proficience and Advancement of Learning*. Ed. B. Montagu. London: Pickering, 1838.

Bastard, Thomas. *Chrestoleros: Seven Bookes of Epigrames*. London, 1598.

Boethius, Anicius Manlius Severinus. *Fundamentals of Music.* Transl. Calvin M. Bower. Ed. Claude V. Palisca. New Haven: Yale UP, 1989.

Brahe, Tycho. *Astronomiae instauratae Mechanica.* [Wandesburg, 1598]. <http://digital.slub-dresden.de/werkansicht/dlf/16180/1/>.

Browne, Thomas. *Pseudodoxia Epidemica.* [1672]. Ed. Robin Robbins. Oxford: OUP, 1981.

Browne, Thomas. *Urne Buriall and The Garden of Cyrus.* Ed. John Carter. Cambridge: CUP, 1958.

Bunyan, John. "Grace Abounding." John Bunyan: Grace Abounding, with Other Spiritual Autobiographies. Ed. John Stachniewski and Anita Pacheco. Oxford: OUP, 2008. 1-94.

Calvin, John. *Institutes of the Christian Religion.* Trans. Ford Lewis Battles. Ed. John T. McNeill. Philadelphia: Westminster P, 1960.

Campion, Thomas. *Observations in the Art of English Poesie.* 1602. 1998. *Renascence Editions.* 16 July 2012. <http://www.luminarium.org/renascence-editions/poesie.html>.

Cassiodorus. *Explanation of the Psalms. Vol. 2: Psalms 51-100.* Transl. P. G. Walsh. New York: Paulist P, 1991.

Cicero. *Brutus. Orator.* Transl. G. L. Hendrickson and H. M. Hubbell. Loeb Classical Library. London: Heinemann, 1962.

Clement of Alexandria. "The Instructor." *Ante-Nicene Christian Library.* Vol. IV. Ed. Alexander Roberts and James Donaldson. Edinburgh: T. and T. Clark, 1867. 113-346.

Covell, William. *Polimanteia.* Cambridge, 1595.

Cross, St. John of the. *St. John of the Cross: Alchemist of the Soul. His Life, His Poetry, His Prose.* Ed. and transl. Antonio T. De Nicolás. New York: Paragon House, 1989.

Cusa, Nicholas of. *Nicholas of Cusa on Learned Ignorance: A Translation and an Appraisal of* De Docta Ignorantia. Transl. Jasper Hopkins. Minneapolis: Arthur J. Banning P, 1981.

Cusa, Nicholas of. *De Visione Dei.* Transl. Jasper Hopkins. Minneapolis: Arthur J. Banning P, 1988.

Daniel, Samuel. *The Complete Works in Verse and Prose of Samuel Daniel.* Vol. I. Ed. Alexander B. Grosart. [1885]. New York: Russell and Russell, 1963.

Daniel, Samuel. *A Defence of Rhyme.* [1603]. 15 Mar 2005. *Renascence Editions.* 16 July 2012. <http://www.luminarium.org/renascence-editions/ryme.html>.

Daniel, Samuel and Henry Constable. *Elizabethan Sonnet-Cycles: Delia and Diana*. Ed. Martha Foote Crow. London: Kegan Paul, 1896. <https://www.gutenberg.org/files/18842/18842-h/18842-h.htm>.

Davies, John. *The Poems of Sir John Davies*. Ed. Robert Krueger. Oxford: OUP, 1975.

Davies, John. *Microcosmos: The Discovery of the Little World, with the Government thereof.* Oxford, 1603.

De Bèze, Théodore. *Les vrais pourtraits des hommes illustres* [1581]. French Emblems at Glasgow. <http://www.emblems.arts.gla.ac.uk/french/emblem.php?id=FBEb006>. 31 May 2013.

Dickinson, Emily. *The Complete Poems of Emily Dickinson*. Ed. Thomas H. Johnson. New York: Back Bay Books, 1961.

Drayton, Michael, et al. *Elizabethan Sonnet-Cycles: Idea, Fidessa, Chloris*. Ed. Martha Foote Crow. London: Kegan Paul, 1897.

Drummond, William. *The Poems of William Drummond of Hawthornden*. [1832]. New York: AMS, 1971.

Dryden, John. "A Discourse concerning the Original and Progress of Satire." [1693]. *Essays of John Dryden* II. Ed. W. P. Ker. Oxford: Clarendon P, 1900.

Ficino, Marsilio. *Marsilio Ficino's Commentary on Plato's* Symposium. Ed. and transl. Sears Reynolds Jayne. Columbia: U of Missouri, 1944.

Florio, John. *Queen Anna's New World of Words, or Dictionarie of the* Italian *and* English *tongues*. London: Edw. Blount and William Parret, 1611.

Greville, Fulke. *Elizabethan Sonnet-Cycles: Caelica*. Ed. Martha Foote Crow. London: Kegan Paul, 1889.

Hall, Joseph. *Characters of Vertues and Vices: In Two Bookes*. London, 1608.

Harvey, Christopher. *The Complete Poems of Christopher Harvey*. Ed. Alexander B. Grosart. London: Robson and Sons, 1874.

The Holy Bible: Authorised King James Version. London: Harper Collins.

Horace. *The Odes and Epodes*. Transl. C. E. Bennett. Cambridge, MA: Harvard UP, 1964.

Surrey, Henry Howard, Earl of. *Selected Poems*. Ed. Dennis Keene. New York: Routledge, 2003.

Hudry, Françoise. *Le livre des XXIV philosophes: Résurgence d'un texte du IVe siècle*. [Liber XXIV Philosophorum]. Paris: Librairie Philosophique J. Vrin, 2009.

Hugo, Hermannus. *Pia Desideria*. [1624]. Emblem Project Utrecht. <http://emblems.let.uu.nl/hu1624front007.html#folio_pbxx6v>. 27 January 2014.

Johnson, Samuel. "Cowley." *The Lives of the Poets*. Vol. 1. [1779]. Ed. John H. Middendorf. New Haven: Yale UP, 2010. 3-84.

Junius, Hadrianus. *Emblemata*. [1565]. French Emblems at Glasgow. <http://www.emblems.arts.gla.ac.uk/french/emblem.php?id=FJUb049>. 27 October 2013.

Kepler, Johannes. *The Harmony of the World*. [*Harmonices Mundi*]. Ed. and transl. E. J. Aiton, A. M. Duncan and J. V. Field. Philadelphia: American Philosophical Society, 1997.

King, Henry. *Poems, Elegies, Paradoxes, and Sonnets*. London, 1657.

Lydgate, John. *The Pilgrimage of the Life of Man*. Ed. F. J. Furnivall. Millwood: Kraus Reprint, 1973.

Marlowe, Christopher. *Doctor Faustus: A- and B-Texts (1604, 1616)*. Ed. David Bevington and Eric Rasmussen. Manchester: Manchester UP, 1993.

Marston, John. *The Works of John Marston*. Vol. 1. Ed. J. O. Halliwell. London: John Russell Smith, 1856.

Marvell, Andrew. *The Complete Poems*. Ed. Elizabeth Story Donno. London: Penguin, 2005.

Morley, Thomas. *A Plaine and Easie Introduction to Practicall Musicke*. London, 1597.

Overbury, Thomas. "A Wife." *His Wife. With Additions of New Characters, and Many Other Wittie Conceits Never Before Printed*. London: Laurence Lisle, 1622.

Ovid. *Heroides and Amores*. Transl. Grant Showerman. Cambridge, MA: Harvard UP, 1977.

Paracelsus. *The Hermetic and Alchemical Writings*. Vol. I. Ed. Arthur Edward Waite. London: James Elliott and Co., 1894.

Paradin, Claude. *Devises heroiques* [1551]. French Emblems at Glasgow. <http://www.emblems.arts.gla.ac.uk/french/emblem.php?id=FPAa022>. 31 May 2013.

Peacham, Henry. *Minerva Britanna, or a Garden of Heroical Devises*. London, 1612.

Peacham, Henry. *The Garden of Eloquence*. London, 1593.

Plato. "Phaedo." *Euthyphro, Apology, Crito, Phaedo, Phaedrus*. Transl. Harold North Fowler. Loeb Classical Library. London: Heinemann, 1966.195-403.

Plato. *Plato's Phaedrus*. Transl. R. Hackforth. Cambridge: CUP, 1972.

Plato. *Timaeus, Critias, Cleitophon, Menexenus, Epistles*. Ed. R. G. Bury. London: Heinemann, 1966.

Puttenham, George. *The Art of English Poesy*. Ed. Frank Whigham and Wayne A. Rebhorn. Ithaca: Cornell UP, 2007.

Robinson, Thomas. *The Schoole of Musicke*. London, 1603. <http://www. shipbrook.net/jeff/bookshelf/details.html?bookid=26>.

Rossetti, Christina. *The Complete Poems of Christina Rossetti: A Variorum Edition*. Vol. II. Ed. R. W. Crump. Baton Rouge: Louisiana State UP, 1986.

Scève, Maurice. *Délie*. [1544]. French Emblems at Glasgow. <http://www.emblems.arts.gla.ac.uk/french/emblem.php?id=FSCa032>. 27 October 2013.

Shakespeare, William. *The Complete Sonnets and Poems*. Ed. Colin Burrow. Oxford: OUP, 2002.

Shakespeare, William. *Coriolanus*. Ed. Lee Bliss. Cambridge: CUP, 2000.

Shakespeare, William. *Romeo and Juliet*. Ed. G. Blakemore Evans. Cambridge: CUP, 2003.

Shakespeare, William. *Shakespeare's Sonnets*. Ed. Stephen Booth. New Haven: Yale UP, 1977.

Shakespeare, William. *The Tempest*. Ed. Virginia Mason Vaughan and Alden T. Vaughan. London: Bloomsbury, 2011.

Shakespeare, William. *The Winter's Tale*. Ed. Stephen Orgel. Oxford: OUP, 1996.

Sidney, Mary and Philip Sidney. *The Sidney Psalter: The Psalms of Sir Philip and Mary Sidney*. Ed. Hannibal Hamlin et al. Oxford: OUP, 2009.

Sidney, Philip. *An Apology for Poetry, or, The Defence of Poesy*. Ed. Geoffrey Shepherd and R. W. Maslen. Manchester: Manchester UP, 2002.

Sidney, Philip. *The Poems of Sir Philip Sidney*. Ed. William A. Ringler. Oxford: OUP, 1962.

Southwell, Robert. *The Poems of Robert Southwell, S. J.* Ed. James H. McDonald and Nancy Pollard Brown. Oxford: OUP, 1967.

Spenser, Edmund. *Amoretti and Epithalamion: A Critical Edition*. Ed. Kenneth J. Larsen. Tempe: Medieval and Renaissance Texts and Studies, 1997.

Tofte, Robert. *Laura: The Toyes of a Traveller, or, The Feast of Fancie*. London, 1597.

Vaughan, Henry. *The Complete Poems*. Ed. Alan Rudrum. Harmondsworth: Penguin, 1976.

Wilson, Thomas. *The Art of Rhetoric*. [1560]. Ed. Peter E. Medine. University Park, PA: Pennsylvania State UP, 1994.

Mary Wroth. *Pamphilia to Amphilanthus*. Ed. G. F. Waller. Salzburg: Institut für Englische Sprache und Literatur, 1977.

Wyatt, Sir Thomas. *The Complete Poems*. Ed. R. A. Rebholz. Harmondsworth: Penguin, 1978.

C. Secondary Literature

Alexander, Gavin. *Writing After Sidney: The Literary Response to Sir Philip Sidney, 1586-1640.* Oxford: OUP, 2006.

Anderson, Donald K., Jr. "Donne's 'Hymne to God my God, in my sicknesse' and the T-in-O Maps." *South Atlantic Quarterly* 71 (1972): 465-72.

Archer, Stanley. "The Archetypal Journey Motif in Donne's *Divine Poems.*" *New Essays on Donne.* Ed. Gary A. Stringer. Salzburg: Universität Salzburg, 1977. 173-91.

Asals, Heather A. R. *Equivocal Predication: George Herbert's Way to God.* Toronto: U of Toronto P, 1981.

Asals, Heather. "John Donne and the Grammar of Redemption." *English Studies in Canada* 5.2 (1979): 125-139.

Austin, J. L. *How to Do Things With Words.* Cambridge, MA: Harvard UP, 1975.

Bald, R. C. *John Donne: A Life.* Oxford: Clarendon P, 1970.

Banzer, Judith. "'Compound Manner': Emily Dickinson and the Metaphysical Poets." *American Literature* 32.4 (1961): 417-33.

Bauer, Matthias, *Mystical Linguistics: George Herbert, Richard Crashaw, and Henry Vaughan.* (to appear).

Bauer, Matthias. "Religious Metaphysical Poetry: George Herbert and Henry Vaughan." *A History of British Poetry.* Ed. Sybille Baumbach, Birgit Neumann and Ansgar Nünning. Trier: WVT, 2015. 107-21. (2015a)

Bauer, Matthias. "Secret Wordplay and What It May Tell Us." *Wordplay and Metalinguistic / Metadiscursive Reflection: Authors, Contexts, Techniques, and Meta-Reflection.* Ed. Angelika Zirker and Esme Winter-Froemel. Berlin: de Gruyter, 2015. 269-88. (2015b)

Bauer, Matthias, and Sigrid Beck. "On the Meaning of Fictional Texts." *Approaches to Meaning: Composition, Values, and Interpretation.* Hg. Daniel Gutzmann, Jan Köpping, and Cécile Meier. Leiden: Brill, 2014. 250-75.

Bauer, Matthias and Angelika Zirker. "Sites of Death as Sites of Interaction in Donne and Shakespeare." *Shakespeare and Donne: Generic Hybrids and the Cultural Imaginary.* Ed. Judith H. Anderson and Jennifer Vaught. New York: Fordham University Press, 2013. 17-37.

Bauer, Matthias. "Time and the Word: A Reading of Henry Vaughan's 'The Search.'" *Of Paradise and Light: Essays on Henry Vaughan and John Milton in Honor of Alan Rudrum.* Ed. Donald R. Dickson and Holly Faith Nelson. Newark: U of Delaware P, 2004. 292-308.

Bauer, Matthias. "Iconicity and Divine Likeness: George Herbert's 'Coloss. 3.3.'" *Form Miming Meaning: Iconicity in Language and Literature.* Ed. Max Nänny and Olga Fischer. Amsterdam: John Benjamins, 1999. 215-34.

Bauer, Matthias. "'A title strange, yet true': Toward an Explanation of Herbert's Titles." *George Herbert: Sacred and Profane.* Ed. Helen Wilcox and Richard Todd. Amsterdam: VU UP, 1995. 103-17. (1995a)

Bauer, Matthias. "*Paronomasia Celata* in Donne's 'A Valediction: Forbbiding Mourning.'" *English Literary Renaissance* 25 (1995): 97-111. (1995b)

Bauer, Matthias. "Herbert's Titles, Commonplace Books, and the Poetics of Use: A Response to Anne Ferry." *Connotations* 4.3 (1994/95): 266-79.

Baumgaertner, Jill. "'Harmony' in Donne's 'La Corona' and 'Upon the Translation of the Psalms.'" *John Donne Journal* 3.2 (1984): 141-56.

Baumgaertner, Jill P. "Seventeenth Century Ideas of Harmony in the Poetry of John Donne." Diss., 1980.

Beck, Rosalie. "A Precedent for Donne's Imagery in 'Goodfriday 1613. Riding Westward.'" *RES* (1968): 166-69.

Bednarz, James P. "*The Passionate Pilgrim* and 'The Phoenix and the Turtle.'" *The Cambridge Companion to Shakespeare's Poetry.* Ed. Patrick Cheney. Cambridge: CUP, 2007. 108-24.

Bell, Ilona. "Circular Strategies and Structures in Jonson and Herbert." *Classic and Cavalier: Essays on Jonson and the Sons of Ben.* Ed. Claude J. Summers and Ted-Larry Pebworth. Pittsburgh: U of Pittsburgh P, 1982. 157-170.

Bellette, Antony F. "'Little Worlds Made Cunningly': Significant Form in Donne's *Holy Sonnets* and '*Goodfriday*, 1613.'" *Studies in Philology* 72 (1975): 322-347.

Bennett, Joan. *Five Metaphysical Poets.* Cambridge: CUP, 1964.

Bitton-Ashkelony, Brouria. *Encountering the Sacred: The Debate on Christian Pilgrimage in Late Antiquity.* Berkeley: U of California P, 2005.

Blake, N. F. *A Grammar of Shakespeare's Language.* Basingstoke: Palgrave, 2002.

Bloch, Chana. *Spelling the Word: George Herbert and the Bible.* Berkeley: U of California P, 1985.

Blume, Thomas. "De dicto – de re." *UTB Handwörterbuch Philosophie.* Ed. Wulff D. Rehfus. <http://www.philosophie-woerterbuch.de> 4 Aug 2013.

Boenig, Robert. "Listening to Herbert's Lute. *Renaissance and Reformation / Renaissance et Reforme* 8 (1984): 298-311.

Bowers, Fredson. "Herbert's Sequential Imagery: 'The Temper.'" *Modern Philology* 59.3 (1962): 202-13.

Briggs, Julia. *This Stage-Play World: Texts and Contexts, 1580-1625*. Oxford: OUP, 1997.

Brooks, Cleanth. *The Well Wrought Urn: Studies in the Structure of Poetry*. London: Dennis Dobson, 1949.

Brooks, Helen B. "Donne's 'Goodfriday, 1613. Riding Westward' and Augustine's Psychology of Time." *John Donne's Religious Imagination: Essays in Honor of John T. Shawcross*. Ed. Raymond-Jean Frontain and Frances M. Malpezzi. Conway: UCA, 1995. 284-305.

Brueggemann, Walter. *The Message of the Psalms: A Theological Commentary*. Minneapolis: Augsburg Publishing House, 1984.

Brueggemann, Walter. "From Hurt to Joy, From Death to Life." *Interpretation: A Journal of Bible and Theology* 28 (1974): 3-19.

Buchanan, Colin. *Historical Dictionary of Anglicanism*. Lanham: Scarecrow P, 2006.

Campbell, Harry M. "Donne's 'Hymn to God, My God, in My Sickness.'" *College English* 5.4 (1944): 192-196.

Carey, James W. *Communication as Culture: Essays on Media and Society*. London: Routledge, 1992.

Carey, John. *John Donne: Life, Mind and Art*. London: Faber and Faber, 1981.

Carpenter, Margaret. "From Herbert to Marvell: Poetics in 'A Wreath' and 'The Coronet.'" *Journal of English and Germanic Philology* 69.1 (1970): 50-62.

Carruthers, Mary. *The Book of Memory: A Study of Memory in Medieval Culture*. Cambridge: CUP, 2008.

Caxton, William. *The Golden Legend, or, Lives of the Saints*. New York: AMS, 1973.

Chambers, A. B. "'Goodfriday 1613. Riding Westward': Looking Back." *John Donne Journal* 6.2 (1987): 185-201.

Chambers, A. B. "'Goodfriday, 1613. Riding Westward': The Poem and the Tradition." *ELH* 28.1 (1961): 31-53.

Chambers, A. B. "*La Corona*: Philosophic, Sacred, and Poetic Uses of Time." *New Essays on Donne*. Ed. Gary A. Stringer. Salzburg: Universität Salzburg, 1977.140-72.

Chambers, A. B. "The Meaning of the 'Temple' in Donne's *La Corona*." *Journal of English and Germanic Philology* 59.2 (1960): 212-217.

Clements, Arthur L. *Poetry of Contemplation: John Donne, George Herbert, Henry Vaughan, and the Modern Period*. Albany: State U of New York P, 2011.

Clements, A. L. "Theme, Tone, and Tradition in George Herbert's Poetry." *English Literary Renaissance* 3 (1973): 264-83.

Clutterbuck, Charlotte. *Encounters with God in Medieval and Early Modern English Poetry*. Aldershot: Ashgate, 2005.

Colie, Rosalie L. *The Resources of Kind: Genre-Theory in the Renaissance*. Ed. Barbara K. Lewalski. Berkeley: U of California P, 1973.

Collins, Grace Elizabeth. "The Symbolic Language of Penitential Conversion in Donne's Devotions." Diss. University of Michigan, 1974.

Connolly, Daniel K. *The Maps of Matthew Paris: Medieval Journeys through Space, Time and Liturgy*. Woodbridge: Boydell P, 2009.

Conti, Brooke. *Confessions of Faith in Early Modern England*. Philadelphia: U of Pennsylvania P, 2014.

Cook, William T. "The Development of Change Ringing as a Secular Sport." *Change Ringing: The History of an English Art. Volume 1: Its Development up to 1699*. Ed. J. Sanderson. Morpeth: Central Council of Church Bell Ringers, 1987. 28-39.

Crane, Mary Thomas. *Losing Touch with Nature: Literature and the New Science in Sixteenth-Century England*. Baltimore: Johns Hopkins UP, 2014.

Crawforth, Hannah. *Etymology and the Invention of English in Early Modern Literature*. Cambridge: CUP, 2013.

Cummings, Brian. "The Protestant and Catholic Reformations." *The Oxford Handbook of English Literature and Theology*. Ed. Andrew Hass, David Jasper and Elisabeth Jay. Oxford: OUP, 2007. 79-96.

De Swart, Henriette. "Mismatches and Coercion." *Semantics: An International Handbook of Natural Language Meaning*. Vol. 1. Ed. K. v. Heusinger, C. Maienborn and P. Portner. Berlin: De Gruyter, 2011. 574-97.

Des Harnais, Gaston R. "John Donne's 'The Canonization' and the Alchemic Model. Diss. U of Detroit, 1977.

Diaconoff, Theodore Andre. "George Herbert's Use of the World Harmony Theory in *The Temple*." Diss, 1973.

Dickens, A. G. *The English Reformation*. London: Batsford, 1999.

DiPasquale, Theresa M. *Literature and Sacrament: The Sacred and the Secular in John Donne*. Cambridge: James Clarke, 2001.

Divine, Jay D. "Compass and Circle in Donne's 'A Valediction: Forbidding Mourning.'" *Papers on Language and Literature* 9 (1973): 78-80.

Doerksen, Daniel W. *Picturing Religious Experience: George Herbert, Calvin, and the Scriptures*. Newark: U of Delaware P, 2011.

Draaisma, Douwe. *Metaphors of Memory: A History of Ideas about the Mind*. Cambridge: CUP, 2000.

Duffy, Eamon. *The Stripping of the Altars: Traditional Religion in England, c.1400 – c.1580*. New Haven: Yale UP, 1992.

Duncan, Edgar Hill. "Donne's Alchemical Figures." *English Literary History* 9:4 (1942): 257-85.

Dyas, Dee. *Pilgrimage in Medieval English Literature, 700-1500*. Cambridge: D. S. Brewer, 2001.

Edwards, David L. *John Donne: Man of Flesh and Spirit*. London: Continuum, 2001.

Eisel, John C. "The Development of Change Ringing in the Seventeenth Century." *Change Ringing: The History of an English Art. Volume 1: Its Development up to 1699*. Ed. J. Sanderson. Morpeth: Central Council of Church Bell Ringers, 1987. 40-49.

Eliot, T. S. "Lancelot Andrewes." [1926]. *Selected Essays*. London: Faber and Faber, 1972. 341-54. (1972a)

Eliot, T. S. "The Metaphysical Poets." [1921]. *Selected Essays*. London: Faber and Faber, 1972. 281-91. (1972b)

Elsky, Martin. "Polyphonic Psalm Settings and the Voice of George Herbert's *The Temple*." *Modern Language Quarterly* 42.3 (1981): 227-46.

Ettenhuber, Katrin. *Donne's Augustine: Renaissance Cultures of Interpretation*. Oxford: OUP, 2011.

Fabb, Nigel. *Language and Literary Structure: The Linguistic Analysis of Form in Verse and Narrative*. Cambridge: CUP, 2002.

Falck, Claire. "Purer Spheres: The Space Systems of Donne's Courtly Epithalamions." *John Donne Journal* 30 (2011): 123-55.

Ferguson, George. *Signs and Symbols in Christian Art*. New York: Hesperides, 1961.

Ferrari, Leo Charles. "The Theme of the Prodigal Son in Augustine's *Confessions*." *Recherches Augustiniennes* 12 (1977): 105-18.

Ferry, Anne. "Titles in George Herbert's 'little Book.'" *English Literary Renaissance* 23 (1993): 314−44.

Fetzer, Margret. *John Donne's Performances: Sermons, Poems, Letters and Devotions*. Manchester: Manchester UP, 2010. (2010a)

Fetzer, Margret. "Plays of Self: Theatrical Performativity in Donne." Solo Performances: Staging the Early Modern Self in England. Ed. Ute Berns. Amsterdam: Rodopi, 2010. 189-205. (2010b)

Fiddes, Paul S. *Seeing the World and Knowing God: Hebrew Wisdom and Christian Doctrine in a Late-Modern Context*. Oxford: OUP, 2013.

Finegan, Edward. *Language: Its Structure and Use*. Boston: Wadsworth, 2012.

Finney, Gretchen Ludke. *Musical Backgrounds for English Literature: 1580 - 1650*. New Brunswick: Rutgers UP, c.1960.

Fischler, Alan. "'Lines Which Circles Do Contain': Circles, the Cross, and Donne's Dialectic Scheme of Salvation." *PLL* 30 (1994): 169-186.

Fish, Stanley E. *Self-Consuming Artifacts: The Experience of Seventeenth-Century Literature*. Berkeley: U of California P, 1972.

Fleissner, Robert F. "Donne and Dante: The Compass Figure Reinterpreted." *Modern Language Notes* 76.4 (1961): 315-20.

Ford, Brewster S. "George Herbert and the Liturgies of Time and Space." *South Atlantic Review* 49.4 (1984): 19-29.

Freccero, John. "Donne's 'Valediction: Forbidding Mourning.'" *English Literary History* 30.4 (1963): 335-76.

Fredriksen, Paula. "Paul and Augustine: Conversion Narratives, Orthodox Traditions, and the Restrospective Self." *Journal of Theological Studies* 37 (1986): 3-34.

Freer, Coburn. *Music for a King: George Herbert's Style and the Metrical Psalms*. Baltimore: Johns Hopkins UP, 1972.

Friederich, Reinhard H. "Expanding and Contracting Space in Donne's *Devotions*." *English Literary History* 45.1 (1978): 18-32.

Friedman, Donald M. "Memory and the Art of Salvation in Donne's Good Friday Poem." *English Literary Renaissance* 3.3 (1973): 418-42.

Frontain, Raymond-Jean. "Donne, Spenser, and the Performative Mode of Renaissance Poetry." *Explorations in Renaissance Culture* 32.1 (2006): 76-102.

Frye, Northrop. "Third Essay: Archetypical Criticism: Theory of Myths." *Anatomy of Criticism: Four Essays*. Ed. Robert D. Denham. Toronto: U of Toronto P, 2006.121-223.

Gaiser, Frederick J. "A Biblical Theology of Conversion." *Handbook of Religious Conversion*. Ed. H. Newton Malony and Samuel Southard. Birmingham: Religious Education P, 1992. 93-107.

Gardner, Helen. *The Metaphysical Poets*. Oxford: OUP, 1961.

Garrett, Cynthia. "The Rhetoric of Supplication: Prayer Theory in Seventeenth-Century England." *Renaissance Quarterly* 46.2 (1993): 328-57.

Gaventa, Beverly Roberts. "Conversion in the Bible." *Handbook of Religious Conversion*. Ed. H. Newton Malony and Samuel Southard. Birmingham: Religious Education P, 1992. 41-54.

Gaventa, Beverly Roberts. *From Darkness to Light: Aspects of Conversion in the New Testament*. Philadelphia: Fortress P, 1986.

Gayk, Shannon. "Early Modern Afterlives of the *Arma Christi*." The *Arma Christi* in Medieval and Early Modern Material Culture. Ed. Lisa H. Cooper and Andrea Denny-Brown. Farnham: Ashgate, 2014. 273-307.

Gill, S. D. "Prayer." *The Macmillan Encyclopedia of Religion: Second Edition*. New York: Macmillan, 2005. 7367-72.

Gilman, Ernest. "'To adore, or scorn an image': Donne and the Iconoclastic Controversy." John Donne Journal 5 (1986): 62-100.

Glaser, Joe. "'Goodfriday 1613': A Soul's Form." *College Literature* 13.2 (1986): 168-76.

Goldberg, Jonathan. "Donne's Journey East: Aspects of a Seventeenth-Century Trope." *Studies in Philology* 68.4 (1971): 470-483).

Goodblatt, Chanita. *The Christian Hebraism of John Donne: Written with the Fingers of Man's Hand.* Pittsburgh: Duquesne UP, 2010.

Goodblatt, Chanita. "From "Tav" to the Cross: John Donne's Protestant Exegesis and Polemics." *John Donne and the Protestant Reformation: New Perspectives.* Ed. Mary A. Papazian. Detroit: Wayne State UP, 2003. 221-46.

Gorton, Lisa. "John Donne's Use of Space." *Early Modern Literary Studies* 4.2/ Special Issue 3 (September, 1998): 9.1-27 <URL: http://purl.oclc.org/emls/ 04-2/gortjohn.htm>.

Gorton, Lisa M. "Philosophy and the City: Space in Donne." *John Donne Journal* 18 (1999): 61-71.

Gottwald, Norman Karol. *The Hebrew Bible: A Socio-Literary Introduction.* Philadelphia: Fortress P, 1985.

Greenwood, E. B. "George Herbert's Sonnet 'Prayer': A Stylistic Study." *Essays in Criticism* 15 (1965): 27-45.

Grierson, Herbert J. C. *Metaphysical Lyrics and Poems of the Seventeenth Century.* [1921]. Oxford: OUP, 1995.

Groves, Beatrice. "'Temper'd with a Sinners Tears': Herbert and the Eucharistic Significance of the Word 'Temper.'" *Notes and Queries* 49.3 (2002): 329-30.

Guibbory, Achsah. *Returning to John Donne.* Farnham: Ashgate, 2015.

Guibbory, Achsah. "Donne and Apostasy." *The Oxford Handbook of John Donne.* Ed. Jeanne Shami, Dennis Flynn and M. Thomas Hester. Oxford: OUP, 2011. 664-677.

Guite, A. M. "The Art of Memory and the Art of Salvation: The Centrality of Memory in the Sermons of John Donne and Lancelot Andrewes." *The Seventeenth Century* 4 (1989): 1-17.

Hahn, Juergen. *The Origins of the Baroque Concept of* Peregrinatio. Chapel Hill: U of North Carolina P, 1973.

Halewood, William H. "The Predicament of the Westward Rider." Studies in Philology 93.2 (1996): 218-28.

Hall, Michael L. "Circles and Circumvention in Donne's Sermons." *Journal of English and Germanic Philology* 82.2 (1983): 201-14.

Hamlin, Hannibal. "Poetic Re-creation in John Donne's 'A Litanie.'" *The Sacred and Profane in English Renaissance Literature*. Ed. Mary A. Papazian. Newark: U of Delaware P, 2008. 183-210.

Hamlin, Hannibal. *Psalm Culture and Early Modern English Literature*. Cambridge: CUP, 2004.

Hammond, Gerald. "Herbert's 'Prayer I.'" *Explicator* 39 (1980): 41-43.

Harland, Paul W. "'A true transsubstantiation': Donne, Self-love, and the Passion." *John Donne's Religious Imagination: Essays in Honor of John T. Shawcross*. Ed. Raymond-Jean Frontain and Frances M. Malpezzi. Conway: UCA, 1995. 162-80.

Harman, Barbara Leah. *Costly Monuments: Representations of the Self in George Herbert's Poetry*. Cambridge, MA: Harvard UP, 1982.

Hartwig, Joan. "Donne's Horse and Rider as Body and Soul." *John Donne's Religious Imagination: Essays in Honor of John T. Shawcross*. Ed. Raymond-Jean Frontain and Frances M. Malpezzi. Conway: UCA, 1995. 262-83.

Harvey, Andrew James. "Understanding Mystical Theology in George Herbert's 'Prayer' (I)." *George Herbert Journal* 37.1-2 (2013/14): 131-45.

Haskin, Dayton. *John Donne in the Nineteenth Century*. Oxford: OUP, 2007.

Haskin, Dayton. "A History of Donne's 'Canonization' from Izaak Walton to Cleanth Brooks." *Journal of English and Germanic Philology* 92.1 (1993): 17-36.

Hegnauer, Salomon. *Systrophe: The Background to Herbert's Sonnet* Prayer. Berne: Peter Lang, 1981.

Heiler, Friedrich. *Das Gebet: Eine religionsgeschichtliche und religionspsychologische Untersuchung*. München: Reinhardt, 1918.

Heninger, S. K., Jr. *Touches of Sweet Harmony: Pythagorean Cosmology and Renaissance Poetics*. San Marino: Huntington Library, 1974.

Herman, George. "Donne's 'Goodfriday 1613. Riding Westward.'" *Explicator* 14 (1955/56): n.p.

Hickey, Robert L. "Donne's Art of Memory." *Tennessee Studies in Literature* 3 (1958): 29-36.

Higbie, Robert. "Images of Enclosure in George Herbert's *The Temple*." *Texas Studies in Literature and Language* 15 (1974): 627-38.

Hollander, John. *The Untuning of the Sky: Ideas of Music in English Poetry, 1500-1700*. Princeton: Princeton UP, 1961.

Hooker, Richard. *Of the Laws of Ecclesiastical Polity*. Vol. 5. Ed. Ronald Bayne. London: Macmillan, 1902.

Hotson, Leslie. *Shakespeare by Hilliard: A Portrait Deciphered*. Berkeley: U of California P, 1977.

Hunt, Clay. *Donne's Poetry: Essays in Literary Analysis*. New Haven: Yale UP, 1962.

Hunter, Alastair. "Psalms." *The Oxford Handbook of English Literature and Theology*. Ed. Andrew Hass, David Jasper and Elisabeth Jay. Oxford: OUP, 2007. 243-58.

Hurley, Ann. "Donne's 'Good Friday, Riding Westward, 1613' and the *Illustrated* Meditative Tradition." *John Donne Journal* 12 (1993): 67-77.

Huttar, Charles A. "Herbert and Emblematic Tradition." *Like Season'd Timber: New Essays on George Herbert*. Ed. Edmund Miller and Robert DiYanni. New York: Peter Lang, 1987. 59-100.

"Hymn." *The New Grove Dictionary of Music and Musicians*. 2nd ed. Ed. Stanley Sadie and John Tyrrell. London: Macmillan, 2001. XII: 17-35.

James, Jamie. *The Music of the Spheres: Music, Science, and the Natural Order of the Universe*. New York: Copernicus, 1993.

Järvikivi, J. et al. "Ambiguous Pronoun Resolution: Contrasting the First-mention and Subject Preference Accounts." *Psychological Science* 16 (2005): 260-64.

Johnson, Cedric B. and H. Newton Malony. *Christian Conversion: Biblical and Psychological Perspectives*. Grand Rapids: Zondervan, 1982.

Johnson, Paula. *Form and Transformation in Music and Poetry of the English Renaissance*. New Haven: Yale UP, 1972.

Kalas, Rayna. "The Technology of Reflection: Renaissance Mirrors of Steel and Glass." *Journal of Medieval and Early Modern Studies* 32:3 (2002): 519-42.

Kaske, Carol. Spenser's *Amoretti* and *Epithalamion*: A Psalter of Love." *Centered on the Word: Literature, Scripture, and the Tudor-Stuart Middle Way*. Ed. Daniel W. Doerksen and Christopher Hodgkins. Newark: U of Delaware P, 2004. 28-49.

Keeble, N. H. "'To Be a Pilgrim': Constructing the Protestant Life in Early Modern England." *Pilgrimage: The English Experience from Becket to Bunyan*. Ed. Colin Morris and Peter Roberts. Cambridge: CUP, 2002. 238-56.

Keller, James R. "The Science of Salvation: Spiritual Alchemy in Donne's Final Sermon." *Sixteenth Century Journal* 23.3 (1992): 486-93.

Kent, David A. "'By thought, word, and deed': George Herbert and Christina Rossetti." *The Achievement of Christina Rossetti*. Ed. David A. Kent. Ithaca: Cornell UP, 1987. 250-73.

Kinnamon, Noel J. "Notes on the Psalms in Herbert's *The Temple*." *George Herbert Journal* 4.2 (1981): 10-29.

Kissine, Mikhail. "Why *will* is not a modal." *Natural Language Semantics* 16 (2008): 129-55.

Klein, Lisa M. "'Let us love, deare love, lyke as we ought': Protestant Marriage and the Revision of Petrarchan Loving in Spenser's *Amoretti.*" *Spenser Studies* 10 (1992): 109-37.

Kneidel, Gregory. *Rethinking the Turn to Religion in Early Modern English Literature: The Poetics of all Believers.* Basingstoke: Palgrave Macmillan, 2008.

Kneidel, Gregory. "John Donne's Via Pauli." *Journal of English and Germanic Philology* 100.2 (2001): 224-46.

Knox, Francesca Bugliani. *The Eye of the Eagle: John Donne and the Legacy of Ignatius Loyola.* Oxford: Peter Lang, 2011.

Kratzer, Angelika. "Modality." *Semantics: An International Handbook of Contemporary Research.* Ed. Arnim v. Stechow and Dieter Wunderlich. Berlin: De Gruyter, 1991. 639-50.

Krebs, Robert E. *Groundbreaking Scientific Experiments, Inventions and Discoveries of the Middle Ages and the Renaissance.* Westport: Greenwood P, 2004.

Kronenfeld, Judy Z. "Herbert's 'A Wreath' and Devotional Aesthetics: Imperfect Efforts Redeemed by Grace." *ELH* 48.2 (1981): 290-309.

Krones, H. "Quodlibet." *Historisches Wörterbuch der Rhetorik.* Vol. 7 (2005): 532-49.

Kupfer, Marcia. "Reflections in the Ebstorf Map: Cartography, Theology and *Dilectio Speculationis.*" *Mapping Medieval Geographies: Geographical Encounters in the Latin West and Beyond, 300-1600.* Ed. Keith D. Lilley. Cambridge: CUP, 2013. 100-26.

Labriola, Albert C. "Donne's 'Hymne to God My God, in My Sicknesse': Hieroglyphic Mystery and Magic in Poetry." *Ben Jonson Journal* 2 (1995): 1-7.

Labriola, Albert C. "Donne's 'The Canonization': Its Theological Context and Its Religious Imagery." *Huntington Library Quarterly* 36 (1973): 327-39.

Lang-Graumann, Christiane. *Counting Ev'ry Grain: Das Motiv des Allerkleinsten in George Herberts* The Temple. Münster: Waxmann, 1997.

Lasersohn, Peter. "Mass Nouns and Plurals." *Semantics: An International Handbook of Natural Language Meaning.* Vol. 3. Ed. K. v. Heusinger, C. Maienborn and P. Portner. Berlin: De Gruyter, 2011. 1131-53.

Lausberg, Heinrich. *Handbook of Literary Rhetoric.* Leiden: Brill, 1998.

Lees-Jeffries, Hester. *Shakespeare and Memory.* Oxford: OUP, 2013.

Leimberg, Inge. *Heilig Öffentlich Geheimnis: Die geistliche Lyrik der englischen Frühaufklärung.* Münster: Waxmann, 1996.

Leimberg, Inge. "*If* and *It* and the Human Condition: Considerations Arising from a Reading of *The Merchant of Venice.*" *Connotations* 22.1 (2012/13): 57-84.

Levinson, Stephen C. *Pragmatics.* Cambridge: CUP, 1983.

Lewalski, Barbara Kiefer. *Donne's* Anniversaries *and the Poetry of Praise: The Creation of a Symbolic Mode.* Princeton: Princeton UP, 1973.

Lewalski, Barbara Kiefer. *Protestant Poetics and the Seventeenth-Century Religious Lyric.* Princeton: Princeton UP, 1979.

Lewis, David. *On the Plurality of Worlds.* Oxford: Blackwell, 1986.

Lindberg, Carter. *The European Reformations.* Oxford: Blackwell, 1996.

Linden, Stanton J. *Darke Hierogliphicks: Alchemy in English Literature from Chaucer to the Restoration.* Lexington: U of Kentucky P, 1996.

Linden, Stanton J. "Mystical Alchemy, Eschatology, and Seventeenth-Century Religious Poetry." *Pacific Coast Philology* 19.1-2 (1984): 79-88.

Lobsien, Verena O. "Squaring the Circle: Neoplatonic Versions of the Self in Early Modern Poetry." *Symbolism* 9 (2009): 13-39.

Low, Anthony. *Love's Architecture: Devotional Modes in Seventeenth-Century English Poetry.* New York: New York UP, 1978.

Magnusson, Lynne. "Donne's Language: The Conditions of Communication." *The Cambridge Companion to John Donne.* Ed. Achsah Guibbory. Cambridge: CUP, 2006. 183-200.

Mahnke, Dietrich. *Unendliche Sphäre und Allmittelpunkt.* [1937]. Bad Cannstadt: Friedrich Frommann Verlag, 1966.

Malpezzi, Frances M. "'As I ride': The Beast and his Burden in Donne's 'Goodfriday.'" *Religion and Literature* 24.1 (1992): 23-31.

Marsh, Jan. *Christina Rossetti: A Literary Biography.* London: Cape, 1994.

Martz, Louis. "The Generous Ambiguity of Herbert's *Temple.*" *A Fine Tuning: Studies of the Religious Poetry of Herbert and Milton.* Ed. Mary A. Maleski. Binghamton: Medieval and Renaissance Texts and Studies, 1989. 31-56.

Martz, Louis L. *The Poetry of Meditation.* New Haven: Yale UP, 1955.

Masselink, Noralyn. "Memory in John Donne's Sermons: 'Readie'? Or Not?" *South Atlantic Review* 63.2 (1998): 99-107.

Maurer, Margaret. "The Circular Argument of Donne's 'La Corona.'" *Studies in English Literature* 22 (1982): 51-68.

Mazzeo, Joseph A. "Notes on John Donne's Alchemical Imagery." *Isis* 48.2 (1957): 103-23.

McColley, Diane. "The Poem as Hierophon: Musical Configurations in George Herbert's 'The Church.'" *A Fine Tuning: Studies of the Religious Poetry of*

Herbert and Milton. Ed. Mary A. Maleski. Binghamton: Medieval and Renaissance Texts and Studies, 1989. 117-43.

McCoy, Richard C. "Love's Martyrs: Shakespeare's 'Phoenix and Turtle' and the Sacrificial Sonnets." *Religion and Culture in Renaissance England*. Ed. Claire McEachern and Debora Shuger. Cambridge: CUP, 1997. 188-208.

McGuire, Philip C. "Private Prayer and English Poetry in the Early Seventeenth Century." *Studies in English Literature* 14.1 (1974): 63-77.

McMahon, Robert. "Herbert's 'Coloss. 3.3' as Microcosm." *George Herbert Journal* 15 (1992): 55-69.

Merrill, Thomas F. "Sacred Parody and the Grammar of Devotion." *Criticism: A Quarterly for Literature and the Arts* 23.3(1981): 195-210.

Miller, Greg. *George Herbert's "Holy Patterns": Reforming Individuals in Community*. New York: Continuum, 2007.

Milward, Peter. "'Double Nature's Single Name': A Response to Christiane Gillham." *Connotations* 3.1 (1993): 60-63.

Moog-Grünewald, Maria. "Conversio: Zu einem 'apokalyptisch' figurierten Topos autobiographischen Schreibens." *Was ist Dichtung*. Heidelberg: Winter, 2008. 127-49. (2008a)

Moog-Grünewald, Maria. "Der Sänger im Schild – oder: Über den Grund ekphrastischen Schreibens." *Was ist Dichtung*. Heidelberg: Winter, 2008. 179-96. (2008b)

Morillo, Marvin. "Donne's Compasses: Circles and Right Lines." *English Language Notes* 3.3 (1966): 173-76.

Müller, Wolfgang G. "The Poem as Performance: Self-Definition and Self-Exhibition in John Donne's *Songs and Sonets*." *Solo Performances: Staging the Early Modern Self in England*. Ed. Ute Berns. Amsterdam: Brill, 2010. 173-88.

Murphy, J. Stephen. "Ejaculatory Poetics and the Writing of Ecstasy in George Herbert's 'Prayer' (1)." *George Herbert Journal* 24.1-2 (2000/01): 19-34.

Murray, Molly. *The Poetics of Conversion in Early Modern English Literature: Verse and Change from Donne to Dryden*. Cambridge: CUP, 2009.

Narveson, Kate. "Publishing the Sole-talk of the Soule: Genre in Early Stuart Piety." *Centered on the Word: Literature, Scripture, and the Tudor-Stuart Middle Way*. Ed. Daniel W. Doerksen and Christopher Hodgkins. Newark: U of Delaware P, 2004. 110-26.

Newhauser, Richard G. and Arthur J. Russell. "Mapping Virtual Pilgrimage in an Early Fifteenth-Century *Arma Christi* Roll." The *Arma Christi* in Medieval and Early Modern Material Culture. Ed. Lisa H. Cooper and Andrea Denny-Brown. Farnham: Ashgate, 2014. 83-112.

Nicolson, Marjorie Hope. *The Breaking of the Circle: Studies in the Effect of the "New Science" upon Seventeenth Century Poetry.* Evanston: Northwestern UP, 1950.

Niefer, Janina. *Inspiration and Utmost Art: The Poetics of Early Modern English Psalm Translations.* Münster: LIT Verlag, 2017.

Norton, David. *A History of the English Bible as Literature.* Cambridge: CUP, 2000.

Nuttall, A. D. *Overheard by God: Fiction and Prayer in Herbert, Milton, Dante and St John.* London: Methuen, 1980.

O'Connell, Patrick F. "'La Corona': Donne's Ars Poetica Sacra." *The Eagle and the Dove: Reassessing John Donne.* Ed. Claude J. Summers and Ted-Larry Pebworth. Columbia: U of Missouri P, 1986.119-30.

O'Connell, Patrick F. "'Restore Thine Image': Structure and Theme in Donne's 'Goodfriday.'" *John Donne Journal* 4.1 (1985): 13-28.

Ohly, Friedrich. "Deus Geometra: Skizzen zur Geschichte einer Vorstellung von Gott." *Ausgewählte und neue Schriften zur Literaturgeschichte und zur Bedeutungsforschung.* Ed. Uwe Ruberg. Stuttgart: Hirzel, 1995. 555-598.

Oliver, P. M. *Donne's Religious Writing: A Discourse of Feigned Devotion.* London: Longman, 1997.

The Oxford Dictionary of English Proverbs. 3rd ed. Rev. F. P. Wilson. Oxford: OUP, 1970.

The Oxford English Dictionary. <http://www.oed.com>.

Pando Canteli, María J. "The Poetics of Space in Donne's Love Poetry." *John Donne Journal* 19 (2000): 45-57.

Patterson, Annabel. "Donne's Re-Formed *La Corona.*" *John Donne Journal* 23 (2004): 69-93.

Pebworth, Ted-Larry. "The Early Audiences of Donne's Poetic Performances." *John Donne Journal* 15 (1996): 127-39.

Pebworth, Ted-Larry. "John Donne, Coterie Poetry, and the Text as Performance." *SEL: Studies in English Literature, 1500-1900* 29 (1989): 61-75.

Peters, Ursula. *Das Ich im Bild: Die Figur des Autors in volkssprachigen Bilderhandschriften des 13. bis 16. Jahrhunderts.* Köln: Böhlau, 2008.

Pickering, F. P. *Literature and Art in the Middle Ages.* Coral Gables: U of Miami P, 1970.

Pollock, John J. "The 'Harmonious Soule' in Donne's 'Hymne to Christ.'" *American Notes and Queries* 17 (1978): 2-3.

Potts, Christopher. "The Expressive Dimension." *Theoretical Linguistics* 33.2 (2007): 165-98.

Poulet, Georges. *The Metamorphoses of the Circle.* Baltimore: Johns Hopkins P, 1966.

Powrie, Sarah. "Speculative Tensions: The Blurring of Augustinian Interiority in *The Second Anniversarie*." *Connotations* 25.1 (2015/16): 1-20.

Pruss, Ingrid. "George Herbert's 'Prayer' (I): From Metaphor to Mystery." *George Herbert Journal* 12.2 (1989): 17-26.

Questier, Michael C. *Conversion, Politics and Religion in England, 1580-1625*. Cambridge: CUP, 1996.

Quinn, Dennis. "Donne's Christian Eloquence." *ELH* 27.4 (1960): 276-97.

Riemer, A. P. "A Pattern for Love – The Structure of Donne's 'The Canonization.'" *Sydney Studies* 3 (1977):19-31.

Robbins, Jill. *Prodigal Son / Elder Brother: Interpretation and Alterity in Augustine, Petrarch, Kafka, Levinas*. Chicago: U of Chicago P, 1991.

Rudrum, Alan. "God's Second Book and the Regenerate Mind: Some Early Modern Conversion Narratives." *Renaissance Ecology: Imagining Eden in Milton's England*. Ed. Ken Hiltner. Pittsburgh: Duquesne P, 2008. 201-16.

Ryley, George. *Mr. Herbert's* Temple *and* Church Militant *Explained and Improved*. [1715]. Ed. Maureen Boyd and Cedric C. Brown. New York: Garland: 1987.

Sabine, Maureen. *Feminine Engendered Faith: The Poetry of John Donne and Richard Crashaw*. Basingstoke: Macmillan, 1992.

Salenius, Maria. "The Circle and the Line: Two Metaphors of God and His Works in John Donne's *Devotions upon Emergent Occasions*." *Neuphilologische Mitteilungen* 102 (2001): 201-10.

Sanchez, Reuben. *Typology and Iconography in Donne, Herbert, and Milton*. New York: Palgrave Macmillan, 2014.

Sanchez, Reuben. "'First the *Burden*, and then the *Ease*': Donne and the Art of Convertere in Four Texts." *EIRC* 36.1 (2010): 119-46.

Scarisbrick, J. J. *The Reformation and the English People*. Oxford: Blackwell, 1984.

Schiller, Gertrud. *Ikonographie der christlichen Kunst. Band 2: Die Passion Jesu Christi*. Gütersloh: Gütersloher Verlagshaus, 1968.

Schleiner, Winfried. *The Imagery of John Donne's Sermons*. Providence: Brown UP, 1970.

Schliebs, Gisela. "Die Funktion der Strophenformen in George Herberts *The Temple* im Rahmen des literarhistorischen sowie des musik- und dichtungstheoretischen Kontextes." Diss. Universität Gießen, 1970.

Schöne, Albrecht. *Emblematik und Drama im Zeitalter des Barock*. München: Beck, 1993.

Schoenfeldt, Michael. "'That spectacle of too much weight': The Poetics of Sacrifice in Donne, Herbert, and Milton." *Journal of Medieval and Early Modern Studies* 31.3 (2001): 561-84.

Shami, Jeanne. "John Donne: Geography as Metaphor." *Geography and Literature: A Meeting of the Disciplines.* Ed. William E. Mallory and Paul Simpson-Housley. Syracuse: Syracuse UP, 1987. 161-67.

Shami, Jeanne. "Anatomy and Progress: The Drama of Conversion in Donne's Men of a 'Middle Nature.'" *University of Toronto Quarterly* 53.3 (1984): 221-35.

Severance, Sibyl Lutz. "Soul, Sphere, and Structure in 'Goodfriday 1613. Riding Westward.'" *Studies in Philology* 84.1 (1987): 24-43.

Sharpe, Kevin. *Remapping Early Modern England: The Culture of Seventeenth-Century Politics.* Cambridge: CUP, 2000.

Sherman, Anita Gilman. "Fantasies of Private Language in 'The Phoenix and Turtle' and 'The Ecstasy.'" *Shakespeare and Donne: Generic Hybrids and the Cultural Imaginary.* Ed. Judith H. Anderson and Jennifer C. Vaught. New York: Fordham University Press, 2013. 169-84.

Sherwood, Terry G. "Conversion Psychology in John Donne's Good Friday Poem." *Harvard Theological Review* 72 (1979): 101-22.

Sherwood, Terry G. *Fulfilling the Circle: A Study of John Donne's Thought.* Toronto: U of Toronto P, 1984.

Sherwood, Terry G. *Herbert's Prayerful Art.* Toronto: U of Toronto P, 1989.

Shoulson, Jeffrey S. *Fictions of Conversion: Jews, Christians, and Cultures of Change in Early Modern England.* Philadelphia: U of Pennsylvania P, 2013.

Sicherman, Carol Marks. "Donne's Discoveries." *Studies in English Literature* 11.1 (1971): 69-88.

Siegel, Paul N. "Christianity and the Religion of Love in Romeo and Juliet." Shakespeare Quarterly 12.4 (1961): 371-392.

Simpson, Percy. *Shakespearian Punctuation.* Oxford: Clarendon P, 1911.

Slater, Michael. "'Invoking' Donne: A Grammatical Reconstruction of 'The Canonization.'" *Notes and Queries* 53 (2006): 159-64.

Slattery, Dennis Patrick. "Poetry, Prayer and Meditation." *Journal of Poetry Therapy* 13.1 (1999): 39-45.

Song, Eric B. "Anamorphosis and the Religious Subject of George Herbert's 'Coloss. 3.3'" *SEL: Studies in English Literature 1500-1900* 47.1 (2007): 107-21.

Soubrenie, Elisabeth. "Conversion et Poésie chez George Herbert." *Bulletin de la Société d'Etudes Anglo-Américaines des XVIIe et XVIIIe Siècles* 45 (1997): 35-55.

Spear, Charles. *Names and Titles of the Lord Jesus Christ.* Boston, 1841.

Spenko, James L. "Circular Form in Two Donne Lyrics." *English Language Notes* 13.2 (1975): 103-07.

Steele, Oliver. "Crucifixion and the Imitation of Christ in Herbert's 'The Temper' (I)." *George Herbert Journal* 5 (1981): 71-74.

Stein, Arnold. *George Herbert's Lyrics*. Baltimore: Johns Hopkins UP, 1968.

Stelling, Lieke. "'Thy Very Essence is Mutability': Religious Conversion in Early Modern English Drama, 1558-1642." *The Turn of the Soul: Representations of Religious Conversion in Early Modern Art and Literature*. Ed. Lieke Stelling, Harald Hendrix and Todd M. Richardson. Leiden: Brill, 2012. 59-83.

Stirling, Kirsten. "Liturgical Poetry." *The Oxford Handbook of John Donne*. Ed. Jeanne Shami, Dennis Flynn and M. Thomas Hester. Oxford: OUP, 2011. 233-41.

Strahle, Graham. *An Early Music Dictionary: Musical Terms from British Sources, 1500-1740*. Cambridge: CUP, 1995.

Strier, Richard. "Going in the Wrong Direction: Lyric Criticism and Donne's 'Goodfriday 1613. Riding Westward.'" *Divisions on a Ground: Essays on English Renaissance Literature in Honor of Donald M. Friedman*. George Herbert Journal Monograph (2008): 13-27.

Strier, Richard. *Love Known: Theology and Experience in George Herbert's Poetry*. Chicago: U of Chicago P, 1983.

Stubbs, John. *Donne: The Reformed Soul*. London: Viking, 2006.

Sullivan, Ceri. "Seventeenth-Century Wreath Poems." *George Herbert Journal* 19 (1995/1996): 95-101.

Sullivan, David M. "Riders to the West: 'Goodfriday, 1613.'" *John Donne Journal* 6.1 (1987): 1-8.

Summers, Joseph H. *George Herbert: His Religion and Art*. London: Chatto and Windus, 1954.

Sutherland, Annie. *English Psalms in the Middle Ages, 1300-1450*. Oxford: OUP, 2015.

Tadmor, Naomi. "The Social and Cultural Translation of the Hebrew Bible in Early Modern England: Reflections, Working Principles, and Examples." *Early Modern Cultures of Translation*. Ed. Karen Newman and Jane Tylus. Philadelphia: U of Pennsylvania P, 2015. 175-88.

Thomas, John A. "The Circle: Donne's Underlying Unity." *"The Need Beyond Reason" and Other Essays*. Provo: Brigham Young UP, 1976. 89-103.

Tiffany, Grace. *Love's Pilgrimage: The Holy Journey in English Renaissance Literature*. Newark: U of Delaware P, 2006.

Todd, Richard. "Donne's '*Goodfriday* 1613. *Riding Westward*.': The Extant Manuscripts and the Group 1 Stemma." *John Donne Journal* 20 (2001): 201-18.

Tuve, Rosemond. "George Herbert and Caritas." *Journal of the Warburg and Courtauld Institutes* 22 (1959): 303-31.

Tuve, Rosemond. *A Reading of George Herbert*. Chicago: U of Chicago P, 1952.

Tuve, Rosemond, "Sacred 'Parody' of Love Poetry, and Herbert." *Studies in the Renaissance* 8 (1961): 249-90.

Ure, Peter. "The Looking-Glass of Richard II." *Philological Quarterly* 34.2 (1955): 219-24.

Veith, Gene Edward. *Reformation Spirituality: The Religion of George Herbert*. Lewisburg: Bucknell UP, 1985.

Vendler, Helen. *The Poetry of George Herbert*. Cambridge, MA: Harvard UP, 1975.

Von Fintel, Kai and Irene Heim. "Intensional Semantics." Ms. Massachussetts: MIT, 2011.

Walker, D. P. *Spiritual and Demonic Magic from Ficino to Campanella*. London: Warburg Institute, 1958.

Walker, Julia. "The Religious Lyric as Genre." *English Language Notes* 25.1 (1987): 39-45.

Weiss, Roberto. *The Renaissance Discovery of Classical Antiquity*. Oxford: Blackwell, 1969.

Westerweel, Bart. "The Well-Tempered Lady and the Unruly Horse: Convention and Submerged Metaphor in Renaissance Literature and Art." *Convention and Innovation in Literature*. Ed. Theo d'haen et al. Amsterdam: Benjamins, 1989.

Westerweel, Bart. *Patterns and Patterning: A Study of Four Poems by George Herbert*. Amsterdam: Rodopi, 1984.

White, Helen, C. *The Metaphysical Poets: A Study in Religious Epxerience*. New York: Macmillan, 1956.

Wilcox, Helen. "Herbert's Musical Contexts: Countrey-Aires to Angels Musick." *Like Season'd Timber: New Essays on George Herbert*. Ed. Edmund Miller and Robert DiYanni. New York: Peter Lang, 1987. 37-58.

Williamson, George. "Mutability, Decay, and Seventeenth-Century Melancholy." *English Literary History* 2.2 (1935): 121-50.

Wilson, G. R., Jr. "The Interplay of Perception and Reflection: Mirror Imagery in Donne's Poetry." *SEL: Studies in English Literature* 9.1 (1969): 107-21.

Wilson, Gerald H. "Shaping the Psalter: A Consideration of Editorial Linkage in the Book of Psalms." *The Shape and Shaping of the Psalter*. Ed. J. Clinton McCann. Sheffield: JSOT P, 1993. 72-82.

Windelspecht, Michael. *Groundbreaking Scientific Experiments, Inventions and Discoveries of the 17th Century*. Westport: Greenwood P, 2002.

Yearwood, Stephenie. "Donne's *Holy Sonnets*: The Theology of Conversion." *Texas Studies in Literature and Language* 24.2 (1982): 208-21.

Yeo, Jayme M. "Converting England: Mysticism, Nationalism, and Symbolism in the Poetry of John Donne." *The Turn of the Soul: Representations of Religious Conversion in Early Modern Art and Literature.* Ed. Lieke Stelling, Harald Hendrix and Todd M. Richardson. Leiden: Brill, 2012. 177-98.

Young, Alan R. *The English Prodigal Son Plays: A Theatrical Fashion of the Sixteenth and Seventeenth Centuries.* Salzburg: Institut für Anglistik und Amerikanistik, 1979.

Young, R. V. "Donne's Catholic Conscience and the Wit of Religious Anxiety." *Ben Jonson Journal* 16 (2009): 57-76.

Young, R. V. *Doctrine and Devotion in Seventeenth-Century Poetry: Studies in Donne, Herbert, Crashaw, and Vaughan.* Cambridge: Brewer, 2000.

Zirker, Angelika. *Stages of the Soul in Early Modern Poetry.* Manchester: Manchester UP, c. 2018.

VIII. Index

IX. Summary

This study investigates how the notion of turning is connected to and reflected in the language of religious Metaphysical Poetry, where turning is a pervasive and recurrent topic. "Turning" is understood as a turning towards someone or something and simultaneously as a turning away from someone or something else. To this is added the motion of turning back to someone or something, which often creates a circular movement. In addition, in the poems considered here, turning is always a double and reciprocal motion: the speaker of a poem turns towards God, and at the same time he images God's turning towards him. Thus, turning is closely connected to the notion of spiritual conversion, which is marked precisely by man's turn to God and the perception of God's turn to man, and in fact most of the poems discussed show the speaker's conversion experience.

Turning is also an inherently spatial concept, based on a speaker's movement and orientation. As such, turning depends as much on basic geometrical principles as on the larger world picture that links an individual speaker to the world and to God. Moreover, religious turning is often connected to ideas of musical order and harmony. In this respect, there is a close conceptual relation between turning (as a linear or circular movement) and the notion of musical tuning. Circularity and circular turning, while being part of both spatial and musical concepts, deserve special consideration, since they are often emphasised in relation to turning towards God.

The notion of turning is a central aspect in religious Metaphysical Poetry, and the focus here is on the poems of John Donne and George Herbert, two of the most prominent and typical Metaphysical Poets. The various aspects of turning under discussion here are approached through close analyses of single poems; a detailed analysis is necessary because all of the poems discussed are highly complex and can only be understood in their entirety.

The introduction outlines the various conceptions of turning under consideration here and their relation to concepts of space and music, and shows how the pervasiveness of the notion of turning in metaphysical poetry is conditioned by the circumstances of the poets' life and time and

generated by a general anxiety about man's spiritual fate and the salva-
tion of his soul. It also serves to show to which extent the notion of turn-
ing has already been regarded in analyses of Donne's and Herbert's
work.

The next chapter focusses on Donne's "Riding Westward, Goodfriday
1613." The main focus of this chapter is on turning in the sense of spir-
itual conversion, but the analysis of this poem also serves to give an
overview over all aspects of the notion of turning. In the poem, the
speaker turns to God through a reinterpretation of his movements. His
conversion takes place on a literal (westward) journey, and while the
speaker initially sees this as a turning away from God (only in his mind
he looks east towards Christ), he comes to recognise his westward
movement also as an approach to God, carrying him closer to death and
his afterlife. Through merging the world of the speaker with that of
Christ, the poem creates a spatial and temporal state in which both speak-
er and Christ are simultaneously present and converging, and allows the
speaker to establish a connection to Christ and experience his conversion.
The chapter also shows the relevance of spatial constructions and musical
notions for a speaker's turn to God, and it shows how language is em-
ployed in presenting and creating turning.

The following chapters are each dedicated to another aspect of turning,
examined through the detailed analysis of one representative poem and
complemented by shorter discussions of other poems. The analysis of
Herbert's "The Search" serves to put the spatial aspects of turning in fo-
cus. The poem is about the speaker's spiritual search for God, which is
depicted as a literal searching for God (the speaker seems to wander
around) that is linked to the speaker's metaphorical and spiritual motion
(and to his perceived distance and closeness to God). The speaker's im-
agined union with God at the end of the poem is likewise depicted in
spatial terms. At the same time, "The Search" can be understood as a
sacred parody: it takes elements of secular love poetry and uses them in
the context of sacred poetry. In this way, the possibilities to express rela-
tionships and movements of turning in love poetry become available in a
religious context. The chapter also treats the concept of life as a pilgrim-
age, essential to the notion of turning towards God in Metaphysical Poet-
ry.

The chapter on Donne's "The Canonization" focusses on the special use of language and on the potential of language in bringing about turns and transformations. In the poem, two lovers are transformed into saints because of their love and with help of the poem's language. At the same time language itself (speaking, singing and writing) is constantly brought to the fore. Although "The Canonization" is a poem about the love between two people, the lovers' relationship is explicitly characterised as a sacred one, so that the poem can be considered a love poem as well as a religious poem.

The next chapter, on Herbert's "The Temper (I)," foregrounds the relation between music and turning, and shows how an individual speaker's turning experience is embedded in a world picture based on order and harmony, and on harmonic principles. A speaker's turn towards God and a desired union with God is often perceived musically as a tuning of the speaker in order to achieve a harmony with God, which is especially prominent in "The Temper (I)."

The last chapter focusses on the relation between turning and circular motion, using Donne's "La Corona" as an example. The speaker progresses through Christ's life and death from annunciation to ascension, and links his own fate to Christ's. In the end, due to the poem's circular form, he ends where he began, with a repetition of the poem's first line. This repetition marks not only a return to the beginning, but also a progress to a higher level as the speaker and his relation to Christ have changed through the poem, and the repetition cannot be read in the same way as the initial beginning.

This study highlights the fundamental importance of turning for Metaphysical Poetry and analyses the diverse ways in which language contributes to the conceptualisation of turning. By showing how turning is presented and brought about in the language of the poems under consideration, this work also adds to the understanding of Early Modern poetry in general and of a number of Metaphysical Poems in particular, and offers deeper insight into how the mechanisms of language work.